# POLICE

## Streetcorner Politicians

# POLICE

## STREETCORNER POLITICIANS

WILLIAM KER MUIR, JR.

THE UNIVERSITY OF CHICAGO PRESS
CHICAGO   LONDON

The University of Chicago Press, Chicago 60637
The University of Chicago Press, Ltd., London
© 1977 by The University of Chicago
All rights reserved. Published 1977
Paperback edition 1979
Printed in the United States of America

09 08 07 06 05 04                    9 10 11 12

*Library of Congress Cataloging in Publication Data*

Muir, William K.
    Police: streetcorner politicians.
    Bibliography: p.
    1. Police.   2. Power (Social sciences)   1. Title.
HV7921.M84        363.2      76-8085
ISBN 0-226-54633-0 (paper)

**To Pauli, Kerry, and Hattie
with Love and
to the Chief
with Respect**

[A]fter Hannibal had defeated the Romans at Cannae, whilst all Italy rose up in consequence of this defeat, Capua still remained in a state of insubordination, because of the hatred that existed between the people and the Senate. Pacovius Calanus being at that time one of the supreme magistrates, and foreseeing the dangers that would result from the disorders in that city, resolved by means of the authority of his office to try and reconcile the people and the Senate; with this purpose he caused the Senate to be assembled, and stated to them the animosity which the people felt towards them, and the danger to which they were exposed of being massacred by them if the city were given up to Hannibal in consequence of the defeat of the Romans. He then added, that, if they would leave it to him to manage the matter, he would find means of restoring harmony between the two orders; but that, for this purpose, he would shut them up in their palace, and by seemingly putting them into the power of the people he would save them. The Senators yielded to his suggestion: whereupon Pacovius shut the Senate up in their palace, and then assembled the people and said to them that "the time had arrived when they might subdue the pride of the nobles and revenge themselves for the injuries received at their hands, and that he held the Senate shut up in their palace for this purpose. But believing that they would be unwilling to allow the city to be without a government, it would be necessary, before killing the old Senators, to choose new ones; and that therefore he had put the names of all the Senators into an urn, and would proceed to draw them in their presence, and that one after another those who were drawn should die, after their successors had been elected." And when the first was drawn and his name proclaimed the people raised a great noise, calling him proud, arrogant, and cruel; but when Pacovius asked them to choose another in his place, the whole assembly became quiet, and after a little time one was named by the people; but at the mention of his name some began to whistle, some to laugh, some to speak ill of him in one way, and some in another; and thus, one after another, those that were named were pronounced by them unworthy of the senatorial dignity, so that Pacovius took occasion to speak to them as follows: "Since you are of the opinion that the city would fare ill without a Senate, and as you cannot agree upon the successors of the old Senators, it seems to me it would be well for you to become reconciled with the present Senate, for the fear to which they have been subjected has in great measure humbled them, and you will now find in them that humanity which you in vain look for elsewhere." This suggestion prevailed, and a reconciliation between the two orders followed, and the people, when they came to act upon particulars, discovered the error into which they had fallen in looking at the subject in general.

*Niccolo Machiavelli*
Discourses, 1520

On passing from a free country into one which is not free the traveler is struck by the change; in the former all is bustle and activity; in the latter everything seems calm and motionless. In the one, amelioration and progress are the topics of inquiry; in the other, it seems as if the community wished only to repose in the enjoyment of advantages already acquired. Nevertheless, the country which exerts itself so strenuously to become happy is generally more wealthy and prosperous than that which appears so contented with its lot; and when we compare them, we can scarcely conceive how so many new wants are daily felt in the former, while so few seem to exist in the latter.

*Alexis de Tocqueville*
Democracy in America, 1835

# Contents

# Acknowledgments

My first acknowledgment must be to the men of action whose lives I have studied in writing this book. I found I was often little more than the transcriber of the experiences and reflections of men too busy to write down their own recollections. They took the time to educate me and share their insights. In doing so, the twenty-eight young police officers and their ten "old-timer" colleagues have given me a lot of memories.

I am also indebted to the administration of the Laconia Police Department, particularly to its chief, whose intelligence and integrity caused him to open the department to outside observers, whether they concluded with applause or condemnation.

Three men, through their interest in the problems of police, helped me considerably with their perceptions, questions, and thoughtful research: Professor Lief Carter, now of the University of Georgia Political Science Department; Professor Byron Jackson, now of the California State University, Chico, Political Science Department; and Linus Masouredis, now of the Harvard Law School. A fourth, Professor Frank Levy, now of the University of California, Berkeley, School of Public Policy, diagnosed two major problems in the first draft of the book and then showed me how to cure them.

I appreciated, more than they may know, the abundant criticisms and suggestions of many friends, among them Bill Cavala, John Gardiner, Alexander George, Fred Greenstein, Bill Kahrl, Irving Lefberg, Jim Newman, Doug Perez, Jeff Pressman, Martin Shapiro, Jerry Skolnick, and Bill Zinn.

Finally, I owe much to two other persons whose part in this study was more indirect but more fundamental: Harold Lasswell, who first posed the issue of power and personality elegantly enough to catch my fancy, and my wife, Paulette Wauters Muir, who always mixed in just the right proportions healthy skepticism, powerful human insight, and affectionate support.

To all of them, my deepest respect and thanks.

# The Problem of Coercive Power 1

Policemen are the subjects of this case study, but I beg the reader to view them as exemplars of a much larger group of individuals. Policemen are instances of powerful persons. In observing the behavior and development of policemen, the reader witnesses at a more abstract level the effects of coercive power on the human personality. He can learn much from the police experience to enhance his understanding of political figures, with their unique agonies and special dilemmas. This book is about the problem of coercive power, and Part I, after introducing the reader to the police world and four policemen who inhabit it, describes what that problem is.

# 1      "What Is a Good Policeman?"

Power tends to corrupt, and absolute power corrupts absolutely. Great men are almost always bad men, even when they exercise influence and not authority: still more when you superadd the tendency or the certainty of corruption by authority.

*Lord Acton*
1887

The office makes the man.

*Anonymous*
Political folklore

## I

What is a good policeman, and what does he think and do differently from a bad one? Does police work corrupt, or does it expand a policeman's horizons and magnify his soul? Can anything be done to avert the potential for his moral breakdown?

This book speaks to these questions. It describes the moral and intellectual perspectives of twenty-eight young men who served as police officers in a sizable American city in the early 1970s. The point of the book is to explain the interplay between a policeman's most fundamental attitudes and the violence he recurrently faces in fulfilling his powerful office.

In a nutshell, the conclusions are these. A policeman becomes a good policeman to the extent that he develops two virtues.[1] Intellectually, he has to grasp the nature of human suffering. Morally, he has to resolve the

---

1. This book deals with both the descriptive and normative aspects of the policeman's lot. I have tried to give as much attention to the question of what constitutes a good policeman as to understanding what happens to him. Readers who wish to understand the reasons for selecting the particular criteria of goodness (or "professionalism") should turn to chapter 4.

3

contradiction of achieving just ends with coercive means. A patrolman who develops this tragic sense and moral equanimity tends to grow in the job, increasing in confidence, skill, sensitivity, and awareness.

Whether or not he develops these two virtues depends on the choices he makes among alternative means of defending himself against recurrent threats. Those self-defensive reactions to violence and madness influence the very core of his being. The responses he has to make to what I have called "the paradoxes of coercive power" challenge his basic assumptions about human nature and his conventional notions of right and wrong.

Achieving a tragic sense and a moral calm under the threatening circumstances of patrol work depends in part upon developing an enjoyment of talk. Eloquence enriches his repertoire of potential responses to violence and permits him to touch the citizenry's souls—their hopes, their fears, their needs to be something worthwhile, their consciences. Equally important, a policeman's penchant to talk provides him the chance to associate with his fellow officers. A department can create institutions within it to capitalize on his sociability. Two institutions in particular, the Training Academy and the patrolman's squad, are crucial in this regard. In being thrust together in training and in squads, policemen have unique opportunities to talk out the intellectual and moral issues inherent in the paradoxes of dispossession, detachment, face, and irrationality—the four paradoxes of coercive power. The chief of a department can have great effect on his men's capacity to avoid moral breakdown by seeing that effective training is developed and that good sergeants lead patrol squads.

On the other hand, in the paradoxical circumstances in which the policeman is forever working, of being powerful but not absolutely powerful, the absence of either the inclination or the opportunity to talk is likely to isolate him from both the public and his fellow officers. This isolation impedes developing a tragic outlook in combination with a moral equanimity about coercion. As a result, he tends increasingly to habits of avoidance, brutality, or favoritism. In turn, these unacceptable performances tend to compound moral and intellectual disorientation, leading to ever increasing isolation from human companionship and, eventually, to personal deterioration.

## II

The remainder of the book attempts to establish these conclusions. Chapter 2 introduces the reader to four policemen and what they thought and worried about, particularly their preoccupation with the dilemmas of coercion. Chapter 3 analyzes the concept of coercion. I examine an abstract model of a coercive relationship, something I have called the extortionate transaction.

Using that model, I identify four paradoxes inherent in the effective exercise of coercive power. I have called them the paradoxes of dispossession, detachment, face, and irrationality. They are paradoxes because they contradict other "truths" by which the affairs of the civilized world are generally conducted. Chapter 4 addresses the crucial methodological question of defining the nature of the "good" policeman, the professional officer. It also insists (as does chapter 3) on the essential point that the policeman is the victim of coercion, "absorbed," as Tocqueville remarked about politicians in general, "by the cares of self-defense."[2]

Chapters 5 through 9 explore how each of the four paradoxes of coercive power manifests itself in the policeman's daily work. For each paradox, I have distinguished four possible means of self-defense, and I have discussed the conditions and consequences of a policeman's choice among them.

Then, in chapters 10 and 11, we come to the dynamics by which these paradoxical events affect a policeman's intellectual and moral development. These two chapters involve a minute examination of how a policeman's experience causes the growth of character. Chapter 12 goes on to deal with three factors, language, leadership, and learning (i.e., the education given to an officer on the job by his sergeant and squad members), and how they can be manipulated to affect the direction of character development. Chapter 12, thus, is about the way human effort can artificially alter the "natural" consequences of the policeman's lot.

Chapters 13 and 14 look at two sets of implications of the study: What does an understanding of these twenty-eight young policemen suggest about improving American police organizations? And what does the study teach us about coercive power as a universal phenomenon?

The rest of this chapter sketches the context in which the events of this book took place and discusses the selection of the sample of twenty-eight young officers.

## III

The peculiar characteristic of police departments in the United States is that they are local and very different one from the other. An observer of a single police department must constantly check against a tendency to overgeneralize.[3] A literate person surfeited with police stories emanating from New York

2. Alexis de Tocqueville, *Democracy in America,* trans. Henry Reeve (New York: Vintage, 1945), 1:140.
3. In *City Police* (New York: Farrar, Straus & Giroux, 1973), Jonathan Rubinstein so respected this limitation that he insisted on identifying Philadelphia as the specific site of his observations. His book is much the better for its humility, and he admonishes others who study police that "the question of evidence is crucial" (p. xiii). Because

and Chicago may find it hard to comprehend that some local police departments operate without significant graft and illegitimate political influence. But there are many graft-free and professional police departments in this country. Likewise, a middle-class citizen, used to the operations of suburban police departments, may completely overlook the vital counseling role which city policemen play in lower-class urban areas. But dealing with intimate family problems is often the most significant part of the work of a metropolitan police department. Similarly, the law-abiding reader who encounters an ill-trained (and unpaid) police *reservist*[4] on duty at county fairs and ball games may doubt that American police get any training at all, much less good training. But the training given to regular policemen in the better police departments in the country is sometimes intellectually sophisticated and effective.

Departments differ most importantly in seven respects: the *homogeneity* of the citizenry they serve, the extent of *illegitimate political influence* to which they are subject, the pervasiveness of *graft* within them, their *size* and the organizational efforts to cope with size, their *history*, the investment in professional *training*, and the philosophy and skill of their *chief*. Each of these seven factors may have a crucial effect on the character of a police department.[5]

Take the Laconia Police Department, for example, the one in which this study was undertaken. In at least one of these seven respects, it fulfilled the popular stereotype of an American police department. Laconia, the city it served, had half a million people—some rich, some poor; some established families, some recent immigrants; some black, some white; some sanguine, some without hope. Its substantial minority-group population—black, Latino, Asian, and Amerindian—was geographically concentrated in one-half of the city. Laconia was rectangular in shape, fifteen miles long west to east, and five miles wide south to north. Practically none of Laconia's 200,000 nonwhite citizens lived in the hilly southern half of the city. Rather,

---

a book about individual policemen depends upon those policemen's revealing the confidences of their hearts, assurances of confidentiality became crucial, and so my study has regressed to the conventional rules of anonymity.

4. The police reservist in the United States is a "volunteer" cop, outfitted with a uniform, a star, and even a gun, given little training even by the most professional departments, and placed on duty on weekends on occasions when the regular police department has insufficient manpower to meet every need. Their motivations are suspected by regular policemen, and their actions cause their regular colleagues the gravest amount of rue. But they save cities vast sums of money, and because of that fact the tradition of the reservist is not likely to die quickly.

5. James F. Ahern, the former Chief of Police of New Haven, Connecticut, describes the effects of pervasive graft and undue political influence on the police institution in the first several chapters of his book, *Police in Trouble* (New York: Hawthorn, 1972).

they lived in the "flatlands," the lower, older half of the city that bordered the river. By no means were all the people who lived in this northern, or level, half, poor and minority. For instance, there was Lafayette Park, in the exact center of the flatlands, with its stylish commercial and swank residential developments. But a substantial fraction of the neighborhoods consisted of bleak public housing projects, where no citizen was a homeowner and where the typical family was broken, on welfare, and almost invariably under serious medical or emotional stress. In contrast, the new subdivisions spotting the hillsides to the south were filled with white, middle-class families, who enjoyed suburbanlike luxuries (and deprivations)—vistas, open spaces, and privacy, but no sidewalks, mass transit, or nearby stores. Not atypically, Laconia was a city of contrasts and varieties of cultures.

But in other respects Laconia and its police department differed sharply from the stereotype. For one thing, there was an almost total absence of illegitimate political influence applied to the department. Elected politicians in Laconia accepted the widely understood taboo against seeking favors and interfering in the administration of the department. No Laconia policeman that I met ever suggested that someone other than his uniformed superiors would affect his promotion or his duties. The elective political system of Laconia during the time of this study was conservative and business-oriented. (For a variety of reasons, the political efforts of the nonwhite population had not yet become effective. No black, for example, had even been elected to the city council.) The city manager dominated the policies of city government; elected officials deferred to him on practically every significant matter. As for political parties, they were simply nonexistent in the reform politics of the municipality, and labor was surprisingly inept in making its influence felt. The bar dominated the appointment of judgeships, and the basis of selection was more likely to be professional accomplishment and connections to the state political system than political participation within the city. The police chief, the city manager, and the civil service director agreed on the need for a professional police department; each insisted on "merit" as the sole basis for employment and promotion; each insisted that no citizen should get covert special favors. In the vacuum of city politics, they had the influence to enforce their good intentions.

Nor was there, generally speaking, any corruption within the department. In the 1950s, the department had suffered serious scandal, in which several policemen had gone to prison for shakedowns and bribery. Long since then, graft had been rooted out. Even a free cup of coffee transgressed departmental regulations, and the chief had made several harsh examples of policemen who violated the rules against accepting gratuities. Moreover, the relatively high salaries of Laconia policemen made graft unnecessary.

The result was that there were no embarrassing skeletons hidden away in the recesses of the department and no necessity to keep things secret from outsiders. Citizens and researchers, friendly and hostile, had ready access to every aspect of the department. To an extent limited solely by a concern for safety, the chief made the department's operations open for all to see. The chief's open policy had been in effect so long that patrolmen were fully accustomed to recurrent "outside" observation.

The police department was sizable—it had to be, to cover the seventy-five square miles within the city limits. In all, there were 800 uniformed personnel. Despite the relatively large size of the department, however, all administrative activities were centralized in a single building, known as "Downtown." There were no precinct stations in Laconia. The nearly 400 men who constituted the Patrol Division of the department arrived every work day at Downtown, drove out to their beats in marked cars, thereafter responded to citizens' calls dispatched by radio from Downtown, and at the conclusion of the watch returned Downtown.

Patrol officers were organized into three watches, or shifts. Each watch worked eight and a half hours a day, with a new watch coming on at 7AM (day watch), 3 PM (third watch), and 11 PM (dog watch). Every six weeks the watches rotated, so that in an eighteen-week period each officer in Patrol normally worked an equal number of weeks in the morning, evening, and night. All the men on a given watch, no matter what part of the city they patrolled, dressed in the same locker room, met in the same lineup hall, and worked out in the same gym.

Each watch was under the command of a captain. To cope with the geographical extent of the city and the frequent overload on the radio system, the department subdivided Laconia into an east area and a west area, each with its own radio channel and each supervised by a lieutenant. In turn these two areas were further subdivided into two or three districts, each of which was patrolled by a squad of eleven men led by a sergeant. Individual squad members, working alone or in pairs, were assigned to particular beats within their district.[6]

The other 400 men in the department were assigned to specialized details

---

6. Traffic and Special Operations also did Patrol work and hence met the public at large. Traffic consisted of thirty men who patrolled the city's main thoroughfares. Three features made Traffic attractive for some officers, outweighing the boring, dangerous, and relatively useless character of the work. The hours of work were stabilized; the majority of Traffic officers had weekends off; and all Traffic officers rode motorcycles, a welcome relief from the radio-ridden, claustrophobic existence inside a patrol car. Special Operations was slightly larger than Traffic and constituted a specialized Patrol operation. SOS officers (as they were called) worked parts of the city where crime was high. Their exclusive job was to fight crime, searching the streets for malefactors, and devising ways to catch the muggers, the burglars, the purse-snatchers, and the troublemakers of the world.

like the Investigative Division (consisting exclusively of men who had "made" sergeant), Training, the Juvenile and Vice Units, and Internal Affairs (which conducted investigations of allegations of police misconduct). These parts of the department, which never met the public at large the way Patrol did, were also concentrated within Downtown.

The present condition of the department was affected by its history. Events twenty and thirty years old were remembered by Laconia citizens, who passed on remembrances of the past to newcomers—in bars, on streetcorners, at family gatherings. In the past of Laconia, a riverfront and industrial city, the department was mixed up in the violence of the Great Strike (in the Depression), the Military Curfew (in the middle of World War II), and the Riot (in the middle of the "other war," in Vietnam). It was in the light of these dramatic and tumultuous events that the public at large developed its notions of the toughness, the relentlessness, and the physical massiveness of the Laconia policeman. No one in Laconia, or nearby, of any seniority, ever attributed meekness to the Laconia Police Department.

Even as late as the mid-1960s, the department was making history infected with violence. A vigilante band of black youths, called the Overseers, had organized in the early part of that decade. As a part of their self-appointed duties, they tried to modify the behavior of police within black areas—through surveillance, threats, and firearms. Deadly shoot-outs erupted half a dozen times, and there were victims on both sides. History preserved the hatreds bred by this open warfare, and it shaped dogmas, understandings, and stereotypes which did not give way quickly to changes in reality.

Moreover, history was handed down within the department. For example, in the scuttlebutt of the locker room, incoming rookies would be regaled with the stories of the free-for-alls between the department and the Devil's Men, a notorious motorcycle gang. This group of hoodlums, virulently anti-black and defiant of civilized standards, profited by narcotics traffic and partook of the violence inevitably connected with the business. Those stories abounded with powerful images and homilies; thus, the realities of history transformed themselves into lessons for today.

In police circles the department was regarded as a model in the extensive professional training it provided its officers. In 1972, the schooling period for a recruit lasted a full thirty-eight weeks. It consisted of twenty weeks of classroom work, where the new men mastered the criminal code, learned how to observe human events and write police reports about them, discussed (for six intensive weeks) the sociology of the city, took part in simulations of critical street incidents, and underwent training in using firearms. In the succeeding eighteen weeks, each rookie received individual instruction from a specially trained recruit-training officer who chaperoned and evaluated him in the field.

Thereafter, in the course of his career, a Laconia police officer would return again and again to Training. He might take several short special courses (e.g., in narcotics, alcoholism, bilingualism, first aid); he would also periodically get a more general educational course longer in duration and offered to advanced officers, recruit-training officers, and sergeants.

A final significant factor affecting the Laconia Police Department was its chief of police. During the part of the 1970s when this study was being completed, a constant topic of conversation in the ranks was the chief. His policies and his personality aroused strong feelings. He evoked hatred and respect, and often from the same men. Whenever the officers spoke well of him, they admired the undoubted clarity of his mind. They referred to his philosophy as "progressive." He tolerated no brutality, no illegality, and no graft among his men. He imposed the strictest controls on the use of firearms. He publicly applauded the due process revolution effected by the United States Supreme Court, and he took steps to explain to all his men how to adhere to the new restrictions on interrogations and searches and why adherence was a good thing.

When his men spoke bitterly of him, as a general rule they referred to his personal quirks and particularly to the unnecessary humiliations he inflicted on them, in his public disparagements and private scoldings of them. Because of his personality, he was not a popular chief. Under his tutelage, his men were often sullen, full of animosity, and increasingly resentful of his brittle, acerbic, and denigrative style.

But no man among the officers I met doubted that he had turned the philosophy of the department upside down, from a legalistic, arrest-prone, evenhandedly repressive department in which a policeman's arrests (as quantified on his weekly "activity sheet") were the unchallenged measure of his worth, to a service-oriented one, where too many arrests were treated as a signal of police ineptitude and where anything novel was assumed to be better than the old police methods.

## IV

These seven characteristics of the department—its chief, its history, its size, its training, its incorruptibility, its independence, and its clientele—affected every police officer who was working there in 1971, the year in which my researches began.

1971 was a year in which relative quiet returned to the streets of Laconia. Not that crime appreciably diminished, but policemen sensed that the violent spirit of the late 1960s was beginning to abate. National and international factors had combined to calm the communities within the city. So had the chief's "progressive" policies, at least to the extent that spokesmen for some of the minority groups which had been most critical of the police could begin to make public acknowledgment of the chief's efforts. As already noted, during the 1960s several policemen and citizens had been killed in street encounters with strong racial overtones. By 1971 large-scale battles in the streets had been transmuted into election campaigns.

In 1971 there were more than 400 policemen in the Patrol, Traffic, and Special Operations units of the Laconia department. Nearly all of them were nonsupervisory personnel. They met the public daily in the field, available on call for whatever job came up. A majority of these nonsupervisory officers were relative newcomers to the department, under thirty years old, with eight or fewer years of experience. They had all been recruited since 1963, the year the department overhauled its selection and training procedures.

Under the selection procedures instituted in 1963, each candidate faced a series of hurdles. He had to pass a battery of written intelligence exams. He submitted to a medical and physical agility evaluation. He met with a psychiatrist, who, through written and oral tests, checked for problematic emotional characteristics, principally "schizophrenic" symptoms. Police personnel investigated his background for any pattern of debts, violence, criminal behavior, or nonachievement. He submitted to a one-hour interview by a panel of three persons, consisting of a civilian examiner from civil service and two members of the police department. Only if he negotiated every one of these obstacles did he become a police recruit. For every successful candidate, thirty-three failed.

At the same time that the department was revising its selection procedures it was also formalizing its recruit-training program. In 1963 the department for the first time established a six-week course, largely consisting of practice in report writing and drills in the nuances of the criminal code. By 1971 the training had lengthened to thirty-eight weeks, including a six-week "seminar" in the sociology of Laconia and an eighteen-week field course under the tutelage of a police instructor.

## V

I wanted to find out how policemen developed in the first few years of their careers. For that reason I focused my study on those newcomers to the Laconia Police Department who had been policemen no more than eight years and who had all been selected and trained under the sophisticated procedures initiated in 1963. I took a sample of twenty-eight of these young officers in the following way.

Alphabetical lists were prepared of all nonsupervisory policemen in Patrol, Traffic, and Special Operations. I picked a random number between one and ten. Counting down the alphabetical list to the random number, I selected that name and every tenth name thereafter, giving me thirty-eight officers in all, only one of whom was nonwhite. I then listed alphabetically all nonwhite patrol officers and selected two of them randomly. Furthermore, I added arbitrarily a pair of men whom I had known earlier and whose distinctive police styles were widely appreciated in the department. By adding these last two men, I lost a degree of scientific purity, but the two gave me a kind of bench mark which I found useful in orienting myself to the sample as a whole.

This total of forty-two officers included fourteen "old-timers," men who had come on the department before 1963 and who had not taken the extensive battery of selection tests used after that. The remaining twenty-eight officers all had been appointed and trained under substantially the identical post-1963 circumstances. They made up the sample for purposes of this study, a young police department in miniature. So far as can be seen, they did not differ appreciably from their contemporaries on the department, at least at the time they were recruited. The distribution of their scores on civil service tests and their averages in the Training Academy matched that of the men not sampled. In no respect did they appear unrepresentative.[7]

Each of the twenty-eight newcomers was interviewed; they responded to a structured schedule of open-ended questions. These interviews lasted from two to five hours and averaged four hours. All interviews were conducted in privacy, in the police building (Downtown), usually after the men finished their watches that day. All men were assured absolute confidentiality.

After the passage of a year, I began riding with each of the twenty-eight officers constituting this young sample. By that time three of the original twenty-eight had left the department; one was severely injured in a motorcycle accident, and two had joined other law enforcement agencies. I spent no less than eight hours more with each of the remaining twenty-five, accompanying him as well as I could on each assignment.

As for the old-timers, they were interviewed for the perspective their lives provided for the careers of the newcomers. In fact, four of the fourteen old-timers were excused, two because they refused and two others because personal developments in their lives occurred which made interviews inconvenient to them. No substitutions were made. Moreover, I did not systematically follow up the interviews of old-timers with field observations of them.

What were the twenty-eight young policemen like? How did they size up the world? What did they worry about?

7.  Comparisons are made in the methodological appendix.

# 2

# Four Policemen

And there's no one looking over your shoulder. You've got to function by yourself. You're a little island out there. Whether over time you turn good like wine or turn bad like a pickle is up to you. Whether you go one way or the other, you get paid just the same.

*Officer Al Tennison*
Laconia Police Department
1971

The knowledge of things in particular removes from people's minds that delusion into which they ... fall ... by looking at things in general.

*Niccolo Machiavelli*
The Prince
1513

## I

To introduce ourselves to these twenty-eight young policemen, let us talk about four of them in particular—Jay Justice, John Russo, Bob Ingersoll, and Bill Tubman.[1]

Each of the four was a young man. They were in their twenties at the time of the first interview. None had been a Laconia policeman for longer than three years. Each had undergone the same departmental training program. All were married; all were white; and all described themselves as "average middle class." All were breadwinners, bringing home the same pay. All worked under the same laws and were formally obliged to do the same work. Each was a Laconia policeman, patrolling the same flatlands in 1971.

---

1. These sketches are based exclusively on my first interview with each of them. The reader should bear in mind that policemen, particularly young ones like these, were likely to change their philosophies over time. Indeed, the significant point of this book is to define the dynamics of the intellectual and moral changes policemen undergo as a result of their police experience. Nevertheless, by seizing a moment, by limiting our focus to a single snapshot of the past, we can capture the range of outlooks within a police department at a particular historical time.

Historically, none had fathers who had gone to college. None had been the oldest child in the family he grew up in. None had completed a year of college except Jay Justice, who had completed two. All were intelligent; each scored well on standard intelligence tests except Bob Ingersoll, whose test-taking skills had rusted a bit in the nine years between high school graduation and appointment to the police department.[2] Each said he had become a policeman out of a desire to help "others."[3]

But in philosophy they differed. They differed in their vision of reality and, more particularly, in their views of human nature. To the great questions, What is man? and, What is society?, they supplied different answers. Moreover, they were dissimilar in their feelings about the propriety of power. Some accepted the use of coercion in human affairs; others felt extremely uncomfortable about the employment of threats and reacted to power as a bad and unfortunate phenomenon.

The products of these two factors, one intellectual and the other moral, were differing standards of personal success. These four men had dissimilar notions of "the police role," of what they expected of themselves in doing their police work. Some had exalted and perfectionist standards of accomplishment; some developed less exacting definitions of success.

These three elements—their intellectual outlooks on the world, their emotional feelings about power, and their self-imposed moral definitions of

2. Each had taken the Otis Self-Administered Intelligence Test and the Army General Classification Test upon applying to the department. Their scores were: Justice, 62 and 113; Ingersoll, 45 and 98; Russo, 55 and 113; and Tubman, 54 and 131. For what it is worth, each also submitted at the time of appointment to an ersatz 21-question F-scale measure of Authoritarianism. Their raw scores on this methodologically problematic but intellectually provocative test were: Justice, 2; Ingersoll, 2; Russo, 10; and Tubman, 6. The higher the score, the more "authoritarian" the personality. See T. W. Adorno, Else Frenkel-Brunswick, Daniel J. Levinson, and R. Nevitt Sanford, *The Authoritarian Personality* (New York: Harper & Brothers, 1950), chap. 7. For examples of the criticism to which this measure has been subjected, see Richard Christie and Marie Jahoda, eds., *Studies in the Scope and Method of "The Authoritarian Personality"* (Glencoe, Ill.: The Free Press, 1954).

3. Throughout the interviews with each of the twenty-eight young policemen, I was reminded of one of Ross Macdonald's law enforcement protagonists when asked, "What sort of a man are you?": "I feel more strongly for other people than I do for myself. For one thing my parents had a bad marriage. It seems to me I spent a lot of time when I was a kid trying to head off quarrels, or dampen down quarrels that had already started. Then I started college in the depths of the Depression. I majored in Sociology. I wanted to help people. Helpfulness was like a religion with a lot of us in those days. It's only in the last few years, since the war, that I've started to see around it. I see that helping other people can be an evasion of oneself, and the source of a good deal of smug self-satisfaction. But it takes the emotions a long time to catch up. I'm emotionally rather backward" (Ross Macdonald, *Meet Me at the Morgue* [1953; New York: Bantam, 1972], p. 130). The chronology did not apply, the family background often was extremely different, but "helpfulness *was* like a religion" for many of the young Laconia policemen.

success—were systematically interrelated. The character of any one element—circumstances, means, or ends—had implications for the other two, just as, when one corner of a polygon is moved, the other corners must rearrange themselves.

In "general," these men were all policemen, but seen up close and more completely, they were very unlike one another.

## II

Officer Jay Justice was the oldest of the four (twenty-nine), had been longest on the department (thirty-three months), and was the only one with prior police experience. He was a powerful man. With his police hat on, he seemed taller than his six foot three; and in his down-filled police jacket he looked even more massive than his 235 pounds.

Justice's brief life story was the stuff from which Hollywood scripts were made. His father, a Texan, a truck driver, and "a straight shooter," raised him in a Gulf Coast city, in "a pretty tough neighborhood" of navy men and longshoremen. Justice did a hitch in the army, won the service's boxing championship, and then went back home, where he joined the local police department on a "whim" while going to junior college. He remained on the department for two years before he was fired "for conduct unbecoming an officer while off duty." Justice was a man who liked his drinks, and he was dismissed for being involved in a barroom brawl. He went to Alaska and got a job as a heavy-equipment operator, but quit soon after to join a police department in a nearby town. He quickly was promoted to sergeant, but after two years gave up his seniority there to enter the Laconia Police Department. As a policeman, he was imperturbable and superior: "a great officer, one of the best there is," as one proud old-timer put it.[4]

Justice was an attentive observer of human nature, and what he looked for were the pressures which people were under, their suffering from the conflict between those pressures, and the efforts they made to cope with their internal torment.

To him all human nature was one: he looked on humankind at a

---

4. If the reader feels a sense of skepticism, of déjà vu—if this portrait of the swashbuckling, hard-drinking, misunderstood, gentle giant, who embraced the good and kayoed the bad, sounds like a stereotype—it may be some consolation to know I shared those same reactions. Indeed, I worried lest certain artistic preconceptions born of seeing too many Clark Gable and Pat O'Brien movies in a misspent youth simply blinded me to life. As Jonathan Rubinstein has pointed out, however, mystery writers long have drawn on the real exploits of policemen. Art has been more influenced by life than the other way around. Jonathan Rubinstein, *City Police* (New York: Farrar, Straus & Giroux, 1973), p. ix.

sufficiently abstract level that he could see uniformities and discover what the psychiatrist Erikson once called "the simple truths of existence hidden behind the complexity of daily 'necessities.'"[5] Sensing what was common "behind the complexity," he developed a reflexive quality of mind. He applied knowledge about himself to infer the problems of others and in turn used what he learned about others to increase his own self-knowledge.

An illustration will make the discussion clearer. I asked him to tell me about "one of the more difficult spots" he had been in as a police officer. Here is his description:

> We had a warrant—a felony warrant—to make an arrest out of a family situation. We reasonably felt he was there, in a big Victorian house. I went to the front door; my partner went to the back, and my partner heard him scrambling around. About twenty people, relatives and in-laws, were living in the house. They denied he was there. We decided to go in and get him. The whole family offered resistance. Most of the people were arrested—12 or 13 arrests, including a pregnant mother, who stood blocking the doorway. She was also the mother of the person we were looking for. To me, that's the worst scene. She's involved in her family, emotionally involved.
>
> We ended up giving a call for assistance. That ended up in Internal Affairs. In that situation we pleaded for ten minutes. It was impossible to handle that well. By "well" I mean without a big hoorah. We could have backed off.
>
> Now my guess is that would not have happened ten years ago. The mother would have turned her boy in. Like I said before, we are in the middle of a social revolution. No one's sure. People are rights-conscious. They think they don't have to be pushed around, and there have been groups telling them about rights. People are real confused. The police represent, so to speak, the Establishment, and this may be the one chance they think they have to get back. They get their kicks defying us.

Notice the unitary quality of his conception of human nature. First, individuals were essentially social. They were always getting "involved" in the lives of one another, complicating their own sense of self-interest with a concern for others. As a result of empathy and interdependence, their inner feelings became identified with the well-being of others. In this particular incident, for example, all the "relatives and in-laws" developed such a sense of mutual responsibility that they all "offered resistance" to save one member of the family. They sacrificed their own security to secure someone else.

Second, this sense of social responsibility created complications. These

---

5. The phrase is Erik Erikson's. See his *Identity: Youth and Crisis* (New York: Norton, 1968), p. 32.

self-inflicted pressures to respond in terms of what was good for others inevitably conflicted with one another. People were always getting caught between incompatible responsibilities. As a result, they became "real confused," often bothered by feelings of inadequacy, and sometimes they responded erratically to the qualms of conscience. In this incident, the decision to defy the police was made in confusion, executed with misgiving, and justified in the name of equivocal principles.

Third, moral confusion was more likely to occur in some periods than in others. Historical cycles occurred; standards of right and wrong fell into dispute from time to time, challenging personal solutions to the problem of moral confusion and undermining established codes of self-restraint. The older rules by which the mother had governed herself were being undone "in the middle of a social revolution," when arguments against self-control and in favor of kicking back at "the Establishment" were current.

Fourth, Justice applied the same analysis to policemen as to citizens. In other comments Justice noted the social nature of policemen, the moral complexity of their lives, and the unsettling influence of events on their old certitudes. For one thing, policemen had a reciprocal concern for one another: they got "involved"—his word for that involvement was "camaraderie" ("After all we're dependent on each other"). Moreover, policemen also got "real confused" about the many "responsibilities" they felt, and consequently some behaved unpredictably (they began "using their job to work out their own hang-ups, . . . using people as scapegoats more or less"). Furthermore, young policemen went into and out of periods of uncertainty; they sometimes got told "about their rights" by malcontent policemen, unsettling their self-restraint and sense of responsibility.

It was man's fate to suffer doubt and to shape his answers to these conflicting pressures in anguish about what was right and wrong. The only certainty was that individuals suffered doubt and confusion. This understanding of mankind's uniform lot permitted Justice to respond to others intuitively. By force of habit, he resorted to a natural reservoir of information in order to size up others—his own self-understanding. He told me how he handled ticklish situations:

> I'll tell you what I do generally: I always try to preserve the guy's dignity.
> I leave him an out. I make it so that it's his idea to sign the ticket. Especially in a crowd situation, I leave him his dignity. My philosophy in the thing is a combination of, the fact I like to think that I thought of it myself, plus over the years I've watched. . . . Everything I do falls within that category of saving his dignity.

He would do what he would have others do unto him. He did not have to learn about others who were unlike him. On the contrary, he was one of them. His substance and theirs was the same. He had "a common sense."

That a man needed to preserve his "dignity," his sense of ethical fulfillment, was the "simple truth of existence," the "category" into which "everything . . . falls." All men came from the same mold. He had verified that truth over the years by all that "I've watched"—from the perch of triumph in the army, from the depths of disgrace in his first police job, from the second chance provided by the Laconia department.

Related to Justice's outlook on the human condition was his sense of limited purpose. His own ethical accounting system was satisfied short of perfection. He felt no responsibility for improving things totally. He held no utopian or perfectionist standards. Limited help was all that he required himself to give. In his view a degree of human suffering was inevitable, ineradicable, and perhaps necessary. The thought that a policeman could single-handedly save a neighborhood or regenerate another individual was pretentious and romantic.

Justice provided a simple example. I asked him why delinquents sometimes straightened out? "I've seen a few get turned around," he said, "but not necessarily through my efforts. I can think of a guy who began assuming responsibilities, maybe like a family. He did it more on his own." There was nothing heroic that Justice could have done to turn the "guy" around. Justice was without the means by which he could salvage a man's destiny and felt no qualms about his inability to do so. There were proper limits to his responsibility to release fellow mortals from their suffering. Perfection was not for this world.

Justice saw two reasons for being content with imperfect situations: the interest of the long run, and the complexity of right and wrong.

The long-run question, What will the day after tomorrow be like?, crimped any heroic pretensions. Even if the world could be made perfect for a day, unless it could take care of itself after its rescuer had departed, the extreme effort would have really been wasted. History extended beyond the lifetime of its putative saviors. The conflicts and infirmities of life recurred.

Justice discussed the outlook of policemen he admired who

see the overall picture. . . . To consider one big picture and you are just a part of it. How does this affect the social trend? Not, "I'm making 15 arrests by the end of the day." He questions the system as a whole. What good does this do to pick up a drunk? Foremost in his mind is the problem on hand, but he keeps the overall picture in mind. How does it—whatever he does—fit in? You've got a family beef, and the wife asks you to arrest the husband. But he thinks, Who's going to pay to put the food on the table? You have to keep a lot of things in mind.

The husband and the wife have to suffer out a solution to their own problems. A policeman could stop the beef, but he could not cure its causes.

Justice's goal was not to bring a generation of peace to a family; it was sufficient to preserve the moment from irremediable deterioration so that each party could have a second chance to make amends. Keeping the social enterprise going so that accident, a sober second thought, or new information could have their play was not heroic. In Justice's mind, it was just wise.

Thus, one limit of responsibility stemmed from Justice's knowledge that eternity was a long time. Another limit derived from a complex system of moral considerations. Justice kept his mind on the fact that his job was an "overall" one, consisting of many parts: a law enforcer, a welfare worker, a psychiatrist, a peace-keeper, an executor of the laws, a member of a police team, a private family man, and a part of a generation. He did not confine himself to one role, but compromised all the roles, rationalizing short-comings along any one dimension by denying he was a one-dimensional man. Moderation, he might have said with Aristotle, was all; compromise was optimal. In a world of multiple obligations, the pure pursuit of a single responsibility caused injustice. The conscientious policeman, Officer Justice would say, "is aware he has more responsibilities than throwing people in the bucket or interpreting the penal code."

Then Justice continued his thoughts about the ways he worked through his own moral ambiguities:

> Let me think about it. Right now, we're peace officers. We're trying to preserve the peace. That's how I extend myself. Our job is to protect the Establishment, which is being pressured to make changes faster than it is prepared to cope with them. We're in an area that has not changed much for ever so long. The sciences have changed a lot, but the social sciences have lagged behind. There are going to be a lot of changes, though there are not many so far. So I see our job as protecting the Establishment, which is under a lot of pressure right now.

Let me paraphrase Justice's interesting commentary.

"The sciences" and technology have changed the world. Along with the good consequences, they have brought some secondary harmful effects, disrupting people's lives and magnifying their problems. Furthermore, science and technology have given people the illusion that misfortunes which had been deemed inevitable could now be remedied. These rising expectations have intensified the pressures on government and leadership ("the Establishment") to cure problems for which they have neither the social technology nor the "social sciences." Moreover, the misleading implication of this illusion is that if the problems persist, they do so because the Establishment is cold-hearted and malicious. "The sciences," then, have intensified suffering and at the same time have created the impression that suffering is both easily preventable and also the responsibility of government.

"Our job" as policemen is not to "cope with" and solve these big problems. Rather it is to help individuals survive for the time being, to buy time "right now," to offset the despair of the moment, and to "protect the Establishment" until the people soberly reconsider and recognize the falsity of their expectations.

In these desperate times—right now—Justice was choosing to make his first duty that of calming people. Other obligations had momentarily lesser priority. Calming people was a big enough job to occupy a mortal. It meant he had to be a jack-of-all-trades, a Johnny-on-the-spot. It meant, for example, that he had better learn a little insurance law to help families recover indemnity for malicious damage done to their houses. It meant he had better apply a little knowledge of psychology so that he could get an old man hospitalized before the neighborhood kids taunted and drove him into desperate and destructive actions. In short, his job was "to work his beat."

But he could not take care of everything. He had no illusions that, were he to extend himself, all would be secure and well. Hence, he had no feelings of guilt or regret about what he had not accomplished. On the contrary, problems would always be with us, and it was incorrect to "carry about these guilt feelings.... You did the best you were able to at the time."

In short, Justice tried always "to consider one big picture and you are just part of it." In the phrase of E. B. White's Charlotte, the word for Justice's conception of the police role was "humble." As Justice put it, outstanding policemen "did not hog the show." It was the bad policemen who thought police "alone are waging their crusade."

If Justice's ends were humble, what means did he contemplate as necessary to fulfill them? He always tried to talk: "You try to get the respect of people." He recognized that service to others often got cooperation in return: "You spend the time with people in trouble spots." But he also was comfortable about exercising force. We turn to Justice's understanding of coercion.

Throughout the interview Justice returned frequently to the efficacy of "fear." Of certain youths he would say, "You can't do much when they don't fear the law, ... when they are not afraid of anything." Coercion was essential to gaining control of individuals who were otherwise ungovernable. Active men, men who wished to lead events rather than be led by them, had to master the techniques of evoking fear in others. Justice had learned that lesson a long time ago, "in the pretty tough neighborhood" in which he grew up. He had learned that making others fearful required action, frequently painful, difficult action. As a child, "you learn—you fight back because you do find—... you let 'em push you today, they'll push you more tomorrow. They pick on you less, the more you fight back and make them sorry." Fear implied harsh examples sometimes, making bullies "sorry."

To Justice, a policeman could not be "afraid" to fulfill his threats. "If the situation warrants it, you can take whatever action you deem necessary"—necessary to make others regret their bullying ways. Justice was aware that a policeman was set apart from his wife, his friends, his fellow citizens, by his authority to hurt others. The license to use force imposed responsibilities on the policeman which no other men had: to act "aggressively," not passively, not avoiding the pitfalls of power, not being personally prudent.

The word for Justice's understanding of the police job was boldness. Boldness amounted to an unwillingness to remain passive in the face of what was wrongful, no matter what the risks involved. To be bold was to overcome the fears ordinary men submitted to. Boldness was "sticking your neck out in any situation."[6] It was the audacity to try to dominate events when events were out of control.

Justice perceived a relationship between the limited ends he pursued and the extortionate means he used in that pursuit. He had defined for the policeman a modest responsibility. The goals were limited, the aspirations modest, the claims unpretentious. On the other hand, he seemed to have no qualms about using the extreme means of coercion to bring about results in accord with those limited aims. He felt no guilt for making the bully "sorry" or acting without charity to achieve these modest goals. He enjoyed seeing force used well when it was "proportionate"—in keeping with the limited purposes policemen fulfilled. He had no fear that he might be tempted to use extreme force, because he had no taste for extreme objectives. In Justice's mind, the best guard against misusing coercive means was to limit himself to human-sized ends.[7]

### III

Now contrast John Russo at the time I first met him, two years after he had joined the department. He was a compact, agile, twenty-three-year-old man, who spoke and thought quickly. He knew judo, had studied karate, and rode

6. One eloquent Laconia officer described the boldness of two policemen he admired:"They both will step out into the bright lights. 'Here I am,' they'll say; 'You know who I am.' They'll step into a situation and announce their presence, as opposed to not wanting to get involved. You have to be willing to expose yourself. You personify the law, and if you identify yourself and stand out, then people can react to you. They can run away from you or they can run to you, but there is no mistake that you represent the law."

7. Cf. Robert F. Kennedy, *Thirteen Days* (New York: Norton, 1969), p. 104: "President Kennedy dedicated himself to making it clear to Khrushchev by word and deed—for both are important—that the U.S. had limited objectives and that we had no interest in accomplishing these objectives by adversely affecting the national security of the Soviet Union or by humiliating her."

his own motorcycle to and from work. He was the child of a broken marriage: "My parents separated, and I went to a lot of new schools, and I had to fight at each one." Russo had a stepmother who was an alcoholic, and a tempestuous one by his account. His father was a carpenter and a small-time building contractor, who praised his son for his toughness and manhood, "even at age eleven." Russo's father "thought there was nothing better than a workingman," and he employed his son on construction jobs and encouraged the boy to earn money in whatever other employment he could get. Russo wanted the dignity his father heaped on him; he even gave up high school sports so he could work after school, hauling in "workingman's wages" and his father's "respect." Russo apparently hated school, and whenever he had time between jobs, the local police were likely to pick him up, suspecting that he had perpetrated some prank against the school or respectable society. Russo never went to college. He married young, had children, worked hard on riverboats on the Mississippi for several years after high school, and at twenty-one joined the department. The older officer who called Justice "a great officer" characterized Russo as "an eager beaver," "a hot dog," and "a young kid."

Russo's outlook on the world was expressed in a carpenter's metaphor: "Being a policeman is like building a house. You frame it, then during the night someone comes along and tears it all down." It was a roughhewn image, but it revealed much about Russo's roughhewn vision.

The world was divided into two camps, the builders, who "like to see progress," and the "night people," the predators, the destroyers. On the "good" side were the "family men," who "hustled," were ambitious, had "pride," got the "job done," could handle ruffians, kept their defenses up and their powder dry. They were pure of heart, heroic, "adult." They were workingmen. They were "We."

On the other side was the enemy: the "runners," the "fighters," the "big-mouthers," the "crowd-gatherers," the "rats," the "SOBs," the "jail-birds," the "felons," "the guys who get my goat," the "bad asses," the "pretty bad characters," the guys who "by all rights ... should be in jail," the "dirty." They were "conwise," villainous. Their only "handiwork" was crime. They were "They."

The events of life were explicable in terms of the war between "Them" and "Us." The house that was vandalized, the city that deteriorated, the chief's regulations that restricted effective police work, the anger which the citizenry directed at the department, the mellowness which the older cops developed, the "weak decisions" which the judges made—all had implications within this outlook. "Smart-ass little punks" undid the "progress" the city would otherwise have been making. The chief had bowed to "agitators." A lenient cop "did not carry his own load." The judges encouraged the enemy by "teaching" the "punks" they had nothing to fear: "it's 'continued probation' every time."

The police job was to win the war—to eradicate the impure of heart, to take back "our streets" from the barbarians and return them to the workingman citizenry. It was a series of fights to the finish, and "I've never lost one." "My dad didn't ever want a son of his to lose one. He read me his plaque he hung over his desk: 'Don't ever let anyone bully you, or they will keep right on bullying you.'"

Russo's explanation of the world was shaped not by insight but by indignation. It was part of the paraphernalia of battle. Russo was no more ready to give up this vision than he was to surrender his .38. Any educational effort or training program which would challenge his dualistic perspective was a "bunch of huckledy-buck," "public relations," a "waste of time."

The war outlook which Russo had, however, was not so firmly in place as one might have expected. Perhaps it was because Russo was only twenty-three. For whatever reasons, he did not have his world view completed. There were gaps. The structure of the jigsaw puzzle was not firm and resistant to hard knocks—yet. He was surprised by people. He was "confused" by human motives, particularly in "routine matters," between battles, when the "shit was not hitting the fan." Listen to the bafflement of his description of his beat: "The children in an apartment building, they welcome you by singing Old MacDonald, only except they only know one verse—Old MacDonald had a pig. And there's no reason for it to occur. You have not done anything to them." Nor was he able to understand his own department. The surprise, the inability to predict accurately, overwhelmed him from the first day he was interviewed for the job: "The oral board is a good idea except you don't know what they want. It's a wonder anybody gets by." He was in the dark about why police officers had so many family problems, why so many citizens in Laconia had family problems, why people were on welfare, why kids didn't go straight after they were given a break, what caused crimes of violence, why commanding officers would "whittle down" their men. The dualistic vision pitting the good against the bad could explain some, but not all, the "great, blooming, buzzing confusion" of city life.[8]

Russo described his puzzlement about a routine family disturbance.

You know, the parents call and say their kid is out of control, and all they want you to do is come and get him out of there. So you go in, and they tell you Junior is in the back room. Go get him. You go in, and Junior swings at you, and suddenly it is on the ground. Then suddenly it's no longer you and the parents against Junior. Now it's you against

8. The phrase is William James's, quoted in Walter Lippmann, *Public Opinion* (1922; New York: Macmillan, 1961), p. 80.

the world. If a guy swings at you, you should swing back, the way I see
it. You can't let him swing at you, or let him hit you, yet the parents say,
You can't use force. They'll say, Take him to jail, but don't hurt him.

Compare Russo's description of this family with the one Justice gave of the
household which had defied him. It is easier to see Russo's confusion in the
perspective of Justice's intellectual certainty.

Never once did Russo draw upon his personal experience for insight
about what was going on. The omission was even more remarkable because
Russo's own parents had so many disruptive and violent encounters with
one another. Where Justice would incorporate the learning from his private
life into the problems of the beat, Russo separated the two, drew on neither
to illuminate the other.

Quite the contrary, Russo maintained independent explanatory systems
for himself and for others. He originally placed the family encounter into
his dualistic categories. The hero-rescuer came aboard to save the victimized parents from their uncontrollable predatory son, Junior. But instead of
the knight errant's getting his due appreciation, the parents jumped all over
him. His expectation proved dead wrong. The results disconfirmed his
theories. He suffered disillusion.

Russo made no attempt to explain the erratic behavior of the parents in
terms of their "involvement" with others, the central insight feeding
Justice's outlook. The relationship of the family members was insignificant.
Russo was unaware of its implication. Nor did Russo put the event in
historical perspective. He was ignorant of what had caused the child to be
"out of control," and he was not much interested in what would happen
once he had got the son "out of there." There was no sense of context, no
time frame in which events were bunched and related—no mention of the
civil rights movement, to which Justice referred, for example. Russo closed
his eyes to the circumstances of the situation.

Acting within his dualistic world view of Us against Them, Russo wanted
to help. To him, police work was a simple job: "to put a lot of bad asses in
jail," thereby cutting "down on crimes of violence." To him, that was "all
they wanted you to do": Junior was to go to jail, for he was a malefactor.

Notable were the concerns left out of "the job," what did not have to be
done: concern for the personal consequences for the malefactor or for
anyone to whom he may have been attached, concern for the victims of the
crime or for innocent bystanders, concern for ameliorating the overall
problem, concern for the example of law-abiding behavior he was setting,
concern for equal treatment, concern for securing future public cooperation
with the police. His simple goal was to quarantine the bad characters.

The single task assigned to him was unquestionably morally gratifying.
Russo was called a "hot dog" by his fellow officers and took it as a

compliment. By doing "a lot of work" he derived satisfaction—he was saving lives, aborting burglaries, preventing families from being "cleaned out," and protecting human enterprise. He was confident he was helping this family and the rest of his beat in the only ways he felt appropriate—pacifying it, forcing the rats out of it, doing sentry work on its perimeters.

Preoccupied with his simple task, Russo came to feel that every crime committed within his beat was a personal shortcoming of sorts. A burglary meant that he had failed to scare off a suspicious person; he had ignored his "sixth sense"; he had left unmade a possible car stop. A burglary was a blot on his record. Perhaps, thought Russo, he could have prevented it if he had only worked harder.

Another consequence arose. Since crime-fighting was the only job which was morally legitimate under his one-dimensional scale of values, whenever Russo acted in other capacities, he felt he was wasting his time. Talking with victimized families was "public relations; it couldn't be a bigger waste of time." Resolving family beefs happily through patient talk was "bullshit" or dishonesty. Writing a good report for police or social services was "secretarial work." Each of these achievements counted for nothing; worse, they diverted him from cutting down crime, thus increasing his sense of inadequacy and frustration in the face of continued crime.

Still another consequence of focusing on one criterion of success was to heighten the threshold of achievement which satisfied him. Where Justice was content to protect his beat from criminals as well as he could within the limits imposed by the multiplicity of duties, Russo had no countervailing, legitimate obligations to justify his falling short of perfection. The simpler the morality, the more obsessive became its demands. Keeping the beat as clean as possible transformed itself into keeping the beat perfectly clean. If Justice was concerned about reaching some kind of optimal compromise, Russo was driven by an assertive maximization principle. Justice had human limits imposed on him by the obvious incompatibility of his tasks; Russo set himself a superhuman job to perform: perfection along a one-dimensional moral scale.

There was a similarity between Justice and Russo. They both were "unafraid" of using force. Manipulating people by making threats was not incomprehensible, immoral, or difficult for either of them. Russo had a sophisticated understanding of deterrence theory, learned in the two "toughest" high schools in town and at his father's knee: "Don't ever let anyone bully you, or they will keep right on bullying you." He understood the value of a harsh example: "a show of force is a deterrent," he would insist. He appreciated the value of a nasty reputation: "Being a good guy does not work in Laconia." In short, Russo had worked through a great deal of the intellectual meaning of coercion.

Likewise, he found force a moral means. Resort to threats was proper.

With pride, he talked of his detached technique of calming a family dispute: "I say to her, 'There's no need for you to be screaming in front of us. We've got better things to do'": That's what I tell them. That kind of upsets them. But I've had luck with it. I've had very few return calls. Usually I threaten people. With a firm tone I say, 'I don't want to take you to jail. If I have to come back, someone's gotta go to jail.' "

Finally, Russo was, by his own lights, skillful in coercion. "I've had luck with it." As we shall see, other policemen differed from Justice and Russo; for them, coercive means were distasteful, wrong, and full of pitfalls.

Russo sounded a theme absent in Justice's discussion of force. Russo felt morally compelled to use force when laws and departmental regulations forbade it. As a result he "was getting in the shit six times a year." Worse, when he behaved according to the officially approved code, he had a vague sense of double-crossing himself: "You can't treat anyone out there as you know they should be treated—as a jailbird. You have got to treat them as an average person." He found himself "pushing aside the rules a little bit"; he bent the truth on occasion ("What I do is lie"); he was flirting with the idea of "padding" reports "like a lot of policemen do," to cover up the discrepancy between what he knew was legal and what he felt was morally justified.

Why? I suggest it was the compulsion of the ends he felt obliged to achieve. Russo's moral philosophy, his stringent standard of success and failure, was so one-dimensional, so uncomplicated by contradictory purpose, that it made imperative the use of the policeman's fullest capability. The urgency of the job undercut any excuse for moderation in the employment of force. There was no moral excuse for restraint. The law may have forbidden maximum force, but Russo perceived it to be an act of betrayal and cowardice to knuckle under to the law. His need for moral worth, his "pride," would eventually overcome his timidity; defiance of the laws and the regulations would be the hallmark of good police conduct. "I worked dredges before I came on the department, and one supervisor would say, 'If you don't fall overboard six times a year, you're not doing the job.' It's the same way here. If you're not getting in the shit six times a year, you're not doing the job."

## IV

Bob Ingersoll was a big man; he weighed 220 pounds and he was six feet four inches tall. His voice tended to break in the treble register, yet his size and calmness overcame any implication of anxiety or weakness. His father had been murdered by a strong-arm robber when Ingersoll was one year old. His mother had raised him and an older brother, who later became a professor of engineering.

The family was very poor: "I guess my childhood ambition was to be rich; not rich, but wealthy." Ingersoll had had polio, and he still limped discernibly when he was tired. Ingersoll had become a handyman and worked steadily and responsibly for seven years before becoming a policeman at age twenty-six. With only a high school diploma, and several years removed from the classroom to boot, he had difficulty with the department's intense training program. Despite his poor academic rating, however, officers who evaluated his field performance came away impressed. For his own part, Ingersoll was modest: "I don't really know much. I've only worked a year."

Ingersoll was intensely interested in the problem of human motivation. "On a family call you try to understand what caused the people to get to the point where they had to call you in the first place, to get the big picture, I guess." Note the detail of the "picture" of human behavior Ingersoll could recall:

A fight between the husband and wife. The guy had come unglued. There was no way to reason with him in the field. That's what bothered me. Usually you can make heads and tails of what is happening and why it's happening. His wife spent all the month's welfare money. He was trying to make good, trying to toe the mark. He had been laid off, and he was in Sparta [a public housing project] and giving his welfare check to an organization to pay off all his bills and rent and what not. He was trying to keep his head above water, and he had come home and his wife had spent the check. There was no way to calm him down. Alcohol, maybe drugs had played a part. We're out there to preserve the peace, and the fact that we were no way near doing that really bothered me. When we arrived, it was not a criminal matter yet, although the pots and pans were really flying. We were not being able to relieve the situation at all, being there. We just had to take him in. As I said, drugs and alcohol maybe had played a part. I kind of understood the guy's problems. He had made an honest effort to make good. He had two children and he had come home and the money's not there. I understood, but I couldn't solve the problem. He was sure tearing up the place, which was sad because they were nice furnishings. I've come across three or four situations like this, where the guy—it's always the male—where there's no way to get to him. . . . The problems are so immense. The guy can't get a job. He doesn't have a high school diploma or he has a record. He has no money. He lives in a crummy house. It's dirty. His kids are real unfortunate. It's not gratifying, these family beefs.

He took in "the whole situation"; he bothered about causes, the underlying "problems" which would compel a man to become other than his usual "decent" self. Drugs, alcohol, difficulties, even a youthful lark, could cause people to act up. However, if a police officer could "slow down the pace of things," decency could reassert itself. With a second chance, the experience of the earlier debacle would teach the man something. All mankind profited from its mistakes: "We all make mistakes. When I was young, I swiped a couple of candy bars. I was taken downtown once and put into jail for putting soap into the water fountain on Broadway." With a second chance, persons cooled off, calmed down, slept on it, solved the problem, got things straight.

There was no separation between Us and Them, no dualism. Policemen and citizens alike were put in the same bag: "All put on their pants in the same way," he said of his fellow officers, but he meant it to apply to all mankind.

This monistic, reflexive view of human nature as born good, bolted down as it was in the "ten years of life before I came to the department," bore a resemblance to Justice's, except in one respect. There was no accounting for the differences in human nature across space or over time. Justice saw human beings as being "involved" in codes of moral responsibility, but the substance of these codes was constantly changing and could be altered by culture, the nature of the crowd, the family setting, changing relationships to persons and things. Ingersoll's picture of human nature was more fixed and less dynamic. Mankind was basically decent, had been, and always would be, whatever the setting. Aberrations might occur in individual cases, depending on the extent and severity of the problems which eroded that decency. But the historical setting made no great difference. Hence, Ingersoll made no allusions to history, to the "trend," to the "overall picture," things which concerned Justice.

Ingersoll's vision was in no way like Russo's. He did not lump people into legal categories, as "felons" or burglars or car thieves, or their colloquial equivalents. On the contrary, the Laconia citizen was like Rousseau's noble savage or the Hebrew Poet's Job, sorely tried, clinging to life, capable of rallying from self-pity, rekindling his energies, and thrusting his decency into the face of terrible oppression.

In a world full of such tragic figures, Ingersoll's moral duty was clear: to assist them in coping with their individual oppressions. It made no difference that they were malefactors or victims. Relieving problems—getting an ambulance, giving consolation, getting a workman his payment, finding a shelter for a drunk, calling an expert in—was the police equivalent of the handyman's fixing a leaky roof. His standard of success was his client's happiness. "I don't know whether being a police officer differs from any other line of work. What makes him liked in any line of work makes him liked in police work." Ingersoll had a talent for helping and consoling, and he dispensed his services for "gratifying" consideration: thanks, recognition, cooperation, inner pleasure. He sought out ways to provide these services. "It's gratifying to me to talk with business establishments and stores to let them know you are out there and to assure them that they should call you, not their cousin or their bosses." He was the true servant of the people.

But by no means was he a compulsive rescuer. If his offer to help was turned down, or if his compassionate, consoling, empathetic approach was insufficient to rekindle the strength to set things straight; if "all I can do" failed to relieve the difficulty, it was not a personal failure on his part. As he liked to repeat, he did "not take the tragedies of others home with me." Ultimately, it was the individual citizen's responsibility to "forget it," to rally around, and to make an accommodation with his own problems. Ingersoll was content to assist only those who wanted his assistance. It was enough to lend a hand to those who wished to save themselves in a trying world.

What Ingersoll did "take . . . home with me," what really bothered him, was not his inability to rescue everybody, but the problems of force. He was truly relieved to find that older policemen regarded him as a good cop, because the assurance permitted him the luxury of "being too easy." For his part, he wanted to "reason" with the citizenry; he was bothered when reason failed to calm a situation and could not understand the justification for wielding authority against the people rather than helping them.

> So many people are low income. They can't get jobs. There's a big circle there. They drive old, beat-up cars. And you issue citations. Their head-light is out, their taillights don't work. He's emitting excess smoke. He can't afford to fix it. But if he gets a warrant, he'll have to go to jail. And there's a tremendous lot of bail. It's a vicious circle. . . . We give him a mechanical citation, and it costs to get it fixed. And if he doesn't it's a $44 traffic warrant. So you take him to jail.

Threats were "a strange way to operate"; they led to paradoxical results, putting decent people into jail, "locked up, confined."[9] Coercion was an intellectual enigma and a moral evil.

Several consequences flowed from his remedial outlook and emotional aversion to force. One was his joy in coming on a citizen who aroused his indignation, who deserved to be coerced, who was a moral arrest, like a dangerous man performing a "hot activity." Interestingly enough, included in this category of moral arrests, against whom threat and force might be used legitimately, were citizens who tried to deceive. In Ingersoll's mind the ultimate sin was personal dishonesty. "I really get mad. I don't know why I do." Ingersoll expected others to avoid fraud. The obligation not to cheat was the key clause in the social contract. In this suffering world, one might do violence, be careless, lapse into self-pity, but one lived up to one's word. If a suspect betrayed his trust, Ingersoll's indignation overrode any misgivings

---

9. On a grander scale, Ingersoll talked of war and how he hated it: "If I were president, I would get rid of all weapons."

he had about making the arrest, about jailing people in "a little room, by yourself, with no way out."

Another consequence was frequent personal discomfort on the job. Presupposing that the best in people would ultimately surface gave Ingersoll a frame of reference in which to preserve a great many memories of citizens who eventually redeemed themselves: the irate woman who turned contrite, the juvenile motorcyclist "you ... got through to," the husband and wife who saw the light after "sleeping on the situation." The presupposition that "people are decent" sifted out disappointing memories and stored corroborating ones. Yet some surprises occurred: truthful-appearing people gulled Ingersoll into errors. If outsiders, particularly fellow officers, were present, and if they thereafter reminded him of his false prediction through their silent or explicit criticism, it nettled him. He was especially vulnerable because he did not enjoy justifying his outlook. He was a man of action, and he was content to let his overall results speak for themselves. He was not willing to create a time and place to explain a prediction which had gone awry. A more eloquent officer might have said to his partner, "Let's go for coffee" and then explained, as Justice did, "It's more important not to lose the chance than that I'm right. I believe people more than some of the other guys do." Ingersoll would not. Rather he would just fall back within himself. Often criticism got under his skin, however, and his resentment would burst out in the next incident on some surprised or rebuffed citizen. Despite his considerable confidence in the way he saw life, disappointments were a source of considerable discomfiture, the more so because he lacked the extraordinary verbal skills which could have persuaded his fellow officers to see the world his way.

Ingersoll's philosophy contrasted with Justice's in another respect. Both described the good policeman as one who saw a larger picture. Despite the similarity of language, they actually were speaking of different things. For Justice, the "overall picture" consisted of social repercussions: the implications of police action for the city, the society, the general welfare, the future, the "Establishment," the institutions of leadership and education and finance, the foundations of law and morality on which confidence, reliance, and hope depended. For Ingersoll, however, "the full picture" consisted of the immediate causes of what he could see was happening. What was meaningful to him was the individual and his problem—its causes, its consequences, and its remedy. "Society" was an abstraction that meant little to him.

In fact, in Ingersoll's view of human nature as decency beset by corrupting impersonal forces, society was not worth much. Rather it had to be defended against, beaten back, throttled to preserve the individual. On the contrary, Justice's view of human nature made the "Establishment" essential, for the individual was enlarged by human association, enriched by civilized culture, and ennobled by the higher responsibilities society imposed on him. "Society" had meaning for Justice; it determined human behavior for good or ill.

With such different understandings of the consequences of society, Justice and Ingersoll approached the concept of coercion with contrary emotions. Ingersoll thought the policeman was obliged to help the individual, to cure him, to treat him solely as an end, never as a means. His job was clinical in nature, between cop and client. To make an example of the malefactor, to hurt him as a way to convince others to live up to their social responsibilities, made no sense to Ingersoll. It was an unjustifiable use of people as means. For Justice, however, the short-run well-being of an individual might properly be sacrificed to preserve the going concern, the "society," the long run. Ingersoll's concept of the beneficent individual made it much more problematic to justify deterrent coercion than did Justice's concept of the "civilized man," according to which civilization had a value apart from any one individual.


## V

Bill Tubman was five feet nine inches tall and weighed 160 pounds, but he looked thinner. He was twenty-three. He had been raised in a peaceful town in rural Kansas, where his father had owned a service station and his entire family busied themselves making ends meet. Hard work and family unity were the values of the Tubman family; the intellectual bounds were confined: "My dad and mom didn't talk to us much about public service and all that. His service station usually kept him busy."

Halfway through his first year in college, Tubman quit and came to Laconia to join the police department. Upon completing his training, he began to go to college again. He therefore obtained a permanent assignment to the third watch (3-11 PM). As a result, whenever the regular squads rotated every six weeks to a different watch, he began working with a new group of men. Always working third watch was an unsettling and rootless experience. For a diffident and somewhat frightened young man like Tubman, it compounded his isolation from the department. It meant that he had no ready access to the locker room bull sessions among friends; he could not participate in those recurring conversations which would help develop a gift of gab, permit the airing of experiences, and sharpen the eye for detail.

Bill Tubman was intelligent. He had one of the highest scores on the mélange of vocabulary, math, and spatial perception questions which the department used to evaluate police candidates, and in his training class he ranked at the midpoint. The world, however, especially the big-city world of

Laconia, was hard for him to understand. Although he had been a policeman for two years when I first met him (the same length of time as Russo and a year longer than Ingersoll), he still got "lost up there" on his beat. He recalled seeing the city on his first visit there: "We looked at Laconia, and it seemed so big, so overwhelming."

His incomprehension was even greater at the human level. He had little intuitive understanding about people; he had nurtured no presuppositions about what made society tick; he made frequent wrong guesses about what was going to happen.

Unlike Ingersoll, who inquired about the personal details of his citizenry, Tubman never hankered for that kind of information. He had no concept of human nature into which he could organize his experience. As a result, the human aspect of events dribbled right out of his mind.

To be sure, he did sort policemen into two types: those whose daring "panicked" him and those officers who were "cautious." Moreover, he had begun to notice interesting "similarities in the job," which made things "easier . . . the next time around." Yet he could not put words to the kinds of similarities he was seeing; he could not create pigeonholes into which he could file human events and history. He labored under a learning incapacity, and he never recognized that his problems in understanding existed and could be worked on. Because of his timidity and his organizational isolation on a permanent third watch, and because no one was formally obligated to talk within the department, no one engaged him in dialogue to hammer out the meaning of his experiences.

Nor did he have a historical perspective, of how things changed and why they developed as they did. In the entire eleven hours I was with him (three hours of interviewing and eight hours of field observation), he made not one allusion either to the past or the future, with the single exception of this bit of baseless optimism: "Maybe people are getting wise, and the use of narcotics will go down." He was at sea in speculating on the causes of crime: "Burglaries and robberies are going up, and that's due to narcotics, but rape is going up too. I don't know what explains the rising crime rate."

His inability to anticipate events caused him to be surprised and often humiliated. Here is his own description of how he handled one family row:

> It was a day watch, and I got a 975, stand by and preserve the peace. It
> was on the third floor of this big apartment building. I was alone and
> had no transceiver. I went in, and things had quieted down. She wanted
> to get her stuff. So anyway in the course of the deal, I found a marijuana
> joint. I found a little more grass around. Anyway I found it. It was the
> man's anyway. He was there, and she was there. I saw it, and she had
> showed it to me and wanted him to go to jail. I was alone and had no
> transceiver. He was a real big guy, and he had some friends around the

apartment. I didn't arrest him. I was just out of recruit school. I might
have done the same thing now. I would have tried to get a cover unit, and
if I had waited for it, he might have still been around. I just let it slide.
She took off with all her clothes. The decision was whether to arrest him
or not. He got a little upset about it. I told her to hurry and get her stuff
out. I didn't want to make anything of it.

There was a bumbling quality about this piece of police work. No transceiver
(a portable two-way radio), no cover, no anticipation of what was likely to
happen. It was not as if Tubman had just happened on an incident to which
he had to adapt quickly. The activity stemmed from a radio call.

What really happened is not clear from his description. But it says all that
Tubman knew. He had almost no perception of who the girl was, who the guy
was, why they were fighting. All he saw was that the guy was "real big" and
"got a little upset" about the prospect of being arrested for having
marijuana. The girl was small and friendless and wanted to make "something of it"; so Tubman became gruff with her. Might was right, and
weakness was wrong.

This humiliation occurred in his first year on the department. Yet after
another year of police experience, he still "might have done the same thing
now": failed to get cover and to carry a transceiver, let things "slide," lack
control, be gruff with her, be abjectly humiliated in front of that "real big
guy" and his friends. In that story one can see why an older officer could say
of Tubman, "He sometimes comes on too hard with suspects, and other
times too easy with the wrong ones."

Under the pressures of his daily encounters with the public, Tubman
began to develop a dualistic view of human nature. The similarity to Russo's
vision of mankind ended there. The categories were not Us and Them, the
builders and the wreckers, but the "nonintimidating" and "the intimidating." His antennae were out, picking up cues by which he could make the
necessary identifications in each case. He did not ask himself why some
individuals fell in one category and some in the other. The terrors of police
work gave him little time for such detached reflection. He had enough on his
mind just to survive.

Tubman liked the idea of being a policeman because he had "always
wanted to help people," and he found that being a policeman had its
satisfying moments. He liked being on the scene of automobile accidents,
helping the injured. He liked doing investigations after a crime. He liked
testifying in court. He liked the pleasure of being useful to others, of having
"a part in the overall picture." He enjoyed bringing to the nonintimidating
segment of the public the experience of security which the unintimidating
citizens of his Kansas town had shared. When the opportunity arose to
re-create rural Kansas in Laconia, no task was too time-consuming, no detail

too small, no job too unusual. He wanted to help—and to receive the gratitude due the full-spirited public servant.

However, in the presence of the intimidating, he was intimidated. He lacked the skill and the knowledge to use coercion successfully. I asked him how he handled young juveniles on his beat. "If you mean the teen-age burglar, a young criminal, a guy who breaks the law, then you say, 'This is my beat, man; keep it clean.' " The way he said it convinced me that he had rehearsed that remark many times in his fantasies but never delivered it on the street. He had not thought through what could happen when his bluff was called and when his motivation to follow through on his threat was challenged. His interview was laced with memories of when he "backed down," "let things slide," did "not follow through," "did not want to make anything of it," "had not been involved enough," "accomplished nothing." He was not competent in governing others who initially resisted him. He was not bold.

Nor did he understand the psychology and the ethics of force. In his prosaic and busy peaceful childhood, people were hardworking and God-fearing. There was no need for force, and his parents had never talked about its utility. I asked him if his parents had ever advised him about bullies, and he responded, "If they did, I don't remember, but they probably said, 'Just ignore them.' " Tubman had taken this advice to heart and had proceeded to ignore situations where skillful use of force might be necessary.

The personal necessity to ignore danger, however, eventually eroded his desire to help. His fears began to preoccupy his sense of responsibility. Success in police work became the job of staying alive, of keeping aware of possible dangers, of finding ways to fill time with uneventful safe activities, of justifying staying out of harm's way.

Thus, despite the fact he "always wanted to help people," he developed distinctions which justified his avoidance of danger. For one thing, he began to define police work as dealing only with matters defined as criminal by the penal code. "Civil" matters were not his business (despite the fact that accident investigation was archetypically civil): "A lot of calls don't belong to us. A lot of civil problems. Landlord-tenant problems and the like, which are civil problems. They don't even belong to us. They could be channeled elsewhere. Maybe they could be taken care of over the phone." Many officers made a distinction between civil and criminal matters, but for them it had a meaning different from the implication it had for Tubman. For officers like Russo, the distinction permitted them to economize on time, to give them more minutes and hours each day to put the bad guys into jail. Justice, and others like him, appreciated the distinction but accepted both spheres as their job, seeing the connection between the two. Arbitrating disputes between citizens and helping them settle disputes produced information about the people of Justice's beat, permitted him to set a good example, earned him friends. In short, civil problems were his opportunity to work his beat. Tubman, on the other hand, found the distinction a handy way to avoid a vast assortment of potential entanglements which he could not govern. "Policing," to Tubman, "was often a matter of knowing how many ways to tell them, 'We can't help you.'"

With "civil" matters defined as out-of-bounds and "criminal" matters defined as too dangerous for the "cautious" policeman, one might wonder whether Tubman would ever have involved himself in police work were there no activity sheet requiring him to account for his time. He wanted to act only where his safety and self-esteem were out of danger. To avoid a sense of falling short, he cut his sense of public responsibility down to size, whittling away at the part of the population to whom he had to respond. Lacking the skills, the motives, the courage of public life, he pulled back within himself, avoiding power, hating much of his work, despising the diversity and the challenge of the world, fleeing from the confusions to which much of his work exposed him, and suppressing the memory of obligations unmet. He could get away with it by changing squads every six weeks, working a one-man patrol, keeping a sharp eye out for safe jobs, and maintaining a low profile. He was, as a professional put it, one of "those fellows who got their fingers burnt" and thought that the best way was to avoid risky situations altogether.

## VI

These four men differed from each other intellectually and morally.

Intellectually, Justice and Ingersoll both looked at human nature as one: they had "a common sense," a unitary conception of mankind, in which the uniformities between individuals permitted one person to walk in the shoes of another. Russo and Tubman, on the other hand, each held dualistic conceptions, divided people into categories essentially and ultimately different from one another.

Morally, the four had opposed conceptions about the means of coercion. Justice and Russo alike were comfortable using coercive means to manipulate others. Each had an understanding of the utility of force in society; each felt that threats were a proper means to bring about worthwhile ends; each felt he was competent in using force to govern others. In contrast, Ingersoll and Tubman were uncomfortable with coercion. They knew of few, if any, circumstances under which force could produce good results. They would rather deal with people than dominate them.

As a consequence of these intellectual and moral differences, the men differed in what gave them satisfaction. They disagreed about the proper goals of police work. Justice and Ingersoll, with their unitary visions of mankind, set limits on the policeman's responsibility for rescuing his fellow man. But Ingersoll's distaste for coercion led him to isolate a set of enjoyable responsibilities different from the limited social obligations Justice assumed. In Russo's and Tubman's cases, the responsibilities they owed to individuals were more total—to rescue a certain segment of the populace from the sources of their unhappiness. But they had different feelings about coercion, Russo wanted to stand up and fight the victimizers; Tubman wanted to give succor to the victims.

The moral and intellectual diversity of these four policemen was representative of the diversity among the men in the ranks, as we shall see. The causes of the philosophical and emotional variation among them undoubtedly flowed from many sources. Long before they became policemen, they had been shaped by influences of every kind. Yet the effect of their police work on their most deeply held attitudes was undoubted. One could see that, but for their police experiences, they would not have laced their discussion of the basic intellectual questions about man's nature and society's function with the same richly textured illustrations. Had they not become policemen, they would not have responded so feelingly to the big moral questions of guilt and courage, honesty and loyalty. And but for the fact that the tools of their occupation included that ultimate weapon of coercive power, the gun, they would not have been so bothered by, or thought so deeply about, the problem of force—of the relationship between cruel means and worthwhile ends.

The next two chapters explore the notion of coercion and why it has come to play so large a part in the development of a policeman's outlook on the world. They will be more difficult and more remote chapters, seemingly unrelated to the fiber of police life. If the reader keeps two problems in mind, however, the direction of the book may become a bit clearer. The first is to analyze what makes a policeman's life so abnormal, so difficult for a layman to appreciate. The second problem is to develop a conception of what a good policeman is, a definition which takes into consideration the unique circumstances within which a real cop really works.

# 3

# The Extortionate
# Transaction

I'm just giving fair warning, if anybody throws
at my hitters, they will get the same in return.
Pitchers have got to protect their hitters.
You've got to do this, or they'll be knocking
you down all season.

*Gaylord Perry*
Cleveland Indians pitcher
1972

War is Peace.

*George Orwell*
1984
1949

## I

What is coercion? What makes it unique in human affairs?

Coercion is a means of controlling the conduct of others through threats to
harm. Coercive relationships exist everywhere in every society: in families, in
the marketplace, and, characteristically, in political institutions. Civilization
tolerates, even makes possible, many uses of coercion. Most notably, it
delegates to its public officials the license to threaten drastic harm to others.
Some societies, particularly free countries, assure private subjects the right to
exercise significant threats within a framework of law. This legal license to
coerce is frequently referred to as authority, to distinguish it from the
unauthorized and prohibited practices variously called tyranny, blackmail,
and criminal extortion.

The practice of coercion, whether in its lawful or in its unlawful aspect,
involves complex application and has troublesome consequences. To appreciate the nature of coercion more profoundly, I am going to look at a
simplified model of a coercive relationship. I shall call this simplification the
extortionate transaction. I use "extortion" throughout, not in its illegal

sense, but neutrally, describing both authorized and unauthorized forms of coercion—authority as well as hooliganism.[1]

## II

When we construct the extortionate transaction, two facts stand out. First, an extortionate relationship is an antagonistic one. In a world in which relationships are based on threat, everyone is either a victim or a victimizer, one party perceiving that the other is trying to get something for nothing. Therefore the oppressor must instinctively anticipate resistance from the oppressed. Extortion is the classic vicious cycle. *The victimizer is always a potential victim of counterthreats,* ever on guard against the moment his victim retaliates. Both parties to an extortionate relationship have to be preoccupied with the problem of self-defense. The process of extortion in this sense is symmetrical.[2]

Second, extortion depends upon the victim's possessing two things: a *hostage* and a *ransom*. A threat is made by the victimizer committing him to injure the hostage (something the victim values very much) unless the victim will pay a ransom (something he prefers to give up to save the hostage from harm). In the absence of either hostage or ransom, the extortionate relationship will break down; it ceases to be symmetrical. The truly dispossessed—those who have nothing to lose, the life prisoner in solitary,[3] the deadbeat, the bankrupt, and the visionary whose life is worth less than his martyrdom—are not vulnerable to extortionate power. (In the legal profession, the phrase for the dispossessed is "judgment-proof.") Let us call this curious freedom from coercive threats the paradox of dispossession. *The*

1.  The following discussion derives from the work of five major social scientists of this century: Peter Blau, Ralf Dahrendorf, Harold Lasswell, Thomas Schelling, and Max Weber. See generally Peter Blau, *Exchange and Power in Social Life* (New York: Wiley, 1964); Ralf Dahrendorf, *Essays in the Theory of Society* (Stanford, Calif.: Stanford University Press, 1968); Harold Lasswell and Abraham Kaplan, *Power and Society* (New Haven: Yale University Press, 1950); Thomas Schelling, *The Strategy of Conflict* (Cambridge: Harvard University Press, 1960); and Max Weber, "Politics as a Vocation," in *From Max Weber: Essays in Sociology,* ed. and trans., H. Gerth and C. Wright Mills (New York: Oxford University Press, 1946).

2.  Machiavelli, quoting Titus Livius, discourses on the motives and fears of individuals in politics: "And thus the desire of liberty caused one party to raise themselves in proportion as they oppressed the other. And it is the course of such movements that men, in attempting to avoid fear themselves, give others cause for fear; and the injuries which they ward off from themselves they inflict upon others, as though there were a necessity either to oppress or to be oppressed" (*Discourses,* trans. Christian E. Detmold [New York: Modern Library, 1950], bk. 1, chap. 46).

3.  Gresham Sykes, *The Society of Captives* (Princeton, N.J.: Princeton University Press, 1958), chap. 3, has an especially illuminating discussion of the paradox of dispossession in a maximum-security prison.

*less one has, the less one has to lose.* One cannot picket barren ground, Cesar Chavez used to warn his followers.

As a general rule, in the dynamics of extortion, the victim's position worsens the more precious the resources he accumulates. There are two reasons for this. First, the more valuable—that is, the more difficult to replace—any one possession, the more distressed will be its owner by its potential destruction. When the Spartan king Archidamus urged his countrymen not to lay waste the Athenian farmlands, his argument rested on the fact that "The only light in which you can view their land is that of a hostage in your hands, a hostage the more valuable the better it is cultivated.[4]

A second reason is, the more possessions a victim has, the more ransom he can pay to preserve the hostage and the less reasonable it becomes for him to refuse to pay. The rational kidnapper abducts the prince, not the pauper. Extortion makes us the victim of our possessions, the captive of our things.

As a consequence of the paradox of dispossession, parties in an extortionate relationship must engage in either self-minimization or self-defense. The victim himself may destroy his own embarrassment of riches. The political economist Schelling sums up the matter, "In bargaining weakness is often strength, . . . and to burn bridges behind one may suffice to undo an opponent."[5] Soldiers who sacrifice their means of retreat destroy the enemy's potential hostage. By voluntarily relinquishing their escape route, they may save themselves the ransom they might otherwise have had to pay to preserve their escape (the enemy, seeing that coercion will not avail, may fall back, not willing to pay the cost of using brute force).[6]

## III

If dispossession by self-minimization is impossible, then the victim must, as Machiavelli admonished, "fortify well." The victim's possessions are less likely to be seized as hostages the more dearly the victimizers must pay to seize them. Potential victims therefore create *sanctuaries* inside which possessions are no longer vulnerable to easy seizure as hostages. The sanctuaries may be based on custom, law, or force.[7]

---

4. Thucydides, *History of the Peloponnesian Wars,* trans. Richard Crawley, in *The Greek Historians,* ed. M. I. Finley (New York: Viking, 1960), p. 262.
5. Schelling, *Strategy of Conflict,* p. 22.
6. Similarly, Tocqueville, that brilliant and prophetic observer of nineteenth-century America, noted the extortion-proof advantages of Puritan austerity. Alexis de Tocqueville, *Democracy in America,* trans. Henry Reeve, (New York: Vintage, 1945), 1:35.
7. Moralized customary taboos exist in the class structure, professional practices, and occupational arrangements. The aristocrat does not "betray his class" by exposing the dirty linen of his peers to public view. Politicians do not defile the reputations of their colleagues,

However, the more the sanctuaries depend on force alone, the more the victims's energies are expended on the tasks of self-defense. If an individual relies on self-fortification, he tends to develop what is termed "the minimax strategy": his object is to minimize the maximum risk by forgoing every opportunity to be gainful and creative. He ends up burying his talent instead of putting it out at risk, because the perils of seizure are too great outside the sanctuary and the sanctuary's perimeters are too confined to accommodate more than the solitary individual. Thus, the paradox of dispossession has some important effects: it makes a virtue of waste and self-minimization and penalizes creation and accumulation.

The extortionate transaction implies several more interesting paradoxes. One is the paradox of detachment. The victimizer needs to take hostages, but he cannot always perceive clearly what value a victim places on his own possessions. The kidnapper of the king's daughter can never be sure whether the king loves or hates her; if the king is glad to get rid of her, the kidnapper will have succeeded only in taking custody of a shrew. Analogously, voters may threaten an irresponsible senator with prospective defeat at the next election, their hostage being his hopes of retaining office; but if he is indifferent about reelection, their threat will have no effect on his conduct. Likewise, the shopkeeper who has adequately insured his shop may be indifferent to extortionate bomb threats (although his insurance company may feel otherwise).

If the victim can make it clear that he could not care less about losing his daughter, his elective office, or his shop, his indifference for it renders this possession a very indifferent hostage. In dealing with extortion, then, one way one can safeguard a possession one really cares about is to show indifference toward it. This irony is what we mean by the paradox of detachment: *the less the victim cares about preserving something, the less the victimizer cares about taking it hostage.*

The paradox of detachment applies equally to persons and to things to which a victim is attached. The rule that a prison guard must shoot at escaping prisoners who have taken other guards hostage makes sense only if in the long run it convinces prisoners that society regards with indifference the lives of prison guards taken hostage. We kill guards to save guards' lives;

---

even if they philander, get drunk, or moderately pocket some dubious profits. Even in the Mafia, the wife and children of a gang member are not deemed to be "in the business." As for legal sanctuaries, the usual method of providing a citizen with protection for his possessions is to designate them as "property," entitling him to invoke the public force for his protection. A property right is nothing more than the dependable and gratuitous assistance of judges, policemen, and public attorneys in providing a refuge for a person's possessions.

reducing the utility of kidnapping them, we hope to reduce the frequency of such kidnappings.

Detaching oneself from the reciprocal and moralized relationships of human friendship makes a great deal of sense in the extortionate transaction. For the considerate participant in extortion (be he victim or victimizer), it is better to sacrifice his friendships than to have to ransom his friends. Furthermore, a renunciation of his attachments decreases his own vulnerability to victimization. For one thing, his friends may be more susceptible to seizure than he himself. The child lacks the prudence of his parent in fending off the blandishments of the kidnapper. And a victim with a great many friends is as vulnerable to extortion as the least careful of them. For a second thing, under most civilized circumstances, the victim may be under a moral compulsion to pay a ransom to save innocent third parties, whereas he would be morally free to assume the risk of his own destruction. [8]

Detachment, by eliminating the moral compulsion to surrender and by diminishing the dangers of vicarious carelessness, reduces exposure to extortion.

But personal detachment from human friendships poses peculiar difficulties not present in developing an indifference to things. Detachment must be continually dramatized. The victim must convince his predators that he really does not value individuals for whom the normal person would feel human sympathy. It is hard to belie normal attachments. The victim may have to "make an example" of the fact that he is cold and uncaring: he may have to live with the responsibility for the dead guard in the prison case, a spurned friendship (think of Hamlet's extravagant ways to dramatize his detachment from Ophelia), or a devastated hamlet in a war zone. Such are the perilous implications of the extortionate life.

A second costly consequence is that personal detachment isolates the individual from the strengths and the assistance of the friends he renounces.

We now come to a third paradox of extortionate behavior, the paradox of face. We say a person or gang or country has "saved face" if it has gained and preserved a reputation for being mean and meaning it. Just as having "goodwill," a reputation for fair dealing, is an asset of the marketplace, so having "ill will," a reputation for severe retribution, is invaluable in an extortionate relationship. The paradox of face—*the nastier one's reputation, the less nasty one has to be*—holds for both parties in the extortionate

8.  See George E. Reedy, *The Twilight of the Presidency* (New York: World, 1972), p. 24: "Every reflective human being eventually realizes that the heaviest burdens of his life are not the responsibilities he bears for himself but the responsibilities he bears for others."

transaction. The nasty extortionist finds he never needs to execute his threats because his reputation for vindictiveness persuades his victims to capitulate without calling his bluff. On the other hand, the potential victim who is vicious discovers he never needs to retaliate against an attack because his infamy frightens off all would-be attackers. The theory of the balance of power is that two adversaries with reputations for implacability, who mean what they threaten, will coerce each other not to coerce. Peaceful behavior under mutually drawn guns may then transform itself into a profitable set of reciprocal transactions, which in time will make the parties oblivious of the guns which induced them to cooperate in the first place. A notoriety for doing evil may be the only practical means for accomplishing good.

The paradox of face originates in the fact that extortion is elementally psychological. The successful practice of coercion is not to injure but to employ the threat to injure. For example, the threat of a labor strike is an act of extortion; actually going on strike, however, is a failure of sorts. The successful strike is the one not called, the one to which the employer surrenders in anticipation of the event. There is neither profit nor victory on the picket line. Union members invariably endure far more personal distress during a strike than management. For another example, in major league baseball (for professional baseball is of all sports most like the extortionate process), no pitcher wants to bean the dangerous home run hitter. He merely wishes to intimidate the batsman so that he will not dig in comfortably at home plate.

The great risk of extortion is having one's bluff called or having one's ill will questioned. Then the only way to save face is to manifest malevolence and to respond cruelly and destructively, even if it means risking one's own destruction. To be kind, to be forgiving, or to be prudent after making or receiving a threat is to lose face. In extortion, the pressures to carry through threats and counterthreats once uttered are quite relentless. The future depends on the record of the past. Just as in a courtroom, so in extortion we apply a presumption of impeachment: *falsus in uno, falsus in omnibus,* false in one thing, false in everything. Consequently, to prevent further humiliation, one may have to make a harsh example of one's cruel determination. The danger of escalation inheres in the paradox of face—the incapacity of mutually threatening parties to lose face results in deadlock.

Violence and vendetta, or rather a reputation for them, are the qualities of the successful extortionist. Yet there are times when even the meanest reputation will not suffice to effect a successful act of extortion. Sometimes only ignorance will do, a circumstance which I shall call the paradox of irrationality. Irrationality has two distinct uses in an extortionate relationship. For one thing, it enlarges the seriousness of a threat. If a man says, "Stay away or I'll kill us both," he is most likely to be left alone if there is blood in his eyes and madness on his face—in short, if he looks crazy enough to destroy himself. If executing a threat is so self-destructive that no sane man would execute it, only an insane man poses the threat credibly. The rationality of irrationality is how Schelling would sum up the function of pigheadedness in successful extortion.[9]

There is another sensible, self-defensive reason for not having all one's senses. Victims who are, for some reason or another, ignorant of the threats being made against them, will not be deterred by those threats. It is impossible to practice extortion on a deaf man over the telephone. The participant in extortion who deafens or blinds himself to the destructive capabilities of his adversaries deprives them, once they become aware of his ignorance, of their will to take hostages. In extortionate relationships, a fool sometimes can tread where angels fear to go, because the obvious fool really has less to fear.

The point is that being sensible and appearing so may be a liability in an extortionate world, and not knowing enough to know better may be an asset ("studied ignorance" is the conventional phrase for this virtue). We can sum up the paradox of irrationality in this way—*the more delirious the threatener, the more serious the threat; the more delirious the victim, the less serious the threat.*

As in the practical resolution of each of the paradoxes of coercion, making a dramatic example of one's irrationality is crucial and difficult. Its difficulty grows out of the fact that there is a heavy presumption that every individual is *Homo sapiens.* Hence, the burden of proof that one is really nutty is a heavy one. It may be impossible to feign madness. It may be necessary to become sincerely irrational and to believe what is otherwise illogical, to become, in a word, ideological, so that one's adversaries come to believe that one has the will to do things that are senseless in terms of economic efficiency, civilized decency, and human awareness. The politician breathing fire and brimstone, the Ku Klux Klan member with his devout belief in apartheid, and the American Civil Liberties Union zealot with his convictions about moral absolutes—each in his own way has overcome his opponents' presumption that he is reasonable. The risk of this resolution of the paradox, of course, is that if it is rational for each party to become irrational, the result may be the ultimate illogic—a suicide pact.[10]

---

9. Schelling, *Strategy of Conflict,* pp. 17–18.
10. On the inversion of virtues when civilization breaks down and coercion becomes the predominant means of power, see Thucydides's description of the Corcyraean revolution (427 B.C.): "Revolution thus ran its course from city to city, and the places which it arrived at last, from having heard what had been done before, carried to a still greater excess the refinement of their inventions, as manifested in the cunning of their enterprises and the atrocity of their reprisals. Words had to change their ordinary meaning and to take that which was now given them. Reckless audacity came to be considered the courage of a

## IV

The extortionate model makes it possible to see the pitfalls of coercion more clearly, particularly the paradoxes of coercive power:

1. *The paradox of dispossession:* The less one has, the less one has to lose.

2. *The paradox of detachment:* The less the victim cares about preserving something, the less the victimizer cares about taking it hostage.

3. *The paradox of face:* The nastier one's reputation, the less nasty one has to be.

4. *The paradox of irrationality:* The more delirious the threatener, the more serious the threat; the more delirious the victim, the less serious the threat.

How do these four paradoxes apply to the policeman? How may they help explain his professional development? The answer may appear obvious. The policeman's authority consists of a legal license to coerce others to refrain from using illegitimate coercion. Society licenses him to kill, hurt, confine, and otherwise victimize nonpolicemen who would illegally kill, hurt, confine, or victimize others whom the policeman is charged to protect.[11]

But the reality, and the subtle irony, of being a policeman is that, while he

---

loyal ally; prudent hesitation, specious cowardice; moderation was held to be a cloak for unmanliness; ability to see all sides of a question inaptness to act on any. Frantic violence became the attribute of manliness, cautious plotting, a justifiable means of self-defense. The advocate of extreme measures was always trustworthy, his opponent a man to be suspected. To succeed in a plot was to have a shrewd head, to divine a plot still shrewder; but to try to provide against having to do either was to break up your party and be afraid of your adversaries. In fine, to forestall an intending criminal, or to suggest the idea of a crime where it was wanting, was equally commended, until even blood became a weaker tie than party, from the superior readiness of those united by the latter to dare everything without reserve; for such associations had not in view the blessings derivable from established institutions but were formed by ambition for their overthrow; and the confidence of their members in each other rested less on any religious sanction than upon complicity in crime. The fair proposals of an adversary were met with jealous precautions by the stronger of the two, and not with a generous confidence. Revenge also was held of more account than self-preservation. Oaths of reconciliation, being proffered on either side only to meet an immediate difficulty, held good only so long as no other weapon was at hand; but when opportunity offered, he who first ventured to seize it and to take his enemy off his guard, thought this perfidious vengeance sweeter than an open one, since, considerations of safety apart, success by treachery won him the palm of superior intelligence" (Thucydides, *History of the Peloponnesian Wars,* trans. Richard Crawley, in *The Greek Historians,* ed. M. I. Finley [New York: Viking, 1960], pp. 296–97).

11. Whenever a citizen recognizes that a police officer is properly authorized to use coercion, he may submit willingly and without resistance. The sight of the uniform alone may remind him of his responsibilities. However, some citizens refuse to cooperate because they see the police exercise of coercion as unauthorized, a perception strongly influenced by what the legal philosopher Kelsen calls the apparent "antinomy" of the policeman's lot—that the cop's licensed tools of coercion, deadly force, injury, and confinement, are the very weapons he is expected to prevent others from using. Kelsen's description of the nature of a coercive legal order is as follows: "Among the paradoxes of the social technique here characterized as a coercive order is the fact that its specific instrument, the coercive

may appear to be the supreme practitioner of coercion, in fact he is first and foremost its most frequent victim. The policeman is society's "fall guy," the object of coercion more frequently than its practitioner. Recurrently he is involved in extortionate behavior as victim, and only rarely does he initiate coercive actions as victimizer.[12] If he is vicious, his viciousness is the upswing of the vicious cycle inherent in an extortionate relationship.

Contrary to the more unflattering stereotypes of the policeman, it is the citizen who virtually always initiates the coercive encounter. What is more, the citizen tends to enjoy certain inordinate advantages over the policeman in these transactions. The advantages derive from the four paradoxes of coercion. The citizen is, relative to the policeman, the more dispossessed, the more detached, the nastier, and the crazier. Add to these natural advantages the fact that most police-citizen encounters are begun under circumstances which the citizen has determined, and the reader may begin to feel some of the significant limits placed on the policeman's freedom to respond in these encounters. The policeman is the one who is on the defensive. What is interesting about him is that he demonstrates how difficult it is for the self-restrained person to defend himself against the bully. What will distinguish one policeman from the other are the techniques he invents to defend himself in his position of comparative vulnerability.

The irony of the policeman's lot is that his authority, his status, his sense of civility, and his reasonableness impose terrible limits on his freedom to react successfully to the extortionate practices of others. His alternatives are sharply foreclosed; he works within a much smaller range of choices than do his illegitimate and nonofficial adversaries. If Lord Acton was right that power tends to corrupt, at least it is also arguable that the corrupting influence of power stems from the way that the power of a powerful person attracts the practice of coercion against him, placing him on the defensive. Power tends to confine, frustrate, frighten, and burden the consciences of its holders.

---

act of the sanction, is of exactly the same sort as the act which it seeks to prevent in the relations of individuals, the delict; that the sanction against socially injurious behavior is itself such behavior. For that which is to be accomplished by the threat of forcible deprivation of life, health, freedom, or property is precisely that men in their mutual conduct shall refrain from forcibly depriving one another of life, health, freedom, or property. Force is employed to prevent the employment of force in society. This seems to be an antinomy" (H. Kelsen, *General Theory of Law and State* [New York: Russell & Russell, 1961], p. 20).

12. Some may argue plausibly that the citizen may have had to take the coercive initiative because of the policeman's potential coercive capacity. Because he is frightened that the policeman will misuse his authority, the citizen has defended himself by striking preemptively. In this sense, they allege, the citizen is not the real aggressor but is merely retaliating. Perhaps so. But when they speak of the preemptive strike as retaliation, it sounds as if they are speaking of the kind of "retaliation" Hitler practiced on Poland in 1939.

That is why the preoccupation of the four policemen in chapter 2 with the phenomenon of coercion was so pervasive and so important. Or, to put it more candidly, it is why I gave it such importance in the construction of the argument of this book. This the reader will soon see, when we examine the methodological problem of defining the "good," or professional, policeman.

# 4    The Professional Political Model of the Good Policeman

He who lets himself in for politics, that is, for power and force as means, contracts with diabolical powers and for his action it is *not* true that good can follow only from good and evil only from evil, but that often the opposite is true. Anyone who fails to see this, is, indeed, a political infant.

*Max Weber*
"Politics as a Vocation"
1918

At this point I reveal myself in my true colours, as a stick-in-the-mud. I hold a number of beliefs that have been repudiated by the liveliest intellects of our time. I believe that order is better than chaos, creation better than destruction. I prefer gentleness to violence, forgiveness to vendetta. On the whole I think that knowledge is preferable to ignorance, and I am sure that human

sympathy is more valuable than ideology. I believe that in spite of the recent triumphs of science, men haven't changed much in the last two thousand years; and in consequence we must still try to learn from history. History is ourselves. I also hold one or two beliefs that are more difficult to put shortly. For example, I believe in courtesy, the ritual by which we avoid hurting other people's feelings by satisfying our own egos. And I think we should remember that we are part of a great whole, which for convenience we call nature. All living things are our brothers and sisters. Above all, I believe in the God-given genius of certain individuals, and I value a society that makes their existence possible.

*Kenneth Clark*
Civilisation
1969

## I

Coercion, the power of the sword, is not the only means of power. There are the power of the purse and the power of the word as well. We should keep these two other fundamental techniques of controlling others, reciprocity and exhortation, in mind to get a perspective on the moral implications of coercion.

*Reciprocity* is a distinct kind of power relationship. Instead of resorting to threats, one individual overcomes the resistance of another by making an attractive exchange. He gives up something he values less and gets in return something he thinks has a greater worth to him. His exchange partner, meanwhile, because his scale of values is different, receives something that he desires more than what he has to surrender. Thus, both are reciprocally enriched.

There is something extremely civilized about the notion of reciprocity. Persons with different possessions and diverse value systems exchange voluntarily in fair and mutually satisfactory trades. Because there is no antagonism on either side, the motives to welsh on a deal or to resist the terms of reciprocity are inhibited by the prospects of continuing the profitable relationship. Diversity, trustworthiness, constructiveness, empathy, self-improvement—all these virtues have their rewards in reciprocal relationships.

The other technique of power is exhortation. Individuals act, not because they are coerced or tempted, but because they think their action is right, because they are persuaded by the "truth" of the matter that they have a duty to fulfill. They will sacrifice gladly, even kill or be killed, for a cause they believe in, even though, without that dedication, they would have resisted the tortures of the barbarian and the blandishments of the devil. Exhortation is a noble form of human control. There is something inspiring about persons working harmoniously, coordinated by their inner convictions, identifying with the well-being of the larger group, bound by words of honor, certain of purpose. When one thinks of the exhortative relationship between a leader and his followers, numerous virtues leap to mind—solidarity, community, selflessness, conscience, inspiration.

Of the three techniques of power—trade and "truth" and threat—only the last, the means we call coercion, seems on first acquaintance mean and barbaric. To be sure, reciprocity and exhortation are not unmitigated goods. In fact, if the powers of the purse or word were to be examined in detail, they would present as many paradoxical and troublesome aspects as does the power of the sword. Each promotes, in the extreme, highly questionable qualities—for example, selfishness (reciprocity) and conformity (exhortation).

But coercion seems of a different order. The human qualities which appear to be required for the practice of coercion seem incompatible with any civilized notion of the good. The moral realm of the person who must recurrently deal with the paradoxes of dispossession, detachment, face, and irrationality is turned topsy-turvy. Coercion creates a situation in which what is effective is at odds on every point with what Lord Acton called "the inflexible integrity of the moral code."[1] The gap between being a good man and a good practitioner of

___

1. Lord John Emerich Edward Dalberg-Acton was born the year before Queen Victoria took the throne and died a year after her death. He believed passionately both in the inherent

coercion appears unbridgeable. Even if the person in authority would prefer to act in conventionally fair and gentle ways, he can be sure that self-minimization, detachment, remorselessness, and ignorance will be practiced against him, necessitating his self-defense and more, if his desires to put his authority to good purpose are to avail. The tendency of coercive power to corrupt its wielder seems nearly unavoidable.

## II

But are there ways to prevent persons in authority from becoming wicked? In his essay, "Politics as a Vocation," the German social theorist Max Weber (1864–1920) probed that question.[2] He framed the problem of coercive power and personality as follows: "He who lets himself in for politics, that is, for power and force as means, contracts with diabolical powers and for his action it is *not* true that good can follow only from good and evil only from evil, but that often the opposite is true. Anyone who fails to see this is, indeed, a political infant."[3] Or, as Weber said elsewhere in the essay, "Whosoever

---

weakness and wickedness of mankind and in the uses of history to hold mankind accountable. For Acton, history recorded the deeds and misdeeds of individuals; it taught future generations about the evil consequences of doing evil; and it punished in perpetuity those men who had escaped punishment too long during their lives. Among the targets he attacked most devoutly were men of politics and men of the cloth; state and church alike, in his eyes, had done immeasurable disservice to mankind.

When Acton's friend Mandell Creighton concluded, in his *History of the Papacy during the Reformation,* that the late-medieval papacy had "been tolerant and benevolent," Acton disputed the point in a review submitted to the *English Historical Review,* of which Creighton was the editor. Creighton's kindly nature made him willing to publish the review despite its "ill-natured" quality, and in the correspondence between the two men concerning some revisions prior to its publication in 1887, Acton remarked, "Power tends to corrupt and absolute power corrupts absolutely." The tenor of Acton's argument is revealed in these excerpts: "I cannot accept your canon that we are to judge Pope and King unlike other men, with a favourable presumption that they did no wrong.... Historical responsibility has to make up for the want of legal responsibility ...; if what one hears is true, then Elizabeth asked the gaoler to murder Mary, and William III ordered his Scots minister to extirpate a clan. Here are the greater names coupled with the greater crimes.... I would hang them, higher than Haman; for reasons of quite obvious justice; still more, still higher, for the sake of historical science.... The inflexible integrity of the moral code is, to me, the secret of the authority, the dignity, the utility of history. If we may debase the currency for the sake of genius, or success, or rank, or reputation, we may debase it for the sake of a man's influence, of his religion, of his party, or the good cause which prospers by his credit and suffers by his disgrace. Then history ceases to be a science, an arbitration of controversy, a guide to the wanderer, the upholder of the moral standard which the powers of earth and religion itself tend constantly to depress.... Then history ... serves where it ought to reign, and it serves the worst cause better than the purest."

2.  Max Weber, "Politics as a Vocation," in *From Max Weber: Essays in Sociology,* ed. and trans. H. Gerth and C. Wright Mills (New York: Oxford University Press, 1946), pp. 77–128.
3.  Ibid., p. 123.

contracts with violent means for whatever ends—and every politician does,"
exposes himself to the "ethical paradoxes of coercion" and "endangers the
'salvation of the soul.'" Those paradoxes, summed up by Weber as the
"irreconcilable conflict" between the "demon of politics" and the "god of
love," produce consequences "for his inner self, to which he must helplessly
submit, unless he perceives them." If political persons do not anticipate them,
if those who undertake coercive power "do not fully realize what they take
upon themselves," then the consequence is bitterness, banal self-acceptance,
or flight.[4]

Weber constructed a model of "a *mature* man," one who would not
"crumble" under the ethically paradoxical pressures which afflict the
"professional politician." For purposes of reference, I shall call this construct
the professional political model, using "political" in Weber's limited sense to
refer to matters involving coercive threats and violence, and "professional" to
indicate that the encounters with coercion occur so recurrently as to become
routine. Weber's model of a professional politician had two characteristics
which in combination reduced the chances of corruption. Weber called them
the virtues of "passion and perspective."

1. *Passion: a capacity to "integrate" coercion into morals.* Weber insisted
that the "genuine man," the professional political model, harmonized his
standards of innocence and his willingness to "stand up arms-in-hand" for the
general welfare. He did not suffer disabling pangs of guilt about the harmful
consequences which flowed from recourse to threats and violence. He
reconciled the irreconcilable. He felt good about coercive power; he made the
consequences of his recourse to threats consistent with those moral codes
which regulated and gave value to the conduct of his total life; he knew that his
involvement in violence was "principled." Having accomplished "the integration of violence into ethics," the professional political model achieved the
"passion" necessary to endure the antagonisms aroused by politics, by
coercive power. (The ethical basis for coercion lay in the "causes" served by it
and not attainable without it.)

2. *Perspective: intellectual "objectivity."* But an ethic of "principled
violence as a means" was not enough, since moral equanimity about coercive
means could be achieved not by reconciling but by rejecting the ethical
concerns of civilization. Then there would be no guilt because there would be
no conscience. For Weber such fundamental moral rejection led to a "really
radical Machiavellianism," in which the world was distorted to appear

4.  Weber summed up these three harmful developments this way: "Will you be bitter or
    banausic? Will you simply and dully accept world and occupation? Or will the third and
    by no means the least frequent possibility be your lot: mystic flight from reality ...?"
    (ibid., p. 128.)

hateful, thereby justifying the violence being used against it. In a word, cynicism was possible.

The model professional politician, however, fought the temptation to distort by cultivating "objectivity." By this Weber meant "the knowledge of tragedy with which all action, but especially political action, is truly interwoven." The professional political model possessed a sense of the meaning of human conduct—a comprehension of the suffering of each inhabitant of the earth, a sensitivity to man's yearning for dignity, and, ultimately, "some kind of faith" that no individual is worthless. In short, the professional political model nurtured a persistent contact with reality. He developed a cognitive efficiency, a "perspective," a capacity for seeing rich implications of meager cues. He developed an inner understanding of the motives of men, a sense of life's rhythms of cause and effect, and a self-suspicion that drove him to find out for himself when what he had been told by frighteners and flatterers did not square with his inner "knowledge of tragedy."

The secret of avoiding corruption by coercive power—i.e., wickedness, banality, or cowardice—was to combine passion with perspective. Once again, to resort to Weber's language, the "good" politician was defined by an ability to forge together "warm passion and a cool sense of proportion . . . in one and the same soul."

## III

What is the point of discussing Weber's professional political model in a book on policemen? It turns out to be of the utmost utility in solving the crucial methodological problem inherent in this study. I ask the reader's patience to indulge me in a short excursion into technical matters which may strike him or her as a bit pedantic. I think the point is important enough to take the time.

Recall that what I am trying to do is to explain the development of *good* policemen. The reader and I both know that to derive any value from such an inquiry, we must come up with a sensible definition of what we mean by "good." The problem is a sticky one. Any solution to it is both pivotal and also most deserving of critical scrutiny.

I urge that a reasonable definition of "good" will have to satisfy three criteria: (1) *Independence*—is the definition grounded in terms of a relatively broad range of social concerns and as free of police organizational bias as practical? (2) *Realism*—would a reasonable policeman agree that any assessment made of him in terms of the definition was taking into consideration many of the substantial constraints affecting him? and (3) *Timeliness*—assuming the definition was relatively independent and realistic, could a researcher gather evidence on how a policeman currently measured up to the definition?

In view of these three standards, let me explain why I flirted with, but ultimately rejected, five apparent solutions to the problem of defining the good policeman.

1. *Good is what a policeman's supervisors say it is.* Performance ratings by supervisors were made annually in the Laconia Police Department. Each supervisor reviewed them with both the rated officers and his own superior. The evaluations tended to be knowledgeable and were taken seriously by all parties. The merit of an inside, informed appraisal, however, was undermined by its lack of independence. In making ratings, policemen were writing their own report cards, not only in the sense that an officer's promising development reflected well on the supervisor's abilities but also, and more important, because the evaluations were based on the Laconia Police Department's criteria and not demonstrably on the larger society's.

Under ideal circumstances the administrator's definition of good police work might have been appropriate for the larger society. But it was not necessarily so. In any organization a tendency exists to displace the needs of its clientele for its own good, and the Laconia Police Department was unlikely to be an exception to this general rule. To know whether the organization's goals were congruent with the social welfare, it ultimately was necessary to anchor the evaluative standard outside the organization. For these two reasons, self-inflation and self-deception, I rejected supervisors' ratings as a measure of good police work.

2. *Good is measured by a policeman's performance in recruit school.* Recruit-school grades of the individual patrolmen were tempting because they were so precise in appearance and the recruit school was, to me, so sophisticated. The grades, however, lacked timeliness (as well as independence). Unless one presupposed that good trainees eventually made good police officers, classroom performance was either obsolete or irrelevant. In fact, one of the inquiries made in this research was whether good trainees turned into good police officers.

3. *Good is standing at one extreme or another on a scale created by the police organization for other reasons.* Certain secondary indicators had the merit of automatic and timely collection. Injuries on the job, days of absence from work, censures and awards, and public complaints about police misconduct were recorded systematically in the department. The difficulty in using these statistics as gauges of merit was their empirical remoteness to the quality of police work. For example, both good and bad policemen could be injured. Injuries were often explicable in terms of beat assignment (and selection for a tough beat, at least arguably, was related to the quality of a police officer). Absences resulted as much from a good officer's having an

unbearable supervisor as an unbearable officer's having a good supervisor. And so on. No matter what the secondary indicator, every policeman I met thought it too remote or too equivocal in the individual case to be a decisive measure of police work.

4. *Good is the number of arrests a policeman makes.* The Laconia Police Department required each policeman to summarize his accomplishments on weekly activity sheets. However, it limited the recordable activities to issuing tickets and making arrests. This indicator of activity obviously lacked comprehensiveness. Ticketing and arresting were not the quintessence of police work in most men's minds. The activity sheets omitted to record the family beefs handled well, the crime prevented, the information gathered, the stolen goods recovered, the friends made, the potential delinquents set straight, the commercial relationships ameliorated, the racial cleavages bridged, the hope infused, the help given. Such activities, which frequently animated the policeman, never were tabulated administratively. The activity sheets were, in a word, unrealistic.

5. *Good is a psychiatrist's finding of "not being abnormal."* Psychiatric examinations were made of Laconia policemen initially when they were recruited and followed up a year or two later. The reports of the psychiatrist resulting from this series of examinations overcame some of the liabilities of the first four definitions of a "good" policeman. They were more independent than the ratings of supervisors, more timely than recruit-school grades, more decisive than secondary indicators, and more comprehensive in assessing the whole policeman than the department's activity sheets.

A psychiatric evaluation was based upon a medical "model" of a "bad" man. A Laconia police officer was deemed "bad" if he approached the sick state of schizophrenia, "good" if he was not so sick. The "model" was sensitive to the individual's attitudes, not to his behavior. It searched out his understandings and emotions, and if they resembled those of the "sick" psychiatric model, then he was considered problematic and hence a problem cop. If he saw things with an "unrealism," if he evaluated matters too autonomously, without an adequate appreciation of the complex interrelationships of others around him, then his resemblance to the psychiatric model of the schizophrenic was marked, and he was characterized as abnormal, hence "bad."

Problems with the psychiatric model, however, occurred in two directions. Defining a bad policeman in terms of whether or not he was a sick man was at once too broad and too narrow. Too broad, because it presupposed that "bad" men would be "bad" policemen, that unhealthy attitudes would produce socially destructive behavior. Conceivably, however, "unrealistic" ideas and autonomous value systems might produce beneficial behavior. Martin Luther and Mahatma Gandhi might well have looked sick to the psychiatrists of their day. This is the problem of the attitude/behavior relationship, and we shall come back to it in the next section.

Even more important, the definition of a "bad" policeman was too narrow. By confining itself to detecting "bad" men, it might not identify a great many "bad" policemen. Arguably, the police job could be so demanding that more than a nonsick condition would be required of an individual if he were to do good police work over the long haul. An individual adequate to manage his own affairs might prove inadequate to govern the lives of others. A good man, as determined by civilized standards, able to cope well within the reciprocal and moral conventions of civilization, might be out of his depth in the uncushioned and frightening circumstances of the coercive world. Thus, application of the psychiatric model failed the test of realism.

## IV

That is where the professional political model came in. By accepting Weber's assertions, I could identify a "good" policeman in terms of how his "passion and perspective" resembled the qualities of the professional politician. If he felt morally reconciled to using coercion and at the same time he reflected empathetically upon the condition of mankind, he measured up to being a professional, a good policeman.

To be sure, the professional political model was no less based on attitudes than the psychiatric model, which we have just rejected, had been. It did not solve the problem of the attitude/behavior relationship any better. Singling out "passion and perspective" as important assumed, but never proved, that the personal attitudes of a policeman and the actual results of his public actions were somehow positively related. I think there are both logical connections and a factual correlation between the two, but the reader should remain skeptical. Comparing the professional political model with the psychiatric model, however, I must repeat one point. They are both attitude models. The question is, which is the better attitude model for assessing policemen?

The professional political model had some virtues. It was independent of organizational bias, capable of using timely information, and, above all, realistic. Every policeman I asked insisted that the critical and recurrent part of his job occurred when he was the object of the threats of others and when he, in turn, had to influence people to do those things they were little inclined to do of their own accord—to desist from an antisocial act, to give humiliating information, to go to jail. At those times, he could give little in the way of positive inducements to compensate the citizens for their pains. He had only his authority, the threat to harm, to defend or assert himself. He had to extort cooperation because often he could not obtain it by any other means. In that a Laconia policeman often had to rely on his power to harm to prevent himself from being harmed by others, Weber's model of the professional politician seemed to fit the problem of measuring the man to the police job.

Moreover, a further advantage of the two-dimensional professional political model was that it could, theoretically at least, generate three types of nonprofessional policemen: (1) enforcers—police who had passion, but lacked perspective; (2) reciprocators—police who had perspective, but lacked passion; and (3) avoiders—police who lacked both passion and perspective.

## V

I carefully analyzed the contents of the first interview of each police officer, young man and old-timer alike. I characterized his attitudes about the motives of mankind and the acceptability of coercion. I looked for clues particularly, but not exclusively, in his answers to these five questions.

1. Now let me get a feeling for what it is like being a police officer in Laconia today. Can you tell me about a particular incident which turned out to be one of the more difficult spots you've been in as a policeman in the field in Laconia?

2. Did anyone ever tell you how to deal with bullies—a pal or a minister or teacher or father or someone?

3. Let me shift gears a minute. I was reading a story of a first-year New York policeman named Gene Radano, and he told of an incident when he pulled over a car, an expensive-looking car, for running a stoplight. Radano said to the young guy who was driving, "I'm sorry, sir, but you just went through that red light. Can I have your license, please?"
The driver was pretty rude, but the policeman kept on being polite and said, "I'm sorry, but from where I was standing you had ample time to stop." The driver wouldn't turn over his license and told Officer Radano to go ahead and arrest him; his father who was a bigwig would have his job. A crowd gathered—about eight or nine people, and when the driver even refused to give his name, Radano decided to take him to the station to be booked. Well, it turned out the guy who was arrested had claustrophobia, a fear of closed places, but nobody knew about it, including him, and when he refused to cooperate even at the station, the lieutenant decided to lock him up and cool him off. When the kid saw the bars of the lockup, however, he began fighting hysterically. In the fight a couple of officers got hurt, but, of course, the young fellow got hurt worst of all, and he ended up in the hospital. Radano's reaction was to blame himself. "If only I'd spoken with more authority in the beginning. Maybe if I'd been stern, it might not have happened. Maybe my courtesy was inter-

preted by the man as a sign of weakness. Maybe that was what started the snowball rolling downhill." One thing that interested me was the way Officer Radano felt about himself. What do you think of the way he blamed himself for what happened?

4. I have heard policemen talk about each other, and invariably they seem to talk about how one group of men will do things differently from other groups of police officers. What are the different types of police officers which you see, and what are they like, and how do they differ?

5. Let me ask you a personal question: Have you ever had a tough problem in your police work where a decision of yours was right from one angle but wrong from another: say, from a personal or religious viewpoint it may have been right to do something, but from a police angle it was wrong, or the other way around: right from a police angle but not from a personal one.

Among the twenty-eight young policemen, ten (36%) appeared to be professionals. They resembled Jay Justice, whom we met in chapter 2, with his general notion about the dignity and tragedy of human nature and his ability to integrate the use of "proportionate" force into his principles of morality. Five (18%) could be characterized as enforcers. In their first interviews, at least, they resembled John Russo, whom we saw earlier as thoroughly confident in the efficacy of force but somewhat cynical about human society. Six (21%) could be typed as reciprocators, officers like Bob Ingersoll, who had moral conflicts over the necessity of coercion ("hated it," Ingersoll said) and were sympathetic with the citizenry. Finally, seven (25%) fell into the category of avoider. Bill Tubman, with his suspicion, cognitive bluntness toward the subtleties of human detail, and puzzlement about the ethics of force, illustrated this group of policemen.

A tabulation of the twenty-eight young officers would look like table 1.

In the course of this book, you will become acquainted with most of these individual policemen. Before you do get to know them better, let me utter two essential reservations about the classifications.

First, some men did not readily fall into categories. Some officers were uncertain about their perspectives. Rockingham, for example, a giant, motorcycle-riding ex-military policeman with a musician's sensibilities, was still trying to make sense of a hazy world filled with human suffering, and he wavered almost day to day. Because he had not resolved this conflict in comprehension, his perspective was treated as if it were cynical. Some officers who usually felt good about exercising coercive power (and hence were labeled as having an integrated passion) still evinced considerable discomfort about coercion in some situations. And vice versa: some officers usually troubled by force could take coercive action without the slightest qualm when the conditions were right.

Table 1                              Classification According to Professional
                                     Political Model

|                      | Morality of Coercion | |
| --- | --- | --- |
|                      | Integrated | Conflicted |
| Tragic perspective | *Professional* | *Reciprocator* |
|                      | Justice | Ingersoll |
|                      | Andros | Haig |
|                      | Bentham | Hooker |
|                      | Chacon | Hughes |
|                      | Douglas | Lancaster |
|                      | Patch | Wrangel |
|                      | Peel | |
|                      | Rolfe | |
|                      | Tennison | |
|                      | Wilkes | |
| Cynical perspective | *Enforcer* | *Avoider* |
|                      | Russo | Tubman |
|                      | Bacon | Booth |
|                      | Carpasso | Garfield |
|                      | Kane | Longstreet |
|                      | Kip | Nary |
|                      | | Rockingham |
|                      | | Thayer |

Second, these men were young and, by and large, developing. Some had just begun the domesticating experience of having their own families. Some were taking college courses and confronting systems of ideas in their sociology and history courses that allowed them to recompose their perspectives. Each was increasing in police skills, and each was encountering new aspects of the city and of humanity. Some were likely to encounter difficulties which were going to overwhelm and destroy their development as professionals. Others, like John Russo, thanks to maturation, reassignment, and accident, appeared to change their outlooks and moralities so perceptibly in the several years I observed them as to begin the transformation into professionals.

This last point is the essential one to recall. Development and change were not easy, yet paradoxically were very likely. Development occurred daily; some was constructive, some destructive. One object of this book will be to identify a few of the crucial factors affecting this development.

## VI

We have just begun the inquiry by measuring twenty-eight young policemen against the professional political model. Assuming for sake of argument that this typology is "correct" in some way, I want to emphasize that it is still nothing more than a starting point. We need to discover three things.

First, we have to know whether the typology is *useful.* Do policemen whose attitudes place them in these different categories behave differently? Specifically, did the professional policeman, the "good" cop, perform differently (and in some sense, respond more desirably) from the nonprofessional officer? This question, as we shall soon see, produces some very complex answers, and some readers may believe (as I do) that, sometimes, in some situations, the professional may behave *less* desirably than the nonprofessional policeman.

Second, there is the question of *explanation.* What is the dynamic process by which the recurrent use of coercive means produces the perspectives and passion to which the professional political model is sensitive? How does the resort to force build and destroy the attributes measured by Weber's scheme?

And third is the question of *engineering.* How can the corrupting effects of confronting recurrent coercive situations be modulated by human artifice so that desirable development will more probably occur and bad effect will be less likely? Those three questions—usefulness, explanation, and manipulation—constitute the final three parts of this book.

# The Four Paradoxes of Coercive Behavior  2

The work of policemen differed from one day to the next. "Doing something different every day" made police work satisfying to a large majority of officers in Laconia. The men frequently mentioned "variety" in distinguishing their job from those of white- and blue-collar workers. "I'm not the type to sit behind a desk pushing paper around or in a plant doing something over and over again." "No two days are the same ..."

On the other hand, the men talked of the value of experience, of seeing the same things recur. They developed classifications for similar-appearing events: the skid row confrontation, the family beef, the crowd scene, the juvenile caper. The policemen themselves treated events as variations on a theme, not sui generis.

Like any job, a policeman's work consisted of both the routine and the critical. The routine work involved taking reports of burglaries, lost dogs, and missing persons; carrying messages; serving warrants; teaching in school; testifying at trials; and driving the streets. Yet very little of the policeman's energies were absorbed in the routine; the work of a policeman was coping with critical

events, or looking for them, and they performed that work ceaselessly, even when they were concurrently doing the routine.

A critical incident occurred whenever a citizen enjoyed, or could have enjoyed, an initial advantage over the policeman in controlling the course of events. If we resort to political terms, a critical incident involved a rebellion, or a potential one. (A rebellion occurred whenever the citizen threatened or attacked a policeman; a potential rebellion, when a policeman might reasonably anticipate aggression against him.)

The likelihood of rebellion increased significantly under any of these conditions: (1) if the citizen were likely to suffer a *less severe injury* than he could inflict on the policeman or on persons with whom the policeman identified; (2) if the citizen were *less vulnerable to injury* than were the policeman and persons with whom the policeman identified; (3) if the citizen were *less remorseful* about any injuries he caused than the policeman; and (4) if the citizen were *less aware* of any injuries he caused than was the policeman.

Handling these four dangerous situations was the basic theme of police work. These four types of critical events corresponded to the four paradoxes of coercion—the paradoxes of dispossession, detachment, face and irrationality. The policeman had much to fear whenever he had to protect hostages who were more valuable or vulnerable than his adversary had to worry about or whenever his motivation to inflict harm was checked by more remorse or more knowledge than was his adversary's.

Variations on these four themes sounded and resounded during my years of talking with and observing policemen. Against each kind of peril each policeman had to develop defenses. But different policemen developed different kinds of defenses. In the several chapters which constitute this part of the book, I want to describe an illustration of each of the four paradoxes and the various means by which the policemen defended themselves. I have referred to these varied reactions as the avoidance, the enforcement, the reciprocating, and the professional responses.

# 5

# The Paradox of Dispossession: Skidrow at Night

In the United States where the poor rule, the rich have always something to fear from the abuse of their power. This natural anxiety of the rich may produce a secret dissatisfaction; but society is not disturbed by it, for the same reason that withholds the confidence of the rich from the legislative authority makes them obey its mandates: their wealth, which prevents them from making the law, prevents them from withstanding it. Among civilized nations, only those who have nothing to lose ever revolt; . . .

*Alexis de Tocqueville*
Democracy in America
1835

Up in the hills there are some very important, very influential and very rich people, whom you don't treat the same as people in other areas. You don't run a car check on a guy who lives on Lookout Peak. There may be a few who don't pay their tickets, but most do.

*Ed Andros*
Laconia Police Department
1972

## I

In 1835 Tocqueville wrote that the rich inevitably were timid and hence presented little threat to democracy. Because they had so much to lose from an attempted revolt against political authority, they would endure their frustrations and submit. They were the victims of the paradox of dispossession: "The less one has, the less one has to lose." They had too much to lose.

In 1972, Ed Andros, a Laconia policeman, made a similar observation: because the wealthy "up in the hills" would suffer so many subtle injuries if hauled before a traffic judge for nonpayment of traffic violations, it was a practical certainty they were not scofflaws. They would have paid for their past violations of the laws despite their dissatisfaction with them. It was

usually only the poor who would flout the law, not pay their tickets, and be
fearless enough to rebel.[1]

The very poorest citizenry in Laconia inhabited skid row. In the daytime,
in the commercial area near skid row, Laconians exchanged goods and
services and lived up to moral standards of conduct, sensing that they were
going to benefit from an unbroken system of mutual obligations. They hardly
noticed the inhabitants of skid row, who slunk and got drunk and looked on
at a world which had no commerce with them.

At night, things changed. Laconia's dispossessed became more obvious
and more ominous. The center of their activity was at Michigan and
Commerce, the hub of a dozen bars which hardly closed except for five hours
in the early morning. Nearby business establishments also remained open
throughout the night—cheap movie houses and hotels. In the recessed
entryways of these dark buildings, prostitutes, pimps, and their clientele
hung out, along with drug traffickers, winos, thieves, and robbers. While
they might appear to the uninitiated to be transients, each of these
individuals inhabited a limited territory. The stranger stood out, and the
news quickly spread through the community grapevine about who he was and
what his business was. Every citizen in nighttime skid row had a business of
sorts.

In civilized terms, however, the people whose ways of life took them to
Michigan and Commerce each night were "judgment-proof." They had no
money, no family, no job, no property, no respectability, no health, no skills,
and no hope. Without denying the significance of loss of liberty, the
humiliations of jail, and the dangers of prison life, we can fairly say that in
jail they would eat better, sleep more warmly, be cleaner, and have safer
companionship. A few of them were probably due to go to jail eventually
anyway; warrants were out for their arrest for some previous infraction from
which they had fled. They were life's losers; they possessed nothing except
their links to a free world in which they were misfits.

They characteristically lacked something more—a moral compulsion to
comply with the constituted authorities. Breaking the law pricked few
consciences on skid row. A sense of mutual obligation between skid row
denizens and the world which shunned them was nonexistent.

1.   The reader might first interpret Officer Andros's statement as an illustration of a dual
     system of justice—leniency for the rich and severity for the poor. In fact, however, Officer
     Andros was *not* talking about whether he would ticket a wrongdoer "in the hills": he
     would and did. Andros was discussing the question whether he would *also* run a "car
     check" on the "very rich" driver. A "car check" was a procedure which took up to five
     minutes and involved a call to a central computer to discover whether there were any
     outstanding warrants for the driver's arrest. Andros was saying that the probabilities that
     a rich man would ignore a warrant for his arrest were so low that it was not worth
     further delaying the ticketed "guy who lives on Lookout Peak" to run a fruitless car
     check on him.

Skid row was so close to anarchy at night that the Laconia Police Department assigned foot patrolmen to it. By 1970 the walking beat had disappeared from most city streets, and for good reasons: increased police responsibilities, intensified reliance on technology, the diminished density of the modern city, and the high costs of police labor made greater efficiency mandatory, and so policemen were assigned to patrol in cars.

In densely populated parts of the city where the crime rate was high, however, the foot patrolman retained an advantage over his motorized counterparts. The department felt that his presence more effectively suppressed the extensive purse-snatching and mugging and vice than a passing patrol car.

The foot patrolmen in Laconia were almost invariably veteran police officers; selection for such duty was regarded as an honor. They were likely to be big men (over 74 inches and 200 pounds). They worked in teams of two. They usually visited each bar three times a night to see if things were orderly and whether the owner still had affairs under control. The last nightly visit was to close the bar and to protect the owner from being robbed of his night's receipts. In passing from bar to bar, the pair of officers dealt with trouble as they saw it. They also could respond to radio calls dispatched over the small portable transceivers they carried on their belts.

Some time during the night, there would be trouble. A veteran walking patrolman described this typically dangerous incident: "It was Michigan and Commerce. This colored prostitute was chasing three whites with a knife around a car. Naturally five colored men came in to help her, and suddenly about fifty or sixty colored people in a crowd were all around. We arrested her, and she was hollering prejudice and that she was being arrested because she was black." The lawful goals of the policemen in the short run were to disarm the woman, find out what had caused the problem between her and the "three whites," settle it one way or another, and pacify the crowd. In the long run their goals could probably be defined in terms of diminishing violence and injury on the beat: what means would best reach this general objective was a subject of disagreement.

The goals of the men and women of skid row often were unknown to the policemen. At a minimum, the woman wished to retain her knife and coerce the white threesome to satisfy their obligation to her. The latter wanted to save their skins and escape arrest and notoriety for their misdeeds. For reasons of loyalty, money, revenge, or excitement, the prostitute's five assistants wanted to stop the policemen from arresting her. Some in the crowd, carried away by the solidarity of the moment or the hope of anonymity, might have wanted to hurt the two policemen or, at least, hoped to frighten them enough to hamper them in performing their appointed duties in the future.

In short, the objectives of the policemen and of skid row were incompatible. Whose goals would obtain, those of the authorities or their antagonists?
Which side would control the encounter and the human behavior in it? What
means could cops use to govern the situation and to defend themselves?

## II

At Michigan and Commerce, the policeman was the man of property. He had
a job and if he kept it for twenty-five years, he would have a generous pension
coming. He had a family which depended on him. He had many possessions,
and he had been taught from childhood the value of owning things (and
indeed the importance of his job of protecting the property of others would be
diminished if he believed otherwise).

Jim Longstreet was typical. He had been on the department for four years.
Son of a railroad man, a breezy-talking, well-muscled, somewhat undisci-
plined athlete, Longstreet had only a high school diploma and lacked
confidence that he could ever amount to much in a world where knowledge
and cleverness were crucial: "I don't have the education." He enjoyed
physical challenges, and in police work he had enjoyed mixing it with the
citizenry—going "into some of the bad places" which trafficked in dope and
stolen goods "and jacking them up." "As far as I'm concerned, what I like is
the worst beat with a little leeway. That's when I'm happiest."

But Longstreet did not get leeway. While his job was technically protected
by civil service, any citizen could complain to Internal Affairs that Longstreet had violated a law or regulation or had acted without good judgment.
Internal Affairs could recommend that he be fired or reprimanded. To be
sure, a police officer had some protection by virtue of the procedures of the
department. The complaint had to be in writing; the complaint could be
challenged by the policeman. An officer could appeal an adverse decision of
Internal Affairs to the Civil Service Board and to the courts thereafter.
Moreover, to make the complaint in the first place, a citizen had to have
some faith that his effort to follow through would be worthwhile—a faith
which many self-proclaimed victims did not have (erroneously, in light of the
severity of Internal Affairs in Laconia). Nevertheless, the sanctuary of civil
service was by no means invulnerable. Policemen had been discharged for
alleged misconduct sufficiently frequently to be ominous, and a suspension
or even a reprimand could adversely affect chances for assignments to good
details, departmental respect, and promotions. Longstreet himself had been
before Internal Affairs several times and had had to shave the truth in
disconcerting ways when he found that the administration was out of step
with his police philosophy and would not back him up. He had received
written reprimands. He had undergone an extensive FBI investigation for

alleged violations of the civil rights of another and was being sued for $25,000.

What was more, he was married, had a child, and owned a house in the suburbs. He had begun to work part-time as a security officer in a department store to keep ahead of his debts. With a stake in the future, he found himself no longer "going the route" with citizens who revolted against his authority. Worried about sticking his neck out, he found himself doing "nothing" for a week, making just enough arrests to keep the sergeant off his back, and taking a walk when a guy said, "Screw you." "I'm not without worry about the repercussions," he said at one point. "My rule is no ticket is worth it if he's going after my job, and I'll let him have his way. I'm sickening; you shouldn't have to do it. But I'm paranoid about this stuff," he blurted at another point.

> A guy worries about the repercussions if you did get into a hot situation.
> ... I'm lucky. I've just bought a new house. I got a family. If I got fired,
> I don't know what I'd do. I could get a job. I'm still young, but when I get
> older and get fired, what could I do. The salary, it's good, and you live
> right up to it. Two or three hundred dollars less, and I'd be in a real bind.
> I earn fifteen thousand dollars but I've got no savings account. If I were to
> make less money, I'd have to make a lot of changes. I worry about security. I
> think of it more and more. My house, my daughter, more and more security.
> So when you see a job that looks like it might blow up, you sometimes want
> to say, "So what?" and move on.

Moving on, however, was easier to talk about than to accomplish. Avoiding hot situations required certain conditions.

First, unless a policeman who practiced the avoidance response was working his beat alone, he had to be in collusion with others; an eager partner could compel him to get involved. It was true that policemen had some choice of partners, and a sergeant was usually glad to defer to their desires to work with personalities that meshed. Sergeants usually tried to alleviate the natural tensions which built up between two large men, cooped up in a car for eight hours, breathing the same air, never out of each other's sight, interdependent for every decision. In this free-selection condition, practitioners of avoidance were likely to find inactive soul mates for partners.

The collusion, however, had to extend beyond the partnership to be foolproof. Since squad members from different beats covered one another, a norm had to exist within the squad not to punish or highlight or talk pejoratively about the noninvolvement of fellow officers. Officers had to agree on a kind of social laissez-faire: Live and let live. On the other hand, if it was proper for one squad member publicly to upbraid the "laziness" or the "cowardice" of another, then any attempt to take a walk would be made public. Each officer and each recruit to a squad had to be indoctrinated with the avoidance philosophy lest he rock the boat.

The supervisor of the squad, its sergeant, would have to countenance noninvolvement by his men. Inaction was significantly more difficult to detect than active misconduct like brutality. In order to perceive nonevents, persons had to have a perspective, a sense of "something missing." The sergeant had a chance to see that his men were taking a walk, for he, alone of all the supervisors, monitored the radio, checked the policemen's logs, and supervised a small enough group of men to individuate them in his mind.

A second condition was that the victims of police noninvolvement had to lack the motivation, perspective, and capability to complain about it. The naturally indignant, the rich, and the aware—the somebodies, in short— were worrisome because they could and did make complaints about policemen who paid them no heed. However, the submissive, the poor, the undereducated—it was highly unlikely that they would ever cast public light on police neglect.

Of course, third persons might act on behalf of the public. Observers accompanying the policeman, curious newspaper reporters, public officials, and political leaders could publicize police shortcomings in meeting their responsibilities. If policemen were to get away with avoidance, these public spokesmen had to be silenced: the police department had to be made a closed organization: city politics had to be kept low-key; and newspaper reporters had to be seduced or intimidated into indifference.

Only if there existed these three conditions—collusion, selective nonenforcement, and suppression—could the avoidance response happen widely. Yet it was possible, and when policemen did take a walk when the situation got hot, what happened as a result?

There were two sets of consequences, one for the community and one for the policeman himself.

On the beat there would inevitably be a number of the dispossessed who would recognize that the beat policeman was not around when the going got tough. They were persons who stood to profit from the policeman's absence—the strong-arm, the bully, the vicious. The grapevine would carry the news to their like-minded associates. When might made right, when the rebels against authority knew they were in control, skid row went to hell in a hand basket.

So did the community surrounding skid row. On the edge of skid row lived good people—old folks, sick folks, hardworking poor, recent immigrants to the city, minorities, small businessmen—struggling to maintain the margin of survival. They improved their daily lot; they raised children; they grew gardens; they cleaned and painted. They depended on police for protection from the predators. When they found that they did not enjoy police protection, they ceased to expose themselves and their possessions. They no longer went out in the evening. They refused to open their doors to strangers. They could not open their windows at night for ventilation. They stopped working in their gardens or maintaining the exteriors of their houses. They shut down their businesses. They turned in on themselves, dispossessing themselves of those very amenities which attracted the vicious to them. They learned to retaliate: they purchased guns and used them. They might even put themselves under the protection of a patron; stores employed private security police; and, as happened in a number of American cities, a community might assemble a vigilante patrol.[2]

In the communities where police permitted the dispossessed to rule by force, freedom became the freedom to prey on others. There was no equality between the brute and the benign. Those who were left in command were civilization's scoundrels. Creativity and civilization disappeared. The pleasure of the moment predominated. Matters that took time to develop had to be forgotten: a business, a garden, even a family would be destroyed before they survived their term or would be seized for ransom as they became more valuable. The long term had to be sacrificed in the name of survival. There was no hope.

As for the policeman who chose to "move on," dependent as he was on other policemen's covering up for him, he stopped speaking out in criticism of his fellow officers. A conspiracy of silence overtook him, requiring him to cover up not only his own avoidance behavior but also that of others—and any more egregious misconduct, including brutality or venality. The cop who avoided difficulty had to cope with feelings of cowardice, of having betrayed those motives to help which emanated from his religion and uprbringing— his deepest self. He derived less gratification from his job because he could no longer hold his whole life up to his previous standards of conduct. These feelings of cowardice and inadequacy led to intense frustration, often resulting in brutality whenever conditions would shield him from repercussion. One old officer recalled with the deepest revulsion a fellow officer who was a habitual avoider:

> I remember walking with him, and an old wino began badmouthing him. Just an old wino in his cups, perfectly harmless, and this guy charges toward him to slam him. I got in his way, and said, "What are you doing with this old man?" His answer was, "He's not that old." I told him, this was not the time when you get tough. "How come you didn't get tough with that big black guy back at Digby's Diner?" I asked; "you didn't get tough with him." "Well, this guy isn't going to talk to me like that," he says. He was going to slam this old man against the wall. "Why didn't

2.  See Samuel Lubell, *The Hidden Crisis in American Politics* (New York: Norton, 1970), chap. 4.

you knock that big black guy over?" I said, and I wouldn't let him past me, but he was going to make that old man toe the line. . . . I knew that he was a coward. He'd use that uniform as a form of bravado. He was always lying, and he was guilty of police brutality.

## III

If the citizen was so dispossessed that he was without even respectability, hope, or freedom, things which policemen might legitimately take as hostages, it was possible for a policeman to threaten things which the law forbade him to threaten. He could defend himself by implacably escalating the stakes; he could begin to take illegal hostages. Even the dispossessed possessed something—their physical integrity. Society, however, conventionally gave sanctuary against bodily assaults. Some policemen violated that sanctuary; in doing so, they became lawless.

The sanctuary for human life consisted in part of departmental regulations: "The policy of this Department is that members shall exhaust every other means before resorting to the use of firearms."

There were also laws against battery and homicide that applied to policemen who used more force than reasonable to subdue a citizen. In part, the sanctuary was provided by the force of moral obligations. Moreover, this moral aversion to injuring or killing another was reinforced by the practical consequences for a policeman of shooting someone: an extensive shooting board inquiry conducted by the department into the discharge of any police weapon, the increased likelihood of a riot, the intensification of community resentment.

Despite these considerable safeguards which civilization created for individual life, some policemen dared the wrath of the gods and recurrently desecrated the sanctuary.

Bee Heywood was "an old-time policeman," as he liked to describe himself. He was a brawny, red-haired Irishman who first joined the department because he loved motorcycles. As a member of the department motorcycle team (which he had organized), he had become national hill-climbing champion. Born out of state, he had come to Laconia in his adolescence at a time when his parents had been divorced and his mother had remarried. "Laconia then was a tough town, especially along lower Wichita Avenue. Besides I had a temper, and I couldn't stand anyone to hit me in the face. I'd always fight if they hit me in the face. I remember one old fella who told me that the big fellas on my paper route always knew I'd fight them, that I ought to turn and walk away. He said, 'They just egg you on, and your temper gets you all that stuff.'"

As Bee Heywood grew up and became a policeman, he stayed the same,

only more so. He retained his temper, and he found that it was prized in the
police department of the 1950s, which had believed in the efficacy of selective
harassment. He had "gone to Knuckletown" with a great many residents of
skid row.

That was half the story. The other half was that Heywood was a
tremendously likable, open, thoughtful, natural, and confident man. He had
begun our interview by warning me that he was a "naturally suspicious"
person, particularly of "pantywaists" from a university, and that he was
likely to refuse to answer many of my questions. Then he proceeded to talk
nonstop on every subject conceivable for four and a half hours. He was a
convert to Mormonism, a member of the John Birch Society, deeply
sentimental, heroically stubborn, and had an uncanny memory for detail. At
bottom, however, he was a physical man who learned about and sensed the
world through his body. A motorcyclist, a stunt flyer, a man who "raced
boats, raced cars, waterskied, rode horses, broke a horse of my own when I
was 14," fisherman, hunter, boxer, football player, he had survived an
on-the-job broken back and was in his twenty-sixth year on the department,
still working despite his eligibility for retirement. Bee Heywood had never
accepted the old man's admonition to "turn and walk away."

Being one who used violence against the dispossessed, living according to
the law of the jungle instead of the laws of civilization, was a wearying,
fearful, soul-searching job. Heywood's own eloquent testament summed up a
dozen years of skid row patrol:

> Sometimes it's real unpleasant; it's a real tough job. I don't enjoy it like
> I used to. As you get older, you don't want bitter fights, quarrels,
> enemies. As you get older, you want a little more peace, friends; you
> want to get away from all the strife. You just mentioned about hippies
> and narcotics addicts. When I transferred out of motorcycles after I broke
> my back, I couldn't take this downtown beat—the pimps and the hypes
> and the hoods and the crims. It really got me down, but as time passed,
> I think I just got used to the habit of staying downtown. It was not
> appalling to me, you might say, after a time. I used to work construction
> before coming here, and I found that often at first I didn't like a job, but
> by making myself stay with it, by giving it a probation, often I grew to like
> it. Well, if I didn't like police work, I would quit. I came to ask myself
> for some reasons why I was put down here. When I was in the air force
> during World War II a chaplain came up to me and said I should
> remember three questions. Well, I didn't think much about it at the time,
> but since those three questions, I've really begun to think more and more
> of them: Where did you come from? What are you going to do here?
> Where are you going after? So I kept asking myself that question about
> my work. And the answer I finally came to was, I was down here to protect
> life and property from the animals, the strong-arm thugs. I was here to

protect the pensioners and the old women, and the young servicemen from the thugs, the prostitutes who'd entice a guy into a room and when she got him there, she'd say, "Pardon me, let me see if my husband is around," and she'd open the door and in would walk two dudes who'd look real mean and send that serviceman running, feeling lucky he got away with his pants. I figured the old people really needed help; they really had to get shielded. So I began to feel I was really doing a job that needed to be done.

In providing the shield, Heywood did not always act lawlessly. If he had the self-restraint or the time to delay, he would investigate exhaustively until he got something on one of the dispossessed which would justify putting "the animal" behind bars. He was a tenacious adversary.

I remember one fella. I made an FC report on the man [that is, he asked the citizen to identify himself]. He started mouthing off, "You silly cops, you can't put me in jail," and acting smart. After that I went through our active vagrancy file, and there was nothing on him. But I take a certain pride in my work, and I finally got him into jail. I had to do it on my own time, but I finally busted him for a burglary of the Rivers Liquor Store. I caught him busting out with a carton of liquor. I had a hunch he would hit Rivers. So each night I'd put on my plain clothes, and I'd wait in the dark, watching the place in the cold. The night I caught him I was about to leave. Boy, it was cold, when sure enough, he comes walking up the driveway with a couple of guys, carrying pry bars, and then they break the lock, and as they're coming out with the liquor, I get a gun on them and say, "Don't run, fellas. If you do, I'll kill you. Just don't tempt me, or I'll have to shoot." After, I told him his mistake was calling me names. "You shouldn't talk to a policeman like that."

But often things were otherwise; he lacked the time and the patience to fulfill his responsibility of cleaning up downtown with the opportunities the law limited him to. So he handled the punks—physically.

I remember once I hit one guy with a club. He had a steel plate in his head, and he went to the hospital. I really sweated that one out. I was in the right, but you really think about it, having a life on your hands. You don't sleep at night. Since then, I haven't used my club. I use my fists instead.

He did use his fists. He also used his tongue to taunt and to egg on the resistance which made it right to use his fists. He beat up the punks and held his adversaries at bay by threat of brutality.

To be able to act violently required a stringent set of conditions. Obviously a policeman like Heywood, who frequently resorted to the enforcement response, had to have the capability—the strength and the cunning to win fights, to suppress by brute force.

When the adversary was one of a crowd, he had not only to fight with savagery but also to appear to be a savage in order to prevent the crowd from acting in concert. Most crucial to having sufficient capability was having another policeman with like habits and capacities as a partner. One man could barely handle a single adversary. Two men patrolling together and willing to respond viciously could take the measure of a crowd.

Second, there had to be collusive backup. The sanctuaries that safeguarded human safety were located in a separation of powers. The legislature created them and the judiciary supervised the administration of these sanctuaries. The policeman lacked control over these independent powers. An officer who practiced the enforcement response against the dispossessed therefore had to cover up his lawlessness. He had to be backed up by his fellow officers, his supervisors, and his chief administrators; and backing him up meant lying, falsification of reports, secrecy, and suppression of witnesses. Violence was far more difficult to hide than inaction, because the victims of the brutality knew what policemen to blame. A victim of the enforcement response had to be perpetually cowed into silence, compounding the need for continuing oppression.

If these difficult conditions could be satisfied, what were the effects on the beat of such police action?

Using lawless force unquestionably escalated the conflicts on skid row. Police violations of the taboo against physical threats licensed the unscrupulous citizen to violate it too. The simplicity and symmetry of the *lex talionis,* an eye for an eye and a tooth for a tooth, had a great attraction on skid row, as if in the absence of the artificial restraints of religion and law, this simple form of retribution would naturally flourish. The ethic of individual equality saturated skid row thought, and violation of principle by one side justified reciprocal violation by the other. In short, one consequence of police brutality was that lawlessness and the taste for vindication spread epidemically.

Moreover, the usefulness of violence was increased by keeping its memory alive within skid row. The recollection of the brutal example reminded the citizenry of the policeman's terrifying capability. If the community forgot it, it had to be repeated. To refrain from the enforcement response would undermine the effects of the policeman's reign of terror. Forgiveness had the effect of unleashing the hatred of skid row, previously suppressed by fear. In the adversary context which brutality created, steps to reconcile differences appeared to be appeasement, cowardice, and an invitation to retaliate. Once terror had been made the means of domination, there was no turning back.[3]

---

3.   Parenthetically, some threats did not create perpetual hatred. When the objective of these threats was the welfare of the person being threatened and he ultimately realized it, the threats received a justification which cut the vicious cycle of power and reprisal. An

Another consequence was that the community of the dispossessed were motivated to remain so. A community oppressed by threats would be worse off the more it developed a stake in the world. As badly off as the dispossessed were under the threat of bodily violence, they would be even more vulnerable to police lawlessness if they got a dog, made a friend, planted a flower bed, tried to become respectable, painted a room, or had hope, for these would become hostages at the mercy of any cop who resorted to brutality. Ever mindful that they had to mistrust the policeman, they felt they were better off low profile and unpropertied, as little vulnerable to police injury or scorn as possible. The policeman's atrocious reputation made a garrison state of his beat.

The personal effects of his atrocity were severe. The nightly work of officers like Heywood became "terrifying." They were preoccupied with the tasks of self-defense. They knew they would get no help "from those bastards . . . when you get in trouble." They were frightened of ambush and reprisal. They were frightened that their methods would be discovered and prosecuted. As one young officer observed, "Hot dogs have much more to worry about; they're always on edge."

Then, too, an officer like Heywood tended to obtain little information about the community. No one except finks and flatterers, hoping for leniency, told him anything, and what information he did get put him on his guard or misled him into lowering it. The news he was given contained nothing insightful about the community, nothing about whom to help and how.

Also, a policeman who ignored the taboo against hurting citizens ran the risk of destroying the very sanctuaries to which he and his fellow policemen entrusted their own lives. Other policemen were aware of the effects of a fellow officer's barbarity and resented it and the counterviolence it begot.

In addition, an officer who was guilty of enforcement responses found himself forced to take responsibility for the abuses perpetrated by his fellow officers. Bound by a conspiracy to cover up each other's brutal acts, Heywood and his colleagues were mutually implicated. Heywood could disclose no horror of any magnitude, lest his own illegalities unraveled in the disclosure. Solidarity alone guaranteed self-preservation. Complicity with his fellow officers complicated matters; it forced Heywood to disregard the difference between countenancing the "necessary" abuses he perpetrated and the "sadistic" abuses of his fellow conspirators.

One final effect must be noted. Men like Heywood, distressed by the undesirable implications of the lawless means to which they resorted,

---

atrocity, such as Heywood's use of force on skid row punks, however, was self-interested; its purpose was inevitably seen to be the policeman's own gain, not the good of the citizens against whom it was used.

urgently looked for good deeds to perform. Heywood sought out people to rescue, and his acts of goodwill were meaningful—vital to him. "The most satisfying feeling is the feeling you are needed, that you are helping." To accomplish these good deeds, he gave inordinate time.[4] He needed to be kind. It was like an urgent search for expiation after having contracted with the devil. Men like Heywood needed opportunities to restore their souls, and his compulsion to alleviate the troubles of his fellow man served as a reminder of the complexity and the redeemability of the human soul.

## IV

Captain Hook was not a Laconia police officer. He was a businessman. His business was providing security services to other businessmen. He sold private police protection to merchants, theater managers, barkeepers, grocers, and landlords. He employed a half-dozen beefy roughnecks like himself to assist him in handling the numerous jobs he had contracted. The Laconia Police Department licensed him and his employees to carry concealed revolvers while acting as security guards. In addition, the captain's men carried blackjacks and steel knuckles, and the captain fondled a menacing spiked nightstick.

Captain Hook did not wear a uniform. In the daytime he strutted around in a dirty T-shirt which stretched over his belly. Two American flags tattooed into his upper arms augmented the impressiveness of his biceps. On the roof of his twenty-year-old Chevrolet was a yellow rotating blinker light, and he had installed a bullhorn system in the front of the car. A bullet hole, prominent and unrepaired, was in the center of the car's rear window, testimony to the violence in the captain's wake.

The captain was tough, unscrupulous, and remorseless. Officer Longstreet said he was "three bricks short of a load," a phrase suggesting the disproportion between muscles and brain. He had served as a bouncer at

---

4.   For example: "The best case to tell is about Joey Lewis. He lived out in Westfield Village. He was a big kid; he'd been kicked out of school a lot. He had a bad temper; he was a bully, so to speak. I remember seeing him first; he was making a lot of noise in the Boston Diner. He had his feet up on the table. Well, there's one thing I can't stand is to have a kid talk back to an officer. I came into the Boston Diner, and I said, 'Son, why are your feet on the table? This is not a pigpen.' He began to mouth back that it was none of my business. I told him, 'This is my business. Get your feet off the table.' I jerked him off the chair, and I kicked him flat. He was a big kid then, but he was young and not coordinated at that time. I told him, 'Look, you're too big for me to fool with. I'm going to treat you like a man. Now you get back in my police car over there, and if you don't, you're going to find yourself in the hospital, and don't be too long about it.' He was real sullen and complained about his rights. 'You've lost all your rights, fooling around with these schoolgirls. I'm going to lock you up on a vagrancy offense. Why aren't you in school?' Well, it turned out that the wagon was tied up; so I decided to take the bull by the horns. I asked permission to take the boy home. So I make out the juvenile citation

numerous Laconia bars, and the punishments he had inflicted on uncooperative or nonpaying bar patrons were legendary in the police department.
When he capitalized on his brutal talents to enter the security policing
business, he continued to apply his barroom techniques and found new
markets for them. For example, the captain was hired by one landlord who

---

on him and took him to his house. I knocked on the door, and I said, 'Mrs. Lewis? I've
arrested this boy of yours. Is his father home?' 'He'll be home in about five minutes.'
Well, it was a beautiful home, the kind of home you could eat off the floor. She says
to me, 'What did he do now?' I said, 'Can't you handle this big monster of yours?' And
she says, 'No, Joey's too big for me; he pretty much goes as he pleases.' I said, 'For pete's
sake, what do you think the police department is for? This boy is going to prison if we
don't get him off the wrong track. He's nothing but a bully; he's surly; he won't talk
with people.' Well, it was a beautiful home, and the people were well spoken. 'We are your
police department,' I said, 'I'm in a hurry now, but we've got to get organized. This boy
of yours: he's idle. He's not doing anything. He's been kicked out of school, and he's been
beaten up enough for today. I'm leaving him in your custody, and I don't want him to
leave this house. You understand, Joey? Meantime, I'll be back Monday on my day off
and I'm going to help you out.' 'Can I go to the show Sunday?' Joey asks. And I say, 'Okay,
but don't bully anyone.' The kid weighs about 215 pounds. I went to juvenile because I
wanted to handle the matter myself. Juvenile had a good talk with the mother. Meanwhile,
I got some paint wholesale, and I said to Joey, 'You gotta learn something. Here's a paint-
brush.' He started on the back of his house, so's if he botched up, it wouldn't show so
much. We had a talk before we got started. 'We have to have a boss,' I said; 'I'll be the
boss, and you go along with it, or I'll thrash the daylights out of you. You've been a
terrible trial to your parents, but I'm not going to wait a minute to fight you. We don't
have the fight if you accept me as a boss. There'll be no hard feelings. I'll be a real
fair boss. In the meantime I'll get you a job.' I went down to a local bar I knew to see if
there was a job available for after hours. 'Is he trustworthy?' I said I didn't know, 'but
he's good at lugging heavy crates.' So he got the job, and I got him some more painting
jobs, cheap jobs. And when he got better, I went to a painting contractor. I told him the
kid was good and he's not afraid to work. Well, after a while, the contractor came to me
and said the kid was damn good. He became an apprentice painter. He was going to Edge-
hill High School meantime, and he finished his school, and they wanted him in the
draft. Well, they drafted him, and for three years, I didn't hear from him. Then one
day I was walking up Michigan, and an officer came by and said, 'Say, Bee, a couple
of big colored marines were looking for you. One's a big son-of-a-bitch.' I went along,
and I saw two guys standing at the Michigan Theater. Both are sergeants, and I hear one
say to the other (it was Joey Lewis), 'This is the man I've been telling you about.' The
other guy is as black as the ace of spades, and he says, 'He thinks you're God.' So I say,
'Let's go down to Johnson's. I'd like to find out what you're doing.' Both are sergeants,
and they're tough. But Joe is six foot five inches, and he must weigh 235 pounds, and
he's got a real physique. He was making a career out of the Marines. I had really
straightened him out. 'Of all the guys I've met on this job,' I told Joey, 'this one instance
with you makes it all worthwhile. Are you going to go to college now?' 'No,' he said, 'I'm
going to make a career out of the Marines.' He had a nice wife and a couple of children.
I was never sure he'd really make it. Belligerent—man, I have never seen such belligerence.
I'd say, 'Why have you got the chip on your shoulder? I came to help you,' I said,
'and I'm going to make you do what nobody else could. I know you dislike me. Let's get it
out on the table. You think I dislike you. Well, you're mistaken.' Later he confessed
to me what was bothering him. 'I didn't know myself what it was,' said Joey. 'It was hard.
I hated white people. I didn't realize I was hiding it all inside me.' I said, 'I can understand,' and we'd talk about things, and we bridged the gap.''

owned a notorious apartment house nicknamed the Taj Mahal. The landlord wanted to get rid of some tenants he deemed undesirable and asked the captain to help. The captain's method allegedly was to go door to door, displaying his spiked baton and ordering the tenants to leave in a day and a half, or else. One day, in front of a half-dozen policemen, without shame or fear, the captain and the landlord congratulated themselves on the fact that "the homos were no longer there." Each policeman had a good idea of the illegal extortion the captain had practiced on the tenants. None of the officers, however, was ready to denounce the captain or cite him for his strong-arm practices.

In fact, a kind of partnership existed between some of the squads and Captain Hook. The deal was that the captain patrolled skid row and the enterprises which served it. He cowed skid row with his bullying tactics. At the same time, he protected the businessmen, who were pleased by his high-handed but effective unofficial procedures.

The key to the deal between the captain, the police, and the businessmen was official leniency. The policemen bent the law, looking the other way from the captain's daily violations of it. By failing to halt him, they unleashed him. As a result of his exemption from legal restrictions, the captain could provide his customers with a unique and brutal service, one for which he could ask a monopolist's premium. It was a good deal for all. Policemen delegated part of the dirty business of keeping the peace on skid row to a nonofficial vigilante. His salary in turn was paid by the merchants and businessmen who profited most from the captain's activity. The police were not obviously implicated; it was just a matter of their never having sufficient evidence to charge the captain and his cronies with the assaults and batteries they committed.[5]

Leniency, studied ignorance, inaction—these were the patronage a policeman could dispense. Absolute secrecy became more important as the size of the favor grew. At one extreme, the minuscule patronage of transporting six juveniles to their weekly jazz band rehearsals in a police car was openly tolerated by the area supervisor because in exchange the kids passed on information about burglaries and muggings in the neighborhood. This patronage was so minimal that few precautions had to be taken to keep the public unaware of it. Other minor forms of leniency which policemen regularly dispensed were permitting kids to congregate in large groups in the parks, overlooking parking violations, countenancing a little dice game behind a fence, and allowing a bar to stay open a few minutes past the lawful

5.   Masao Maruyama provides an intriguing glimpse of the influence in pre-World War II Japanese politics of the *ronin,* those adventurers and soldiers of fortune who bartered their cunning, courage, and readiness to break the law for wealth and influence. Masao Maruyama, *Thought and Behavior in Modern Japanese Politics* (New York: Oxford University Press, 1969), pp. 128-30.

closing time. As a quid pro quo, the peace was preserved and everyone involved was discreetly silent about the arrangements. As the degree of leniency increased, however, the deals became more vulnerable to public criticism, demanding greater efforts at secrecy. Permitting Captain Hook's vigilantes to range unhampered was serious business. Revealing the arrangement would have been devastating to all parties.[6]

The point is that any police department, even one as free from graft as Laconia's, had a great deal of potential illegal patronage to dispense, giving it the power to purchase cooperation and social repression. Such a patronage system required complicity because it was outside the law. In Laconia the system was not so extreme that the department had to close itself off from all public scrutiny. It was a system that applied only to part of skid row activities. However, this corruption of authority was extremely subtle, and it imperceptibly grew. Its utility was so obvious and its initial cost so modest that even the most scrupulous of policemen found it difficult to speak out against it.

The most serious effect of this delegation of power to a vigilante was that he ruled part of skid row outside the rule of law. He had no training in self-restraint, few incentives to practice it, and considerable immunity from legal, political, and police criticism. His unspoken contract with the police placed few real constraints on his conduct; at most, he was to be discreet in choosing victims who would not complain and he was to use some intelligence in hiring employees. Undermining the policemen's efforts to keep the captain in line was their recognition that his effect on skid row would be enhanced by the extortionate advantages resulting from his bizarre behavior, his cruel reputation, and his lawlessness—he acted in ways that official policemen could not. By allowing him to do away with legal principles governing proper standards of police conduct, however, policemen found it increasingly difficult to discern the line between actions which were necessary and excesses which were sadistic. The result was that few policemen ever blew the whistle on the captain, and he knew that his license was, for practical purposes, extremely broad.

Inequality was officially countenanced on the beat. Captain Hook, the guy who did the policemen's dirty work, got away with illegal activity, while men less useful but also less cruel could not. Whether it set a cynical example, whether it encouraged disrespect for the law's supposed evenhandedness, was unknown. What was certain, however, was that policemen on skid row had difficulty asserting that the police did not play favorites.

6. At the extreme to which leniency might go, one could imagine cities where a group was permitted to monopolize the traffic in illegal drugs in exchange for suppressing the crimes of others. Such an extreme corruption of authority did not take place in Laconia, but it would have required utmost conspiratorial silence if it did.

The problem with vigilantism was that the deal between official and nonofficial peace-keepers fell outside the law and social acceptance. Being outlaws, the participants had exchanged hostages; each could be prosecuted if the deal was exposed. The policeman who delegated his job to an outlaw like the captain had escaped the clutches of the dispossessed, but by means which placed him in the captain's clutches. Thus, while skid row may have become more secure, the policeman who resorted to this kind of reciprocity response was less safe. He had to hide the captain's record of misconduct, because the whole arrangement would unravel if that record came to light.

Covering up a delegation of power to vigilantes on any larger scale than was practiced in Laconia would have meant closing the beat and the department to all outside scrutiny. Without the presence of outsiders, the police chief would have been less informed, or at least less certain that he was informed, about the street conduct of his men. If outsiders were forbidden to observe and inquire about department practice, the opportunities for fruitful dialogue and innovation would have materially diminished.

Because a "contract" between vigilantes and official police involved the participants' putting themselves in a mutually extortionate situation, it tended to be worse for the party who had more to lose from exposure. Unquestionably, the policeman was the more vulnerable. Since Captain Hook was both the less vulnerable and the more active partner in the deal, he set the pace. It was Captain Hook who determined the scope of obligation of his passive partners, the police. As he widened the scope of his dreadful activities, the policemen found that they were increasingly required to ignore the calls for assistance from the captain's victims. The moral problems this increasing avoidance presented to policemen who wanted to help the oppressed was extremely great.

## V

Each of the three means of dealing with the dispossessed which has been described thus far required secrecy and complicity between partners, on the squad, throughout the department, and with the community. Each response was lawless or unrespectable. The difficulty of coping with the dispossessed was so great that law-abiding policemen—or, rather, policemen who wanted to perform services within the law—were forced outside the law merely to cope.

The professional response, however, was a way of effectively working within the rule of law. Some policemen developed their beat; they established relationships with their citizenry. They did not pay for it by surrendering their authority, nor did they develop a schedule of inducements and penalties outside the law.

Mike Marshall was a walking patrolman, a rangy ex-basketball player who had played professionally eleven years before putting on a police uniform. His education was acquired through nineteen years of experience in Laconia streets. It was a minimal education, adequate only because he had specialized in patrolling skid row. As he argued so simply, "In this world you pick out what you can do, what you think you'd be good at, and do it."

He neither understood nor tolerated hippies, demonstrators, and people who spoke out against America, but he never met one on his beat. He knew human nature in skid row, where it was "more down to earth." He liked his "bums."

> I think I know everybody on my beat. Maybe 5,000 persons. And I try to learn all their first names and their faces.... I prefer to have them call me "Mike," and they prefer to have me call them that way. A wino comes up, and by calling you by your first name he gets a feeling of equality. By giving them a feeling of equality, you are making a friend of them. Even though I put a lot of them in jail, they are friends, so-called friends. A lot will get drunk for a week; then they'll want you to put them in jail a week or so. They know when they've had enough. Otherwise, they'll die. An awful lot ask to go to jail.

He was not afraid of them because he knew which ones had weapons and which ones did not.[7]

Furthermore, he was respected and trusted because he had worked his beat. He had performed countless good works on skid row, for numerous people, and with equitable regularity. The gravest widespread need of the community of bums was financial. Bums needed money for wine whenever they were caught short. Their problem was Marshall's opportunity. He helped them in their time of necessity and merited their friendship. The citizens of skid row:

> knew that if they were short a few cents for the price of a bottle of wine, they could come to us. Every night they are into me for a couple of dollars. I'd bet I have three or four hundred dollars loaned out. Once in a while one will pay you back. Probably one in five. There are fifteen or twenty of them that always pay you back. The day the welfare check comes out, they pay you the twenty-five cents or dollar they borrowed. How did it get started? I think I probably offered the first few times. I saw them looking at their hand in front of the liquor store, looking for the dime or quarter they did not have. So I'd hand it to them, and you'd see them smile, and you made friends for life. Actually they're not bad people. Whether they

---

7. For instance, he talked of the effects of the Supreme Court's legal restraints on searches and seizures: "There are many pushers on skid row; but rarely will a pusher carry a gun because if he does, we can pat him down and find what's in his pockets. They don't want us going into their pockets."

pay you or not, they'll come by and tell you they will. You don't really expect it. You know what it's going for, but you know you're not going to cure them of their drinking.

Marshall enjoyed what Tocqueville referred to as "that respectable power which men willingly grant to the remembrance of a life spent in doing good before their eyes."[8] The bums trusted him, placing confidence in the humanitarian system of checks and balances which they saw as forestalling any abuse of power. In developing his beat, Marshall neutralized the fear, the distrust, the antagonism which citizens naturally experienced in the presence of unmeasured authority.

Thus, when Marshall and his partner of twelve years disarmed the knife-wielding prostitute and she began "hollering prejudice," no confrontation materialized. "But the citizens knew that was not the reason. And they were on our side. That really helped us. Had they not known us, we would have been in a great deal of trouble. In skid row they were 'good citizens.' They're the winos, the bums, the pimps around the area, and other prostitutes. They knew we were not out to arrest them."

Marshall's development of skid row had transformed the dispossessed of that community into "good citizens," into people who had something to lose and therefore something to protect—a line of credit, a decent friendship, a good public servant, whatever it was that Marshall had come to represent through "a life spent in doing good before their eyes."

The conditions which made this professional response possible were very different from the circumstances required by the avoidance, the enforcement, and the reciprocal responses. For one thing, the professional response depended on mankind's passion for talking to and about one another, not on its capacity to keep a secret. Developing a beat required a grapevine to spread the news of good works far and wide. Doing good without a communication system to advertise it would not have been effective. If only a handful of citizens knew of Marshall's value to the community, or if men did not understand that their own affection for Marshall was widely shared throughout the community, then the sense of solidarity necessary to stand up for him would have been missing. No one man was strong enough to help Marshall against the prostitute and her five assistants. Only action in concert was sufficient to suppress them. Each citizen had to know that his defense of Marshall would be immediately supported by his fellow citizens.

The condition of open deeds openly advertised limited what Marshall could do by way of public service. He had to do the kind of good works which were equally available to all. He had to anticipate that his kindness to one

---

8. Alexis de Tocqueville, *Democracy in America,* trans. Henry Reeve (New York: Vintage, 1945), 1:51.

person would excite everyone else to demand equivalent treatment. His good deeds created a principle of responsibility which no one had felt before. If Marshall fell short of that standard of responsibility thereafter, he was blameworthy, undependable, and unrespectable.

Marshall could and did handle this raising of public expectations by mastering important democratic skills. For one thing, he became eloquent. He mastered the knack of talking with his citizenry and establishing principles of distributive justice. He gave money after expressing the principle of "to each according to his needs," a standard which permitted him to justify denying requests for large sums of money or necessities other than food or drink.

He economized. The service he provided was inexpensive. He gave out nickels and dimes, the kind of support which he could afford when universalized. He did not dispense five dollars at a time, lest he have to discriminate between the favored few and the needy multitude. [9]

He became empathetic and in touch with his citizenry. He found out what they really desired. What he donated to them had to be something they valued, not something he thought would be good for them. Gratitude did not flow from buying a wino a cup of coffee.

Finally, he knew the law so that he could prudently stay within it. An illegal favor, witting or unwitting, would require secrecy. If he had tried to develop his beat by bending the law, Marshall would have been compromised. He would have been in constant jeopardy that someone would call him to account and require him to undo the good works he had done. Only by acting within the law could he have gained the necessary independence from outside intrusion. Of course, he had to have the legal leeway to dispense favors within the law. Marshall could not have developed his beat by nickel-and-diming his winos' necessities in a time of prohibition or under an officious set of departmental regulations prohibiting such loans.

One consequence of this professional response was that the community tended to develop confidence in the beat patrolman. It became more open, had a greater sense of security, and enjoyed a number of little productive happinesses. For the officer himself, one result was that he developed a feeling of safety, a more informed understanding of his beat, and considerable moral gratification from doing the job well. Not all the possible consequences were desirable, of course. A policeman who had developed his beat well often felt a twinge of hostility toward newcomers coming into the area and other sources of social change. He became conservative. To this

9.  In working-class areas, a policeman could give advice on repossession, insurance matters, getting gypped at the store, and how to get help for a child with school problems. Advice was cheap to the knowledgeable policeman. It did require some mental capital, investments in learning the law and mastering the procedures of bureaucracies.

tendency was added a proprietary feeling about "my" beat. A policeman good at the professional response often became so involved with his beat that he failed to see the bigger city-wide picture. If a chief were not aware of this possibility for his most skilled policemen, misunderstandings could arise which caused the chief to be angry with their arrogance and them to be frustrated by the imperception of their chief. Finally, community support had a tendency to give those men who could develop their beats a false sense of well-being; they tended to let down a little or to cut corners. They were flattered, and sometimes they confused admiration for their office with admiration for themselves personally. Overconfidence and a tendency to take some unmerited pleasure in oneself, however, are not problems unique to policemen.

# 6

# The Paradox of Detachment: The Family Beef

Cleon, when he first decided to take up political life, brought his friends together and renounced his friendship with them as something which often weakens and perverts the right and just choice of policy in political life.

*Plutarch*
Moralia
ca.100 A.D.

One police officer I really admired, he'd come into a family beef with a husband and wife throwing and yelling at each other. Then he'd set down on the couch and take his hat off, and he didn't say a word. Sooner or later the couple felt kind of silly. He'd take 45 minutes in each of these situations, but he never had to come back.

*Officer Mark Rockingham*
Laconia Police Department
1971

## I

Cleon was a demagogue, an aristocrat who lived in Greece in the fifth century B.C. and based his political career on the support of the poorly born, the have-nots. According to Plutarch, Cleon anticipated the reactions of his parents and relations to his decision to represent the hated multitude and took prudent steps to safeguard himself. He realized that the leaders of the aristocratic class would apply pressures directly against him—ostracism, scurrilous rumors, disinheritance. Moreover, he was aware that indirect pressures might be more difficult to resist, ultimately forcing him to weaken his attacks and pervert his beliefs. If his friends were subjected to abuse, he would have an obligation to save them, as they were implicated in his troubles only because of their affection for him. Less able to defend himself against these indirect pressures, he publicly and dramatically renounced his friendships, thereby freeing his friends from their moral obligation to assist him and at the same time unburdening himself of a reciprocal responsibility to help them. In effect, he made it clear to his adversaries: "I don't care about attachments you thought I had. My former friends are not suitable hostages, for they are no longer important to me. I am indifferent to their fate. I matter not to them, nor they to me."

Twenty-four hundred years later a Laconia police officer looked on while a desperate husband behaved like Cleon. A family fight was in progress, and the husband appeared to be utterly indifferent to the destruction of his marriage and the worldly possessions fortifying it. The husband had detached himself from his responsibiⁱity to care for his wife or his children. He had renounced any concern for a reputation as a stable and substantial citizen. His renunciation, like Cleon's, was public and dramatic. Perhaps, like Cleon, he had foreseen that obvious attachments to others might make him vulnerable to restraint. Cleon's detachment freed him from his loved ones and the moral influences of his background so that he could follow the "right and just policy" of abating class hatred. The husband's detachment liberated him from the moral influence of others, including his wife, his children, his neighbors, and the policeman.

This curious pattern of behavior illustrates the second paradox of coercion—the paradox of detachment. "The less the victim cares about preserving something, the less the victimizer cares about taking it hostage." The paradox of dispossession presented the problem of how to keep what one cared about; the paradox of detachment raised the corollary question, whether to care about what one has kept. One classic response to the aggressions of the dispossessed, you will recall from the discussion of the extortionate transaction, was to take sanctuary in order to preserve what was important. The classic defense against the aggressions of the detached, on the other hand, was to diminish the importance of things in order to avoid having to create a sanctuary. The reactions were different, not in degree, but in kind. Against the dispossessed, an individual defended himself by asserting, "I care so desperately about injury to my things that I shall fight to the last to protect them." Against detached persons, such as Cleon or the rampaging husband, however, one could simply say, "I don't care either."

In Laconia the recurrent variation on the theme of detachment was the family beef. In the evening, when the fever of life abated and the psychiatrists closed their offices and the clergy had other things to do and the social workers went home, the hush inside a police car would invariably be broken by a radio call, "999," the police code for a family disturbance. You may recall Officer Ingersoll's description of the events leading to a typical fight between husband and wife.

> The guy had come unglued. . . . His wife spent all the month's welfare money. He was trying to make good, trying to toe the mark. He had been laid off, and he was in Sparta [a rather handsome low-income housing

project] and giving his welfare check to an organization to pay off all his bills and rent and what not. He was trying to keep his head above water, and he had come home and his wife had spent the check. There was no way to calm him down. Alcohol, maybe drugs had played a part. . . . He had made an honest effort to make good. He had two children and he had come home and the money's not there. . . . He was sure tearing up the place, which was sad because they were nice furnishings.

At some point the wife or a neighbor had telephoned the police department, and the radio room had dispatched the complaint to the beat officer, usually without details. Unless it were a repeat call, the officer would not know the family. He could only guess how the husband and wife would respond to an officer intruding on their citadel—his castle, her nest. The patrolman would never have been inside the home. He would not know where the guns or the knives were located or what the neighbors would be like. He would have no clue to the background of the dispute or the precipitating event. What he did know was that family beefs were invariably perilous. "I think the toughest situations that a policeman today on the street faces is the husband-wife dispute." That was the unanimous sentiment of the ranks in the Laconia Police Department: "In family beefs more police get killed than in any other kind of situation."[1]

In a family beef things came unglued. The husband and wife were destroying their most precious attachments. Their relationship and the possessions to which they had given so much time—the glue of their joint lives—were the objects of their destruction. His dignity had been bound up in supporting his dependents and providing a home. Her pride adhered to her children, the cleanliness of her household, and the integrity of the family unit. Yet there they were, destroying every one of these valuables.

The wrench of events had been so terrific that they were throwing over their old scale of values. They had become so desperate that everything that had mattered seemed insignificant beside the contention in their lives. They revolted against their inner bondages; they detached themselves from their past. Everything was up for destruction: their windows, their china, their friendships, their children, their very lives. For the moment they (or one of them) no longer cared about anything or anybody, not even the policeman who responded to the 999. If it was the husband who was enraged, "there was no way to calm him down," indifferent as he was to everything, and hence invulnerable to the direst police threat. What could a policeman do?

1.  Family beefs happened every night. They occurred with such frequency that the department established an experimental Family Crisis Unit to reduce the beat officers' overload of them. Several specially trained men responded exclusively to 999s throughout the city. They rarely lacked for calls, and they never completely relieved the beat officers of answering a good portion of them.

## II

If the patrolman who entered the door was young and inexperienced, there was no way he could avoid "getting his fingers burnt," "getting in over his head," "getting in the dogshit." He would start with the disadvantage of being much younger than the couple he was attempting to arbitrate between. Furthermore, if he were married himself, he had not been for very long, and he would lack the direct experience of long-abiding marital frustration. Finally, he would not be detached. He would be anxious about his own value in the world. He would be prepared to lavish his help on any persons who needed it. By meeting responsibilities, he would enlarge his self-respect. He would build an identity on the basis of his successful intersections with the lives of others.

Young patrolmen needed to know that their individuality counted for something. They were in the process of building for themselves an adult "image" by taking advantage of the moral opportunities which presented themselves. A family beef animated them to offer assistance. It involved them. Their identification with the couple's well-being, however, put them at a disadvantage relative to the detached husband or wife. Their concern to protect the family often exceeded their capacities to defend it.

When the policeman was as incompetent as Officer Jim Garfield, the family beef became an intolerable ordeal. Garfield was six foot four, thin, mustachioed, and handsome. His pretentious oratorical style, arrogant strut, and insensitivity created antagonism in every situation which I observed. As one training officer delicately put it, he was "sometimes curt and rude in his manner."

Moreover, he had a learning disability. He had flunked out of college. He had failed the police department intelligence test. The supervisor of the Police Academy had recommended that he be dropped from his class after six weeks. An old-timer noted, "He doesn't seem to have the capacity to retain information or advice given to him."

Finally, he was mixed up. As an adolescent, he had halfheartedly run away from home and the father he reviled. He gloried in his memories of the mayhem of Vietnam. He drank excessively. And he was obsessed with narcotics: "My ambition is to get in the Vice Division. All the way through school, I was attracted, I was interested in narcotics. In the service, I helped out supplying information on hard narcotics." Other policemen hated to work with him. Supervisors made up innocuous tasks to keep him off the streets as much as possible, and if they could not find ways to divert him from critical situations, they asked other officers to stay with him. He was a real albatross—unquestionably the worst officer in the sample.

Why was he on the department? Why did he stay on? His size, his good looks, his military experience, and his persistent desire to be a policeman gave him a series of second chances. Moreover, when he came on the department, civil service had begun to have doubts about the "job-relevance" of intelligence tests. Its extensive testing battery was under attack in a civil rights suit. Paradoxically, then, when this privileged Anglo-Saxon failed the tests, he was given, along with other applicants, a second, less demanding examination, which he passed. After he was accepted on the department, the chief, then needing men, overrode the supervisor's recommendation to expel him from the Training Academy. His field evaluators, lacking a chance to discuss Garfield with one another, separately doubted their individual predictions that Garfield was bound to get worse. These factors all combined to get Garfield through the one-year probationary period, after which he could not be fired except for active misconduct. Garfield, however, stopped being active, and thus he became a permanent, undischargeable liability. "I've got number one to think about before everybody else," he would say, and that meant avoiding any difficult task, "kissing it off." He looked for the slightest excuse not to get involved. He waited to see if other patrolmen would respond to the radio dispatcher. If he had to go to a scene, he would leave it as soon as the opportunity arose. And if a couple were in the middle of a domestic crisis and "they tell me to get out, I have left. If they don't want me, I don't want them. I'm their servant, and it's their prerogative." Having proved incompetent in handling family beefs, he defined them as outside his police responsibilities. By his lights, family beefs were not work for police but for a family counselor whom the city had not yet hired: "He could be especially hired to work with married families' problems: why bring policemen into a family squabble when it's a medical or emotional problem? A doctor or reverend can handle it. They've got to get rid of this petty stuff." Thus, he justified his inaction, leaving the citizenry's "medical or emotional problem" to a doctor whom they could not afford and to a clergyman who might never come except to bury one of them.

Some of the same conditions which permitted policemen who took hikes whenever skid row blew up had to obtain if a man like Garfield was to get away with leaving family beefs to nonexistent nonpolice. There must be complicity with a partner if he had one, secrecy from outsiders, a prudent talent for responding only to those few somebodies who might call him on the carpet for his irresponsibility.

Yet a final condition must be added when a situation recurred as frequently as the family beef. The policeman who habitually responded evasively had to construct a socially unassailable justification for his inaction. For his fellow officers he had to cast his avoidance response into a legitimate (or ostensibly legitimate) perspective. He had to utilize some conventional piece of departmental wisdom for his own purposes. In defining family beefs as outside his responsibility, he drew largely on the familiar admonition, "Don't get involved." This equivocal phrase was the foundation of Garfield's moral defense. It was an imperative to which different policemen responded differently. To the person who responded professionally, it meant, Be fair. To some others, it meant, Don't take other people's troubles home with you. To a policeman inclined to the enforcement response, it meant, Don't be merciful. For Garfield, however, it meant, Mind your own business. "Don't get involved" was ambiguous enough to cover up his irresponsibility and provide him an acceptable principle of conduct. So long as the leadership of the department failed to confront and resolve the ambiguity, it would remain that way.

The personal results were disastrous: nonfulfillment, erratic behavior, and increasing avoidance of police work. Garfield and others who responded in the same way reduced their opportunities to matter in the world, because they had defined so much of what policemen normally had to do as immaterial. Having drawn such a narrow compass around their conception of police work, they had little scope to perform in a worthwhile way. To be sure, Garfield's detachment from the destinies of so many people saved him from having to defend them, but it also left him with no material with which to build a self-image. He was an individual without identity, a man who played no worthwhile part, a wastrel of himself.

The frustration of such self-depletion was intense, and episodically Garfield relaxed the moral confinement to which he had assigned family disputes. Almost whimsically, he would come on a domestic beef and, rather than avoid it, he would treat it within his definition of police work: "stopping ... crime," "giving tickets," making arrests, "cleaning the beat." In his own words, "it was a husband and wife beef. Both started beefing at me. There were eight or nine people standing in the living room. I took them all to jail—even the spectators. I called a unit, and they knew we weren't kidding. It turned the situation around." Thus Garfield turned a "medical or emotional problem" into police work, where some glory, some sense of moral self-fulfillment, was possible. He felt good; he was doing his job; he slaked his need for moral replenishment.

Yet, despite these erratic episodes, the trend to inaction persisted. Declaring that difficult jobs were outside the police job was habit-forming. Once he had excised family beefs from his definition of police work, he next found it easy to put "kids playing baseball in the street" out of his moral ken, then feuds between families. Then he began avoiding any dispute between residents of that part of the city he called "asshole country," those low-income public housing developments where the public peace was so frequently violated. From that point of retreat, the logic of his moral argument led him to exclude all activity in "asshole country," even stopping burglaries and muggings. In that manner the moral blight kept spreading

until the detached Garfield was left with a landscape in which there was no
food for the soul. He became a policeman dead on his feet.[2]

The social consequence of the avoidance response was that the citizens
were thrown back on themselves to solve their own problems. As Garfield
said with misplaced pride, "I never had any more complaints." The
problems persisted unattended. Violence did not abate—just the complaints
concerning it. The weak got hurt, but having no recourse to the law and the
larger society, they protected themselves by detaching themselves from
concern for their family, their friends, their community, in fact, anyone
but number one. Furthermore, in an area without the law, those who were
strong enough to tear down civilization when they became unglued encountered no effective resistance to their brutishness. The values of family life,
love, growth, and responsibility died in the devastation.[3]

## III

Officer Frank Carpasso was not a moral zombi. He was a rescuer. He needed
to be needed. He depended on the attachments of others; he had to have
opportunities to assist the weak, the poor, the luckless, the oppressed. He
was "out there to help people." "It's gratifying for the soul."

He had felt this pleasure in helping people as long as he could remember.
In his boyhood he had idolized the local policeman whose assorted acts of
kindness and patient explanations compensated for the inadequacies of
Carpasso's own father. Like his idol, Carpasso extended a helping hand to
any likely prospect. "I took under my wing" a juvenile offender whose
father, like Carpasso's own, had been an alcoholic. Carpasso had bribed the
boy to go back to school, rewarding him with money and tickets to sports

2.  Parenthetically, Garfield possessed a markedly asocial understanding of life. Whether his
    belief in man as "an island" was cause or consequence of his recurrent avoidance, his
    perception of the world was extreme in the degree to which he blinded himself to man's
    need to be in touch with others. For instance, he justified his difficulties in high school
    as follows: "I got rotten grades for grammar when I was young. I'm like an individualist.
    If I feel a comma should be in the middle of the sentence, that's where the comma is going,
    as far as I'm concerned." This narrow understanding of social responsibility, reflected
    in ignoring the need for clarifying others' confusion, and his inability to see his own
    communication from the point of view of the person who would be receiving it, seemed
    present in his police work. He was, as he said, "like an individualist."
3.  One officer told this story of the avoidance response of a former partner: "He just did not
    want to get involved.... We got a call from a daughter that her mother was trying to
    kill herself with sleeping pills. We drove up to the mother's house; he told me to wait in the
    car, and he got out and rang the doorbell. Nobody answered; so he came back, and we
    drove off. No one answered, and for him that was the end of the call. You can imagine
    the kind of visions going on in my mind, and I told him exactly what I was thinking. But he
    responded, it was 'not our business to get into trouble.' Well, it turned out that the mother
    was actually someplace else, and she did not die, but he didn't know it, and I didn't
    either."

events. He had helped the boy join the YMCA and gave general instructions on how to go straight. But the relationship fell apart. The boy deceived Carpasso about playing basketball and cheated on his promises to return to school. Eventually he was sent to the Juvenile Detention Center. "It did not work out," Carpasso admitted.

Nonetheless, in four years of police work, Carpasso continued to seek out ways to help, and if there was no plea for assistance, he invented one. Family problems between parents turned into opportunities to save their children. He entered every family dispute to separate the child from the wayward parent. He listened to the grown-ups, not to find out what was happening, but to confirm his presuppositions about what was going on. When the confirming clue appeared, he "knew" the whole story. Instead of arbitrating the dispute that was actually taking place, however, he constituted an inquiry to determine which parent was at fault for the assumed injury to the child. Did the mother feed the child, or play around? Did the father get drunk, or was he trying to keep the house together? Once he found out, there were only two alternatives: the "no-good" parent left "willingly—or [went] to jail." Thus, sentimentality developed into an enforcement response.

Carpasso's sense of identity was so involved and his obligation so attached to the family dispute that he drew meanings from it which many other officers never saw. It was the kids to whom he was attached, and he reconstructed each domestic scene, not as the parents saw it, but as a small boy might have felt it. One sensed Carpasso was haunted by memories of his own childhood unhappinesses.

> My father was an alcoholic and in all kinds of problems. My parents had my two older sisters, and then they had split up. After they got back to- gether, they had me. So we were kind of two families. The marriage wasn't too good ever, and I'm kind of from a broken home, you might say. . . . A psychiatrist would have a good time with my story.

The conclusion to which Carpasso jumped could endure as the ground for his conduct in the absence of any information to belie it. The radio dispatcher's laconic message provided Carpasso little in the way of reality. In the fury of the family beef, accurate information was hard to obtain under any circumstances, giving Carpasso plenty of leeway to structure his inquiry so as to render irrelevant any facts which might upset his assumptions.

A second factor contributing to Carpasso's sentimental behavior was his dualistic understanding of human nature. He tended to separate mankind into two groups: the heroic and the miserable, the good and the bad, the best and the ignoble, We and They. Practically any feat was possible to the first group, provided that the "bad people" were put out of the way. In family beefs the latter typically consisted of fathers, perhaps because the mother was the complainant, perhaps for practical reasons (if you jailed the mother, what was the father to do with the kids?), perhaps because it was more likely to be the truth. The dualistic view made it possible to spotlight who was to be rescued and who condemned.

A third condition making this sentimental concern possible was the division of labor in the Laconia Police Department. It meant that Carpasso was always a field officer (who dealt exclusively with confrontation) and never an investigative officer (who developed the full story in the calm of the next day). Carpasso rarely had a chance to check his assumptions against the larger dimensions of the event. As part of this separation of functions he saw only one aspect; as the man responsible only for the initial interview, he was not accountable for any bad guesses. His predictions were never challenged to his face because he had long since left the scene, never finding out if his guesses had been right or wrong. In that sense the division of labor insulated him from intellectual accountability. The psychological contradiction inherent in his hero-and-villain orientation was never put in issue.

The approach, however, worked for Carpasso, although "not all the time with all the people," but his system did give him an analytical perspective, on the one hand, and feelings of success, on the other.

Inquiring about the offspring of a squabbling couple gave him an intellectual focal point for prying open the situation so that he could see into it. In a situation where information was so elusive, helter-skelter, and subjective, asking "Who's to blame for hurting the kids?" centered the matter. Reconstructing the story in terms other than those provided by the disputing parties sometimes gave him an insight which permitted him to calm the situation. His theory of family life amplified the most modest clue into a full-blown story, sufficient for him to act decisively.

The confidence which such decisiveness gave this uncertain man should not be underestimated. Carpasso derived a zest, an exuberance, a moral enthusiasm from certain family beefs which a less presumptuous officer never could enjoy. When he felt he ought to be magnanimous, he behaved magnanimously and with abundant energy and attention to detail. He released himself into the situation. He got involved.

In the long run, one can see how this heroism could be transformed into cynicism. As life shattered his illusions about the purity of the parties he rescued—as the boy failed to straighten out; as the mother, once left on her own, became as "no-good" as the father—Carpasso would learn his lesson. He would realize that he had defined the category of noble persons too broadly; accordingly he would cut its size and raise the standards for admission. With each new disappointment, he would be prepared to attach himself to fewer and fewer until there were not many left to rescue, until he developed serious doubts about the question he put to himself: "Is it possible to help people? You've got to look after your own skin. Sometimes you can help."

The sentimentality of a man like Carpasso tended to create trouble on the beat. His system of guessing who the good people were often resulted in unequal application of the law. As we said, Carpasso tended to approach situations, looking for favorites to pamper. If the boy played his cards right, he could get Carpasso to pay his fee for the Y, intercede with his classroom teacher and the truant officer, and go to bat with the Youth Authority to divert him from jail. If a husband looked desperate enough, he could get pocket money donated to him and an immunity from arrest. But if there were favorites, there were also heels, against whom Carpasso carried out his moral mandate to be forceful. A lieutenant on the department called Carpasso a softy because of his sentimentality, but the lieutenant was only half right. Carpasso was tough against the adversaries of the citizens he was seeking to rescue. Since the adversaries did not always see reality in the same way as Carpasso reconstructed it, his toughness sometimes smacked of tyranny.

This potential for inequality was compounded because some citizens could sense Carpasso's sentimentality and played on it. Finding they were the object of his moral attachments, they manipulated his sense of obligation to them. Assured that he was morally committed to defend them, come what may, they would press their advantage against their own adversaries, entreating retribution, humiliation, a pound of flesh, and Carpasso might accede. If he did not, if he developed second thoughts about their vindictive demands, they "got on his back," heaping scorn on his betrayal and taking the most severe of all reprisals, denying him the moral gratification of helping them.

At the other extreme, some citizens resented being rescued. They felt that Carpasso's assistance was condescending, that his rescue efforts were undertaken to demean their pride and autonomy. Their indignation would then trigger a defensive response in Carpasso to rewrite the script of the situation, transforming the persons he originally wanted to help into "assholes." When Carpasso's theory of the situation was distorted by his reaction to the citizenry's reaction to his rescue efforts, the possibility of a false reconstruction grew by leaps and bounds. In turn, the toughness with which he intervened then became so erratic that it became contemptible. When legal power appeared to be exercised whimsically, the people had to forsake the law as too irrational and insecure, had to look to their own defense, and had to assume the worst whenever they got involved with policemen.

Perhaps the lieutenant had this distressful result in mind when he asserted that a softy would "never make a good cop."

**IV**

Officer Tom Hooker was twenty-six when he joined the department, but looked even more youthful. He had an unlined face, dark, somber, strikingly handsome. Slight in appearance, he was an athlete—a scrappy and intense competitor, an agile and strong gymnast, a tough and well-conditioned fighter. As a middle-class teen-ager growing up in a middle-class small town, he had been the toughest kid around: "I was kind of a bully. . . . It was my middle name." In his adolescence he began to argue with his "hardheaded" father, but mostly he poured his energies into high school athletics, high-powered engines, and motorcycles, interests that he retained through college and his police work. (He continued to ride in cross-country motor-cycle races on his days off from the department, ultimately suffering such a serious head injury that he had to quit the department on medical advice in his third year.)

Hooker was a Mormon, and after high school he went to Ireland for two years—"to please my parents." The experience calmed him down and broadened his horizons beyond the limits of his teen-age. When he returned to the United States, he entered college, where he found sociology and psychology helped him understand himself and the "180-degree turn" which his life seemed to be undergoing. He married "a great wife" who helped him talk about himself. In his junior year, he noticed an ad in his college newspaper inviting him to join the department, and he did, needing the money and the satisfaction of doing something important.

In his first year of police work he suffered a lot of self-doubt. His training officer, a perceptive old-timer, observed, "His greatest difficulty at this point appears to be lack of confidence." Lacking confidence, he reverted to the adolescent patterns of his high school days. He became a tough, active, and physical policeman. He was called before Internal Affairs three times (in each case he was exonerated). Some of his supervisors noted an overeager-ness to respond to "hot calls" (i.e., in-progress burglaries, high-speed chases) and a correlative lack of interest in more routine police work. He even transferred into Special Operations, where the incidence of "hot" activity was higher than in Patrol.

In his second year, however, his confidence grew. He found a way of doing police work which accorded better with his maturing rhythms. Moreover, he learned that his fellow officers respected him for the way he could take care of himself on the street. Most important, he discovered that he was good at something other officers had difficulty with: he could handle family beefs.

Hooker became a clinical psychologist in the field. He thought it unwise to force the husband to leave the house; after all, he was "the man of the house." It would be unthinkable to arrest a party to a family squabble: "to me an arrest is like the last straw." In any beef Hooker's object was more than restoring momentary peace; it was to develop a basis for resolving the future conflicts that would inevitably arise in the course of the marriage. With subtlety and through discussion, he would teach the disputants some techniques for recognizing the signals of disagreement and what to do to head one off. He used humor. He put matters in perspective, so that the couple saw that their anger and disagreement were not abnormal in a marriage between persons who loved one another. He emphasized the necessity of finding ways to deal with irritations, and that meant discussion between husband and wife: finding out how the other felt about things, reconciling the different ways of looking at matters, talking things out, perceiving that compromise was not retreat. But, above all, he listened.

For all his youth, Hooker understood how lonely his citizenry were, how desperate they were for some mediation, some advice, some consolation, some encouragement, some help to put their lives back in order. Despite his small-town middle-class upbringing, he understood how difficult it was for hardworking, disadvantaged city folk to find anyone to turn to for such succor—no doctor, no clergy, no social worker, no family patriarch, no friend.

In family beefs Hooker modeled his own behavior after the conduct of a medical professional who was employed by the family as a whole. He struggled to put words to the clinical posture he sought to strike:

> You hear a lot of stories, of how an officer said that he had been real gung-ho, and today he said that "I don't give a damn." He didn't mean that. He still gives a damn, but he doesn't take it so personally. You have to stand back awhile, not get involved. You have to be aloof, no, not aloof, a little more objective. That still isn't what I want to say. Instead of think-ing everything is personally done to you, you begin thinking, "I've got a job to do. He didn't do it personally against me.

"Don't give a damn," "don't take it personally," "stand back awhile," "not get involved," "be aloof," "be . . . a little more objective," not thinking it was "personally against me," "I've got a job to do"—this onrush of phrases manifested the efforts Hooker made to distinguish between the enforcement response of identifying with one client against his family and his own response of "nonpartisanship," as he called it.

Hooker successfully fulfilled his clinical responsibility: "In family squabbles I have never yet failed to get some kind of peace established." His success meant a lot to him; his pride was profoundly engaged in his ability to pass on his psychological insights, the fruits of his empathy, the lessons he had learned about knitting back unraveled relationships, his methods of getting persons to talk with one another. "I guess I get my greatest satisfaction from that," he said of the family beef.

Hooker's faith that his families actually cared about one another gave him a workable solution to the paradox of detachment. He made himself clinically skillful, and he anticipated a market for his skills. He was certain that a couple in the course of their fight would come to recognize that he had a service they had long wanted. If time and circumstances permitted, their efforts to detach themselves from one another would diminish. Once their attachments to meaningful relationships and things had begun to reassert themselves, then the family would want him around, would be willing to buy his talents, so to speak, would want an appointment with him. In Hooker's mind they had paid for it by dint of their past efforts to develop a family and a home. The services of a clinician were their due.

In order that Hooker could respond in this clinical way, certain factors had to exist. First was an outlook about the oneness of human nature, a perspective that balked at the differentiation between angel and devil. Hooker had to resist the temptation to see the world in terms of Us and Them. On this point, Hooker, only twenty-nine at the time of my first acquaintance with him, was firm: he assimilated policemen and citizens; alike they had inferiority complexes, considerable intelligence, and hang-ups between countervailing tendencies. Moreover, he felt it a serious shortcoming not to practice empathy. Indignation, in his mind, was a bad thing. Moralizing to others was not his job: "I believe in understanding people." Where did that moral imperative come from? A good wife, an adult example like a father or a teacher or someone in the church, a college education, whatever—he had to develop a manhood model in which insight was a virtue.

Second, he had to have considerable interpersonal skills. If he lacked a reasonably profound insight or if he had failed to develop his ability to talk, he would not have been capable of pacifying some of the beefs he encountered. It took talent to bat one thousand in family squabbles, to "get some kind of peace established," and to "get 'em laughing."

Third, using these skills had to be socially acceptable within the department. Not that playing the clinician had to be official policy, yet it had to be decent to have "soft" attitudes. In Laconia, Hooker depended on two bases for acceptability. One was personal to him. He proved to others that his softness did not result from a lack of courage. Here his physical prowess helped him enormously. He handled himself in street melees with great skill. He had earned his right to be soft. Indeed, his trips to Internal Affairs may have resulted from a desire to exemplify his bravery to his fellow officers: as he put it, "You don't want other policemen to interpret what you do as weakness." His reputation as a motorcycling fool no doubt helped too.

The second basis was that others did it, and those others had the respect of their fellow officers. In Hooker's case, the most crucial police model was his training officer, who "was fantastic with people ... easygoing ... didn't have anybody resisting him." Hooker recalled his exact words at the conclusion of the six-week apprenticeship in the field: "Hooker, I know there are a lot of things I didn't show you. We didn't make many car stops or arrests, and we didn't stop people walking down the streets. I don't believe in it. You'll have to learn that from someone else." The fact that the department could select as a training officer an old-timer who liked to patch up family fights helped legitimate Hooker's own inclinations to do likewise. That early memory of a respectable officer vanquished recurring doubts about whether softness was equivalent to weakness.

Finally, Hooker, or any officer who tended to a reciprocating response, needed time to do his job. He needed the luxury of a quiet beat to afford him an hour or more with a family. If his beat was so busy that he had to be on the go yet was not, then other officers had to cover for him, lest the rest of the citizenry be ignored.

With each appointment consuming so much time, what effects did officers like Hooker have on their beats? Acting as psychologist, psychiatrist, child guidance counselor, and ignoring the narrow definitions of the police job which justified an avoidance response, they accomplished fewer tasks. They carried a diminished work load. They took fewer burglary reports; they did less preventive patrolling; they made fewer arrests. They did not "produce," as the saying went.

Who was to say it was a bad thing? Perhaps it could be argued that policemen who responded clinically had a better chance to do effective counseling than the social worker or counselor. The heat of battle might provide a more accurate glimpse into the problems of the family than did the quiet aftermath of an office visit, when second thoughts and selective memories would sift out the reality. Compared with a psychiatrist or family adviser, who had to imagine what the home was like, the policeman made on-the-spot observations. Moreover, the actual tension might make for a better therapeutic situation: anger might break down the deceptions and disguises which "patients" conventionally erect around their problem. Insight into the self might be closest on the edge of fury. I never was sure, but it seemed worth conjecturing that therapy might be most effective when the adrenaline was flowing and the consequences of personal detachment were most manifest. This form of immediate therapy might be particularly important for cutting through the self-conscious inhibitions which befuddle relationships between a middle-class counselor and persons humiliated in his presence by their lack of formal education. In short, policemen in the field might be better counselors than full-time psychiatrists once removed.

Nonetheless, the policeman who acted as a clinician faced a problem of priorities. If he could not serve all, whom would he serve? In this context, the concept of equal protection of the laws became a slippery one. Equality could have three different meanings to a policeman. First, and most conventional, there was equality of treatment: in the beat patrolman's terms, that meant substantially the same availability to perform equivalent services for each citizen. The officer who responded clinically to intensely personal situations, however, did not have enough time to give the same number of minutes and hours to all citizens as he gave to the most favored of them. A second kind of equality smacked of compensation: those who were most needy, who started out with less, were entitled to more help than others. This kind of compensatory assistance worked toward an equality of result. A third meaning of equality was a kind of efficiency. It was justifiable to give help to those who could most efficiently use the kind of help in which the patrolmen specialized. An efficiency concept of equality was comparable to the rate of return in the marketplace. One invested oneself in a situation until the marginal benefits derived from it diminished to a level equal to the marginal benefits derivable from alternative opportunities. A beat officer who was inclined to give intense counseling dispensed his skills according to the capacity of the citizen-client to benefit from them.

Men like Hooker tended to justify their time-consuming behavior in terms of this third meaning of equality, happily serving those who showed the larger measure of improvement. That is why the clinical approach was really a reciprocating response. Hooker did not serve those who had little need for his specialty. Priority went to those with family beefs; less favored were those who might be old, single, small, intimidated. In other words, he and others like him discriminated. It was a reasonable discrimination, and it might even be a correct discrimination. Perhaps the best use of their time was family counseling. Finding ways to instruct families in how to stay together might best cut crime and produce order in the long run. However, the priority was not above dispute.

The clinical approach created serious personal consequences within the department for the officer who resorted to a reciprocating response in family beefs. As he became converted to the psychiatric approach for solving the citizens' problems, he tended to denigrate other approaches and other tasks. He became self-defensive when officers who worked differently expressed their doubts or criticisms. He shrouded himself in the confidential relationships between him and his citizenry and eschewed team policing. He became more of a loner, less of a leader. If the loneliness was essential to his clinical approach, it prevented him from justifying it to his fellow officers and winning them over to it. On the contrary, he found himself retaliating for their attacks against his identity. Hooker, for example, complained: "I think policemen as a whole don't let themselves understand why people act as they do. They'd prefer to think of them as assholes than go deep and develop a compassion toward these types of people." Ironically he was beginning to create the very intellectual distinctions he deplored in other policemen—an

enemy psychology about human nature—except that he was identifying with
the people against his fellow officers. This feeling of estrangement from the
police organization seemed ever on the verge of creating serious dissension
within the department.

## V

Officer Joe Wilkes did not look impressive. He was squat and rough-spoken.
His clothing never seemed to fit properly. He had a physical frame on which
no conceivable uniform could look tailored. On first appearance he struck
people as a little like a punch-drunk club fighter, always fighting out of his
weight because he lacked the discipline to slough off excess pounds. In fact,
Wilkes had been a prizefighter, roaming Central and South American
boxing halls as a youth in pursuit of experience and a meager living.

He had been born and raised in Alaska. His father had been a hard-
drinking traveling handyman, who "had a temper, but used it right,"
thought it important for everyone to "stand up for his rights," and was a
"good man."

Wilkes had emulated his father. Like him, he had traveled around the
world—as a merchant seaman. He had done a hitch as a parachutist in the
army, worked as a bartender, dishwasher, salesman, warehouseman, and
management trainee. He had learned Spanish and attended college at nights.
He eventually had found his way to a quiet Stateside town where he became a
policeman. Confined by the smallness of his life, he quit the job to join the
Memphis Police Department, but within twenty-four months was induced by
the higher salary schedules of the Laconia Police Department to transfer to
it.

Joe Wilkes had spent his life involved with kids. He was no less ardent than
Carpasso about doing good. He had won the Officer-of-the-Year award
several times. Conferred by the local newspaper, the award was given to
Wilkes because of his off-hour work with boys' clubs. His personnel file was
filled with letters of gratitude for some unpaid service or another to local
youth groups. He spent his rare moments of free time devising plans to get
Laconia police officers paid for coaching and working with juveniles.

Despite this devotion to the youth of Laconia, Joe Wilkes had a turbulent
record in Laconia. Even with his broad experience, he was clumsy in some
situations. His timing was off with some citizens. He got into fights with
sufficient frequency to be identified as a "violence-prone" officer and was
appointed to the Violence Prevention Unit. The VPU amounted to a subtle
form of sensitivity grouping. Men who had been involved in a relatively large
number of altercations were brought together to discuss the reasons for their
anger among themselves. In this self-conscious but supportive context, some

officers gained considerable understanding of themselves and their emotions. Joe Wilkes was one of those. He responded powerfully. He contributed to every discussion. He initiated many thoughtful proposals for the department and future VPU units. Through the sessions he came to see that his experiences with youth could logically be applied to his other work. He went through a "humanizing process," as he put it, a realization that men were simply robust boys, that the desire to be productive and engaged in the world's enterprises was as universal among the adults he fought with as it was among the youth he uplifted. The discussions gave him the time and the stimulation to harmonize these two aspects of his experience, at least in that class of confrontation called the family beef.

When Joe Wilkes was called to a domestic fight, he saw the family in a moral context. He perceived each member as the center of a complex of relationships. When those relationships pulled the members in conflicting directions, paralysis set in or frustration erupted. When those relationships pulled in the same direction, they created a force too great for any policeman to counter. He understood the basic weakness of the moral compulsion between citizen and policeman. The latter, not being on the scene twenty-four hours a day, seven days a week, from here to eternity, was of secondary importance in the moral context of a family beef, no matter how devoted he wanted to be. A policeman could not elicit sacrifice.

In short, Joe Wilkes realized that any chance for long-run pacification of a family squabble depended upon the family members' reattaching themselves to those friendships, traditions, and concerns which they had previously felt were important.

So, in a family beef, Joe Wilkes talked. "My own personality is to talk," he said. He articulated a perspective of hope for the husband and wife: "We talk about his possibilities—about everything he had possibilities for." To touch men's hopes, he sought to detect old attachments that had made the past meaningful—to scent out the "glue" that had held together their center. He tried to expand their self-interest, what he called their "ego" and what others referred to as pride or dignity, and he attempted to attach it to the future, for only "the possibilities" justified present sacrifice and forbearance.

He looked for anything that indicated what had once been important to the marriage—a car that was well taken care of, a valuable domino set, a good-smelling soup on the stove, a spotless kitchen—anything which indicated the locus of former concerns, anything which had been beloved, any basis for hopefulness.

He did not act clinically; he did not depend on diagnosis of the causes of the wreckage. Faced with problems of such complexity and magnitude that they boggled the mind, he simply tried to remind his citizenry of their traditions, of who they were, of what had been meaningful to them—and to

assure them that it had been worthwhile thus far and was still worth
persevering for. He worked on their hopes.

In the end, however, after diverting, calming, reminding them of the
meaningfulness of their old attachments, Wilkes took a chance. He left. He
did not explore their problems in any detail. He did not know whether his
citizens would injure one another before their former attachments had had
time to reassert themselves. He reinvested them with their freedom. It was
not the safest course, but it was a calculated one, based on experience and a
willingness to take risks. He saw that he was incapable of erecting sufficient
protections around family members. Such fences had to be perfected by
discord and autonomy. Recall Officer Justice's maxim, when he summed
up, "In those cases when it isn't important if I'm wrong,... I take a
chance. It's more important not to lose the chance than that I'm right." The
chance of strengthening a citizen's indomitability, of maintaining his faith,
of encouraging him to hold to his values even when they were nearly
indefensible—in such unpretentious opportunities lay the secret of governing
a land of free people.

Joe Wilkes's way was a middle path between Carpasso's tendency to act
without listening and Hooker's inclination to listen without acting. He
compromised treatment in the name of time, and I have called this
compromise the professional response. One who responded professionally
gambled on serendipity—on the fortuitous and fortunate happenings which
occur in human society because human beings, once moved to action, tend
to be resilient, crafty, free-willed, and adaptive. Rather than trying to cure a
family's problems, Wilkes was likely to leave it to its own devices, once he felt
that the danger of irremediable physical injury had diminished.

He left the scene before he was sure.

Instead of turning eyes inward and ripping down the deceptions behind
which the citizens' pasts were hidden, the officer who gambled was more
inclined to divert the family's eyes to the future. If empathy summed up the
reciprocal response, challenge characterized the professional response. If
Hooker delved deeply into the soul, Wilkes touched only upon hopes.

What made this kind of response necessary or possible? First was an
awareness of the need to economize on time. Wilkes felt he had other jobs to
do, other people to serve. The cost of more profound treatment—even if he
were capable of it—was nonavailability to respond to others. A readiness to
accept human limitations helped to justify the risks he took.

Second, one who gambled had to have skill with the spoken language, for
the professional response involved a lot of talk. Wilkes spoke more and
listened less than Hooker. He sought to put words to the most profound
feelings of disappointment and aspiration; he formulated moral issues; he
expressed the spirit of the law so as to make it intelligible to the layman. The

ability to catch in a telling phrase the secrets of the human heart was an indispensable precondition for gluing persons back together. Sometimes this loquacious agility sounded like a demagogue's casuistry. In reformulating the meaning of events in terms which rang true to his citizenry, Wilkes had to say what he did not necessarily believe. He was an advocate, a mouthpiece for someone else's soul.

So, as a third condition, the professional response depended on a lawyer's capacity to suspend judgment. Men who responded to family beefs as Wilkes did had to be skeptical about the existence of absolute truths. Their attempt to put their citizenry's case in the best light was not a matter of insincerity. Rather it was a means of helping a family uncover deeper truths—the human desire to matter.

Fourth, they had to be able to bear the risks of their gambles: things were going to go wrong some time or another. A fight might flare up again; someone might be hurt or killed. Officers who gambled had to be able to defend their choices before their sergeants, their lieutenants, their captains, their chief, their fellow officers, their community, maybe even their god. They had to be sufficiently self-confident about their methods and assumptions to convince others of their validity.

The consequences for the beat were hard to define. Perhaps more police service was dispensed and to a greater variety of persons. Certainly officers like Wilkes felt they were helping a great variety of people on a great variety of matters. They were proud of their "productivity," in contrast to the self-condemnation expressed by Hooker and those who tended to the reciprocating response.

Yet everything was so speculative. The virtues men like Wilkes were trying to evoke were self-respect, pride, a taste for accomplishment. Whether their future-oriented methods were more effective than the introspective, analytic devices of a Hooker was not clear.

But in terms of personal development, it was clear that Wilkes felt better about himself. He felt he was doing a rounded job of police work. He saw himself as being versatile, capable of coping with every variety of police work. Consequently, he was less defensive about the softness with which he handled family beefs, assured as he was that he had plenty of opportunities to display other forms of competence in different contexts. He did not lock himself into the role of specialist.

He therefore tended to remain fully confident that he could assume leadership of policemen. He could and did manage many tasks and felt confident he could manage many men. In responding professionally, Wilkes had found a socially acceptable compromise between the multiple obligations of being a policeman. It was an exhilarating success.

# 7      The Paradox of Face:
## The Crowd Scene

We dare not tempt our adversaries with weakness. For only when our arms are sufficient beyond doubt can we be certain beyond doubt that they will never be employed.

*President John F. Kennedy*
1961

There's an old story of the officer who would jump out of his car with his baton waving, and yelling and screaming, and hitting at the trees and garbage cans and lampposts. It always broke the crowd up, and he never had to arrest anybody and nobody ever got hurt.

*Officer Mark Rockingham*
Laconia Police Department
1973

## I

In roughneck politics no task exceeds the difficulty of managing the paradox of face: "The nastier one's reputation, the less nasty one has to be." It involves the politician in preserving his opportunities to employ purposeful threats. He has to defend something of great value to him: his reputation for firmness, remorselessness, nastiness—in short, his honor. What is at stake is his entitlement to control others through intimidation, his very capacity to get things without giving adequate compensation.

Because the paradox of face involves the ultimate right to practice extortion, it contains the most basic peril. Political folklore has it that "The hardest tumble any politician can take is the fall over his own bluff." To avoid that tumble, anyone who has to live by threats subjects his courage to the severest test. The paradox of face demands grace under pressure. It wreaks the greatest havoc with the phonies.

What makes this so is that the paradox of face affects the future. Not only does the statesman have to win the war, he also has to win it with honor. To gain an objective momentarily and yet sacrifice his credibility at the same time is to win a Pyrrhic victory.

For some citizens under some circumstances the same was true, and a policeman recurrently encountered citizens who were fighting to preserve their honor and had the courage to do so. That was why policemen conferred their highest respect on colleagues who could handle "the crowd scene." The crowd scene was the paradox of face incarnate. Typically it looked like this (in the words of one officer): "This guy at the Recreation Center called and said a man had tried to assault him with a baseball bat. This fella calling was a volunteer aide at the Rec Center, and he had been accused by his assailant of raping the 13-year-old sister of the guy with the baseball bat. Everybody was in the act, including the grandmother and the mother of the girl. It was really hostile. Everything was up in the air."

A sizable crowd consisting of bystanders, friends, and relations had gathered. "Everybody was in the act," watching the aide (the accused rapist of "the girl") and "the guy with the baseball bat," her brother.

The paradox of face was played out on two levels—in the relationship between the two antagonists, and in the relationship of the crowd to the two men. The policeman had to perceive both levels.

At one level the policeman had to discover what the dispute was about. Who was the bully? At first glance it appeared to be the assailant with the baseball bat. Until the background reasons for the fight could be pieced together, the fight had all the appearances of just another adolescent predator attacking the protector of the Rec Center. After all, the rec aide was the complainant. A first guess might have been that the aide had tried to foil some sort of shakedown and the extortionist had resented the interference. Playground extortion, after all, was a frequent occurrence, and the policeman had often seen it happen at this center.

Such a sensible guess would have been wrong in this case, and unless the policeman could give himself enough time to find out the real reasons for the altercation, he was going to act on a false impression.

The other level involved the crowd's relationship to the antagonists, what the police called "the psychology of the situation." From the point of view of the brother of the victim of the alleged rape, he was retaliating not merely from a desire for retribution but to deter future marauders. He was acting out of concern for his family's very safety. He was executing the implied and widely understood threat to strike back, which the aide had defied when he raped the girl (if the allegations were true). The brother was establishing face in the neighborhood, a reputation for dogged revenge; in thrashing his sister's rapist, he was making a harsh example for all the crowd to see. He was speaking with public actions, "Don't tread on us." He was publishing his message for those persons that really counted, those who might think they could push his family around. In the brutish neighborhood he and his family inhabited, the brother was making himself "a man of respect." He was establishing a sanctuary for his family by erecting a "sufficient" self-defense system. Since the criminal law and the police were not timely, reliable, or capable enough in the flatlands to be depended upon for protection, the residents had to put up their own security perimeter against predators.

In the relationship between the crowd and the brother, the crowd's definition of honorable conduct became crucial. Depending on its expectations of him, his attack on the aide would have different meanings. What would make the brother respectable: merely attacking the aide? drawing blood? breaking an arm? forcing retreat? causing death? getting him in jail? Anyone who had the talent to influence the crowd's philosophy in this matter could make a great deal of difference to what the brother felt he had to do to establish face. In short, someone who was aware of the importance of the crowd could change "the psychology of the situation."[1]

## II

A few policemen never understood the significance of the crowd. Take Garfield, for example, the officer who proved so inept with family beefs. Called to the incident at the Recreation Center, he would come on with an ultimatum, uttered loudly and publicly to antagonists and crowd alike. "You're supposed to act like normal human beings. Right? Well, you're not doing it, and we've been here time and time again. We've been trying to teach you people how to get along with each other. But the next time I'll take the whole stinking lot of you to jail. You people can't get along. And it'll cost you $100 a head to get out of jail."

His assumptions that "normal human beings" do not assert their rights to bodily security, that they passively accept injury resulting from the negligence and malice of others, that they wish neither revenge nor compensation for wrongs done to them and their loved ones, were explicitly obvious and obviously wrong.

Garfield's tirade did not "teach" the people the following facts: (1)

---

1. In this and in the other three "paradox" chapters, I have used license in the interest of clarity. I have selected a typical instance of each paradox, as described by one policeman, and contrasted his specific reaction to it with the reactions of three other policemen to the same *general* event. I have reconstructed the actual encounters of these three other policemen in terms of the details of the typical instance. For example, the Recreation Center incident described in this chapter arose in Officer Peel's experience. The encounters which Officers Garfield, Kip, and Haig described to me were not with the same vengeful brother Peel faced, but with different antagonists at the center of a crowd scene. But the problem each officer faced was the same, that of defending himself and others against a person whose "honor" was at stake. To enable the reader to see the contrasts between different police responses more clearly, I have assimilated the details of the officers' encounters in terms of the typical instance.

"normal human beings" frequently conflict and get angry with each other;
(2) "normal human beings" should not passively endure injuries inflicted by
others; (3) if it is sometimes true that people appeared "to get along with
each other," it is only because civilized society provides a number of
institutions to protect citizens from victimization; (4) these institutions allow
victims to exact a domesticated but devastating form of revenge in the form
of punishment and compensatory damages; and (5) these institutions provide due process, to deal with the elusiveness of truth and the temptations to
mendacity. Garfield could not teach these facts because he was ignorant of
them himself.

Nor did he see the psychology of the situation—the play between the
antagonists and the crowd. He failed to grasp the necessity of face-saving and
the importance of "respect" in a fear-ridden neighborhood. Therefore, he
could not use the crowd to affect the behavior and the incentives of the two
antagonists.

Having squandered the potential utility of the crowd to quell the dispute,
he had to rely on making himself fearsome when he had no jurisdiction to be
fearsome. He had no legal right to resort to threats. He was without authority
to injure anyone. The crowd had done nothing to warrant being sent to jail.
When he uttered the threat, Garfield was without probable cause to arrest
the recreation aide, nor had he seen "the guy with the baseball bat" take a
swipe at the aide. Garfield had made a phony bluff, and if any person there
challenged it, if anyone refused to "get along with each other" despite the
command to do so, either Garfield would have to back down from his threat
or "hum" them in by resorting to some wobbly legal basis for arrest—refusing to identify oneself or resisting arrest (policemen called these the
"chickenshit sections"). Or he might bend the truth a little, doctoring his
version of what happened to justify an arrest.

Not having a lawful basis for arrest was just one aspect of a larger measure
of phoniness. The fact was, the crowd was not convinced that Garfield had
the fortitude to execute his threat. He had made a threat, but he had no
reputation among the onlookers for ever having mixed it. The threat lacked
personal authority (and the public was terribly perceptive in detecting those
little hesitations and awkwardnesses which betrayed a policeman's bluff). So
long as the crowd felt skeptical about Garfield's firmness, the exasperated
brother was left in a position where he had to defy the policeman. The crowd
expected him to live up to his responsibility to avenge his sister and his
family. If this crowd felt he had not behaved sufficiently aggressively in
accordance with the neighborhood law of revenge, he would be dishonored.

The short of the matter was that Garfield was not a sufficiently respected
policeman to exonerate the brother from criticism for obeying a cop. In the
crowd's mind, a man dishonored himself if he retreated before the ultimatum

of an unworthy adversary. The blue uniform, the badge, the gun provided a presumption of respectability, but in the 1970s it was a presumption rebuttable by evidence of worthlessness or incompetence.

Garfield also had created another incentive for the brother to fight him. He had told the brother he would no longer respond to any pleas for assistance. In so many words Garfield had said he would take the "stinking" lot to jail if he were called again. Consequently, the brother knew he could not employ legal institutions for his self-defense. He had to rely on his own fearsomeness. In the lawless, dog-eat-dog situation which Garfield's ultimatum had created, the brother had a greater need to become a "man of respect" than if he was assured a positive police response. To save his family, he had to develop a formidable reputation for ruthlessness. There seemed no better way to gain such a reputation than to make a heroic fight in front of the crowd against the policeman. To be sure, there was a chance of looking like a fool, but if the policeman betrayed incompetence and lack of firmness, as Garfield did, that chance was much diminished. Going to jail for attacking an officer of the law would save the brother's face.

It was possible for policemen to employ ultimatums in crowd situations, but the conditions for doing so successfully were stringent. First, an officer had to understand what a difference a crowd made. Neighbors involved in fighting each other behaved differently in front of a crowd than in privacy. The policeman had to understand that neighborhood reputations for indomitability were on the line. If the policeman understood that those reputations depended on crowd definitions of satisfactory performance, he could work to lower the expectations of the crowd about how aggressive a neighbor had to be. A policeman who could successfully lower those expectations was taking a crucial step toward closing the gap between an honorable performance (i.e., one which saved face for the neighbor) and a lawful performance (i.e., one which the policeman desired). If an ultimatum was to be successful, that gap had to be completely closed.

Second, a policeman who wanted to succeed with ultimatums had to have a widely publicized reputation for firmness. The reader has already seen the complicated interrelationships between the crowd, the policeman, and the antagonists. The fighters' behavior depended on their perceptions of the crowd and of what that crowd expected each of them to do. The crowd's expectations about the fighters, however, turned on its perception of the policeman and on what he would do if the fighters defied his ultimatum. The policeman's success depended on his awareness of the interrelationship of the fighters' perceptions, the crowd's expectations, and his own determination to put down defiance. In this infinitely reflexive calculus, only a mutually recognized stopping point could stabilize the situation. Inevitably the likely possibility for agreement rested on the extent and certitude of the crowd's information about the policeman's firmness. If the policeman were recognized by the crowd as a man whose words meant something, and if the fighters were certain that the crowd felt that way, then, and only then, could they dare to defer to the policeman without losing face. A policeman might earn a reputation for being severe and firm by his constancy, by his mercilessness, and by his past courage in dealing with hard situations, come what may. A fair-weather policeman like Garfield, who did only the easy jobs, could not build such a reputation.

Third, a policeman could not utter an ultimatum unless he were prepared to follow through if his bluff were tested. Either he had to know the criminal law thoroughly and have something on the persons to whom he had issued the ultimatum, thereby having a proper legal basis for executing his threat to take them to jail, or he had to use his own physical prowess, manhandling the disputants. In the latter case he was using force outside the law and became subject to possible legal action. If physical prowess was the basis on which he depended, it helped if he was grandly endowed in stature, girth, or coordination, thereby discouraging defiance.

If a policeman was like Garfield, neither aware, skillful, dogged, nor knowledgeable, issuing an ultimatum was likely to heat up the situation instead of cooling it off, likely to harden the defiant resolve of the main antagonists instead of increasing flexibility, likely to compel bystanders to take sides in a dispute instead of manipulating them to extinguish the need for further dispute. The result was that the community would be less inclined to call the police in the next situation. Rather than invite in policemen too stupid to arbitrate, the community would invent other methods of resolving neighborhood conflict. If police were unable to channel hostilities, then the neighborhood had to turn to extralegal methods of social control. It might look for nonofficial arbitrators—a clergyman, a politician, a businessman, a patriarch. If none was available, however, then might made right: bullies prevailed over the weaker; the more sensitive had to surrender to the tougher. Respect based on fear became the exclusive mode of self-protection (and one means to establish one's respectability was manifesting a brave defiance of the policeman's authority).

The personal consequences for the policeman of issuing ineffective ultimatums were increased ignorance and apprehension. The community felt he was dishonored; it hid information from him, put him outside its confidence. At the same time, young men and women out to make a neighborhood reputation challenged him. Such a policeman was increasingly likely to begin to withdraw his presence from the community. Why should he continue to answer calls when he always had a fight on his hands, when he was always getting his expensive uniform dirtied and ripped, when the "stinking" lot of them would not learn "how to get along" with each other, when they looked right through his pretenses and saw what a phony-tough[2] he was?

## III

Rudy Kip was a little guy. Too short to meet the five foot nine requirement, he stuffed cotton into his socks to elevate him the extra inch he needed. His height was the frequent butt of kidding in lineup and locker room talk.

Kip was born in a midwestern railroad town and raised in a working-class neighborhood. His father, according to Kip, "did not take the time to explain things to us. He was very meek himself, and would never want anyone to fight." Kip, however, fought his way through high school ("I have my mother's personality"), enlisted in the Marine Corps, fought in Vietnam and Laos, and returned to the States where he got a job as a night watchman.

Discouraged by the dullness and the restraints of the job, he applied to become a Laconia police officer. By the time he was accepted he was twenty-five, married, and terribly determined. With the impulse of a perfectionist, he tackled his studies, worked exhaustively, won praise from his training officers for his initiative, and seemed to find a niche for his doggedness, toughness, and assertiveness. When the Special Operations section was formed, he transferred to it from Patrol. Glad to be quit of the 999s, the neighborhood fights, and taking reports, Kip enjoyed doing "real police work," catching criminals.

In conversation Kip thrust his head forward on his thickly muscled neck in a way which challenged others to fight back. He rankled the average citizens, the ones who thought they were living good lives. (Ironically, in citizens more experienced in the justice system, he did not arouse the same degree of resentment.) He talked rapid-fire, overwhelming his listeners with oratory rather than illuminating them. His conversation was not a tennis match; it was a boxing contest. One of his favorite phrases was, "I can outargue them."

Kip's style in everything he did was to overwhelm others with the might of his tongue, his spirit, his body, and his weaponry. Not that he was unaware of the virtues of explanation, discussion, and manipulation; it was just that when he came on a neighborhood fight, he invariably concluded that the better thing to do was to leap right in. The crowds were too problematic to be trusted to help; it was better to keep them at bay by keeping them "confused" and cowed by a display of might and a preemptive attack. Thus,

2.  The phrase is the late Stewart Alsop's (*Newsweek,* September 10, 1973), p. 94.

when he came on the two disputants at the Recreation Center, he would "put 'em up against the wall." He would "lay it down bluntly" ("If you don't do this, you are going to jail"). He would "buffalo" them with his knowledge of the criminal code and his capacity to classify all their behavior in terms of it. And he was prepared to call in "500 cops" to back up his ultimatums.

He enjoyed fights; they released tensions which built up in him whenever the streets got too quiet. He had to have a sense of total control. The more chaos he created, the greater his sense of self-control. "I feel I have to take complete command immediately." He had an ability to hassle bad guys, which he did as part of his mission of "overcoming a great evil." He was gratified by helping mankind but derived little satisfaction from helping individual men.

He lashed out with both fists and tongue, not only against the public but also against some fellow officers and even his commanders (he received a severe reprimand during training for disputing openly with a sergeant). He was unafraid to do things that made other policemen quail or that embarrassed them. He pulled his gun earlier than most officers, and he was not afraid to use it. Moreover, he was tireless. He tackled any job. He was not a phony. He was brave, and he was fearless to the point of craziness.[3]

If one looked at Kip's angular, compact, lean muscularity, one was tempted to write off his pugnacity to physique. There was an explosiveness about the way his inner dynamo worked, as if the accelerator were constantly pressed to the floor, its effects barely restrained by a Herculean application of the brakes. If an eight-hour watch passed without some trouble to conquer, Kip's nervous energy almost seemed to crackle inside the patrol car. Kip's fingers struck an arhythmic tattoo on the steel roof; his foot beat the floorboards; his exasperation burst through his concentration. Kip was a man in whom inner pressures were considerable.

Yet other factors contributed to his behavior and the reasons he continued to defend himself in the paradox of face as he did. Kip's tactics were to disperse the crowd through terror, neutralizing the crowd as an incentive for the principal fighters to continue their dispute. To manhandle a crowd, however, Kip had to work in concert with one or more partners. It was a rule of thumb that police could handle a crowd in direct geometrical proportion to their numbers. One policeman could control only one person, but two could take on four citizens, three could corral nine, and so on. Kip needed to coalesce with a partner who was as pugnacious, as skilled defensively, and as persistent as he was. Alone, he lacked the might to intimidate a crowd. With an incompetent or unreliable partner, he was vulnerable.[4]

3.  Stewart Alsop's expression for men such as Kip was "crazy-brave," ibid., p. 94.
4.  One of Kip's stories made this clear: "We got another call, two men fighting, the same

The point may seem obvious, but an officer like Kip needed to have the active and skillful assistance of other like-minded policemen if his tactics were to be effective and not imprudent.

In Kip's case, Special Operations provided a niche in the department where he had reliable partners. Consisting only of officers of experience, its members screened by supervisors for qualities of toughness and joy of combat, Special Operations ended up an exclusive group of men who could behave like crazy-braves. Untried officers were ineligible for its ranks. Men who liked to work differently had no taste for transferring to it.

Kip's preemptive terrorist methods often were extralegal and abusive. Tried on some citizens who had the capacity to complain about them, his tactics could backfire into a complaint, either before Internal Affairs or outside the department (a civil rights suit precipitated an FBI investigation, because of which Special Operations terminated its illegal harassment of certain notorious bars where stolen goods were fenced and narcotics were sold). Again, the advantages of a special unit were apparent; it had supervisors who "backed their men up" with strong rebuttal and who softened the consequences of adverse findings. Officers who behaved like crazy-braves had to have supervisors who tolerated crazy-brave behavior.

Then, to succeed with an enforcement response, an officer had to have verbal facility. Kip was able to state his ultimatums with sufficient force that they rang with credibility. An officer who stated things in either/or terms as frequently as Kip did had to practice an eloquence which would intimidate a crowd as well as the immediate antagonists. Successfully to reduce the incentives of others to defy him, he had to speak to the multitudes with conviction. Otherwise, the crowds withheld honor from the antagonists for not defying an unconvincing ultimatum. In short, Kip required demagogic skills. His language had to intimidate. He had to harangue to the point, spontaneously, under pressure, without being tongue-tied. Moreover, being outside the law, vulnerable to internal rebuke and external penalties for his abuses, he had to be able to justify his bullying to his fellow officers, to doctor his reports with apparent sincerity, and to defend himself before boards reviewing his conduct. To be able to talk fast and forcefully was as important to the crazy-brave as were his courage and muscularity. Bravado and bravery were necessary counterparts.

---

evening. It wasn't clear whether any of the men had a gun. So I said to this kid [his temporary partner], 'We'll approach as if he had a gun.' Well, this kid pulled up a half block away from the scene, right in the middle of the street, and opens the door and starts running down the street. 'What the hell are you doing?' I ask. 'I'm not going into anything I don't know something about.' Well, he had made two mistakes. First, his car is his only protection. And second, he had parked so as to cut off all his cover from coming down the street."

Being an officer who recurrently employed the enforcement response in the paradox of face was a bittersweet experience. On the one hand, a deep camaraderie developed among the crazy-braves from exposure to common dangers. Being more vulnerable to severe injury because of their risky and provocative mission, they were more obviously dependent on each other for mutual protection. Common peril and the excitement it generated built an esprit among them not by intention so much as by virtue of being a byproduct of their interdependence. Consensus about the world and the police job in it developed to such a degree that officers like Kip became a community of men. They manifested their solidarity by forming drinking groups and fishing and hunting associations, and gravitating to the same suburbs as neighbors. As a general rule, a policeman's lot was a lonely one, but the least alone were those whose habits were to manhandle crowds.

On the other hand, in a department where the official policy was so squarely against demagoguery and intimidation, men like Kip were unhappy. Their proudest achievements of crowd control were not publishable. The chief's general statements tore at their individual self-esteem, and Internal Affairs constantly threatened them. Only their friends gave them respect. They labored under an atmosphere of repression. Their joys were always partly frustrated, and so they found themselves beginning to hate— first, the policies of the chief, then those fellow officers who adapted to those policies, and finally their job, which estranged them from all but each other. The outlook they developed to justify their extralegal terror was shared only by fellow terrorists; when they were with other officers, they had to watch their step, for they were out of step. The brotherhood was divided; they had to be careful about what they said, always checking against the spontaneous reaction; and they had to be cunning about covering up their innermost thoughts from those they suspected might divulge them to the administration.

Ordinarily, a policeman who was a crazy-brave "heated up" his fellow officers. His bravado seemed to stigmatize more civilized or circumspect conduct as cowardice or phoniness. He would put other officers on the defensive, daring them to prove that they were as courageous and manly as he. This was still true within the discreet enclave of Special Operations, where sympathetic supervisors still held sway. Otherwise, however, the chief's official policy, sanctioned by Internal Affairs and indoctrinated by training, supported a contrary interpretation: terror was defined as intemperate and unprofessional. Thus the silent reproach of men like Kip lost its sting. Persistent policy began to act as a strong counterinfluence, instead. Far from heating up a squad, Kip would suffer rebuke at lineup ("Here comes Hot Dog Harry") or worse—outright ostracism. Police leadership turned off those galvanizing juices of Kip's motor, sometimes to the point where he became demoralized and peevish, momentarily unsure of why he should stick his neck out.

If Kip was unhappy with the oppression he suffered within the department, his beat was unhappy with the oppression he inflicted on it. Not being able to be merciful, having to build an unblemished reputation for nastiness, he continued to make harsh examples not only of the deserving bad but of the exemplary good as well. He left no law unenforced; he became (as Kip declared himself) "feisty, real hard-nosed, and inclined to write every violation" he saw. Such merciless surveillance smacked of malice and created bitter feelings. As one dignified-looking older black man cried out in frustration after Kip had cited his wife for a highly debatable traffic violation, "No wonder everybody wants to kill you cops; I hope you get yours!" Oppression depended on making the public feel impotent to resist, and a beat that felt that downtrodden was a woeful place to live.

## IV

Doug Haig was one of the three members of the sample who came from minority groups. He was soft-spoken, irrepressible, and multilingual. He was also an ex-marine, a former major league baseball prospect, and the coach of the department's baseball and basketball teams (even though, at six foot even, he was shorter by several inches than the next-shortest member of the basketball team). He had been on the department five years, had barely missed passing the sergeant's exam in his first attempt, and wanted to be a sergeant very much. He was a highly respected policeman, particularly by young officers who went to him for fatherly advice even though he was barely thirty. He was well liked among the old-timers too, for he played the straight man for their jokes, which were funnier than his, and he maintained the respect of his contemporaries because of his athletic abilities and personal warmth.

He had been raised in the South, in an impoverished, hardworking, large family. His father had picked tobacco and traveled as a circus handyman. Haig sketched rapidly the context of his boyhood:

On my last visit home I learned a great many things about my dad I had never known before—that he had been married before, but his wife died; that his own mother and father had died when he was young and that he had quit school to take care of his brothers and sisters; he had only a third-grade education as a result; and that his first child of his second marriage had died when she was four months old. He had quite a tragic life, losing his parents, his wife, and his first child. He was strict on us, strictest on me of all the children for some reason. He beat me the most, not roughly, but enough to hurt. We were always poor; I never had anything the other kids

had. I never had a bicycle, never had a gun, never had roller skates. And
when my father saw me using someone else's things, he would thrash me,
and say he never wanted to see me using other people's property. But we
would go off in the woods, and someone would let me use his BB gun to
shoot at rabbits. And I loved to roller-skate. But it got so bad, me borrow-
ing things from the other kids all the time, that they would shun me, they'd
run away from me when they saw me coming. All my clothes were handed
down from my older brothers; I'd go off to school in an old pair of overalls,
no shoes or anything, and it hurt me; I was embarrassed about it. As a
result, I played a lot by myself. When I was a kid, I was musically inclined.
One day in the fifth grade, my music teacher came to me and said, "I want
you to play the French horn." Well, I didn't want to change and play that
big thing; it was bigger than me almost, and I didn't have one and I didn't
have the money to buy one. So I said I didn't want to, but he said, "If you
do, I've got a surprise for you." Well, the surprise was that in the fifth
grade I played in the high school band; I got to use the band's French
horn. And every Saturday the high school bus would come all the way
across town to pick me up and take me to the game. They didn't have a
uniform small enough to fit me; so at first I didn't wear a uniform.

As a teen-ager, Haig developed into a keen football player and devoted his
summers and spare time to coaching younger kids in a variety of sports.
When he graduated from high school, however, his father refused to let him
accept an athletic scholarship to the university ("he didn't think education
was worth my time"), and Haig joined the Marine Corps. Some six years
later, now out of the service, married, living apart from his roots, and
working in an assembly line, he joined the Laconia Police Department.

He was twenty-five at the time. In his first eighteen months as a policeman
his agility and capacity to take care of himself served him well. In those days
he did his work as he was instructed to do it. He enforced every law, made
lots of arrests, stopped suspicious characters, and never lost a fight. Then, in
the middle of his second year, a profoundly disturbing thing happened. A
member of the Overseers, a black youth gang, and a Laconia policeman
named Luke Sever got into a fight. Sever was killed by a bullet from his own
revolver, allegedly fired by the Overseer. Haig was the first officer to reach
the scene:

I'll never forget Luke's last words, "Help me." I'll never forget it. I remember one of the older officers that same day had come up to Luke and
said, "Slow down. Don't bug those people too much, or you'll get hurt."
Well, that really hit me. Here was a person who could not communicate.
He saw all the people as lawbreakers, and he treated them all the same.
As far as he was concerned, they should all go to jail. That's how I became
the police officer I am now. I'll never forget it. The officer who had told
him to "slow down"—I will never forget him. Luke was working beat 1,

and this old-timer knew beat 4; he had worked the area for years and years and years. He tried to get the point across to Luke. I remember hearing some of the prostitutes, who said, as he was dying, "I'm glad that honky got it." That was really hate, not because he was a policeman but because he was a bully. They hated him even as he was dying. Too bad, because Luke Sever in his mind was doing one helluva good job. In his mind he was doing nothing wrong. He was not prejudiced. They were breaking the law, and he was doing what he was being paid to do. He could not see any other way. Too bad.

The effect of the public's hatred set in motion the deepest self-doubt in Haig. He began to question what he was doing on the street, and his unconscious quest for "another way" was stimulated by his supervisor, a sergeant of limited judgment and dull perception, perhaps the most reviled squad leader in Patrol. The sergeant began to ride Haig.

Increasingly Haig found there were days he could not bring himself to go to work, and he called in sick. He drew back from his fellow policemen. He lost his enthusiasm and became morose and introspective. He sulked and grew bitter, and the sergeant took it as a personal attack and railed against Haig vindictively.

Haig, however, was not cast out totally as a result of his supervisor's efforts to punish him. Haig's interests in athletics maintained his association with police officers on other squads and in other lines of police work. Thanks to these reassuring and accessible enclaves within the department, his estrangement was never total. Moreover, and somewhat ironically, the ineptitude of the sergeant impelled younger officers on the squad to come to Haig to express their misery and seek his assistance. Gradually, over three years, his own morale and interest returned. The timing of his spiritual resurgence was perfect. The administration of the department turned over, and the personnel change ushered in a "softer" idea of police work. Seeking to make its training program a more effective instrument of these new policies, the administration began to develop a field-training officer program to give recruits in their first weeks of field experience the benefit of pairing with experienced officers selected for their exemplary "soft" qualities. The previous practice—slapdash assignment of raw rookies according to manpower needs and regardless of training implications—had frequently run into criticism. Working with an embittered or inept partner had got many a rookie off on the wrong foot. In a conciliatory spirit, the chief went through the motions of polling his patrol officers, seeking their nominations for these exemplary FTOs (field-training officers). Haig's clientele of advisees had grown sufficiently numerous by this time that his name was thrust before the chief. Combining high recommendations with a minority background in a department much in need of minority-group officers, Haig was a natural choice. To Haig his selection came unexpectedly, but it served to shore up his growing conviction that the hard-nosed means by which police work had been done in Laconia was unnecessary and destructive and that restraint was preferable. "It takes a helluva lot more guts to back down than to go ahead and bang heads." In his spiritual journey he had arrived at the same conclusion as the new chief and with no less firmness of conviction. Yet despite the accidents of encounter and timing, there was an inevitability about Haig's redemption. He was a man coming home, a police officer who had found his way back to those peaceable methods by which he and all he had admired in the past had worked best.

Haig was aware of the paradox of face. He understood, as some never did, that men must never show weakness in the presence of bullies. "My father's advice was, no matter how big he is, hit him back, even if you have to run after you've done it. And don't cry." He appreciated from afar indomitable determination to carry out one's threats and to avenge one's injuries.

Haig, nonetheless, imposed strict limits on the means he personally would employ. He carried a revolver, but he had resolved never to resort to it. He carried a baton, but he refused to use it. He had the power to arrest people who defied his orders, but threatening arrest was not his style of settling a beef. Haig had limited himself to nonviolent means, and this self-limitation meant that some situations were beyond his ability to handle. This sense of human limitation also implied that, when a situation went bad, it was not necessarily his personal responsibility. "You accept the fact you did the best you could." His self-imposed limit on means imposed limits on his goals.

What did Haig do when confronted with a neighborhood beef which did not stop merely because the policemen had arrived? He first looked about for faces in the crowd, people he recognized as natural leaders of the community or the gangs. "The most effective thing to do is to get one of his [i.e., the antagonist's] peers to come say, 'Cool it.' I like to have them handle the situation, and it usually works." Not only did these community leaders have the power to punish with, for example, ostracism and unpopularity, but they also had positive rewards to confer: friendship, status, jobs, wisdom, safety.

Resourcefulness in devising means to use others to control situations was Haig's hallmark. Knowing the limits of his influence in situations which were escalating, aware of the limited range of hostages he allowed himself under his self-imposed restraints, Haig acted the part of the populist in that he motivated the stabilizing influences within the natural community to "cool it."

To the extent that Haig could and did develop his beat in order to enlist the cooperation of third parties, his response was similar to the professional response of Marshall in the skid row situation.

If there was no help available, however, Haig himself had to intervene and cope. He did so in a markedly reciprocating way: with the appearance not of indomitability but of insight; not from an invincible position of strength, but from a vulnerable display of weakness; with the intent not of hurting another but of being hurt; with the resolve not to use the weaponry he was licensed to use, but to forego such use in order to lose. Without prudently attempting to isolate either of the protagonists from themselves or from the crowd, he openly sought to contrast his reasonableness with the cruelty of the fighters. In abstaining from violence and arrest, in "taking" whatever language or abuse the guy with the baseball bat might send his way, in passively suffering the vulgarity and barbarity of others, he tried to enlist the crowd's sympathy for him and against the fighters. Above all, he was going to be reasonable— even if it meant risking that things might "get out of hand." The moral example of turning the other cheek was the lesson Haig tried to give the crowd. It was necessary to establish the sincerity of the police as assistants of the people, not as their adversaries. In other words, the reciprocating response of Haig was civility at all costs, even under the most aggravated circumstances.

In a neighborhood beef, however, Haig generally would not be the only policeman on the scene. He depended on assisting officers to cooperate with him, to accept his soft style of handling the ruckus. To an extent, the geographical division of the city into beats gave Haig a leadership advantage. When the beef occurred on his beat, officers from adjacent beats who arrived on the scene deferred to him as the beat officer. "You have the responsibility for your beat," and this presumption of local competence meant that the beat officer initially commanded the allegiance of outside officers.

Yet this presumption, this modern adaptation of the Reformation principle of *cuius regio, eius religio* (which might have been translated in Laconia, "Whosoever beat it is, his style of policing") applied only if the local officer displayed worthiness. Signs of incompetence negated the presumption that the local officer would take charge and set the pace. In some police organizations Haig's "softness" would have been so dishonorable that policemen would have felt ashamed (and frightened) to cooperate with it. In Laconia, however, the chief's forceful and unequivocal policies made the situation otherwise.

Undoubtedly the chief was personally unpopular: the effect of his leadership on department personnel as a whole was demeaning and dispiriting. His mode of running the department was markedly coercive. He got his way by making harsh examples, by condemning and punishing bad police practices, and by appearing as an oppressive antagonist of his policemen rather than as their loyal supporter.

Despite this, however, he was the chief, the only one the department had. The chief monopolized the official broadcast facilities; his was the only voice that could speak both to the community and to the entire department at the same time. Moreover, his system of punishments, as it had been institutionalized in Internal Affairs, was frightening in its severity, its omnipresence, and its detachment.

If the chief's practices toward his policemen were harsh, however, his objectives were to make his policemen soft in their encounters with the citizenry. One ambitious and intelligent sergeant summed up his perception of what the chief wanted: "You don't arrest unless you absolutely have to." The chief's leadership threw the hard-liners like Kip into doubt and isolation, a condition which permitted softer fellows like Haig to flourish. Because the chief was at the top, men with nonviolent inclinations were "turned on," galvanized, and men of the opposite bent fell back into muted, but not yet mutinous, condition. Against their better judgment, policemen who disagreed with Haig accepted their duty of going along with him on his beat, in his assigned sector of authority, because they could not launch an effective revolution.

For an officer like Haig to be effective even in these benign circumstances, he had to have two personal characteristics: personal conviction and some compensating virtues.

Haig was convinced of the propriety of his nonviolence. Unquestionably the tragedy of Officer Sever's brutal death and the agony of self-doubt it caused hardened Haig's natural inclinations sufficiently to withstand criticism, backbiting, and put-downs. In his mind he catalogued nonviolent heroes who prevailed in a violent world, the greatest of whom was Jackie Robinson, the Brooklyn Dodgers infielder who broke baseball's color barrier. Both to me and to young people he met, he would recount how Branch Rickey, Robinson's friend and mentor, had warned Robinson of the personal abuse to which he would be subjected and how he had said to Robinson, "I want a man courageous enough not to fight." Robinson's response expressed Haig's own courageous aspiration: "I've got two cheeks."

These nonviolent convictions, present by virtue of his boyhood experience, tempered by tragedy, bolted down by introspection, and reinforced by the example of others, protected Haig from the pot shots of his detractors.

Then too, Haig had virtues which gained the respect of some fellow officers, especially those associated with him informally. He had courage and judgment. He was, after all, the best athlete in the department. Anyone who could play shortstop with the spunk and alertness he displayed had status, a reputation for courage, that forced his detractors to have second thoughts about their presupposition that softness implied cowardice. If a man was soft in his attitudes but was also brave, then the causes of his softness became problematic. Furthermore, it was hard for his detractors to renounce him, because he was so popular. His baseball and basketball friends were always standing up for him in locker room conversations and making an issue of attempts to denounce him. Without informal organizations within the formal police organization, Haig's respectability would have been far more difficult to establish and maintain.

Finally, it was vital that Haig have a relatively permanent relationship to a neighborhood in Laconia and that his citizenry be able to recognize his civilized ways for what they were. We have mentioned the utility of the beat system for conferring local authority on Haig over his fellow officers. The beat system cut a large city into numerous little ones, and his had a population sufficiently small to enable him to know his people familiarly. Because he circulated only within his beat, he could discover the natural stabilizing agents of the neighborhood and how to activate them. Because his neighborhood recognized him, he was not the symbol of the enemy, to be fought as evidence of respectability. If Haig had had to move every month or had circulated throughout the entire city, he would have wasted the very knowledge and status which he needed to practice his reciprocal arts.

Nonviolence gave wider latitude to the citizen to act out his own nastiness. Given the freedom to be vile, the citizen had the chance to see the ugliness of his violent feelings made manifest. At least, that was the underlying premise of the nonviolent policeman. Permitting a person to project frustration and inner hatred out of the shadow of thought and into the light of action sometimes worked as a self-administered antidote to the inner poisons. Self-correction resulting from self-perception was the consummation for which Haig devoutly wished.

Yet, to the victim, Haig's patience was sometimes upsetting. It was one thing for him to practice nonviolence in the face of personal peril; it was another matter where the safety of someone else was involved and especially when that someone did not subscribe to the same nonviolent discipline. In such an event, the victim might just perceive himself deserted enough to undertake his own defense.

But even if the nonviolent strategy worked, what happened to the problem which provoked the beef in the first place—the raped sister, in this case? What happened to the situation when Haig let the fight run its course? Underlying his nonviolent style was the premise that humility and self-effacement were somehow good. To assert one's rights was wrong, uncharitable.

Haig's objective, you see, was rehabilitation, remaking aggressors into less aggressive persons. Compared to other policemen, he was less interested in justice for the victim, less concerned about what was due the injured, less resolved to channel resentments into civilized areas of conflict. Other than resignation and charity, he taught victims little about fending for themselves.

Personally, as Haig became increasingly effective in this noncombative style, he gravitated to noncombative positions within the police department. He accepted the job of Traffic Safety officer, in charge of training and administering the local elementary school safety patrols. He was immensely skillful at it. He was gratified by the moral effects his warmth and example had on the children. In many ways this job was perfectly suited to his strengths. But it removed him from the front line, from dealing with the recurrent neighborhood beef. Furthermore, if he had not had informal contacts with other policemen through athletics, he would have had no association with the rest of the police department. A man as skilled as Haig in practicing the reciprocal arts on the street could find much less trying niches inside the police organization. He had plenty of opportunities to remove himself to one of these diverse and civilized jobs within the department for which he was so well suited. Men with nonviolent inclinations like him tended to disappear from the mainstream of police work. They turned the streets over to their more coercive brethren.

## V

Bob Peel was a highly intelligent man. He had a vigorous, productive, and experimental intelligence. He relished applying ideas and observing the results. He complemented his intellectual vigor with an optimism about human affairs. He compulsively kept an eye out for the good effects of every transaction, the instructive moral, the remote results, the unexpected opportunity thrust forward by human endeavor.

He had virtues in moderation and a capacity to make the best of his talents. At six foot two and 200 pounds, he was not the biggest officer on the department, but in his down-filled motorcycle jacket, his safety helmet, and his high leather boots, he always seemed to stand above a crowd. His speech was not colorful or poetic, but he practiced speaking directly and accurately. He was not the fastest runner, the toughest fighter, the most skillful motorcyclist, the best shot, or the mechanic par excellence, but by persistent practice, he did all these things well. He had a high school education when he came on the department. After high school he became an apprentice and later a journeyman carpenter. He retained a distaste for formal education: "School and I have never gotten along too well ever since a tenth-grade counselor told me not to go to college but to go out and get a job." But since coming to the department six years earlier, he had never ceased to educate himself, earning bachelor's and master's degrees and thinking about starting on a Ph.D. in administration—all at night school. At the same time he pushed himself into departmental activities to school himself in the ways of the world; he became a director of the Police Officers' Association, pitched into bargaining and grievance committees, and chaired the pension retirement committee. He was a learner, an insatiably curious man who believed that experiences were a stimulant to more learning. He learned about commerce, art, law, psychology, history, sports, real estate, literature, dogs, motorcycles, and computers because his police work introduced him to these subjects. Nothing in the city was below him or alien to him, and he felt a responsibility to comprehend and "to appreciate."

Peel was a native Laconian who had grown up in an attractive middle-class urban neighborhood. Peel had joined the department four and a half years before I first met him, signing up on a whim (he had gone to headquarters to pay a traffic fine and had responded to a poster urging men to join the department). He had such an aptitude for police work that he ranked first in his academy class and tutored several classmates through the program. Police work seemed to stimulate his whole being. He loved the mixture of physical and mental work, the opportunities to practice leniency and severity, the dangers which involved courage and prudence. Planning a police career for himself, he transferred himself in and out of the fullest variety of departmental jobs. He worked in Patrol, wended his way into Research, administered several special projects, transferred to Traffic, and performed in Special Operations for a time.

What did Peel do in a neighborhood beef? He became a lawyer, a sidewalk solicitor. He introduced his citizenry to the law in its full panoply. He opened the gate to the entire legal process. In his own words, he told of what he did with the bat-wielding brother, the avenger of his sister's alleged rape:

> I took the guy with the bat into a small cubicle all by ourselves and appealed both to his pride and to his manhood. I told him honestly, If I was the object of his hostilities—I didn't say it quite this way, but this was the general idea—I wouldn't take off my badge and fight it out with him. He was too big for me, and besides I would have to arrest him, and no one wants to arrest him. He didn't do anything wrong. I try to give everyone an avenue of escape. You have got to save his face. Some devices for that are privacy—he can walk out of that cubicle just as big as he went in and as strong as ever. But alone I could advise him to do it the right way. Next day, get on a phone to the police department, and get a policewoman, or a juvenile officer to come out to the house. And interview him, his sister, his mother, his grandmothers. Get statements, even do some medical test-ing on the sister. He went for that eventually. Initially, you see, he would have sacrificed himself, would have gone to jail knowingly. But he had no alternatives in his mind; he had to beat up the guy who had raped his little sister. So you have to offer an individual an escape from his bind. But a policeman cannot afford to lose, and what you have to avoid as a police-man is putting yourself into a spot with a win-or-lose basis. I could have presented an ultimatum. "You shut up or you're going to jail." The final ultimatum is the authority to arrest, and there is a perfect legal right to do

it. But is it going to be a peace-keeping move—and especially in the long run?

Peel perceived the "bind" of the brother, obliged as he was to inflict harm on the one who had wronged his sister. Unless he found "the right way," the legal way, to "beat up the guy," he would have to take action outside the law at the sacrifice of his lawful status. In fact, the brother had no idea a right way was available to him. To find out how to utilize the legal process meant having a guide to the law, and most guides charged at least $25 an hour.

The "right way" tended to be a luxury far beyond the reach of the normal city dweller. Let us reflect upon just how inaccessible the legal system could be for the citizen with whom the policeman normally dealt. In a case of fraud, the amount to be retrieved by initiating a lawsuit would be a pittance compared to the cost of hiring a lawyer. As a rule of thumb, private lawyers in 1971 regarded $10,000 as the absolute minimum stake to make legal action worthwhile to their clients; and action on an ill-made car or against a bad tenant or against a judgment-proof defendant would never pay for itself. If a citizen wanted to abate a neighborhood nuisance or alter a zoning restriction, a $1,500 retainer might start the ball rolling, but if there were an appeal ... Imagine a situation where it was necessary to get one's mother's old-age pension. Suppose the social worker in charge of the case had denied the application for no comprehensible reason. Where would one go if the other knowledgeable persons in the welfare office appeared reluctant to contradict their colleague or to take the time? What if a child's reading problems at school were being overlooked or belittled by a teacher: how would the parents get the school to pay attention? What about medical problems that caused a person to be laid off from work: who was available to interpret the multiplicity of private contracts and public regulations which bore on the problem—the contract of employment, the insurance policy, the unemployment compensation laws, the civil rights legislation, the Constitution? Getting the documents, much less understanding them, provided an insuperable obstacle for the person in whose budget there was no extra money for frills like lawyers.

In 1966 legal aid for the poor increased dramatically, meeting the legal needs for the desperately poor. For those who had an eight-hour job, however, legal aid made no direct difference, for they were ineligible. They lacked the financial surplus necessary to retain a private lawyer but were too industrious to be entitled to a public advocate.

The human animal has always been too resourceful to let important problems persist without developing makeshift remedies. The normal city dweller filled the gap between him and the formal legal process by getting legal advice from lay experts—the political ward heeler, the bail bondsman, the local notary public, the city clerk, the neighborhood bartender, the union steward, even the jailhouse lawyer for those unlucky enough to find themselves behind bars. These paralegal types did their work for small fees, as a form of patronage requiring some reciprocal favor, out of friendship, or because it was their job (as in the case of the union steward). They ushered people through the gates of the law.

Of all the paralegal persons, the most obviously available and the most freely accessible to the modern city dweller was the policeman. It was the policeman who could explain how to register a motor vehicle or to pay a parking ticket. The policeman could explain the importance of placing identifying marks on a citizen's possessions. He could show how to safeguard a dwelling against burglars. No policeman, at least in Laconia, questioned the obligation to provide this kind of legal advice, but officers like Peel extended this function to provide the citizen with more subtle legal know-how, the kind that was necessary to alleviate and control neighborhood conflicts.

Peel saw, in the neighborhood beef, not a problem of disorder but a case of litigation. He knew that to give the beef access to the legal system—to make it justiciable—the parties needed economical legal assistance. As Peel saw it, sometimes the best way to make the neighborhood beef justiciable was to criminalize it. Then the victim, the "plaintiff," obtained a free lawyer (the prosecutor) and free investigative services (usually the police), and the state paid the court costs. In many cases the accused wrongdoer, the defendant, also received free legal services from the public defender.

Peel, however, recognized the considerable disadvantages of resorting to the criminal justice system to resolve private disputes. Procedurally, tough rules of evidence and other due process requirements handicapped the "plaintiff." Moreover, defendants worked under tremendous disadvantages. The "damages" to which they were exposed tended to the Draconian: an arrest record, bail, the necessity of personal court appearance. To alleviate these disadvantages, Peel learned special ways of framing his criminal report in a sufficiently muted fashion to tip off the prosecutor and the police investigators that the matter was not criminal but civil and that it did not require jailing so much as compensation and advice.

In some states the district attorney's office had civil responsibilities, representing the public interest in some areas, acting as an attorney general in educational, regulatory, or ecological matters. Officers like Peel who knew of this potential source of free legal aid could point his citizenry to a "right way" that was practical at the same time.

Were there other sources of free legal talent, free investigative talent, and free judicial assistance? Labor unions were one; they had legal staff for matters that came within the employment contract. There were also the staffs of the numerous legal bodies which touched the city dweller's life—civil rights commissions, alcoholic beverage commissions, city attorneys, legislatures, regulatory commissions, building inspectors, fair trade investigators, judges, grand juries, the military. Cut-rate services, however, had their drawbacks, and invoking them for effective action was no mean trick. Yet it was possible to get legal and investigative help for free without going the criminal route.

In a situation such as the Recreation Center standoff, one citizen had a grievance against another. The brother thought he had a wrong to be remedied, a future danger to be prevented, a right to be asserted, a need to coerce.

The problem was not how to harmonize or how to induce the brother and sister to adapt to the hard knocks of life. The problem was doing justice, giving a man his due, getting payment for suffering.

When Peel talked with the young man with the baseball bat, he acted like his professional solicitor. He explained in private consultation how to get free investigative services: getting a policewoman to examine the sister in order to build up the kind of medical and evidentiary conditions that would entitle his family to the legal services of a prosecuting attorney. For Peel, advising his citizenry how "to do it the right way" amounted to showing them how the legal system could be used to "beat up the guy" who had raped his "little sister," instead of using self-help.

Now, "the right way" did not always work perfectly. The prosecutor often lacked the time and the inclination to pursue what he deemed were inconsequential personal matters. The problem of underenforcement was not a problem afflicting only the lower orders. Rich and poor alike have found that bureaucracies need prodding to do their many jobs. The classic role of the lawyer for the rich man has been as expediter; similarly, in the poor man's case the paralegal gatekeeper had to perform expediting tasks— making sure the bureaucrats kept working at the problem, making sure his client did not get discouraged, maintaining order and patience, and orienting the client to the overall system.

It was not an easy task to make this professional response. For one thing, Peel had to know much more law than just the criminal code. Since the academy gave no courses on civil matters, he had to teach himself about the laws of the people—landlord-tenant law, domestic relations, debtor-creditor matters, Social Security regulations, fraud, property damage, insurance, and so forth. He had to know the popular laws well enough to teach them to the public. Although Peel did not, a few policemen who resorted to the professional response also went to law school to enlarge their legal learning. Most, however, simply got themselves into situations where they picked up an orientation to the various subjects. Men did as Peel did: they joined the police pension committee and got a free introduction to insurance and Social Security concepts. They sought to be placed in the Training Academy where they had time and incentive to master popular laws. They made it a point to ask judges and prosecutors and bailiffs what they would have done about a particular incident; in listening to the solutions, they observed the lawyer's approach to social problems. They sought out sergeants who likewise thought it important to know more than the criminal law.

But more than understanding the law was necessary. A professional response called for the development of techniques for activating the legal system, for getting its members to do what the policemen wanted them to do. One skill crucial to this task was communicating in writing. Through his police reports, a policeman who played the role of legal gatekeeper had to influence a wide range of government employees to do the right thing. He had to get social workers to mediate, investigators to investigate, district attorneys to litigate, judges to negotiate. He had to make good guesses about what the actual effects of his written expression would be in different contexts. Because he did not want to employ the criminal law always in the same way—sometimes he might want punishment, at other times help—he had to frame his official message with great verbal subtlety, depending on his objectives and knowing that he had no power to command his "superiors," only the capability to influence them. Such a skill resulted from extensive, self-conscious experiments.

Moreover, anyone who played the role of legal gatekeeper had to have oral eloquence, public-speaking ability. On the one hand, he had to prevail upon the individual citizen to solve his problem "the right way." On the other hand, and more difficult, he had to cope with the crowd. The paradox of face was created by the crowd's presence. It was the assailant's need to preserve his reputation as an avenger which drove him to defy the policeman in the first place. If doing things "the right way" caused him to lose face, then he could not afford to do things "the right way."

Peel's successful handling of a neighborhood beef depended on his capacity to make the crowd accept a new definition of victory for his client. He had to assume that the crowd would initially perceive victory in terms of the short run, the one-shot vengeful knockdown. Through his eloquence he had to transform those rudimentary criteria of success into more sophisticated ones. He had to increase the crowd's consciousness of how much more dire long-term legal remedies really were. When the brother put down his baseball bat to pursue the "right way," the crowd could not be allowed to think it was out of cowardice. The crowd had to know it was out of nastiness, that it was because the "right way" afforded a more certain and cruel method of gaining vengeance. The professional would never leave the crowd asking, "Who won?" He told them in no uncertain terms who would win if the brother's suspicions were accurate and what the victory would amount to.

Peel needed still another skill. He had to create an appearance of impartiality while playing the advocate's role. Such impartiality was a difficult pose to strike. After all, the very act of privately advising the brother with the baseball bat on how to do things the right way might appear highly partisan to the recreation aide. Worse, to many policemen such unilateral help bordered on provocation, not neutrality. Being a sidewalk advocate made many policemen feel uneasy and hesitant.

Peel developed successful rebuttal to such charges of bias. Neutrality, he would explain to his critics, did not mean having no opinions about right and wrong. It only meant having opinions about right and wrong which were in accordance with the lawmakers' authoritative determinations of what was right and what was wrong. An impartial attorney general was entitled to bring actions against one element of the public on behalf of another element because statutory and common law provided for such actions on grounds of public policy. Likewise, Peel would explain, a neutral policeman must be biased in favor of one citizen's freedom of speech against another's claim of privacy because the Constitution told him he should be inclined to weigh these values differently. And similarly, he should help rape victims get vengeance and compensation because the law says such victims are entitled to them.

While it might sound easy to accept this reasoning, application of this idea in a police context had many pitfalls. For example, stirring up litigation, which was what Peel was doing, sooner or later could develop into the police version of champerty and barratry. Directing a citizen's attention to particular legal forms of redress might eventually conclude in directing the citizen to particular legal offices. Neutrality in a conflictful world was hard to achieve.

Finally, Peel had to live with his conscience. The nub of the matter was that in a police context it always seemed more questionable to provoke conflict, legal or otherwise, than to impose peace upon a community. To carry a legal briefcase was not the policeman's bag, according to the conventional police wisdom. On the other hand, it was acceptable for a policeman to limit his duties to restoring order and be quit of the matter. If violence broke out later, it was not his fault, He had given the community the chance to be peaceful, and the community had blown it. Restoring peace was the police equivalent of washing one's hands clean of guilt.

To buck this police orthodoxy, Peel personally had to accept the blame if things went wrong. While it was acceptable for him to act outside normal expectancies, he was on his own. The buck stopped at him. It was he who had contributed to the conflict; it was he who had induced the brother's reliance on "the right way"; it was he who had excited hopes of proper vengeance. If "the right way" turned out badly, if the district attorney failed to pursue the matter, if the investigator failed to act, the citizen was now in a much worse position in terms of honor in the neighborhood than if he had attempted vengeance when he could. Having depended on the legal system to execute his threats, he looked foolish if the legal system failed to back him up.

Thus, Peel and men like him took on a larger and higher responsibility for resolving the crowd scene. They put themselves in a position of having to follow through on a variety of old business, because, as the sidewalk advocates who gave the advice in the first place, their responsibility continued. The responsibilities accumulated, and gave their duties a complexity and a burdensomeness which were distinctly more time-consuming and heavy than those of officers who handled crowd scenes differently. Men who responded professionally to the paradox of face had to have the strength and the quickness to cope with these added responsibilities.

# 8

# The Paradox of Irrationality: The Juvenile Caper

I have always thought that in revolutions, especially democratic revolutions, madmen (not those metaphorically called such, but real madmen) have played a very considerable political part. At least it is certain that at such times a state of semi-madness is not out of place and often leads to success.

*Alexis de Tocqueville*
Recollections
1848

I'd much rather chase burglars or robbers because they're scared of us.

*Officer Bill Douglas*
Laconia Police Department
1973

## I

Tocqueville's observations about the political success of "real madmen" were connected with 15 May 1848, when supporters of several extreme political clubs overran the French Assembly and caused its temporary dissolution. The boldness of the leaders of this insurrection unsettled Tocqueville. They felt no fear. They commanded with assurance. They took action which portended disaster in everyone's eyes but their own. Centered on the moment at hand, they ignored the dangers they were setting in motion. They worried not at all about the incredible odds against their successful flouting of the Assembly's authority. They lacked fear of self-destruction and chaos. They marched to the beat of a different drummer. And they were victorious—temporarily at least.

Irrationality, the ignorance of fearful prospects, resembled courage, the conquest of fear. The difference turned on the degree of forethought and calculation at the root of an individual's actions. The brave person understood the trouble that was in store but accepted the risks with full knowledge of the probabilities of success and failure. He convinced others that he saw the prospects and had the fortitude to cope with them. The foolhardy person, however, assessed the conventionally perceived risks with indifference. He did not prepare for the foreseeable consequences. He had no prudence, in a word. The irrational man miscalculated, like an accountant who never checked the cost side of the ledger. As a result, his undertakings often violated conventional taboos and common sense, and his words and deeds convinced people that he did not know better.

Despite the differences between them, however, irrational men were no less formidable adversaries than courageous ones. Perhaps they were more so. Irrational individuals posed terrifying problems for those who had to contend with them. They were like no other adversary—different from the dispossessed, who became prudent after they had been invested with something to lose; different from the detached, who became careful when they had been reinspired with hope; and different from the remorseless, who regained a sense of constraint once they had been removed from a position of personal insecurity. Irrational men remained fearless because they were certain they had nothing to fear. Convincing them that their confidence was misplaced, that they were blind to important consequences, that their nonawareness of threats raised great perils, was a task of enormous difficulty.

The policeman faced irrational persons every day—drug addicts, drunks, infuriated citizens, the deranged, and the zealots of our time.[1] They were persons who were so single-minded, so one-dimensional in their perceptions of the world, so selective in what they heard and comprehended, that normal communication broke down. The ultimatum, "Stop or I'll shoot," meant nothing to a wino too drunk to hear. The assassin whose ideology required him to die a martyr was an implacable and terrible foe. They all lacked the self-concerned prudence on which threats worked effectively. In contrast, the accomplished criminal was almost admirable, for he had fears but coped with them in predictable ways.

The juvenile caper embodied the paradox of irrationality: "the more delirious the threatener, the more serious the threat; the more delirious the victim, the less serious the threat." Not that juveniles were fiends or zealots: the young simply foresaw their actions' having consequences different from those which adults anticipated.[2] Blind to some of the implications of what

---

1. Some officers thought the chief and his disciplinary institution, Internal Affairs, were irrational.
2. The classic representation of this phenomenon is Joseph Conrad's novella, *Youth,* about a youth who chose to sail aboard a rusty, leaky ship, in the worst season of the year, with the scruffiest crew in the Bangkok trade and a dangerous cargo of coal on board. After a series of calamities, the cargo caught fire, and the ship sank in the Indian Ocean, more than a hundred miles from land. What were misfortunes for others, however, were adventures for the young man, and none was more stimulating than the prospect of

they were doing, they were insensate to some of the fears. They roman-
ticized,[3] invited martyrdom, wished to suffer like heroes because only heroics
could absolve them from their adolescent sense of unworthiness. If they were
fearful, they were most fearful that their fearfulness would be detected by
others. They did not fear chaos or destruction, for their self-centeredness
preoccupied them. Misery was a purely personal phenomenon to them, and
the more misery they endured, the more certain they became of their own
worth.

Imagine the scene at Caesar's, a soda fountain and confectionary store
across the street from one of Laconia's five high schools. In the 1960s
truancy and disciplinary suspension reached such magnitudes that the
numbers of teen-agers not in school became unmanageable. "At Caesar's
there were a lot of kids in there. I talked with the woman in there when I first
came on the beat. They cut school, she tells me, and play the pinball
machines all day. Business was going way down. Families no longer came
in." Teen-agers all, these "kids" had a faulty judgment of what the world
was like. Their inexperience led them to misjudge the possible real effects of
their misbehavior: their ineligibility for college, their putting Caesar's out of
business, and even their arrest. To the adult a policeman posed a threat of
endless trouble—arrest meant expenditures for fines and lawyers' fees,
inconvenient court appearances, loss of liberty. Of these and other implications, youth were oblivious. They simply did not know in their hearts what
terrors the law could visit on them, what perils an arrest presented in terms of
future jobs, a driver's license, social stigma, and a regretful lifetime. They
were inclined to emphasize the glory of it all; the snares were not perceived.
They lived in the security of thinking jail was a playpen. That delusion gave
them a powerful advantage when the policeman entered Caesar's to put a
halt to their antics. The question was, how could a policeman correct those
miscalculations inside their teen-age heads? The different answers can be
understood more clearly if we first examine the professional response of
Officer Bill Douglas, the patrolman who said, "I'd much rather chase
burglars or robbers because they're scared of us."

---

being adrift at sea in a flimsy lifeboat with no sanctuary for life or sanity: just youth
against the elements, without any of civilization's securities. Conrad concluded with this
thought: "And, tell me, wasn't that the best time, that time when we were young at sea;
young and had nothing, on the sea that gives nothing, except hard knocks—and sometimes
a chance to feel your strength—..."

3.  Karl Popper, *The Open Society and Its Enemies* (Princeton, N.J.: Princeton University
    Press, 1950), p. 164: "Aestheticism and radicalism must lead us to jettison reason, and to
    replace it by a desperate hope for political miracles. This irrational attitude which springs
    from an intoxication with dreams of a beautiful world is what I call Romanticism." Popper
    defined aestheticism as a desire to build a world which was not only a little better and
    more rational than ours, but one which was free from all its ugliness.

## II

Bill Douglas was a minister's son. His father was the "hardest-working man I've ever known," restless, Methodist, preacher for the poor, and a sometime political organizer. Douglas's most abiding memory of his father was the latter's involvement with the family problems of his parishioners: "Dad had settled a lot of them. He was a big, solid guy, six foot, 200 pounds. He was very calm.... My father would discuss with my mother the family beef he saw, but he always would say, 'You follow God's rules; you turn the other cheek.' He'd take abuse. I thought he should become physical a lot of times, but then three or four days later, along would come that abusive person, and he'd apologize."

Douglas was a fine high school athlete, an all-county football player, compact, balanced, highly intelligent. The adolescent temptations incident to good looks and personal popularity had diverted him from applying himself in high school, and he passed up a chance to go to college, to his father's bitter regret. Douglas went to work as a warehouseman and then as a hashslinger at a local hamburger joint, but out of boredom, at the age of twenty-two, he applied to the department and was accepted.

Meanwhile he had fallen in love and married. Over the course of the next four years his wife grew to dislike the dangers of her husband's job and, just when his spirits were lowest and his outlook most troubled, persuaded him to quit and become an insurance salesman. That life lasted less than two years. Douglas rejoined the department and had been back on Patrol for a year and a half when I first met him. (His wife divorced him soon thereafter, taking the two children and leaving this complete family man without a family.)

Douglas enjoyed his work more and knew his beat better than any other policeman I met. "I now know," he once said, "that I can work this job without getting bitter." Douglas always wanted to be a teacher and coach, but felt he would never have a second chance to go to college. In his own mind the only second chance he was going to have to make something valuable of his life was his police work: "The job ... is one way a fellow with my education can help."

By his lights he had miscalculated when he was young; he had not thought about the next step while he was blowing his early opportunity to attend college. Man's weakness, Douglas saw, was this tendency not to think about the next step. Everywhere he saw confirmation of this insight. Certain policemen who bullied juveniles never reflected on the implications of making enemies for a lifetime. Some officers shot their guns off wildly, giving little thought to where the bullet might end. Similarly, young people took drugs for the kicks of the moment or spurned education, forgetting that without it they enslaved themselves to the life of a drudge. The prize example of imprudence, of course, was Douglas's own adolescent wasting of opportunity.

Douglas was outspoken. Unlike the average policeman, he would chew out fellow officers about the "dumbbell things" they did. With juveniles, he "put it on the line," telling them directly about their responsibilities. "I learned at my job in the warehouse that if a guy can get away with sloughing off, he will, and he will get worse off. So you watch him, and let him know what's expected of him, and he'll do it, and do it well."

What led persons, particularly young persons, to accept responsibility and to stop doing things without thinking? According to Douglas, people had to be scared enough to force themselves to think things through—they had to be sobered by the realization that their trespasses were harmful enough that the damage might never be undone. A kid might overdose on drugs, or he might pass his "breaking point" in other ways sufficient to make him see that he was only a mortal. Fear was a great teacher, an indispensable one. It conditioned the mind wonderfully to lessons about self-restraint and concern for the long term.

But Douglas's analysis did not stop just at this point. For if fear got people to pay attention, there had to be a worthwhile and accurate lesson to pay attention to. The brutal policeman, the kind Douglas despised, forgot that the citizen had to channel his fear into self-improvement.

What did Douglas do to restore rationality to the juvenile caper? Basically Douglas talked juveniles into feeling that they were responsible for all the effects of their actions, not just for the desirable consequences they envisioned. That took time: a policeman could never be in "too big a hurry"; the sober second thought had to have a period to develop and come to the fore. It also took an ability to create fear "to make people pay attention." As Douglas remarked several times, a policeman usually began every encounter with a personal advantage, "an edge of fear," but through clumsy use of that edge, he could squander it and panic citizens into trapping themselves in their own miscalculations.

Douglas used his "edge of fear" with great subtlety. To a greater extent than any other officer in the sample, he maintained a notebook on the juveniles on his beat. In it he kept photos of the more notorious ones; and of the notorious and not-so-notorious alike, he recorded their deeds and statements: "I'll remember everyone I've run into before. You've got to keep book on them: who's running around? who's committing crimes on your beat? You note down what they say. The next time you meet them, and they tell you a different story, I say, 'You lied to me.' It's embarrassing, getting caught in a lie." "Getting caught in a lie" was embarrassing because of the undeniable personal responsibility for speaking the lie. Douglas, the historian of his beat, reminded his subjects of the gap they created between their pretenses and their practices. He preserved a record of their miscalculations, their mistakes, and their shortcomings; he reminded them of that record and the reminder was fearsome.

In each encounter with juveniles Douglas anticipated miscalculation on their part and made allowance for it, giving them psychological room to readjust their initial estimates of matters. When Douglas walked into Caesar's, he allowed for the probability that they would misjudge him. He also concentrated on purposefully using time to dispel any irrationality. "So the next few days I walk into Caesar's, and I get myself about fifty names, and I tell each one, 'You do not play the machines. You go to school, and if you don't, I'll run you in.' So the first time down goes their name in my book. The second time I catch them, I make a little check right beside their name, just as big a gesture as I can. And the third time, I tell them 'they go to jail.' Well, I only locked up one. And I had no more trouble."

That was Douglas's pattern: a clear statement of his objectives, a gradual increase in pressure to evidence his determination to prevail, the presence of fear, the reminder by word and deed that the ultimate responsibility for any arrest was the citizen's, and time to recalculate and take stock of prospects.

There were five conditions which made this approach successful. First, Douglas cultivated certain personal qualities useful in applying fear surgically and incrementally. One was humor. It relaxed tense situations. His jokes often contained an allusion to some past event, reminding juveniles just how much he knew about them. Moreover, humor dignified adolescents by giving them credit for having a sense of humor. That is what Douglas meant when he said, "Kids dig you dropping down to their level—or thinking you are." Kids dug cops' dropping a sincere and subtle compliment. Douglas had other personal traits which helped. He had a power of dramatization; he could amplify his words with dramatic deeds, with the big gesture. And he had patience. His model, of course, was his father, an example which invested his own behavior with a certainty that patience and cowardice were not the same thing. Each of these qualities—humor, a sense of the dramatic, and patience—Douglas practiced and developed.

Second, if he was forced to work with a partner, Douglas had to have one who was equally willing to move deliberately. Douglas's reminiscences were checkered with painful stories of overeager partners who came on too fast and tried to do too much in a hurry. Douglas preferred to work alone, without a partner, and rarely even called for cover (he said he could not find another officer who worked like him).

Third, because he so often worked alone and because working by oneself created perils which working in partnership avoided, Douglas appreciated the need to be fearsome and appear so. He cultivated every opportunity to dramatize the fact he was not "Joe Nice Guy." He would flourish his

notebook in the presence of juveniles; he would quietly talk about how he had
hounded into jail some individual who had not shaped up. He recognized
that juveniles needed "to test you," to see if a policeman would "goodguy it"
and back down; Douglas responded to those tests with an unequivocal
firmness. Then, too, he appreciated the usefulness of the department's
reputation for being tough and unflinching, "the reputation as supercops: we
really benefit from that."

The fourth condition of success was a personal philosophy of pursuing
limited objectives only. Douglas concentrated on rectifying the most urgent
evil on the beat. He set aside time for it: in one season, Caesar's might be the
priority problem; the next season, it might be a rash of purse-snatchings by a
juvenile gang. These priority goals did not change from night to night. They
were persistent commitments, to which Douglas would return again and
again, giving him time to cut them down to size. He did not avoid other
matters, but he weighed their urgency and committed his time to solve the
most urgent one, deliberately.

What were the standards by which he defined whether a problem was
"urgent"? To a degree, the choice was whimsical; urgent problems were
matters which upset him the most. On the other hand, the choice was often
predetermined: one matter seemed to stand out uniquely because of the
numbers of victims involved or the severity of the injury. But always the
problem involved extreme suffering; on Douglas's beat there was widespread
public agreement that the "big thing on the beat" *was* a big thing, not trivial.
It might be physical danger (as in the case of purse-snatching) or the
bankruptcy of a business. Taking drugs, parking, gambling, drinking,
family beefs, car thefts, traffic accidents—all these things happened, and
Douglas would be on the spot to deal with them if they occurred. But
whenever he had time, it was back to the "big thing" which all of human
society could agree was wrong.

It was infinitely simpler to make time for a single objective of top and
undeniable priority than to respond to all problems as if they were equally
pressing. For one thing, it was easier to develop techniques which wore down
a case of irrationality on a small scale than to find ways of coping with social
irrationality on a big scale. For another thing, Douglas could define
measurable goals: to increase Caesar's genteel patronage, to reduce the
number of purse-snatchings. Such goals gave him a finite measure of
progress.[4]

---

4.  See ibid., chap. 9, where Popper contrasts "historicism" with two kinds of social
    engineering, "utopian" and "piecemeal." At pp. 155–56 he discusses the advantages of
    limited objectives, "of searching for, and fighting against, the greatest and most urgent
    evils of society, rather than searching for, fighting for, its greatest ultimate good." Those
    advantages are: (1) a limited remedial objective is more likely to obtain wider approval

Finally, Douglas's approach succeeded because it was realistic. His assumption that individuals were ultimately reasonable led him to search for the circumstances under which persons did not "grow out of" their irrationality. In the case of the gang at Caesar's, his search for impediments to rational calculation focused quickly on the anonymity enjoyed by members of a large crowd.[5] The juveniles were miscalculating the threat posed for them by Douglas's presence because they believed they were not individually identifiable; hence they felt they had nothing to fear, and that, Douglas thought, was the cause of their mistake in judgment.

Thus, Douglas's unhurried identification of each of the fifty truants at the pinball machines was aimed at dissipating the confidence they had in their anonymity. The series of deliberate steps Douglas took—to make a first identification, to reaffirm soon after that he could recognize the individuals in the crowd, and to make the first, climactic (and only) arrest—effectively altered their estimate of the odds of getting away with the injury they were inflicting on Caesar's. Douglas's tactics caused them to start thinking of themselves as identifiable, responsible individuals. In filling them with fears of prospective and real dangers, he restored their rationality.

The community benefited from Douglas' abilities to bring juveniles back to reason. Juveniles, because of their numbers and the free time at their disposal, wreaked havoc with a neighborhood. Irrationality—unrealistic fearlessness—throve in collectivities like juvenile gangs. A policeman with a talent for altering this destructive and irrational force was of great value to a community. By making a juvenile crowd more deliberate, by scaring it enough to divert its enormous energies out of destructive channels Douglas solved a problem which no community could handle by private means alone.

For Douglas, the results were extremely gratifying. By playing the historian of his beat and its people, he personalized his work. He began to feel he mattered in their lives. Moreover, his records kept in his memory the varied developments of the characters on his beat, some of whom "grew out of" their adolescent madnesses and some of whom did not. The record helped convince Douglas that "fear" had a useful place in human society, that at worst it was necessary and at best it was benign. The written record disposed of any last vestiges of misgiving about using his "edge of fear."

---

and agreement because it is a more obvious end and the technology of means is less problematic and simpler and less risky; (2) hence persuasion rather than suppression can be effective, and a reasonable compromise is more likely, i.e., dispersed influence is a condition which can be tolerated; and (3) criticism can be tolerated.

5.  Social psychologists have long been interested in explaining irrational crowd behavior and have pointed to the importance of anonymity in producing conditions in which individuals can act injuriously and be free of punishment or stigma. See Roger Brown, *Social Psychology* (New York: The Free Press, 1965), pp. 735-36.

He also came to feel content that he was just "an ordinary human ... with an interest in kids and people" and that to be a good policeman he did not have to brandish his gun. He found that he could do a valuable kind of police work with his combination of flaws and virtues—his easygoing manner, his intellectual concern about human development, his skills in detecting the fears of people who appeared to have none, his storytelling abilities, his humor, his own personal background of failure and missed opportunity. He knew he could do a respectable police job in the way he wanted to do it.

## III

Consider Douglas's opposite, Mike Bacon. Bacon stood six foot three, weighed over 200 pounds, and was as stiff as a poker. He frequently described himself as "tense." He had come on the department on his twenty-first birthday and had been a policeman for four years when I first met him. He had no college education and no desire for one. He was, in his own eyes, a policeman, and his ambition was to be recognized as a very good one, which meant he wanted to become a sergeant and ultimately an administrator within the department. To be a good policeman meant having those traits conventionally acknowledged to be important: toughness, cunning, and persistence, along with a mastery of any skills which the department announced as desirable.

Bacon, like Douglas, was an athlete who let his athletic potential lapse on his decision not to go to college. There the resemblance between the two stopped.

Bacon fought his citizenry; he took part in sufficient "resisting" incidents that he was sent to the first class of the Violence Prevention Unit. He also paid no attention to his citizenry: he ignored the personal details of the individuals on his beat; he forgot their names, ignored their lives, and was not concerned with the dynamics and objects of their fears.

Typically, he handled the juvenile caper in a turbulent, impatient, temperamental, and impulsive way. Just the sight of a crowd of adolescents aroused his "sixth sense": his hunch was always, "whatever it was, it was clear there was a crime in it." Playing that hunch, he knew he had "every right" to stop the crime. Knowing that he had a right to intervene tempted him into striking preemptively without calculating whether the conditions existed to make the arrest acceptable to the juveniles, the law, or the public. He acted without laying either a legal or a moral basis for his actions. He did not publicly establish the elements of the crime. He did not publicly identify the wrongdoers. Nor did he work to enlarge his ability to make the arrest effectively. He paid no attention to whether the juveniles were acting irrationally—without fear and without a sober second thought. Hence, he took no steps to manipulate the situation so as to educate them out of their miscalculations. Quite the contrary—he wanted to dumbfound them.

He knew better, and sometimes he behaved better. He knew it was important to leave citizens some alternatives other than retaliation: his training had taught him that. But his impulses often overrode his training, unsupported as that training was by any intellectual understanding of human nature. He never understood the importance of time. Consequently, he acted abruptly, panicking his juveniles and leaving them with a feeling of being trapped. He also acted with such impulsiveness that he lacked the time to observe his quarry and learn their names, their outlooks, their habits. They remained anonymous to him. Hence, while he frightened his juveniles, he did not develop a focused fear in them, a sense they had more to fear if they retaliated or fled than if they shaped up.

Why did Bacon behave as he did? In largest part, the answer boiled down to his basic assumptions about human nature. Here the contrast with the professional Douglas proved instructive.

Douglas, as we noted, anticipated that juveniles were likely to miscalculate the costs of acting harmfully toward others; thus, he gave them time and space to adjust their initial estimates. Bacon's approach to juveniles was that they acted purposefully and with full awareness of the injury they were doing; to give them time and space was to give them something which they did not deserve and which would imply weakness and appeasement on his part. Douglas assumed that time would dissipate irrationality, Bacon that time would increase villainy. Douglas feared dumbfounding his adolescents further; Bacon feared not doing so. Douglas would educate; Bacon would fight.

If a policeman approached a situation preoccupied with the problem of "appeasement" and worried about appearing weak, he tended to convince himself of the efficacy of the "preventive attack."[6] He tended to comprehend events in "intentional" terms: all human action, particularly injurious action, was presumptively purposeful. A surgical strike at the source of this purposefulness removed the source of injury. With such a view of humankind, the policeman perceived his adversary as more fearsome because more malevolent. He also saw his remedy as simpler and more immediate to execute.

Allied with this preoccupation with appeasement was a second condition—a bluntness of perception in observing human detail. Bacon did not bother to look for what lawyers have called the presence of *mens rea*. In criminal law the issue of *mens rea* raised the question of whether the underlying motivation of an injurious act was of such an evil or premeditated nature as

6.   See Robert F. Kennedy, *Thirteen Days* (New York: Norton, 1969), e.g., p. 97.

to convince society that the criminal process ought to be invoked against its perpetrator. Bacon presumed *mens rea* from the injury. This presumption was part of a world view in which human nature was divided into "smarts" and "dumbs," victimizers and victims. The consequence of this outlook was to do away with any need to look for motives and fears. Injurers were presumptively rational, malevolent, and unchanging. The short of the matter was that Bacon treated extremely complicated problems of human motivation with a simpleminded presumption.

Bacon, of course, depended on the toleration of his fellow officers. The chaos his impulsiveness caused had to be acceptable to the "district of guys" with whom he worked, for they so often had to bail him out. He found acceptance in squads whose sergeant made members indifferent to the rough and tumble. A sergeant who encouraged his men to play hunches had to cover up for mistaken hunches. If he did so successfully, he attracted Bacon-like men who liked such a mode of policing. The district system which allowed sergeants to select congenial officers made it possible for a man like Bacon to find a tolerant niche within a police department with an organizational purpose defined so differently from his own.

Bacon's behavior fed the expectancies of the worst elements of the community he served. His impulsive activities—performed as they were without laying an adequate moral basis for their comprehension or justification—reinforced those juveniles who believed that cops were savage, malevolent, self-interested, and power-hungry. Bacon fulfilled the prophecies implied by this devil-theory, and his actions thus enhanced the reputations of those who professed it. Conversely, those juveniles who argued that cops were human, helpful, and sometimes worth cooperating with were undermined by Bacon's counterirrational strategy. In short, Bacon's conduct brought out the worst in everybody.[7]

Bacon suffered personally. Among other things, he had had to defend himself in a number of judicial inquiries. The attorney's fees were expensive, even though the Police Officers' Association was likely to pick up some of the costs and the city attorney might defend him in civil suits (because the city was joined as codefendant in civil suits against policemen). The worry was considerable.

Furthermore, he was torn internally. Bacon retained his ambition to rise in

7.  See Richard McCleery, "Correctional Administration and Political Change," in Lawrence Hazelrigg, *Prison within Society* (Garden City, N.Y.: Doubleday Anchor, 1967), pp. 113–49. "Arbitrariness in the management of the old prison had given experienced inmates an advantage in their ability to predict and explain the events of that hostile and mysterious environment. Using a 'devil theory' to explain every unfortunate event as the work of 'rats,' old cons, like a primitive priesthood, based much of their status on an ability to provide coherent and psychologically satisfying explanations of official action. By focusing the characteristic hatreds and hostilities of the inmates on nonconforming individuals, these leaders were equipped with a powerful instrument of social control" (p. 127).

the department. He had learned that his record of violence constituted a serious handicap to fulfilling his hopes for promotion. Thus he tried to restrain his impulses. The result was that he felt equivocal and ambivalent. He learned the letter of community relations, but he fought the spirit. He worried that he was acting restrained out of cowardice, and he began to worry that his ambition to be a good policeman was illegitimate. The result was that he asserted greater control over his impulses but acted with greater intensity when those impulses periodically overcame the barriers erected by his ambition.

## IV

How did others respond to the paradox of irrationality? One of the distinctive features of this paradox was the asymmetry of communication between the parties: the irrational citizen could communicate to the policeman, but the policeman's messages and threats did not penetrate the awareness of the citizen. The officer who was overly civilized, who was concerned about exchanging ideas on values and consequences, would predictably be stymied by this paradox more than any other.

Dean Lancaster tended to deal reciprocally with his citizenry. He did not use his six foot three intimidatingly. He was too nice a guy. Adopted as an infant by a gentle grocer and his wife, he had had a pleasant, responsible childhood. As a legacy of that childhood, Lancaster carried about with him guilt feelings about certain "bully habits" he had developed when he was an extremely fat little boy and was taunted about his size. In early adolescence, however, he began working with his father at the grocery store. He was paid well, gained an early sense of financial independence, and found at the same time that his body was maturing and his self-confidence growing. By the time he was eighteen he had taken on managerial responsibilities at the store and was an assured, well-rounded young man.

Lancaster's view of being a policeman was not much different from his view of himself as a store manager. The people paid him to serve them, and he did—to everyone's benefit. More than any of the other policemen, he thought of himself as in a process of reciprocity, a retailer of police services. He tried to give his customers the services they needed: being a middleman, brokering disputes between citizens; talking "reasonably"; explaining and giving information he had special knowledge of; hearing and respecting "other points of view"; "helping the community"; teaching the public the value of mutual trust and goodwill; and "giving them what they want." Even the most obnoxious members of the public were "gentlemen" and "respectable."

His capacity for perceiving what others wanted from him was great: he saw their points of view, and he liked the feeling that others relied on him.

When he spoke of incidents involving irrationality, however, never once did he talk of the utility of fear. On the contrary, in dealing with the irrational citizen, he stressed that while "the blue uniform affects him and the way he looks at you . . . you can make him forget it and have it so that it's a man talking to a man." In contrast to Douglas, who capitalized on the "edge of fear," Lancaster preferred to establish a relationship of two reasonable people, to treat the other person "like a human being."

The trouble was that the approach did not always work. He sometimes failed to get across his message: "But if a guy is really disoriented, I can't do anything about it." That is, the ignorantly fearless citizen did not respond reasonably to "the man-to-man approach." Unlike the customer in the grocery store, the irrational citizen lacked the incentive to listen to reason. Furthermore, the time which Lancaster took to work out a deal often made things worse. His attempt to be sincere and fair—so effective in the marketplace or even in the family beef—sometimes backfired. Fights occurred: "I don't know what happened," Lancaster remarked of a rough-and-tumble few weeks when his partner and he had tried to clean up a pool hall which a gang of juveniles had taken over. He found he was stymied by their pointless pugnacity and their stupid fearlessness.

The reasonable approach seemed to excite violence under unreasoning circumstances. Such a result bothered Lancaster no end. Yet he stuck to his approach. Despite the fights, he remained calm, reasoning, trying to convince people by his soft approach that he was trustworthy and well intentioned.

What enabled Lancaster to work this way? I was struck by how important his commercial experience was in determining his behavior. It was often asserted by old-timers that young policemen who had had no work experience made the worst policemen, that they were too harsh, too intolerant, too naïvely perfectionist; and that the best officers were former workingmen. Such may have been the case, but Lancaster's personal history provided a reminder that different work experiences taught different lessons. An experience in retailing, being a middleman between supplier and consumer, taught lessons which were distinctly different from what Russo learned in dredging the Mississippi. The give-and-take experience of retailing was so much more immediately involved with the public; the philosophy that the customer was always right was so much more ingrained and reinforced; the need to work with people and to sense their point of view was so much greater in sales work than in a craft. In Lancaster's case, having been a manager in a retail grocery business since adolescence had made a permanent mark on him; it was not easy for him to throw over all the habits acquired thus.

Then there was Lancaster's size. He was large enough to take care of himself if he ended up fighting the fight his reasonableness invited. Because he was big, he escaped annihilation, which meant he could risk being a nice guy.

A third factor enabling him to remain reasonable was the leadership of the chief. As we have noted, the chief was known throughout the department as an administrator who wanted his officers to take the soft line and the risks such an approach created. [8] The chief's willingness to take the heat for his soft line made it much more acceptable and safe for an officer in the ranks to assume the same outlook. Lancaster never had to take official criticism, and the informal disappointment of some of his colleagues about his style lacked the force which official rebuke might have added to social murmurings. The chief's support also encouraged open alliances among reasonable men like Lancaster, providing a kind of social sanctuary for them.

Finally, Lancaster was eminently educable, and he was not going to stay a patrol officer the rest of his life. He had no doubt that he could make sergeant in a department where appointment to sergeant depended on passing an examination with a high score. He was sharpening his test-taking tools by going to college. Because his patrol job was short term, he was not so upset by the way a few episodes blew up. He would have felt otherwise if he had known that patrol work was a lifetime proposition. He did not enjoy his discomfort about using force (it reminded him of his childhood "bully tactics"), but he did not get discouraged by this discomfort. His eyes were on the future.

This point invites a comparison between Bacon and Lancaster. You will recall that Bacon was anticipating the day when he would reach a respectable level within the department where his career ambitions no longer could be held hostage by his superiors. Then he could resume playing those hunches which he restrained with such effort while his career was in the making. Lancaster, on the other hand, looked to the day when promotion would remove him from a variety of street situations which stymied him. In both cases promotion would be important, because it would have the effect of releasing their personal inclinations from career constraints. In police departments a much greater opportunity existed at the sergeants' level to

---

8.  Bacon, who despised the chief for his "weakness," told this story, the organizational import of which was widely understood: "Then we . . . had a series of problems, a critical-incidents test. They [the instructors in the Violence Prevention Unit] would give you an incident; a guy running down the street, someone yelling after him he's stolen something, running into the house and slamming the door: that type of thing. Then they ask you only two questions about what you would do. Would you take further action? Would you make an arrest? And you had to answer exactly: no hedging around. Then they rated the incident itself for potential violence, 1 through 15. If you said you'd go and break in the door, push into the bedroom and horsecollar the guy and take him down to jail and pull your gun if he didn't cooperate, that would be '15.' If you said, you would just go up and try to arrest him, that might be less, but still there was a lot of potential for violence. If you said, 'I don't know what he did; so I'd just let him go,' that would be a '1.' Well, everybody in the department had to take the test. You know what happened? The chief came out with a '2,' while the average officer was '13.' That'll give you some idea of the difference between the men and the chief."

express individual idiosyncrasies. In that sense a police department reflected the tastes, the values, and the opinions of the men who became sergeants.

Lancaster lacked the fearsome skills of men like Douglas who could professionally manipulate irrationality: the skills of threatening talk and dramatization, a feeling for the propriety of force and for establishing a moral basis for using fear. More often than not, his genuine decency, his size, and the edge which his authority as a Laconia police officer established carried the day anyway. Not always, however, and it was then that he had to resort to manhandling the citizen or else retreat from the problem. Whenever Lancaster felt the community was serious and of one mind about strict law enforcement, he felt justified in resorting to brute force. If, on the other hand, community feeling was divided or not well mobilized, he tended to avoid the problem—to ignore it—if he found it beyond his reasonable capabilities. The notables, who could more easily shape community opinion, thus tended to get the service they wanted. The nobodies did not.

Lancaster did not like the feeling of being unable to do anything about matters where irrationality succeeded. As he began to see that fear sometimes worked where reason did not, he sought out some way to understand the phenomenon he found so baffling. His studies at college, particularly in sociology, provided him with just such a chance. In the classes he attended in his spare time, he found an outlet to talk with others detachedly about his personal qualms regarding threat. As he probed the moral problems of coercion, he began to be reassured that he was not alone in feeling equivocal about the problem of power. He began to feel comfortable with the idea that it was man's fate to face problems which were ultimately insoluble but had to be confronted nonetheless. For a young policeman, particularly one with the gentle and civilized qualities of Lancaster, a college liberal arts education was a vital complement to his early years of police work. Without it, he would have been gored by the dilemma—whether to pull back from difficult spots, dispensing his services selectively only where his reciprocal talents proved useful, or to turn to increased force without guidelines or understanding. The paradox of irrationality buffaloed the likes of Lancaster, because the efficacy of purposeful ignorance defied the common sense they had absorbed in the marketplaces of life. The classroom gave them perspective on their bafflement and made their personal limitations more acceptable to themselves.

## V

Claude Nary fitted no mold. If he had, the policemen of Laconia would have taken immediate steps to shatter it. Nary was an Appalachian, a Fundamentalist, short, uneducated, ungrammatical, garrulous, an ex-soldier who could not hold his liquor, and utterly inadequate as a policeman. In one eight-hour period while I was riding with him, he (1) forgot his lunch box and went home to retrieve it, then panicked when he received an emergency call from his beat five city miles away; (2) went to the wrong site while responding to a robbery in progress and prematurely told the radio room that nothing was going on; and (3) ran out of gas on a main city thoroughfare while responding to a silent alarm. Personally, he had some very appealing characteristics: he was curious and somewhat observant; he was philosophical, friendly, enthusiastic, kind, and folksy; he was forgiving, trusting, generous, and filled with goodwill.

But he was a hapless policeman.

Nary could not deal with juveniles. If he talked with them, he increased their fearlessness, and they taunted him or ignored him. He was unable to make them fear him; so he feared and avoided them. If the situation was such that he had to respond to a call about juveniles, he became angry, not at the juveniles but at the complainant.[9] Typically, in Nary's own words,

> There are a lot of rock-throwing capers—juveniles who go in gangs and break windows. We got a call from a lady whose windows had been smashed for weeks in a row, and all you can say is, "Look, lady, these kids just live in that turn-key apartment. There are 25 kids over there, and you can't identify which ones broke your window, and it just is that you are certain one did it. But I can't arrest them all for it." The people —they don't understand this kind of thing. All they know is, My windows got broke last week. That's what's irritating, mainly their ignorance of the law is what irritates me.

That pattern occurred over and over again: do nothing about the aggressions of frightening gangs except blame the timid and downtrodden victim. That was "all" Nary could do.

Claude Nary lacked Douglas's linguistic skills. He lacked Lancaster's impressive size and strength. He lacked Bacon's brazenness in taking charge. He lacked a sense of maturity. He lacked patience. He lacked sophistication. He lacked a sense of "the police role." He lacked a sense of the city. He lacked a sense of how people worked. He lacked a knowledge of how people felt—their despairs, their hopes, their tragedies, their triumphs, their fears, and their resolution. He lacked the kind of humor which relaxed people and made them laugh at themselves. He could not "relate" to people, he could not cause them to do what he wanted them to do. He had no inner calm. He

9.  See Kennedy, *Thirteen Days*, p. 52: "Bertrand Russell sent a message to Khrushchev praising him for his conciliatory position and a message to President Kennedy castigating the United States for its warlike attitude. The President took time out of his other deliberations personally to compose an answer: 'I think your attention might well be directed to the burglar rather than to those who caught the burglar.'"

lacked a will and a determination. And he lacked an ability to teach himself how to overcome all these shortcomings.

When he was appointed to the department, danger signs were evident. Among those who were accepted on the department, he ranked at the bottom on every test of eligibility. His interviews turned up obvious problems as well. His education was so poor that his contract of employment especially stipulated that he must take some courses in college. His street performance during probation was pathetic. For a variety of reasons, however, he passed through, and his appointment was regularized. As we mentioned about Garfield, another policeman who more and more adopted an avoidance response, public attacks on particular aptitude tests undermined the confidence of civil service in all such tests. Moreover, Nary was a resident of Laconia, and pressures were being applied to get persons who resided in Laconia on the department. His enthusiasm, his friendliness—in short, his civilized virtues—looked good when considered in the one-dimensional light of the late 1960s when the public focus was on police brutality. So he stayed.

Once his training had been completed, however, the sergeants of the department did not want him. He was consigned to the pool, a loose reserve of officers without permanent squad assignments who filled in briefly for absent policemen. Unlike other rookies, Nary was just left there. In his own words, "I must have ridden with fifty different officers in my first year." He worked the wagon. He was assigned jail duty. He was forgotten, suppressed, ignored, and left to get worse. As long as he did not actively perpetrate some disaster, however, he was not going to be discharged from the department.

Why did his development as a policeman stop? After all, in the army he had become a sergeant. He had proved a good mechanic. He coped in other organizations. Police work, however, overwhelmed him; it asked much more of him, much too much. A policeman lived in a world colored by the antagonism which his authority evoked. The police job was a coercive, extortionate job and therefore, first and foremost, terrifying. Only when a person had the ability to cope unfailingly with frightening incidents could that terror be alleviated. The police job put demands on persons with civilized virtues to develop political skills and morals—or else.[10]

What were the consequences? Nary was ostracized by his fellow officers. No policeman would ride with him and be dependent on him. He became the object of ridicule. He had no friends from whom he could learn or to whom he could confide. His judgment became affected: any citizen who was friendly with him, who could relax his constant high-strung condition, could manipulate him. In one case, a con man befriended Nary and sold him a stolen television. Fortunately for Nary he discovered that he had been

10. As Peel expressed the point, "A policeman can never afford to lose."

deceived and admitted his mistake to supervisors before the affair became
public knowledge. As a result, the administration decided, tentatively, not to
fire him but to send him through retraining. For almost a year, Nary was
assigned to Haig for special schooling. Eventually, however, the department
needed Haig for other duties, but still another tentative decision was made to
give Nary one more try.

Haig, in his kindly way, described how Nary policed his beat:

> This officer was so awful, you cannot imagine. He didn't know what he
> was doing; what a police officer should do; he didn't know the penal code;
> he was afraid when he walked in on a family beef; he was so awful. . . .
> You know, the officers wouldn't work with him. They didn't want to get in
> a jam he created. God, he was afraid. He'd walk into a family beef, and
> they kept on fighting, just as if he weren't there. They walked all over him.
> And he was scared, a sign of immaturity, but he just didn't know what to
> do. When I recommended he be kept on, I urged that he be closely ob-
> served. I watched him for about a year, but now I don't know what he's
> doing.

No one else knew "what he's doing" either, hidden away in his one-man car,
avoiding the terrors of irrationality, remorselessness, detachment, and
dispossession which policemen confronted every day. The community was
left to handle its own affairs "as if he weren't there."

# 9

# The Responses to
# the Four Paradoxes
# of Coercive Power

We cannot fully understand the acts of other people, until we know what they think they know.

*Walter Lippmann*
Public Opinion
1922

Why is "Thou Shalt Not Covet" the very last of the Ten Commandments? Because one must first avoid doing the wrong thing. Then, later on, one will not desire to do them. If one stopped and waited until all the passions ceased, one could never attain holiness. And so it is with all things. If you are not happy, act the happy man. Happiness will come later. So also with faith. If you are in despair, act as though you believed. Faith will come afterwards.

*I. B. Singer*
The Spinoza of Market Street
1961

## I

Table 2 summarizes the range of defensive reactions to the paradoxes of power recurring in street situations.

The common attribute in the variety of professional responses to the four paradoxes was the methodical teaching of the citizen that he had much to fear from the law if he stepped outside its framework and much to gain if he adapted to it as a free person. The professional response depended heavily on talk, talk which helped to take charge of events. Sometimes an officer could fashion events because of his previous actions, by developing his beat, as Mike Marshall did on skid row. More typically, however, because of the relatively temporary assignments of policemen, their shaping events depended on the ability to talk, on a readiness to explain and exhort, to establish hope, understanding, and fear. The professional response never involved an indefensible violation of the law. Any apparent illegality, if there was one, was always put in an understandable and acceptable light, openly and publicly justified. Nor did the professional response amount to the

Table 2                                 Defensive Reactions to Paradoxes of
                                        Coercion

| Type of Defensive Response | Paradox of Dispossession ("Skid Row") | Paradox of Detachment ("Family Beef") | Paradox of Face ("Crowd Scene") | Paradox of Irrationality ("Juvenile Caper") |
|---|---|---|---|---|
| Professional | Developing the beat | Gambling on the future | Playing the legal gatekeeper | Using the restorative powers of time |
| Reciprocating | Delegating to vigilantes | Being the clinician | Turning the other cheek | Getting stymied |
| Enforcement | Behaving brutally | Becoming sentimental | Playing the crazy-brave | Becoming counter-irrational |
| Avoidance | Taking a hike | Defining out | Playing the phony-tough | Blaming the victim |

naked assertion of the law. The law was invoked after careful preparation of a foundation of knowledge, or fearfulness, or both. The professional response characteristically involved teaching through talk.

In contrast, the reciprocating response depended on nurturing the citizen's sense of personal obligation to the particular police officer. It depended on the officer's touching some personal compulsion of gratitude, on the return of favors. Those favors were a policeman's open ear or, more often, his leniency. Frequently, the reciprocating response seemed to fall outside the law, and the difference between the reciprocating response and the professional one was that things were left unsaid in the reciprocating response. It let deeds speak for themselves; the justification was left implicit. The reciprocating response let people get away with illegal activity: assaulting a policeman, employing a posse, acting out their adolescent impulses, even destroying property. It was essentially passive resistance to the coercion of others and depended on the citizens' conscious understanding of their moral obligations in the course of time. And sometimes, as in the family beef, the reciprocating response was extremely effective.

The enforcement response was aggressive, somewhat like the professional response but more impatient and unenlightening, unresponsive to the possible changes going on inside the citizen's head and heart. Words were used as weapons or to incite, never to probe the soul. And sometimes the enforcement response, when skillfully performed, worked—swiftly and aptly. Recall Officer Rockingham's piece of departmental lore which headed chapter 7: "There's an old story of the officer who would jump out of his car with his baton waving, and yelling and screaming, and hitting at the trees and garbage cans and lampposts. It always broke the crowd up, and he never had to arrest anybody and nobody ever got hurt."

Finally, the avoidance response, almost invariably passive, ineloquent, unintimidating, was none of these—not luminous like the professional, lenient like the reciprocating, or lunatic like the enforcement response. Merely lifeless, unresponsive to human suffering.

## II

In the last four chapters I have made repeated note of the critical and obvious importance of three influences: the policeman's language skills, his police colleagues (and in particular his sergeant), and the pervasive leadership of his chief. The responses to each paradox were facilitated, or impeded, by the patrolman's relationship to these three factors. In turn, the patrolman's development of customary responses to the paradoxes made a difference in his subsequent dealings with his chief, his attitudes toward his fellow officers, and his appreciation of the effects of language. His habits of action soon forced a choice—between supporting the chief or reviling him; between accepting the friendships of his squad mates and his sergeant or isolating himself from them; between being motivated to practice eloquence or to denigrate it.

We have also repeatedly emphasized the interplay between the officer's attitudes and his actions: the cause-and-effect relationship between what he did and what he believed. My methods of research were too crude to establish with certainty that attitudes and behavior were directly and perfectly related. My impression was that policemen who had a given perspective on the human situation and who were bothered by similar notions about right and wrong behaved predictably and similarly. They repeated the same choices among means of defense. A policeman would often let his perspectives and feelings be affected by his colleagues and his chief. If his attitudes changed as a result, my strong impression (but it is only an impression) was that his customary responses to the paradoxes changed. In this sense, attitudes caused behavior.

But in a deeper sense, we must continue to ask, where did his attitudes come from, especially those feelings and outlooks which let the policeman accept (or forced him to reject) the guidance of his colleagues and his chief? The ultimate sources of these attitudes were deep. The character sketches indicate that hindsight can enable us to see the roots in adolescence, childhood, and even infancy.

Yet if hindsight permits us to trace present attitudes back to their roots, it does not help us account for the directions not taken, the equally plausible but different attitudes which could have developed from the same origins but did not. Foreseeing how feelings and beliefs will grow is much more complicated than looking back on how they did develop.

To one certainty I cling, however. Being a policeman changed attitudes. What impressed me were the crucial moral and intellectual effects stemming from a policeman's choice of defensive responses to the four paradoxes of coercion. These active decisions accumulated over time and shaped his thinking in ways he had never intended. The deals a patrolman had to make with the devil of coercion had unforeseen consequences for his perspective and passion. In this sense, behavior caused attitudes.

In the next part of this book, we turn to examine the reflexive dynamic between a policeman's actions and his intellectual and moral development.

# The Development of Policemen

# 3

Let me make a few comments about the moral axiom underlying the next few chapters. Throughout the preceding chapters we have talked of "moral attitudes," or some equivalent expression like "morals," "morality," "morale," or "values." What is meant by a "moral attitude"? And what assumptions are implicit in the notion of one?

To speak of a moral attitude assumes that persons are essentially moral animals and are governed by moral attitudes. (This assumption we shall call the moral axiom.) Three things must be said about this assumption. First, an assumption is just that—a presupposition, a postulate made prior to inquiry. This book will not satisfy the skeptical reader that there are such things as moral attitudes. On the contrary, the best I can do on this score is to convince the reader to withhold judgment and focus his curiosity, not on whether the axiom is valid, but whether it is useful: whether the reader increases his understanding of policemen by presupposing that they have moral attitudes.

In dealing with his skepticism, the reader might be consoled by the history of physics. Physicists have always started their inquiries by basing their work on unproved assumptions about matter. At the bottom of all physical explanation have lain assumptions about some elemental building block which has been presupposed but never explained. Not too many years ago it was the molecule. I understand that physicists have come some distance beyond the assumption of the molecule as the basic building block—past the atom, past even particles of atoms. Yet in the end the physicist has found he has reached the limits of his science and has set down the superstructure of his explanation upon the foundation of some ultimately unknown and unanalyzed subparticle. The historian E. H. Carr called this need to take something as axiomatic "the unavoidable vice of circularity."[1]

Second, any presupposition necessarily puts blinders on the investigator and biases inquiry. Human life is invariably more complicated than the sim-

---

1. Edward Hallett Carr, *The New Society* (Boston: Beacon, 1957), p. 10.

plistic assumptions we make about its "essential" nature. Purposeful simplicities may be valuable in order to avoid intellectual befuddlement. They are nonetheless simplicities. If we begin with other assumptions as starting points, other insights will inevitably result. The reader may want to reflect on what could be concluded about police if we were to start out with different presuppositions. To name only the two which have most effectively seized our imaginations in the past 100 years, we might begin with the Marxian assumption that man is an economic being, or with the Freudian premise that the individual, at bottom, is an irrational or subrational creature.

Third, by investing in the assumption that humans are moral beings, we acquire a great deal of experience and know-how, as part of this view—implications about moral conflict, responsibility and indifference, the proliferation of moral codes of conduct, guilt, and redemption. These terms may sound a bit quaint. The contemporary reader may want to translate them into more current vocabulary—ego-split, neuroses and anomie, inner-direction, identity crisis, and self-actualization.[2] By whatever name, if we adopt the moral axiom we make this abundant body of observations pertinent to police. It also sharpens our focus on a few selected features of a policeman's life, as we try to understand why he grows or, at least, changes.

Now, what do we mean when we speak of a moral attitude? We envision a thought containing four elements: a "thing," a value, a relationship between the two, and a normative implication.

An *attitude* contains three of these elements. Its form is a simple, active sentence, containing a subject (the thing), a verb (the relationship), and an object (the value). A *moral attitude* is an attitude-sentence, to which is added an injunction, ". . . and therefore I should (or should not) further the thing by liking, assisting, or doing it (or hating, hindering, or halting it)." As an example of a moral attitude, you recall that Officer Justice said, in chapter 2: "I always try to preserve the guy's dignity. . . . My philosophy in the thing is a combination of, the fact I like to think that I thought of it myself, plus over the years I've watched and it works. . . . Our job is to protect the Establishment, that is being pressured to make changes faster than it is prepared to cope with them. . . . Our big job is keeping the peace." Justice's moral attitude, his "philosophy," consisted of a thing ("the guy's dignity"), which was positively related ("I've watched and [preserving it] works") to a value ("the peace" of a civilized society, "the Establishment"), and the purposive implication ("our job") enjoining him to "preserve" the thing ("the guy's dignity").

This simpleminded notion of a moral attitude as thing-relationship-value-injunction is the elemental building block of any analysis of men as moral creatures. The point to remember is that such an attitude has both a cause-and-effect aspect and an evaluative aspect. It is at once understanding and belief, both explanatory and purposive; and its intellectual and moral characteristics are mingled inextricably.

In the next two chapters we shall

---

2.   Morris Cohen, *A Preface to Logic* (1944; New York: Meridian, 1956) p. 58, speaks of the "equivalence of expression": that is, these terms "denote or point to the same object."

analyze the explanatory and purposive aspects separately. We shall talk of a policeman's intellectual growth as something distinct from his moral growth. This separation of intellectual understanding from moral feeling is analytic only, and we shall try at the conclusion to show that explanation and purpose are related in a mutually reflexive pattern of cause and consequence.

One last remark, and then a warning. According to the moral axiom, the function of moral attitudes is to permit self-government. A moral attitude is the law to which an individual holds himself, under threat of guilt. The moral being confronts himself with the choice of behaving responsibly or suffering guiltily. His problem is self-imposed, of his own making, for he is at once law-maker, defendant, prosecutor, judge, and executioner. The remarkable thing is that this conflict of interest more often tends to severity than leniency.[3]

The warning is that the next two chapters will have a slower pace and a more microscopic focus than the chapters we have just finished. If the reader can adjust to these changes, however, I think his patience will eventually be rewarded, and the foundation for the concluding chapters will be more soundly laid.

---

3.  In this respect, I refer the reader to the work of Joseph Wambaugh, a former member of the Los Angeles Police Department, whose books develop with great insight the moral aspect of the police profession. On the point of self-blame and severity, see particularly his *The Onion Field* (New York: Delacorte, 1973), the true story of a policeman who condemned himself for "permitting" his partner to be assassinated—when in fact the murder was unpreventable.

# 10 The Development of Understanding

One of the features of what is sometimes called "understanding" is to grasp the context of an event, that is, temporally to know what went before and what is likely to follow, spatially to know the terrain, in human terms to see the play of the many motives involved.

*Robert E. Lane*
Political Ideology
1962

The prime criterion of whether a guy will make a good police officer is this ability to make judgments. And make 'em constantly, over a long period of time. . . . We all are judges, all the time.

*Officer Al Tennison*
Laconia Police Department
1971

## I

"To make judgments" was to anticipate the future. Judgment referred to the capacity to make accurate predictions of future events. To anticipate what was going to happen, policemen developed a sense for the patterns in human affairs. They formed *concepts,* or classifications, which helped them to assimilate and distinguish discrete persons and events. Concepts were attended by visual procedures by which policemen processed the details of the moment into these abstractions.[1] This mélange of classifications and procedures gave their powers of observation focus, so that they paid attention to telltale clues about human behavior and ignored other things less likely to be informative about the future.

The methods by which policemen developed their judgment were intricate, and their procedures and categories changed "over [the] long period" of their careers. As they matured in their jobs, however, their concepts became

1. Walter Lippmann's felicitous phrase for visual procedures was "the habits of our eyes." See *Public Opinion* (New York: Macmillan, 1961), p. 80.

habits and got locked more and more securely into place. The shape of these habitual concepts in turn affected their understanding, their intellectual grasp of "the context" of events, and thus determined whether they would suffer intellectual "degeneration" or would grow into better students of mankind.

## II

To understand better the problem of judgment, let us walk in the shoes of a patrol officer and go through the mechanics of anticipating events in his world. Let us introduce ourselves to the problem of police judgment by examining a situation which is mundane, routine, and ever so frequent.

It was dusk on a Friday evening. Friday was payday, and businesses always boomed in neighborhood grocery and liquor stores on payday. The stores stayed open later than usual and invariably stockpiled greater amounts of cash to help their customers cash paychecks.

Officer Frank Benjamin noticed a black Thunderbird coupe parked in front of a liquor store which had been robbed several times in the past year. "Benjy" was an old-timer. Born in Laconia, a policeman for twenty-five years, high school educated, Irish, and unexcitable, he knew his beat—its kids, its parents, its business establishments, its family relationships, its church, the members of its high school basketball team, its scoundrels, and its good citizens. He did not recognize the car, however.

In the car, a man appeared to be sleeping in the front seat behind the steering wheel. A floppy hat was lowered over his eyes. His clothes indicated that he was young—early twenties at most. He was black. These attributes were quickly ascertainable.

Benjamin approached the parked car from the right side and tapped on the passenger window. As the driver appeared to arouse himself, Benjamin waited outside, casually removing a package of cigarettes from the left pocket of his pants. As the driver stretched across the front seat to open the door, Benjamin offered the cigarettes to him. The driver's first words amounted to a mumbled refusal of the policeman's offer. Things went smoothly. The driver identified himself; he explained that he had pulled over for a doze, thanked the officer, started the car, and moved on. Benjamin, in fact, could never be sure that the driver had been asleep. He could be certain, however, that the driver had no intention then to act dangerously.

When Benjamin first sighted the inactive driver, he wanted to know two things. First, what was the driver doing? Was he suffering a heart attack? Was he drunk or high on drugs? Was he asleep, or only feigning sleep? Was he waiting for somebody? Was he casing the liquor store, inconspicuously keeping an eye on something?

Second, Benjamin was interested in what was going to happen. He had to make a guess about the future. Was the citizen going to die unless he was rushed to a hospital within minutes? Was he going to arouse himself and try to drive his car, too inebriated to be safe in traffic? Was he going to receive stolen goods or drugs? Was he going to rob or burglarize the store? Would he be rebellious, or restrained, when Benjamin came into his life? In short, Benjamin needed to discover the driver's purposes.

Detecting the purposes of human beings was treacherous business. The will of another was beyond direct observation; it was highly variable among different individuals; and it was subject to change from one moment to the next under the influence of events.

Since purposes were inward matters, they had to be inferred from those outward actions which could be observed—words, gestures, configurations of activity. The implications of these observations were invariably ambiguous. Pulling one's hat over one's eyes and huddling behind the steering wheel of a parked car constituted an equivocal act. It was consistent both with being sick and with an intention to sleep one off before going home. It was equally consistent with a second theory of intention: an attempt to mask some larcenous purpose. It could even imply a come-on, a purposeful scheme to appear suspicious and thereby attract a policeman to the car, from which a hidden gang of juveniles could jump and "get themselves a policeman." Detecting purposes before they were acted upon involved a difficult problem of inference. A policeman could make himself more certain only through means of indirect proof, by disproving plausible alternative purposes.

Moreover, the complexity of indirect proof made for an intellectually staggering burden because of a second characteristic of human nature: the range of conceivable purposes was very great. An individual's will was affected by so many remote, lifetime influences. It was affected by what the citizen "knew," by the concepts with which he cut up his world, by the emotions which blocked or amplified what he saw and heard. It was also affected by his larger purposes, his goals in life, his history of frustration and success in pursuing those goals. In human beings, ways of thinking and hoping could differ to extreme degrees.

Furthermore, purposes were altered by changing circumstances. The situation affected what a citizen was likely to do, and Benjamin, for example, was going to affect the circumstances simply by entering the situation. What he wanted to know was the driver's will after it was affected by the policeman's presentation of himself. Was the driver going to be snappish and churlish if awakened? Was he going to reach for a hidden firearm upon seeing the policeman? Was he going to be frightened, or angered, by questioning?

To a limited extent, Benjamin retained some control over the circumstances of the encounter. By being sensitive to how he "related" to citizens, how he affected their reactions, he could neutralize the likelihood of surprise or panic. Extending a cigarette might make the encounter less threatening to the driver, for example.

The policeman, however, could not manipulate all the circumstances. He could not hide his gun, his blue uniform, or his towering height. Those features accompanied him, willy-nilly. In the larger context he could do very little about any sudden formation of a crowd behind him, or about the diminishing daylight. Moreover, the departmental regulations kept him from turning off his police radio, which could blurt out something provocative at any moment (the description, "male Negro," was a radio term which often upset the citizenry in tense circumstances). Finally, the policeman's partner might independently influence the situation. In other words, Benjamin had to worry about the influence of accident, the chance factor, over which he had little or no control.

## III

How did Benjamin perform those crucial and complicated tasks of detecting the purposes and predicting the actions of others? He did three things. He *formed* concepts: that is, he invented a series of pigeonholes into which he slotted similar persons and events. He *applied* the concepts: that is, he developed a series of observational procedures which enabled him to consign a particular person or event to a particular pigeonhole. And he *confirmed* the concepts: he doublechecked against mistaken predictions. Let us consider these operations one at a time.[2]

In inventing his concepts, Benjamin used his long experience. According to his testimony, it was easier to make judgments now that he was one of "the older officers." He had "been around," worked a lot of "different areas," and had worked some kinks out of his judgments on human affairs. But to make his experience a good teacher, he had had to organize it into concepts. He had made "groupings," as he put it. He had "broken down" human activities according to whether they followed one recurring pattern or another.

What concepts did Benjamin invent to sort out his citizenry? The elemental grouping, upon which more subtle but less basic breakdowns depended, was the separation of people into the governables and the rebels.

2. See R. B. Braithwaite, *Scientific Explanation* (New York: Harper Torchbook, 1960), pp. 255-92. For a particularly lucid and comprehensive discussion of the problem of judgment, see Robert W. Axelrod, *Framework for a General Theory of Cognition and Choice* (Berkeley, Calif.: Institute of International Studies, 1972).

The paramount judgmental task was separating those who might revolt against police authority from those who would not. It was to define a situation according to whether it might embody any of the four paradoxes of power. The governable person was a citizen who was not dispossessed or detached or remorseless or irrational. The rebel was his opposite: in Benjamin's vernacular, it was anyone whom you could not "talk with" or whose past attachments you could not "straighten out" or who was an "SOB" or was "goofy."

What was the source of this judgmental concept of governability? It originated in the occupational setting of the policemen. As the anthropologist Banton and the sociologist Skolnick and so many others have pointed out, policemen lived amid dangers.[3] Even in the calm of Friday evening, "when the fever of life is over and the busy world is hushed," as the prayer goes, even when Benjamin was approaching a harmless-looking, ostensibly sleeping man ready to offer him a cigarette, dangers abounded—of rebellion, of defiance, of injury and death.[4] The potential of danger was always requiring a policeman to form a rapid first impression, to group people quickly according to whether they were likely to behave rebelliously or cooperatively. Because his job was to control the people's use of dangerous violence, he made judgments of mankind in terms of their potential for violence. Because he was a governor, he grouped the governed according to their governability. The philosopher Morris Cohen stated the matter of concept formation this way: "All perception depends on the problems that we set ourselves."[5] A policeman's concepts served the purposes "set" by him and the society with which he identified; they "fulfill[ed] a concrete and specific task requirement"—governing the threats of men.[6]

Each policeman in the sample depended on the same basic judgmental concepts. They described situations with adjectives and phrases like "governable," "controllable," "cooperative," "under control," or their opposites, like "out of control" and "extremely volatile." They grouped people according to whether or not the police could "calm down," "control," "handle," "depend on," "get the upper hand on," "keep on the defensive," or "manipulate" them.

3. See bibliographic essay, pp. 293–98.
4. The professional Wilkes put the matter this way: "You know, nobody deals with people like a policeman does. Not a social worker: they walk into a situation, and it's all set up for them. But in police work, in any situation lives are at stake—the life of you and your partner and of the victim."
5. Morris Cohen, *A Preface to Logic* (1944; New York: Meridian, 1956), p. 71.
6. Jerome S. Bruner, Jacqueline J. Goodnow, and George A. Austin, *A Study of Thinking* (New York: Wiley, 1956), p. 5.

## IV

While the basic concept (or concept-pair) of the "governable/rebel" was in
virtually universal use throughout the police community, individual policemen differed from one another on how they applied it. The virtue, after all,
of the concept-pair of governable/rebel was that it was exhaustive; it fitted
all citizens. Its exhaustiveness, however, meant that it was highly abstract,
grouping together in its two categories a broad range of concrete events
which looked very different in detail. The problem for the policeman was to
develop a skill in detecting the cues which permitted him to pigeonhole
persons and events properly. This process of establishing and detecting
harbingers involved what psychologists have been wont to call "attaining the
concept."[7] Attaining a concept involved the development of procedures and
rules of evidence whereby these defining cues could be detected in the real
world and then used to group matters relatively quickly, unambiguously,
invariably, intelligently, and correctly. In the ways they attained the concept-
pair of governable/rebel, policemen differed appreciably.

The first imperative in attaining the concept was quickness. Under police
field conditions, the best cues were those that provided the longest lead time
preceding the behavior which the cues had indicated would occur. The more
obvious and immediately perceptible the signal, the better the cue in terms of
providing time to prepare in anticipation—what we shall call judgmental
time.

Ideally, from the point of view of police certainty, each citizen would wear
an insignia accurately characterizing his governability. In a world where
deceit was impossible and human nature unchanging, a policeman could size
up the occupants of a car by its bumper stickers. The very futility of thinking
up a nonabhorrent system of insignia in a free country may emphasize the
great difficulty police have in exercising judgment where no single cue is very
certain.

In an unsophisticated police department, it would have been tempting to
teach policemen to rely on such cues as skin color, hair length, and
clothes—the backgrounds of the lives of the citizens. Such cues had the
virtue of being readily perceptible. They had obvious defects, however, and
in Laconia most policemen agreed with the officer who said, "People are
different, regardless of their similar backgrounds."

For a policeman, the importance of being familiar with his beat became
clearer in this context. The time the policeman had invested in knowing his
people created a capital fund of identification tags. Time expended to
become familiar with a beat on earlier occasions was thus conserved to

7. See ibid., passim.

increase judgmental time at critical moments. The experienced cop would seem almost leisurely in approaching a crisis on a familiar beat. He had the assurance of a multitude of identifying cues.[8] In contrast, a policeman who had no familiarity with a neighborhood had to start from scratch in detecting who was governable and who was not. He could not see the hidden and reliable insignia which an experienced officer could recognize.

For every policeman, however, there were going to be times when no cues were immediately perceptible. The policemen then had to take steps to elicit from the citizen signals which would foreshadow future behavior.

Benjamin faced this necessity in the case of the sleeping driver. He did not recognize the citizen, and the citizen's obvious attributes—his huddled posture, his blackness, his youth, his clothing, his car—added up ambiguously. Benjamin needed to evoke additional cues. He needed to magnify the driver's activity to generate additional observations.

That was where the cigarette offer came in. The cigarette was an instrument of an experiment which Benjamin conducted on the spot. By tendering his package of smokes, he induced discernible reactions from the driver. The cigarette offer was scientifically experimental in three respects. First, it was a subtly controlled and skillful alteration of the status quo. Benjamin effectively limited the driver's perception of the changes in the situation to a single nonthreatening factor—the offer of cigarettes. Of course, much more had really changed; the policeman, accompanied by his gun and other symbols of his authority, had entered the picture, for one thing. Yet, by focusing the driver's attention on the decision to accept or decline the invitation to have a cigarette, he distracted the citizen's attention from those other factors. He manipulated the situation so that the driver reacted to the reciprocal act of the cigarette offer, not the threat of the police presence. Benjamin's offering him a cigarette did not force the driver toward the demands of self-defense. It did not add appreciably to his fright, fury, or frustration—emotions which could change a governable citizen into a rebel.

It also resembled a scientific experiment in a second way. Under the controlled conditions Benjamin established, it was possible for him to begin obtaining indirect proof effectively. Indirect proof involved the disproving of alternative hypotheses about the citizen's purposes. He proceeded by making suppositions about how the driver would react to the cigarette under each of several plausible theories—the sleep assumption, the heart attack assumption, the drunk assumption, the danger assumption, the casing-the-joint

8.   Peel was assured at the Recreation Center in the middle of an angry crowd: "It was really hostile . . . but nobody had anything against me, and I did not feel alone. They were all black, and I was the only whitey there, but there were plenty of people around to help me out, and I felt that."

assumption, and so forth. Comparisons of the actual response with the various supposed consequences then permitted him to reject a few of the theories. But it is important to note that if Benjamin had not taken pains to keep all the significant factors in the situation constant except the experimental offer of cigarettes, he could not have rejected any of the hypotheses with much confidence even when the outcome did not square with the suppositions. Without making careful preparation of the experiment, he would not have been sure whether extraneous factors, ones which he had not carefully controlled, had produced the discrepancy. In this case, however, the prudent procedures of his experiment beefed up his confidence in the dependability of his conclusions.

Third, the experiment was scientific because it did not contaminate any future relationship between the experimenter and the subject. The cigarette offer did not necessarily alter the original purposes of the citizen. Particularly if he was initially inclined to be governable, the offer did not upset matters. It left the citizen's original purposes intact.

Ever since God investigated Adam, policemen have performed "attitude tests" because they have always had to make judgments. Policemen have differed from one another in the skill with which they engineered the experiments and in the confidence they felt in the results. The time-honored test, applied in the not so distant past to lower-class citizenry, was for a policeman to bark, "Hey, you, c'mere." Doubtless, this test elicited revealing attributes of the citizen. It was, however, experimentally deficient in several ways. First, and most obviously, the command was likely to alter the relationship between test giver and test taker permanently. The citizen was likely to infer that the policeman was overbearing, partial, and indifferent, and he was probably going to remain convinced of it thereafter, notwithstanding any efforts by the policeman to make amends. Second, it was not clear what the citizen was reacting to: the command, the rudeness, the supposition of subordination, or the blue uniform. No inference of purpose could be made with certainty unless the policemen knew what experimental factor the citizen was affected by. Third, the citizen's response could be easily faked. The con-wise citizen could deceive the police officer by responding ingratiatingly. A fourth objection rested on different grounds: the responses it evoked were ambiguous. A bitter response to the "c'mere" might indicate either a remorseless soul or a proud one. It was consistent with both theories and rebutted neither. A cue which indicated that a person was both a governable and a rebel was no help; in that sense, the results of the test were irrelevant.

This point introduces a second requirement of cues: they must be as unambiguous as possible. No matter how clear the observation, no matter how well an attitude test might have been engineered, a residual degree of ambiguity invariably remained. A citizen who failed to respond to "c'mere" might be deaf. In Benjamin's tender of a cigarette, a sleepy driver might misperceive the cigarette package as a revolver aimed at his head.[9] The trouble with indirect proof was that a policeman had time to reject only the most plausible counterhypotheses, not every conceivable one. Thus some ambiguity was always present.

Then, there was the problem of variability. The harbinger was not the event itself. The present response was not the future behavior. The relationship between the indicator of what was to come and actual rebellion or submission was only probable. The citizen who had every earmark of respectability might have had a bad day and therefore be totally ungovernable. Conversely, the citizen with the smoking gun in hand might have been the victim and be glad to have the policeman arrive on the scene.

To cut down ambiguity and variability, policemen, like scientists, searched for multiple harbingers. They looked for a number of attributes which, taken together or combined in some distinct way, indicated the future more accurately than a single clue.

Learning theorists distinguish three kinds of patterns among multiple attributes. Let us call these different patterns conjunctive, disjunctive, and relational. A concept which was indicated by a conjunctive pattern of attributes was defined by the *joint* presence of several cues; that is, the characteristics were additive. For example, what made the sleeping driver a suspicious person was the combination of the facts that it was Friday (payday), his car was close to a liquor store where there was abundant cash on hand, and he had positioned the car so that he could easily observe any movements within the store through his front windshield while feigning sleep. Likewise, in determining whether a citizen were a rebel, some policemen felt it was crucial to observe him at several different times. This prudent desire for more than one reading was summed up by Benjamin: "Sometimes . . . if he's acting like an asshole, he will get over it, and you can help by not arresting him." An asshole indicated that he was one by behaving like an asshole at two separate times.

A disjunctive pattern was different. Here the attributes were not additive but alternative. Different harbingers substituted for one another. For example, a policeman who resorted to the classic attitude test often treated either an aggressive defiance or a sardonic unction as an indicator of ungovernability. What was confusing about disjunctive patterns, however,

9.   Stories of mistaken inferences abounded in police lore. The eloquent Tennison summed up the matter of mistaken inferences: "Most of the things in the real world are really nothing. If you see a guy halfway inside a window, it turns out it's his house and he's forgotten his key. You come on a guy wiring up a car, it turns out he's lost his car key and he's just trying to get home."

was the frequent "arbitrariness" of the substitutes.[10] Often in disjunctive patterns any apparent relationship between one alternative attribute and another was lacking.[11]

As a consequence of the multiplicity and arbitrariness of conjunctive and disjunctive patterns, a policeman tended to employ relational patterns involving pairs of attributes.

A relational pattern, like the conjunctive one, consisted of the *joint* presence of certain attributes, but in the relational pattern the attributes were in a specified relationship to each other: larger, smaller; before, after; above, below; proportional arithmetically or geometrically. To illustrate: to be eligible to be a Laconia policeman, a person had to meet minimal height and weight standards, but in addition weight and height had to be proportional. The five foot nine individual could not weigh 250 pounds; the six foot four giant was not eligible if he weighed only 150 pounds.[12]

You will recall that Benjamin's concept of a rebel or ungovernable person was indicated by a disjunctive pattern of attributes ("transient types" *or* "upset families with weapons" *or* persons caught up in "a major caper" *or* "deranged" persons were all likely to be ungovernable). In action, however, he defined "ungovernables" in relational terms. He had abstracted the various attributes of rebels into a pattern combining two attributes with a specified relationship between them. In his words, ungovernable individuals were those "persons who [did] not perceive 'You have him.'" That is, they were persons who perceived the situation to be one where the benefits of rebelling outweighed its costs. Benjamin had transformed the indicators of

10.  Bruner, et al., *Study of Thinking*, p. 41.
11.  The best example of a disjunctive pattern involved the legal problem of searches and seizures. During some of the years of this study, the police were faced with the problem of applying a concept of a "constitutionally reasonable search." This concept was archetypically disjunctive: the Supreme Court of the United States had defined it as a search made pursuant to a judicial warrant, *or* one made without such warrant under any of four conditions: *either* (1) incident to a lawful arrest; *or* (2) in an "emergency" to prevent the destruction of evidence; *or* (3) in "hot pursuit" of a dangerous suspect; *or* (4) when the suspect consented. To the average young police officer, who could detect no "relationship" thematically equating all these alternative attributes of a constitutionally reasonable search, this concept was confusing. Because it seemed without pattern, it became a matter of rote and quite unnatural.

     What made it particularly difficult was the number of attributes which a policeman had to check out in order to classify the search. There was real cognitive strain in remembering to look for the presence of the various attributes of a constitutionally reasonable search: *five elements were hard to recall and apply, particularly under severe stress.* It was, as one professional said, easy to "lose the concept of search and seizure. It's a delicate concept."
12.  In the case of the "constitutionally reasonable search," policemen tended over time to redefine it in relational terms: a search was reasonable when the value of preventing loss of evidence (i.e., the difficulty of replacing it) outweighed the danger of abusive exercise of police discretion.

"ungovernability" into a two-factor relationship. In short, Benjamin calculated the problem of rebellion in terms of the citizen's perception of the likely payoff of rebellion.

Economizing on the number of factors which had to be scanned created two difficulties for Benjamin. First, each of the two factors tended to be highly abstract, and a series of procedures had to be developed to convert concrete reality into "costs and benefits" which fitted into the abstractions of the formula. For example, think of the cost-benefit calculations which had to be performed to classify a citizen approaching with his hands in his pockets (where a weapon might be hidden) according to the formula of rebelliousness.

Second, the factors had to be in a specified relationship to one another, and determining the direction of the relationship set the policeman a new task. If the question was whether one factor "outweighed" or was disproportionate to the other, then the policeman had to develop measures of the values of the attributes in question. He had to discern degree. The question became how much of the attribute was present, not simply whether it was present.

For example, policemen looked for a citizen's weakness. What was meant by "weakness" was the importance which the individual attached to certain other persons (e.g., his wife), things, status, or hopes, and his perception of how policemen could retaliate against them as hostages. Policemen developed terms to describe the citizen's perception of the likely costs of rebellion, like "remorse," "pride," "buttering up," and "ready to sacrifice himself," to express degrees of "weakness"—from a lot down to none at all.

In assessing degree differences, the policeman needed measurements, and it was crucial that he be able to articulate those measured differences. As a general rule, if he did not have an adequate vocabulary of degree, a policeman ceased to sense differences of degree over the long run. On the other hand, if he developed a language signifying degree difference, then he tended to perceive acutely.

The absence of words to express nuance diminished the individual's perception of nuance and hence handicapped him in his use of relational patterns. According to police testimony in the interviews, some policemen on coming into the department seemed intuitively adept at distinguishing matters of degree even though they lacked the ability to label the differences: their background gave them an initial advantage over their fellow recruits ("innate judgment"). However, over the long run, learned familiarity with linguistic distinctions tended to heighten perceptual acuteness and narrowed the gap between those policemen who started with "innate judgments" and those who did not. Conversely, over time, for those men who remained linguistically obtuse, the capacity to make fine judgments, to discriminate between discernibly different situations, diminished. It was as if their mental filing system were not sufficiently indexed to handle the increasing overload of fieldwork.

A policeman's vocabulary did not necessarily have a great elegance. They used prefixes like "ultra-" as in "ultraprudent," or "super-" as in "supernice," "supernasty," "superhonest," or "superbrutal." These linguistically rough diamonds helped to cut up the world into groupings on the basis of relational attributes. Some policemen had relatively simple measuring devices of an Aristotelian sort: two extremes and a mean position. It allowed them to distinguish between citizens who were sober, "drunk," and "had been drinking"; between behavior which was prudent, "a danger," and "a hazard"; between situations where one "stuck to a decision," "backed down," and "reassessed the situation"; between conduct which was "mousy," "overbearing," and "aggressive"; between "letting your beat go to hell in a hand basket," "bounty hunting," and "traffic enforcement." Far from being mere semantic quibbles, these characterizations of nuance sharpened a policeman's discriminatory powers no end. As in every other scientific enterprise, police judgment of the future was predicated upon a technology of measurement, a vocabulary of degree.

Policemen gravitated to using relational patterns of attributes notwithstanding the difficulties of using them. Why? In the end, a relational pattern was the most economical intellectual compromise. Given the cognitive strain of managing a substantial number of attributes, on the one hand, and the costs of making mistaken predictions, on the other, the best trade off was to focus on a pair of attributes that had a "natural," i.e., nonarbitrary, relationship between them.

In reducing cognitive strain, it increased judgmental time. After all, the function of judgment was to increase the time available to prepare for the anticipated event. Focusing on two attributes and the relationship between them consumed less time than checking for the presence of many attributes, and if the prediction was no less accurate, the officer had a better chance to prepare his first remarks or to get his hand closer to his gun or to alert the radio room to have the ambulance ready or to evaluate the options available to protect himself and his citizenry.[13]

## V

A policeman's judgments were beset by uncertainty. He could not avoid acting on the basis of predictions, and often he did not have adequate

13. It needs to be said that one of the frequent functions of prediction is to prevent the prediction from coming true. Contrary to historicist prophecy, judgment, like social

information to make an accurate judgment at the outset. In short, he was likely to make many mistaken first judgments about a matter.[14]

Thus, a policeman had to learn how to *confirm* his first predictions. Confirmation involved two distinct operations. He had to doublecheck whether his observations were accurate. That was the question of *reliability*. Had he correctly scanned the harbingers? He also had to be sure that the harbingers denoted the concept. Was the association between cue and consequence sufficiently uniform to support the inference from part to whole? In short, were the presuppositions about the connection between indicator and what was indicated correct? That was the question of *validity*.

Let's return to Benjamin and his effort to define the situation of the sleeping driver. Instead of dusk, let's put the time later in the evening. Darkness would have fallen, and the streetlight would not have penetrated the interior of the car.

In those circumstances the expression on the driver's face and even his first reactions to the policeman's knock on the window would not have been clearly visible to the policeman. Benjamin might guess their nature from the sketchy shadows he discerned, but his observations would necessarily be less reliable than in daylight. It was a greater gamble to identify the man as a governable or rebel late at night because of this unreliability.

Were Benjamin to use a flashlight to illuminate the inside of the car, this effort to increase the reliability of his observations would diminish the validity of the results of his cigarette test. Using a flashlight meant that he would have intruded not only the pack of cigarettes but also a dazzling beam of light into the driver's focus of attention. Under these less controlled circumstances, did anger or panic signify "ungovernability"? Decreased validity resulting from this alteration of the pure cigarette test aggravated the uncertainty of judgment.

It might appear obvious that the less reliable the scanning or the less valid the test for harbingers, the greater the policeman's incentive to try to confirm his earliest predictions. That truism turned out to be more obvious than true. In a policeman's life, doublechecking had far greater value under some conditions than under others.

In Laconia from time to time a citizen was mistaken for a rebel when in fact he was not rebellious. Once in a while policemen misjudged and would "waste" a citizen by being overly suspicious. Justice described a case where

---

science prediction, is a tool which permits men to take steps to facilitate *or* avoid the anticipated outcome.

14.  Peel, by overstating the point, underscored the bafflement of the patrol officer: "The good policemen never avoided anything. They have gotten used to the idea that their predictions will be wrong 99% of the time."

he nearly made an error of oversuspicion: "I had a drunk one time. He complained he was real sick. His liver was spent. I decided, finally, to call the ambulance instead of the wagon. It turned out he was sick, and he did die eight hours after he arrived, but at least he did not die with us thinking he was a phony. He was sick even though he smelled of booze." As unfortunate as mistaken suspicion would have been, however, the personal repercussions for Justice if he had presupposed that the drunk was faking it would have been confined largely to the moral realm. Justice might have felt a degree of guilt, but legal or professional sanctions would not have been visited upon him for the "reasonable" mistake of suspecting that a wino's complaints were phony.

On the other hand, mistakenly trusting a real rebel, taking him for being "under control" when he was not, involved far graver perils for the policeman. Peel described something very close to a mortal error of judgment on his part.

> Once deep in West Laconia I saw a car on the side of the road with its wheels jacked up. As I looked at it, all I could see was a forehead and a nose in the front seat. There could be a couple fooling around, or smoking pot, or someone in trouble. So I parked my car across the street, turned the radio up loud to make a lot of noise, and walked over from my car, leaving my door open. I knocked on the window, and there were four guys in there. And they all came out, and they were all bigger than I was. And they all were intent on beating themselves up a cop. It took a lot of talking. I kept talking futilely and backing up as best I could. But those four were bent on attacking me. They had gotten around me. I was trying to back up. I had already concluded the fact I was going to be beat up and that I wasn't going to use my gun. Well, it turned out all right because a night watchman, who is real friendly with all the policemen—a big black fellow who is called Big Willie—was returning home from work. He had a big dog, and all policemen know him. He saved my tail then.

These two incidents, one involving what nearly was an overly suspicious assumption and the other involving an overly trusting one, illustrated what Bruner and associates called the "asymmetry" of the risk of mistake.[15] Let us sketch the problem of the uncertain policeman in a payoff matrix in table 3.

The matrix reveals the nature of the asymmetry of risk in the policeman's case. In the event that an assumption was erroneously suspicious, the policeman ended up unhappy but at least had the consolation that he was alive to appreciate his unhappiness. In the instance where the mistaken assumption was initially trusting, the policeman's mistake was not redeemed

15. Bruner, et al, *Study of Thinking,* pp. 113 ff. The payoff matrix is directly taken from their discussion of the problem of asymmetrical risk.

Table 3                                The Uncertain Policeman

| Policeman's assumptions were initially | Citizen was really | |
|---|---|---|
| | Governable | Rebellious |
| Suspicious: policeman was | alive and unhappy* | alive and unhappy |
| Trusting: policeman was | alive and happy | dead* |
| Likelihood | .80 | .20 |

*Consequences of being mistaken.

by the fact of personal survival. The mistaken oversuspicion meant wasting a citizen; the mistaken overtrust meant death. There was a qualitative difference (which all policemen appreciated) between being wrong and being disastrously wrong.

In international politics, policy makers often talk of the minimax strategy. To undertake a course of action so as to minimize the maximum risk constitutes such a strategy. The minimax strategy for the policeman, under the conditions sketched in the payoff matrix, was to adopt the suspicious assumption, thereby reducing the chances of the worst injury, his death, from 20% to zero.

The minimax strategy in a context of risk asymmetry, however, had a peculiar side effect in police behavior. It eliminated any incentive the policeman might have had to check whether his initial assumptions were correct or not. Another look at the payoff matrix would confirm that it made no difference to the suspicious policeman whether his judgment was right or wrong. Whether or not he observed the harbingers correctly, and whether or not he drew the correct inferences from them, were matters of indifference to him. In both cases he was "alive and unhappy." The trusting policeman stood in contrast. Here, being right or wrong made a world of difference. The incentive to doublecheck the reliability and validity of his judgment was compelling. Where the risks of mistake were asymmetrical, the incentives to confirm were also asymmetrical. In the case of the minimax strategy, for example, confirmation of the suspicious assumption was a waste of time.

When we talk about a policeman's inclination to doublecheck his judgments, we are, of course, talking about his *skepticism.* Under the conditions of the minimax strategy, at least, a policeman was likely to develop an imbalanced skepticism, one that would check his optimism but never his pessimism.

In fact, instead of the suspicious policeman's having an incentive to confirm the accuracy of his judgments, he had an incentive to develop the reality to conform to his assumption. A prevalent mistake among policemen, one professional remarked, was "becoming too aggressive in the beginning.

Those fellows who don't allow things to progress on their own, those who don't experiment. It's like they've got tunnel vision. They start by predicting the end results, and that's the way it's going to be."[16]

What produced these incentives to make reality conform to one's worst predictions? What induced some policemen to make a pathology out of their prophecies? The answer was that some policemen preferred to produce a violent world in which they had some mastery over techniques of controlling violence than live in an uncertain situation where their special techniques did not give them an advantage. In the worst war between governors and rebels, these policemen felt they were at least equipped to protect themselves. In a world where it was not certain that their physical prowess and forceful skills were appropriate, it was also not certain which persons would be in control of events.

One way to alter this pathological structure of incentives was administrative surveillance. By intensifying organizational punishments for mistaken oversuspicion, for example, the chief, through Internal Affairs, sought to make the consequences of mistaken oversuspicion more closely equivalent to the dire results of mistaken overtrust. The chief established a system to investigate any officer who got involved in more than a minimum number of violent public altercations, thereby penalizing unchecked pessimism and making the risks of mistake more symmetrical.[17]

We will want to examine whether other means existed to influence policemen to acknowledge and cope with these four problems of judgment, i.e., the problems of clumsy experiments, blunt perception, unbalanced skepticism, and pathological prophecy. More particularly, we will return at the end of this chapter to the importance of learning as a way of building in restraints on the minimax strategy, with its nonscientific and antiskeptical implications.

## VI

So far the argument has run as follows. First, police judgment depended on grouping individuals into classifications according to their rebelliousness or

16.  The "tunnel vision" emanating from the minimax strategy was not a phenomenon which occurred only in the policing world. Robert Kennedy noted it in the sense of "betrayal" felt by the Joint Chiefs of Staff when Krushchev backed off from Cuba, contrary to their suspicious assumptions. Kennedy, *Thirteen Days* (New York: Norton, 1969), p. 97. As the professional Peel observed, "They make a prediction and it's a personal attack if the prediction doesn't come out."

17.  It was the necessity to restore some symmetry to the risks of erroneous judgment which led one officer to observe: "A police officer has to be chastised, has to receive a reprimand when he makes a bad judgment. . . . What makes an institution strong is that this kind of supervision gets institutionalized."

governability. Second, the act of grouping depended on the discernment of certain anticipatory cues, or harbingers. Third, discernment depended on the visibility of these harbingers, and when they were invisible or observation was uncertain, officers sometimes experimented with the situation so as to develop some perceptible harbingers. Fourth, as a general rule, the reliability and validity of the grouping were directly related to the number of harbingers discerned, yet multiple harbingers became increasingly unmanageable and time-consuming; hence, the police tendency was to scan for a smaller number of harbingers that had a specified relationship among them. Fifth, detecting relationships between harbingers depended on discerning differences of degree, which in turn depended upon a vocabulary of degree. And sixth, when the correct character of the harbingers was uncertain, the direction in which the guesses were made depended upon the asymmetry of the risks of mistake.[18]

To obtain perspective on the problem of police judgment, let us observe it in a context different from the quiet Friday evening involving Officer Benjamin. Let us examine a "hot caper," one in which the circumstances were more obviously dangerous—a crime had been committed, a crowd had assembled, and drugs had diminished the governability of the situation.

Moreover, the policeman involved was younger, less experienced, and of a more intense temperament than Benjamin. What made the two situations interesting parallels, however, was that the problem of police judgment abided in both. The task for both policemen was to predict. Much depended on that judgment: the officers' safety and that of their citizenry.

Here in the cops-and-robbers language of a then relatively inexperienced patrolman is the account of the hot caper. It was Mike Bacon speaking:

> We had to make an arrest of a rape and kidnap suspect. We had gotten the story from the victim, but her girl friend ran off to tell the suspect we were coming. It was a race between us and her to see if we could reach him before he split. The girl beat us to him. We had to go in after the suspect. We decided not to wait until our cover came, a one-man unit. It was 6 A.M. New Year's Day. It was bad police procedure, but our cover was one of those bad cops I was telling you about. Who knew when he was going to show up! The suspect's father answered the door. He was a huge man, as was the suspect, who was six foot three. We asked, "Was Marcus home?" "Yeah, and he's in his room sleeping. What do you want him

18. Bruner, et al., in *Study of Thinking,* summarized the factors which made a concept and the attendant procedures for attaining it effective: "the defining and criterial status of attributes, their immediacy and proneness to masking, their linguistic codability, the nature of their ranges and transition values,... the manner in which they may be combined, ... the number of attributes ..., and the number of attribute values that are actually used by an individual in discriminating one class of objects from another [p. 45]."

for?" "We want to talk with him." "Yeah, what do you want to talk to him for?" "Well, he may have done something wrong, and we may have to take him in to talk it over." Just at that moment Marcus appeared at the bedroom door in the back of the house and yelled to his father, "Hold them at the door while I get a shotgun." The father slammed the door in our face. By this time we had every right to bust in. The suspect was in the house. For all we knew he was going after a shotgun. The suspect had been accused by his victim. So we broke in, and there we were inside, and there were five adults and about nine kids in that house along with us. We sent out immediately a 940A, and meanwhile the big sister, there's that big sister again, she had picked up a broom and commenced to belt my partner's shins, and a couple of others started in on him from other angles. The father meanwhile had picked up a cast-iron pot cover and was advancing toward me. I had my gun out on Marcus trying to keep him away from the shotgun. The old man was coming at me, and I let out a call for a 940B. Well, we fought and fought. Unfortunately I had to bonk the old man with my club, right square on his head, and broke the skin and it started bleeding all over the place. It didn't seem to bother him none, however; he just kept at me with that cast-iron pot cover. Foster, my partner, meanwhile got out the Mace and was spraying it everywhere. He started shooting, and he squirted me full in the face. I lost my club, my bullets, my handcuffs. Finally, the cover unit showed up, and we got the handcuffs on Marcus and his father. We were losing, and we had to do something, but it's the last time I do that. We'll wait till four men are there. But it was a tough situation. Marcus had made up his mind, he wasn't going to jail. And he had just shot up on heroin. That was another bad police procedure. We even knew he had just taken heroin. But—, Well, it turned out we arrested his sister, father, and the suspect. It still would have been a fight. They had said he was in the house, and in effect you were not going to enter the house to get him. That's an ultimatum. We just had to go in. Then he had threatened us about going to get a shotgun. . . . I could have legally shot the old man. I was seriously in danger, and I could have shot the suspect. But I've never shot anybody, not even a round, and I hope I never have to. I could have put life in danger, however, by withholding my fire. We were real lucky. If this were typical of police life, I would resign today.

The critical figure in the episode was the father.[19] Bacon knew little about him or about what he was going to do. He saw his size and knew that he was

19. The concept of the critical figure had its best expression and illustration in the comments of Officer Wilkes. His remarks provide an instructive perspective on what Bacon did not do—namely, he did not look for the governable person who could turn a rebellious situation around. Wilkes was talking about a question he had been given by an interview board when he applied to become a policeman. "The second situation, and this was the greatest question of all. . . . You're off duty (and in Memphis, you had to carry your gun with you at all times), and you're walking home and you're walking by a bar, and you hear

the father of "a rape and kidnap suspect." Bacon could not detect with any certainty whether the father had been alerted by the girl friend's warning, whether he knew about his son's alleged misdeeds, or whether he appreciated that heroin was circulating in his son's system. Bacon was not even sure that the father knew the son was awake in the house. Nor could Bacon perceive the father's purposes: what other family members he was concerned about, whether he was confused or determined, whether the avoidance of physical injury to life and property was important. In short, when the father first opened the door, the harbingers were insufficient for Bacon to make a good judgment about whether the father would be governable or rebellious.

Like Benjamin, Bacon did not immediately jump to conclusions. He experimented to get more harbingers of governability. To evoke cues he presented a question and an explanation: "We asked 'Was Marcus home?' 'Yeah, and he's in his room sleeping. What do you want him for?' 'We want to talk with him.' 'Yeah, what do you want to talk to him for?' 'Well, he may have done something wrong, and we may have to take him in to talk it over.'" Bacon's engaging the father in conversation had several functions. One was to evoke sufficient reactions from the father to determine his uncooperativeness. As an experiment, however, it contrasted clumsily with Benjamin's experimental offer of cigarettes.

First, in tone and in content, Bacon's remarks constituted a threat. They established a relationship between the policeman and the father which was coercive, not reciprocal or moral. Second, Bacon required as a harbinger of governability that the father back down unconditionally—permit his home to be violated, surrender his son. Since the experimental factor was an ultimatum with a single proper response, Bacon was not ready to discern the father's reactions in terms of degree. Bacon's receptors were not attuned to nuances of equivocation, uncertainty, ignorance, hesitation, or internal

---

wild noises from within. You look into the bar, and there you see a larger man fighting with a smaller man. At this point the large man gets on top of the man and is pummeling him. You enter the bar in plain clothes. You enter the bar, and you identify yourself as a police officer, and you order the big man to get off. He refuses and keeps on beating the guy. And the crowd comes at you menacingly. What do you do? One guy, he said he would pull out his service revolver and fire into the air. If the crowd wouldn't stop, then he'd start shooting. He actually said it.... He didn't make it. I still remember my answer. I would seek help. There was only one guy in that bar—the one guy I could depend on is the bartender. He depends on us for him to run the place. After all, I could close his joint down. Those are the exact words I used, as a matter of fact. And even though the crowd wouldn't necessarily believe I was a police officer in plain clothes, he was going to pay attention. I would tell him to call for assistance. But the fact was also I have a life in jeopardy. That little guy: he's being beaten up, and the next blow might kill him. So I would give a tremendous order for the crowd to stop. And I would order them to assist me in saving this guy. Then if that didn't work, I'd take the guy on, and probably I'd get my ass kicked in. I've thought about that question since then, and even now ... I would do the same thing probably."

moral conflict. His measuring tools were too blunt to evaluate anything but a simple "yes" or "no" reaction.

Third, the response which Bacon would accept as the correct one was so narrowly defined that it did not constitute a valid basis for an inference about the concept-pair governable/rebel. An "incorrect" response did not persuasively point to the inference that the father was going to be ungovernable.

And fourth, the procedures which Bacon developed to detect harbingers ignored the importance of time. If the father had been ambivalent in purpose when he came to the door, if he had been confused or surprised, the tilt of Bacon's procedures forced him to become decisive under the most adverse of circumstances: without a chance for appraisal of the situation, without a sober second thought, without the effects of subtle police manipulation of the context of decision. The method of Bacon's experiment presupposed what was really problematic, namely, that the father's mind was already "made up" when it may not have been.

Bacon knew that time was of the essence, that he was in a "race." When Marcus appeared at the back of the house, Bacon had even less time to judge the father's stance in the matter than he might have counted on. When the father slammed the door, however, Bacon drew the inferences that the father was a rebel and would "fight."

Now this inference of a rebelliousness might have been correct. Its validity depended, however, on a number of assumptions: (1) that Marcus really had a gun and ammunition; (2) that the father would let him use the gun; (3) that the father did not care about the danger to the other members of the family; (4) that the father was willing to have his house destroyed in a shoot-out; (5) that the father was in complicity with his son; (6) that Marcus was cunning, not confused, scared, and uncertain; (7) that the effects of Marcus's heroin would not wear off; and (8) that the extension of time would aggravate the dangers inherent in the situation.

All these assumptions were plausible, but, interestingly enough, they were identical to the same suspicious assumptions which the policemen would have made if they had adopted a minimax strategy. Given the asymmetrical risks of mistaken assumptions about the father's purpose—to cooperate or to rebel—Bacon's suspicious assumptions worked to minimize the maximum danger (Bacon's loss of his life), even if the best possible outcome had to be sacrificed to the "bust-in" implied by these suspicious assumptions. Bacon interpolated the most pessimistic guesses to fill the gaps in his judgment. He predicted the most dire contingencies, with the intention of preventing the worst outcome. Without doublechecking whether reality confirmed these assumptions, he took steps which made a more benign result impossible.

A policeman always had it more within his capacity to bring about destruction than to produce a constructive result, to create the "worst" he feared rather than the "best" he hoped for. He had a measure of control over fulfilling prophecies of doom, and if he would rather be prophetic than productive, he could almost invariably succeed.

## VII

The intellectual work of a policeman consisted, not of one, but of two distinct jobs—judgment *and* understanding. He not only had to predict the future but he also had to explain the past. The policeman was always confronting himself with two very different questions. On the one hand, what will people do? On the other, why do people act as they do? In Lane's terminology, in addition to needing "temporally to know what went before and what is likely to follow," the policeman acted as if he also needed "spatially to know the terrain, in human terms to see the play of the many motives involved."[20]

Why did policemen need to supplement their judgment with understanding? What prompted them to expend energy to "see the play of the many motives involved" if they already had the judgment to know "what is likely to follow"? For one thing, judgment was predominantly a passive and receptive activity. It took the world "as is" and anticipated its flow. It was an adaptive mechanism, accepting events as determined and out of control.

Judgment alone was insufficient to permit a policeman to influence citizens except through anticipating their behavior. Judgment was insufficient in instructing a policeman how to "relate" to persons. It was inadequate to make citizens act differently from what was predicted of them. Judgment was necessary, but clearly insufficient, to govern others.

Thus, one motive to understand sprang from the need to lead events. Once the policeman went beyond detached prediction of human behavior and sought to influence it, he had to understand human nature. Understanding constituted the know-how, the knowledge of cause and effect, in short, the technology of governing.

The imperative to understand had other sources. In a modern world haunted by Greek rationalism, people were always asking one another, "Why?" Thus, understanding was expected of policemen. To avoid the humiliations of falling short of this widespread social expectation, policemen had to respond to ready questions with ready and acceptable answers. One could envision an incurious society where the troublesome legacy of Socrates and the risky presumptions of intellectual freedom did not exist. In such a place the question "Why?" would never be asked, and respect would not be granted on the basis of satisfactory answers to it. Twentieth-century Laconia,

20.   Robert E. Lane, *Political Ideology* (New York: The Free Press, 1962), p. 350.

however, was not such a society; it was more typically rationalistic—and irksomely inquisitive.

Finally, understanding was something citizens and fellow officers alike wanted. As a result they were willing to deal for it. A policeman could trade helpful explanations for cooperation. By increasing his reserve of understanding, a policeman increased his own personal resources of influence. The professional Wilkes referred to the interpersonal value of understanding when he remarked, "Citizens talk about [police]men who understand." Under reciprocal circumstances, at least, sharing an understanding of the human "play" was a way of putting others who wanted a policeman's understanding in a position of indebtedness to him. Like the lending of nickels and dimes on skid row to denizens who were thirsty, so the dispensing of wisdom helped develop beats where the citizens were curious.

In short, the motives to cultivate understanding stemmed from the need to manipulate, social expectations, and self-enrichment in a world which was willing to credit knowledge.

## VIII

Among Laconia patrolmen there existed two distinctly different "understandings" of the human condition. These two outlooks I have called the cynic perspective and the tragic perspective.[21] Policemen developed toward one or the other of these perspectives: their views, often amorphous and inchoate at first, gradually took shape and assumed a fullness identifiable as the cynic or tragic understanding. Let us turn next to a description of these two perspectives.

## IX

The word cynic comes down to us from an historical and respectable tradition of Greek philosophy. Cynicism was an ancient philosophical sect. Its founder was Antisthenes; its major figure was Diogenes, who lived in Athens in approximately 350-323 B.C. as an exile. He was penniless, an ascetic, a wandering beggar. Having been politically disgraced in his hometown, Sinope, he lived in Athens unhampered by family ties, local notions of civil obligation, or social traditions of civility. According to the major modern scholar of cynicism, Diogenes was rootless, austere, indifferent, contemptuous of the public's opinion of him, uncompromising, and remorseless in his ridicule of the simpletons and fools who trafficked in the

21. See above, chap. 4.

world and its marketplaces.[22] In short, he was the epitome of minimization, the ideal player in the extortionate transaction—the dwarfed target. He embodied the classical defenses against coercion: dispossession, detachment, remorselessness, and irrationality.[23]

There were three themes in Diogenes's cynicism. The first was that mankind was not unitary, but dualistic. Mankind was divided into two kinds of people—friends and enemies, cynics and fools, the strong and the susceptible, those with and without "virtue."[24] Virtue was the awareness of the advantages of amounting to nothing and having nothing. Cynicism denied the brotherhood of man and insisted on dividing the world into two classes: the susceptible, made so by their ambitions and possessions, and those who were smart enough to know how to become invulnerable by dwarfing themselves. That was the cynic's starting point.

A second theme which pervaded cynicism was fault-finding. "The fault is always in ourselves."[25] Suffering was always a matter of personal choice, the product of vainly striving to be someone or have something. If an individual had chosen to forego the cynic's virtue, he had only himself to blame. Anyone who suffered simply lacked the self-discipline to train himself in self-denial, indifference, and renunciation of the false currency of civilization—its common materialistic sense and its dainty, civilized values. The sufferer was weak of will, having neglected the stringent training of the cynic and having pursued the insipidities of self-enrichment. Diogenes himself "used to roll in hot sand in summer and in snow in winter, using every means of inuring himself to hardship."[26] One who inured himself to such hardship and thereby developed such absolute self-control did not have to give sympathy or show sensitivity to the foolish persons who were too flaccid or frivolous to accept the imperative of self-sufficiency and its painful implications. If the fool suffered out of greed or weakness, it was his fault and deserved no concern. Cynicism was a one-dimensional world view in which society consisted of injustices, which the foolish lacked the self-control to endure without showing fear and to which the virtuous had the strength to submit without admitting pain.

The third theme was individualism—"the extreme in individualism."[27]

---

22. Donald R. Dudley, *A History of Cynicism from Diogenes to the 6th Century* A.D. (London: Methuen, 1937), pp. 17–39.
23. Legend has it that Plato (who died c. 347 B.C.) used to say of Diogenes, "That man is Socrates—gone mad." (Ibid., p. 27.)
24. Ibid., pp. 5, 97.
25. Ibid., p. 67.
26. Ibid., p. 33.
27. Ibid., p. 37.

The asceticism of the cynic was such that he denied any interdependence with other individuals. Diogenes Laërtius, a later emulator of Diogenes, described his model of the virtuous person: "those who were about to marry and refrained, those who intended to go on a voyage and never set sail, those who thinking to engage in politics do no such thing, those also who purporting to raise a family do not do so, and those who make ready to associate with tyrants and yet never approach them after all."[28] In other words, the praiseworthy cynic was the one who refused all human ties, who exposed no potential hostages. This extreme individualism was intended to make the cynic invulnerable to the coercive influences of others. It was the ultimate in self-defense. It insulated the cynic from moral conflict between the codes of civility and extortion by spurning civility.

Thus, three themes sustained Diogenes's cynic perspective—the dualistic conception of mankind as two warring camps, a simple causal theory presupposing the individual's absolute self-control over his fate, and the defensive virtue of complete indifference.[29]

Officer Chuck Kane was a young Diogenes. He was sufficiently self-conscious about the shape of his "outlook" that he had begun to worry about it.

You become very cynical and tend to lose your sense of what peole are and what they feel. . . . A lot of times you just don't care any more. Most people are cynical. Eight and a half hours, and it's time to go home. In the meantime you're not going to care too much. . . . It seems inherent in the job. I guess it's just a defense mechanism. Day to day you see so much suffering and pain: problems you can't do anything about. If you have any sensitivity, you'll go off the deep end entirely unless you become cynical.

Kane was very young when I first met him; he had just reached his twenty-third birthday. But he had been a policeman almost five years, since he was eighteen. He had been a police cadet, assuming full police responsibilities in a small city police department before he was accepted on the Laconia department at twenty-one. He was intelligent, articulate, graceful.

28. Quoted in ibid., p. 37.
29. Dudley explained the development, popularity, and reoccurrence of cynicism in history in terms of its utility as a reaction to worldly catastrophe. Cynics, in his view, were persons who faced real terrors and had discovered a way to surmount them—by living at the "minimum," by dispossessing themselves of their property, attachments, scruples, and hopes. Where mankind was mean, personal liberty depended upon a mean, i.e., a destitute, existence: to forego the vanity of being or having something. " 'Vanity of Vanities,' saith the preacher, 'all is Vanity'—the author of Ecclesiastes was, like Cynics, a product of the Hellenistic age, a time when old standards had been discarded, and the individual was left to the mercy of capricious but irresistible force." Cynicism was a way of coming to terms with cruelty and danger. In such times, escaping the meanness of others was paramount, and all else in this practical joke of a world was illusory. (Ibid., pp. ix-x, 37.)

On the language, math, and perception tests qualifying him for admission to the department, his scores had been among the highest. He had been the valedictorian of his recruit class. His evaluations during his probation period in the field were of a high order. Moreover, he was taking college courses, on his way to a B.A.

But he had no wife, no family, no attachment to the city, no ambitions in the department. Furthermore, he had no niche within the department. Because he was attending college on a full-time basis, he worked a permanent third watch and was assigned to the pool. He described himself as uninterested and uninvolved, "not very anything about the department" or about anything or anybody.

He reflected the three themes in Diogenes's cynicism. For one thing, he divided the world into two asymmetrical groups, the people who, like himself, "knew better," and the rest. In the "rest" he lumped the citizenry of Laconia ("People are a lot different in the city") and the insincere or pretentiously idealistic police officers in the department: in short, practically everyone he came in contact with. For a second thing, he was blind to causal factors at work in the world other than individual self-interest: there was no mention of accident or the forces of necessity. In his own case he could detect some subtle pressures which made his own behavior "not my fault," but as for the rest, the "different" people, their behavior stemmed from foolish or vain purposes. They were too weak to control their illusions and to stop "building up their egos." Finally, since it was men's perversity which brought about their suffering, victims and victimizers alike were to be ridiculed, not helped. A victim of a car burglary, for example, was a "stupid shit." When I asked him if there was any usefulness in getting to know persons on his beats, Kane responded he had no interest in such activity: "If people get to know you, all they do is call you more often. They come to you with problems they wouldn't ordinarily bother a police officer with."

Nor did he want to become a member of any police squad: "Quite frankly I like to work in a district where men are not close; there is more freedom." Freedom from the irritations of interdependence, of having to care, was everything. Kane was slowly being "dwarfed into sluggishness."[30]

Kane was still extremely young. His cynic perspective was not fully crystallized, and he was equivocal on many subjects. In the year after I saw him, he married and was beginning to make plans to leave the department for work which would be less "monotonous." But the cynic themes still persisted. He had seen the world. It was all the same, repetitious: the cruel and the strong prevailed over the foolish weak, who were dumb enough

---

30.  The phrase comes from Helen Garwood's study, *Thomas Hardy: An Illustration of the Philosophy of Schopenhauer* (Philadelphia: Winston, 1911), as quoted in Richard B. Sewell, *The Vision of Tragedy* (New Haven: Yale University Press, 1959), p. 130.

to care about things they could not protect. It was "boring," observing the stupidity of the simpletons who failed to see that the secret of life was to turn indifferent, to live by the "minimum." He had begun to drive away from the action, going down to the waterfront and watching the river pass by, scorning the illusions of those he could "not do much" for.

To see Kane's cynicism more clearly, however, it is important to analyze the perspective he did not develop: what he did not see and what he did not become. To this problem we now turn.

## X

If in the cynic perspective the experience of pain and fear was both avoidable and shameful, the tragic perspective conceived of such experience as universal and profoundly important. Rather than something to be denied, pain and fear and the self-conscious experience of them which we call suffering were to be admitted and learned from. It was suffering which enabled the individual to learn to feel what wretches feel and which bound him to the family of man. The very measure of an individual was the manner in which he faced and surmounted this terrifying prospect of inevitable suffering. In light of the tragic perspective, the individual who became a cynic, who lived by the "minimum," simply "dwarfed" his humanity. In abstaining from defying "destiny," the cynic failed to press for the "total yield" of life—the knowledge of the potential magnitude of human response to the terror and preciousness of life.[31]

Those policemen who developed this tragic understanding expressed three themes. The first was that all mankind was of one substance. Individuals shared a community of unjust suffering. Their oneness stemmed from their common plight. Every person was faced with the recurrent existential question of whether to give up to his suffering, acquiescing in the futility of illusory values, or to persevere, thereby defying the possibility that life in its irrationality was meaningless. No member of mankind, be he policeman, wretch, or notable, ever permanently and securely settled that question for himself. Persons constantly wavered between submitting to and defying their fates. They might think they had made a final choice, thinking that the spiritual problem had been abated, but it kept being stirred up, quenchless. The tragic perspective was, thus, a unitary conception of mankind; it affirmed the moral nature of the individual and his need to be somebody and to count for something despite vast spiritual uncertainty, despite the doubtfulness of values.

Second, those policemen who developed a tragic perspective affirmed a

31. Sewell, *Vision,* p. 7.

much more complex causal pattern at work in human affairs than cynics perceived. A tragic sense presupposed an "interweaving" of chance, free will, and necessity: accident, self-control, and inevitable factors outside the control of the individual each had substantial influence on his or her life.[32] As noted before, the cynic did not deny that this complex causal pattern existed. He simply dismissed it as irrelevant, since it was absolutely up to the individual to adapt to it. The individual could freely decide for himself to encumber himself, making his worldly baggage and attachments a hostage for others to seize, or he could live by the minimum. In refusing to adapt to suffering in this way, the policemen who developed a sense of the tragic were stimulated to understand the factors of accident, necessity, and human resiliency.

The third theme in the tragic perspective was the precariousness and the necessity of human interdependence: precarious because dependence on others exposed an individual to the risks of undependability, necessary because human solidarity was the foundation of a meaningful life. Self-sufficiency was not possible, for "We are all responsible for all."[33] Responsibility limited an individual's ability to escape pain and suffering. It implied "exposure," as several policemen expressed it. Liberty was not freedom from feeling and suffering. Rather it was the freedom to expand understanding of the human condition and to increase knowledge of how to face and fight against the suffering universally afflicting mankind. Liberty was, as one professional put it, the freedom to have "a lot of memories" and a hard-won wisdom.

Charlie Prince was a young old-timer, thirty-two years old, a veteran of more than nine years on the department. Within a year of my first meeting him, he was severely injured by a motorist who ran a stoplight and rammed his motorcycle. Prince retired from the department with a crippled right leg. He did not have a college education. He had married young, had had children, and then had seen his family dissolve in divorce. He had remarried, and his "optimism" had begun to revive. When I first met him, he was, in the words of one admiring young officer, "the wittiest and sharpest and quickest guy on the squad." In talking with him before the accident, I was struck by the accuracy with which he could reconstruct his own life. In the narrative of his life, the outlines of the tragic perspective were evident.

As I've looked back and observed my own career, I begin to see I had a real good family. There was a lot of sickness in my family, and we all had to take care of each other. I had my first job when I was 12, when I lived with

32.  The word "interweaving" is Herman Melville's; quoted in ibid., p. 98.
33.  Dimitri Karamazov in Dostoevski's *The Brothers Karamazov,* quoted in ibid., p. 114.

my grandmother. When I first came on the department, I had little compassion for anyone. I was a hot dog; I was immature. But one day I looked back and I related to the past, how my family did things. A lot of my thinking—I make judgments from how I feel. When I get in a situation, I ask, How do I feel? I look at the man, and I carry it over to him. You know, I consider myself average, and I ask, How would I react to what I'm doing to him? Would I like to be talked to this way? I remember back to when I got tickets. Now I don't do my job in a way I'd like not to be handled myself. . . . I've been fortunate. I've moved around a lot, and I've been treated nicely by command officers, particularly by the lieutenant in the Vice squad. He liked me. On the Vice squad I saw so much, all the details of life. I was on all the details, homosexual, prostitution, drugs, and they were such sad things. I found myself saying, "Oh, my God, I wonder how they got that way." I got along with the prostitutes. I didn't call them stinking bitches. I'm not one to get on the bandwagon and explain things in terms of economics. In my mind people get that way not necessarily out of economic necessity, but because they had no love. My parents were poor, and they were divorced when I was seven. But I had lots of love. They sat down to discuss why I did things. When you're on patrol, all you do is take reports and handle family beefs. Well, when you're 23 years old, and you referee beefs all day, generally you get tired of hearing about others' marital problems. Most police officers have marital problems of their own. As far as Vice is concerned, most guys who go there, it has an opposite effect of the kind it had on me. You're working with dope fiends and perverts all day, and a guy on the Vice squad usually goes down; he deteriorates; he becomes like the people you work with. But I gained a lot; if I had had to stay there longer, I would have deteriorated. What saved me was I had a commander, a lieutenant. He was a lot stricter with his men than his predecessor, but at the same time he was a fair man, a lot more human. He had a sense of humor, and that means a lot to me. It was hard to be upset with the guy. . . . The lieutenant brought me up from the bottom.

There were the three themes of the tragic perspective. First, there was the unitary conception of man: we are all "average," or, as Prince said elsewhere, "You take the lowest crumb. Basically he doesn't want to be that way. He'd like to be better, and basically he'd like to have things better." Second, there was the interweaving of the three factors of human causation—accidents, like having "lots of love" from his family; the human and freely willed capacity to ask "why I did things"; and necessity, here "economic necessity." And third, he recognized his dependence on human solidarity and the responsibilities it created: because someone had "brought him up . . . from the bottom," he was stirred to "compassion" for the "sad things." What a critic once wrote of the suffering Job could have been written of Charlie Prince: "By now he had come to see his own ways and his own complaints in a different light. He sees his misfortunes not as unique but as typical of man's lot. In one phase of his being, at least, he is becoming a partisan of the human race."[34]

## XI

Thus far we have separated police knowledge into two parts. On the one hand, there was *judgment*, used to predict the specific actions of others, particularly sensitized to anticipate subtle auguries of danger and rebellion inherent in specific situations. Judgment involved the development of the concept-pair of governable/rebel and practical procedures to "attain the concept" in the real world. All policemen who patrolled Laconia streets, where the risk of physical injury was so pervasive, resorted to the same categories of judgment. They differed significantly only in the skills with which each recognized and dealt with the four problems of judgment—(1) the clumsy experiment, (2) the immeasurability of degree, (3) the imbalanced skepticism, and (4) the pathology of prophecy.

On the other hand, there was *understanding*, used to explain the human condition in general, particularly focused on the problem of human suffering. Here policemen differed in their appreciation of the universality of suffering, the causes of it, and the remedies for it. Some policemen developed what we have called a tragic perspective, others a cynic perspective.[35]

How did judgment and understanding relate to one another in the policeman's being? Which was the tail and which the dog? Did the judgments made by policemen to cope with the dangers of rebellion ultimately dictate their choices among competing visions of mankind? Did the strain of judgment amidst dangers inevitably bend their understandings away from the civilized and tragic notions about suffering and produce cynicism?

Or was the opposite true? Was understanding the matrix of judgment? Did a policeman's abstract understanding of mankind determine the skill with which he devised procedures to make judgments about danger? Did the tragic perspective incline a policeman to acknowledge the four problems of judgment, while cynicism led him to ignore them?

On first impression, the problem of judgment, so intimately involved in

---

34. Ibid., p. 18.
35. All the policemen in the sample gravitated to either the tragic or cynic perspective. Perhaps a few recruits had embraced at the outset of their careers a third "outlook," say, an idealistic or a romantic understanding, but these mental constructs of the human situation were temporary and unstable, foundering on the immutable and pervasive condition of human misery.

personal survival, might seem to be the dominant causal factor. In this view, understanding simply amounted to an ex post facto rationalization of an individual's techniques of judgment and the implications of the skills he developed to cope with danger.

For example, there seemed to be a good fit between the policeman's judgmental groupings of mankind into governables and rebels, on the one hand, and the intellectual dualism inherent in the cynic perspective separating the simpletons and the virtuous. Moreover, the policeman's cunning in finding ways to make a potential rebel aware of the costs of rebellion paralleled the cynic's sensitivity to each individual's vulnerability from caring about things. Furthermore, as natural as it was for the cynic scholar Dudley to explain the character of cynicism in terms of the terrifying condition of the Hellenistic world at the time of Diogenes, equally naturally an observer of police was inclined to treat the omnipresence of danger in the policeman's world as the determinant of his personal philosophy.[36]

But for two reasons, one logical and the other empirical, I came to question the plausibility of this cause-and-effect relationship.

The logical basis for doubting the hypothesis was that the fit between the cynic perspective and the judgmental categories of the policeman proved to be less than perfect. True, both the cynic and the policeman anticipating danger divided mankind into different groupings. But if judgment and the cynic perspective were to be logically congruent, the "governable person" became the equivalent of the simpleton, while Diogenes, the policeman, the wino, and the rebel were cloaked in the same "virtuous" cloth. The latter were able to defend themselves from the coerciveness of others because they each lived the same self-denying life of the moral and material dwarf. It was true that the extreme cynics among the policemen—like Kane—came to denigrate the submissive "good citizen" for his susceptibility to suffering, but even Kane never readily grouped himself in the same category of mankind with the dispossessed, the desperate, the cruel, and the crazies— the "rebels," in short. In other words, the intellectual boundary separating cynic and fool did not fall along the same dimensions as the judgmental line between rebel and governable. The fit was illogical; the implications were distressful.

Compared to cynicism, the tragic outlook was at least equally compatible with the imperative of making judgments about danger. After all, the tragic perspective presupposed that all individuals possessed simultaneously qualities of civility and rebellion. Mankind was one, was "average," was of one mold, but the mold contained an inherent dualism. Every man hoped and despaired at the same time; in the face of suffering he wavered between

36.   See Jerome Skolnick, *Justice without Trial* (New York: Wiley, 1966), chap. 3.

responding with magnitude and resigning himself to being a dwarf. The human animal was, in short, both governable and rebellious. The tragic perspective was not at all incompatible with the judgmental problem of discerning whether a person was, *in a given situation,* a subject or a rebel.

The second basis for questioning the hypothesis that danger caused a policeman's outlook to sour into cynicism was empirical. Not all policemen were cynics. Prince coped with the same dangers as Kane and had to perform the same judgmental tasks of concept formation, concept attainment, and confirmation. But he did not see humanity's suffering in the same light as Kane.

The competing explanation—that understanding bent policemen in the direction of one type of judgmental procedure or another—was more persuasive for two reasons.

It coincided with the observations of cause and effect which veteran and sensitive patrolmen themselves made. As the perceptive Prince expressed it succinctly, "I make judgments from how I feel [i.e., understand]"—not the other way around.

Moreover, it explained the results of an experiment in learning which took place in the department. With a description of that experiment we bring this chapter to a close.

## XII

The department did a great deal of teaching. The education of the organization took place constantly, sometimes formally and authoritatively, sometimes informally and extradepartmentally. Its effect was to shape the men's understanding.

To begin with, the Training Academy, with its heavy doses of sociology and ethnic history, was one departmental means of raising questions about human nature, the causes of suffering, and the efficacy of extreme individualism. The academy program, however, preceded the police experience and had to prepare the recruits for it. Consequently, its prime objective had to be the improvement of judgment, not understanding. The academy drilled recruits in scanning reality for danger (and taught them to ignore "irrelevant" factors). The dominant effect on most of the recruits was to make them start "thinking the police way"—to trigger their capacity to anticipate trouble. In stimulating recruits to make prudent police judgments, the academy necessarily deemphasized the function of shaping understanding.

Organizational education did not stop upon the recruit's graduating from the academy. Once an individual became a beat officer, the teaching of understanding took place at lineups and in settings like locker rooms and the local bar.

No influence, however, was more critical than the policeman's sergeant (or, in the smaller specialized units like Vice, his lieutenant). To be sure, many sergeants did not take full advantage of their opportunities to influence; other sergeants made such clumsy attempts to shape their squad's understanding that they inspired a backlash. But some sergeants worked consciously and effectively to instill one kind of understanding or another. Their methods differed, but their purposes were plainly to make the men share their visions of mankind. What follows is a description of how one sergeant proceeded to counter the cynic vision of his squad and replace it with a tragic outlook on mankind. By no means was this sergeant typical. What he did was extreme and unorthodox, but his very deviance suggested how influential a sergeant could be.

The sergeant was Bob Peel, whom we met in chapter 7, coping with the crowd scene. When I began my study, he was a patrolman. In the course of years, he was promoted to sergeant and assigned to supervise a traffic squad.

Sergeant Peel conducted his educational course at line up, in the half-hour which preceded his squad's going into the field each day. Initially, he capitalized on his men's curiosity about the department and their unfamiliarity with the organization. "How did the department work?" he asked. What were the personalities of the chief and the command personnel like? How did their outlooks differ? How did decisions get made? How did their personalities and the different units they supervised all fit together? "To most of the men the chief was like a complete unknown. . . . They felt like basement policemen. . . . They were scared of the rest of the department because they didn't know anything about it." Peel encouraged the lineup discussions about the department to be informal, "two-way talk," and in this obviously useful and nonthreatening context, most of the men joined in. As a result, they perceived a more complicated and strategic picture of the department.

Peel gradually led this analysis of the administration into a discussion of a second topic, the nature of man. He did it in this way. In the midst of discussing the department's method of evaluating its personnel, Peel had each member of the squad do a self-evaluation on department forms. Then, on the pretext of showing how subjective personnel evaluations were, he had each squad member solicit five additional evaluations of himself—one from each of the four members of the squad who knew him best and one from Peel as his sergeant. A general discussion followed about how differently individuals perceived one another.[37]

This discussion of the possible variety of perspectives on human nature

---

37.  In a similar vein, Sergeant Peel took advantage of an upcoming squad party to distribute a list of squad members with the instructions: We are giving a party; at the party each

was merely the beginning. Peel began to explore the complicated psychological and moral nature of human beings, and particularly of men who became police officers. To this end he opened a number of topics commonly considered taboo in the department. What was the "quota system," the implicit imperatives which pressured police to make a minimum number of arrests to indicate their "productivity"? Quotas were a phenomenon within the department which were simultaneously denied and acknowledged but never discussed, hence never evaluated. The topic of quotas led naturally to such "unanswerable" questions as, What did it mean to be a policeman? What were the attributes of a good policeman? From there Peel led the discussion into the topic of "manliness": What did it mean to be a man? What were the attributes of a good man?[38]

The third and final phase of this education was examining the nature of the city. What was a city? Why did people live in Laconia? What made parts of a city live and others die? Knowing that policemen tended to see only the pathologies of a community, Peel convened his squad for lineups in different parts of the city—in the lovely grounds of the cathedral, at the port, the museums, the factories, the parks.

With subtlety he devised ways of having his men test their developing understandings about the department, the city, and mankind. He encouraged them to experiment. Believing in the stimulant of action and application, he encouraged his men to plan and implement new ways in which the squad could better operate. Suggestions ranged from mounting the unwieldy radar equipment on motorcycles (it did not work) to more complex schemes. One was to carry parking and traffic enforcement into "the hills," in the interest of applying justice equally: do unto the wealthy as the poor were done unto. Peel let his men's plan go forward, and his own words tell the story:

One day we went up to the hills and for an hour tagged every parking violation in sight: wheels not curbed, cars parked on the wrong side of the

---

officer will get a prize; for each squad member, write what his prize should be for. "It was amazing to me how skillful these men were in finding the weakness of their fellows, of how accurate they were in applying the needle." By the time this and other self-revealing games were played out, there was little room left for pretenses. In the course of these evaluative exercises, each officer began to realize what the others knew about him; he "knew what he didn't have to try to hide."

38. Sensing that sexual exploits and derogatory talk were conventionally perceived by policemen as indicators of manliness, Peel set out to explore these officially taboo topics. For example, he had his men compile on the blackboard of the lineup room all the vernacular put-downs for blacks, Chicanos, Indians, and Asian-Americans. Listing 120 pejorative terms for blacks on one blackboard had the effect of relieving the stigma and the tensions the officers felt in talking about their feelings about "these people." The discussion flowed to such questions as, Why did policemen feel a sense of comfort in using these characterizations? Where did these characterizations come from?

road, just a multitude of dangerous situations. And the men had a field day: like sticking your hand in a jam pot. Well, the fan really blew. The telephone started ringing in the chief's office, the deputy chief's office, the city manager, and every friend of a friend. I anticipated all that; so I had written a letter to the chief before he called me in, saying that we had done this up in the hills and the parking violations were so out of hand up there that we didn't have the manpower to do our job properly, and that we were ceasing to patrol up there until the department had made a calculated decision as to how manpower was to be allocated for that purpose. Until further orders we were hereby ceasing to go up there. Well, that took the wind out of the criticism. You can't very well tell people to stop doing something they've already told you they had stopped doing.

What was educational about the incident was the insight it provided about the department, the city, and human nature. For example, it raised questions about the accuracy of any possible cynic division of mankind into virtuous and nonvirtuous along economic lines. Thinking that the wealthy and the poor were "different," the one virtuous and the other base, was an easy assumption for Patrol officers to make if they were assigned exclusively to the flatlands and never ascended into the hills except as nonthreatening public servants. The experiment exposed the fact that the wealthy were no more governable than the poor when their oxen were gored.[39] In such ways Peel forced his men to become self-conscious about their understanding, to apply it experimentally, and to reformulate it in light of the results. He was a gifted educator.

The reader should note the difficulty of Peel's being the effective teacher he was. A sergeant, successfully to provide this fundamental kind of organizational education, had to satisfy five conditions.

First, he had to be able to create a kind of "irresponsible" sanctuary for learning, a place where the trials and errors of his men were indulged. Unless he could avert the severe penalties which could be inflicted from outside the squad, there could be no experimentation. Peel had to have the capability of taking the responsibility himself ("riding the heat," "taking the flak," "backing up his men") and surviving. In the ticket spree, for example, he ingeniously anticipated the public's reaction and "took the wind out of the criticism."

Second, he had to reconcile his job as the men's supervisor with his role as

39. John Russo, who was described in chapter 2, was a member of Peel's squad. He remarked to me: "One thing I've learned from this job. On Patrol I used to deal only with poor people, and I thought they were terribly rude and uncooperative. But in Traffic you work the hills a lot more: your major problems are people speeding to and from work. The rich people are three times worse than the poor people in the flats. They expect you to do what they call you for, like getting a cat down from a tree, arrest other people, and not bother them. And they really rise up and call you every name in the book."

their educator. One might think that supervisory power would be an advantage in teaching, but power has a tendency to intimidate and stultify, to produce a rote of acquiescence, when, on the contrary, Peel wanted to encourage his men's initiative to reassess mankind. To overcome this implication of power, Peel created an atmosphere in which the rule of law prevailed. He convinced his men that they had a right to argue with him and could do it with impunity within certain limits.[40]

A third condition was having time for instruction. Peel frequently extended his lineups beyond the allotted half-hour. Because his squad was a Traffic patrol, the periodic absence of his men from the street was not terribly important. In orthodox patrol work, the consequences of under-manned beats would have been more dire.

Fourth, the sergeant had to keep the respect of his men. Touching their understandings as intimately and unconventionally as he did, Peel had to create the legitimacy—the acceptability—of what he was doing. In overcoming the suspicion that he was perpetrating "sensitivity training," he was helped by the fact that he had impressive police skills and was eloquent and clear-minded.

Finally, he had to be a teacher who taught himself how to teach, for the department at that time gave sergeants no training in how to be sergeants, much less in how to counter the cynic perspective of their men.

When these five conditions—of sanctuary, fairness, time, legitimacy, and competence—were met, a sergeant could have significant effects on the understandings of his men. The cynic perspective gave way. Among Peel's men there bloomed a "pride," an appreciation of the meaningfulness of being a person who was doing police work. John Russo, whom the reader met in chapter 2, and Jim Longstreet, who had taken a hike on skid row, both happened to be in Peel's squad and they testified to the effects: a "regeneration" of curiosity, a replenishment of morale and energy, an enthusiasm, and an increase in "self-respect."

But most interesting was the unmistakable impression I had as I watched them work that their judgmental procedures had changed: their experimental probing for harbingers of danger was more subtle, the vocabulary derived from their new understandings was incorporated into discerning subtle degrees of behavior, their skepticism was better balanced, and they were relieved when events did not deteriorate to fulfill prophecies of doom.

On Peel's squad, altered understanding changed judgmental procedures.

---

40. Peel discussed the importance of fairness between teacher and learner: "I try to encourage independent judgment. As a matter of fact, whenever I talk to a man about a mistake he may have made, they always throw that statement back in my face. 'Well, Sarge, I just exercised a little independent judgment.' And that stops me."

## XIII

Does understanding affect judgment, or judgment understanding? Lest the reader be left wondering about the importance of this chicken-and-egg conundrum, the question has significance for policy. The answer to it helps a chief decide what reforms should have priority.

When the direction of cause and effect between two factors can be pinned down, police organizations come to see their opportunities differently. Put yourself in the shoes of a chief with a limited budget and limited personnel. The question he must ask himself is whether he should allocate substantial amounts of time, effort, and money to affect his men's judgment or their understanding. Should he develop an elaborate and expensive mechanism to detect and punish their mistakes of judgment, arising as they do out of an imbalanced skepticism and a pathological inclination to fulfill the worst prophecies? Or should he concentrate on giving his officers an effective liberal education on the nature of human suffering? Both courses involve heavy costs, and choices have to be made about the proper trade-off between punishment and learning, between coercive devices or character-shaping ones.

That is why the question of the relationship between judgment and understanding is so important. For, depending on which determines which, the better choice is to give priority to shaping the dominant one and then fostering the conditions under which it can most efficiently determine the other.

# 11

# The Development
# of Morality

Men are not corrupted by the exercise of power . . . , but by the exercise of power which they believe to be illegitimate.

*Alexis de Tocqueville*
Democracy in America
1835

But with policemen, it's kind of rough to carry about these guilt feelings.

*Officer Jay Justice*
Laconia Police Department
1973

## I

When we speak of morals, we deal with profound questions. What is the meaning of life? Do the risks I run and the privations I suffer matter to society or mankind? Are the sacrifices I make and the hurts I inflict justified in God's eyes, or mine?

Out of hope that life has some meaning, we create bench marks to measure the moral distance we have thus far traversed. Such milestones may be public in nature: How many people have I "helped"? How many potential victims have I saved from harm? How much better have I made a community? On the other hand, our measures may be more private ones: How much have I improved myself? How far have I moved my children toward knowledge, security, or happiness? How closely have I adhered to God's law?

We define these personal objectives as moral milestones because we have faith that they indicate the direction of our ultimate moral destination. As we pass these bench marks, the end of our journey becomes more fully imagined and sharply seen. The better perception of the journey's end confirms the direction of our early course or tells us that the steps we first took were of no or slight account. Negotiating life's course is a cyclical process of checking bench marks against ultimate destination and defining the ultimate in terms of what was learned from attaining immediate bench marks. In this respect we are all moral philosophers.

The policeman was beset by the same profound questions of moral philosophy as any other member of mankind. He was likely to cover these profound and disturbing thoughts with self-deprecating and unpretentious terms. He would talk of his "pride," his "role," his "definition of the job," his "police culture," what made him "feel good," and the way he "sees the job." Underneath these small phrases, however, lay the big, insistent problems of existence. Am I dealing out my life in coffee spoons to no purpose? Or do I matter? He developed short-term goals; he established moral bench marks; he ordered his life according to his moral code. But he was all the while formulating a moral destination which might confirm or undermine the value of the steps thus far taken, the milestones thus far attained. At once, he selected moral bench marks and formulated the ultimate moral goal that made reaching them worthwhile. Or, to use a phrase which Chester Barnard used in another connection, simultaneously and all the while the policeman pursued immediate incentives and also "the incentive that makes other incentives effective."[1] The substance of the policeman's moral philosophy was critical in how he performed his job.[2]

## II

The sources of these moral bench marks—the short-term goals, the tentatively adopted code of conduct—were many and varied among policemen. If asked, the typical officer responded, "I use in my job a lot of my upbringing, my religion, my experiences in my own family situation...." Out of the reciprocal and civilizing ways of their pasts, policemen selected certain ideals to mark their first entry into the police world. These estimates of moral value they brought to the police organization.

Superimposed on these early notions of right and wrong was the learning gleaned from the police life. Anxious about being accepted, the rookie usually took as his first professional guideline the respect of the experienced officers: "A rookie has the problem, how does he show he deserves to wear the uniform and not be considered a hot dog," a sensitive officer said. As

1.  Chester I. Barnard, *The Functions of the Executive* (Cambridge: Harvard University Press, 1938), p. 283. This chapter is largely derived from Barnard's remarkable book.
2.  Elton Mayo expressed the same point: "If an individual cannot work with sufficient understanding of his work situation, then, unlike a machine, he can only work against opposition from himself. This is the essential nature of the human; with all the will in the world to cooperate, he finds it difficult to persist in action for an end he cannot dimly see." Mayo, *The Human Problems of an Industrial Civilization* (New York: Macmillan, 1933), p. 119.

time passed, confidence tended to increase, and the nature of acceptable conduct became clearer and more acceptable internally. "You're ordained as a policeman, so to speak," remarked the thoughtful and devout Haig, and the sign that an officer was ready for ordination was his appreciation of the "policeman's code of honor" and his willingness to make his personal moral code conform to it.

The provisions of the code were numerous. They covered every aspect of the patrolman's activity. Some derived from departmental policy: "Don't backdoor it," for example, restated the regulation against taking any gratuities from a citizen. Some reinforced the civilized morality of childhood: "Refuse to do anything illegal or immoral." But much of the code embodied admonitions and taboos which dealt with the peculiar coercive technology of the policeman—his reliance on threat in defending himself against the paradoxes of coercion: "You cover your men: don't let any officer take a job alone." "Don't get involved." "I'm not going to turn in another officer." "Be firm." "Keep a cool head." "When you've handcuffed a guy, you are taking care of his welfare and his rights, and you have to look out for them and not treat him as if he were in the ordinary situation where he can look out for himself."

To violate provisions of that code was shameful and entitled other officers to be upset with the offending officer and to chew him out. The "code of honor" formed the common belief which made the department a community, and the moral and social compulsions to abide by it were considerable.

An officer felt obliged to "qualify morally" every action he took. Such scruples made policemen extremely reliable. The threat of retribution for violating the code shored up each officer's sense of responsibility.

## III

Whatever the sources of these moral injunctions, however, when the individual policeman came to apply them, he often faced three distinct kinds of difficulties, which I have called the problems of moral conflict, moral discretion, and moral perception. They were problems respectively of contradiction, capability, and characterization.

*Moral Conflict.* The most obvious problem was that of moral conflict. The trouble with the police code of honor, from a patrolman's point of view, was that it had too many provisions in it. It overmoralized. To the rookie the injunctions were stated too categorically and universalistically. One provision often contradicted another when it came to application, and the conditions under which one injunction was more important than the other were left unclarified and inexplicit. Thus the policeman found that any solution he concocted was right from one angle but wrong from another.

It did not take too much acquaintance with what an officer encountered on his beat to appreciate the potential incompatibility of these moral provisions:

| On the one hand | On the other hand |
|---|---|
| "Stick to your responsibility." | "At one time you are crime-fighter, psychiatrist, social worker, minister, doctor—and you're the only one around." |
| "Don't cover a job alone." | "Handle your own load," i.e., avoid making unnecessary calls to other officers for help. |
| "Deter the incidence of crime." | "Don't jack up a neighborhood." |
| "Don't get involved." | "You gotta have empathy." |
| "Don't turn in an officer to Internal Affairs." | "Don't do anything illegal or wrong." |
| "Be firm; don't lose face." | "The first thing . . . you're nice." |
| "Don't break the law to enforce the law." | "Use your discretion." |

For every moral injunction, there seemed to be an opposite one equally applicable. These conflicts derived in largest part from the contradictions between the conventional morality of civilization which the individual carried with him into the department and the extortionate morality of coercion which he learned from his police experience. Thus, the police code of honor contained contradictory admonitions to forgive and be remorseless, to be empathetic and indifferent, to develop a beat reputation for goodwill and for ill will, to be prudent and proud, to be self-defensive and aggressive. The moral conflict to which the policeman could be exposed was extreme.

*Moral Discretion.* A more subtle problem was that of moral discretion. Moral discretion involved means and ends. In the moral realm policemen excused themselves from accomplishing ends where the means were unavailable. They did not blame themselves for being earthbound if they had no airplane. Moral discretion raised the question of whether a conceivable means was practically available and should be employed. If it was too complicated or time-consuming or demanded extraordinary skill, then for practical and moral purposes, it was not available, and the failure to accomplish the end was not blameworthy. Lacking the capability, a policeman was acquitted of responsibility.

For example, juvenile shoplifters presented a problem of moral discretion. On its face, the deciding whether to take a juvenile petty thief into custody or "let him go" after admonishing him to go straight might appear merely to be a problem of moral conflict: to protect the victimized shopkeeper by being severe or to rehabilitate the kid by being lenient. In fact, however, in the typical Laconia case, that conflict was not a real one. The recognized necessity was to save the shop from being pilfered out of business. In reality the apparently "severe" option of arrest usually did not serve efficiently to ensure the shopkeeper's survival. Court-inflicted punishments were likely to be so light and the time in custody so brief that the kid would be back on the streets after a quick ride to headquarters for booking.

More often than not, the so-called lenient approach was the only conceivable means with the slightest chance of helping the storekeeper in the future. But there were risks in an officer's trying to talk a kid into straightening out. If the policeman undertook to rehabilitate the youth but lacked the capacity to "relate" to him, then the officer would suffer abysmal failure in his moral purpose. Having chosen this particular means to the end, he assumed the difficult obligation of handling the juvenile well.

Moral discretion—born of the awareness of the wide choice among means of differing complexity and effectiveness—raised the question of inadequate skills. When a policeman took no action because he doubted his ability to execute practical and permissible means, he felt guilty.

The high degree of skill which Laconia policemen often practiced in discretionary situations was illustrated by an exploit by Officer Joe Wilkes, the former boxer turned policeman, who became so attached to the juveniles on his beat that he devoted a major part of his off-hours to local youth groups.

I'm thinking of a problem that occurred to me, where I used initiative.
There was a recreation building which had been broken into down at the
Saint Anthony Project. There was a tremendous amount of loss—almost
all the sports equipment was taken in the burglary. O.K. I could have
made my report. That would have done it. That could have settled the matter as far as I was concerned. But then I thought about it. If I made out a
report and sent it up through channels, we would never get any of the stuff
back. Then I looked around. A lot of the kids in the area I knew, and I
knew they knew about it. I knew that what had happened was that someone had burglarized the place, for something valuable, and that with the
place open, kids had come along and helped themselves. So I gathered the
kids around, and we talked, and I told them my understanding. I told
them that I really appreciated the fact that they weren't involved in the
break-in, and that they were keeping the equipment for the project. I
was interested in getting the equipment back, not in making any arrests.
Besides there was a good chance that if we couldn't get the equipment
back, that there would be no equipment for the neighborhood at all; not
until the new budget was passed could we get some new equipment. Well,
sure enough, soon about a dozen kids were bringing me the stuff—balls,

bats, the works, They'd say, "I was holding it for you, Joey." I was on a personal basis with all of them. And, I emphasize, that really helped. Sooner or later we got back damn near everything, except maybe a couple of footballs. Then I turned to them and said, "It would be a shame if Mrs. X (she was the lady in charge of the center) came down here and saw all this mess." Some of the floorboards had been taken. Paint and stuff was thrown all over. It was a real mess. A lot of vandalism and all that. So we sat down, and we began to discuss matters. I said, "I thought these things were for them; it was all theirs to play with: it was for everybody in the neighborhood. And it was a shame to have things so messed up." So they cleaned up the whole mess that night, and when the Park and Rec people showed up in the morning, all they had to do was to board up a few windows. And since then I haven't ever had a report on that building being broken in.

Then I did one more thing. I made them understand that the individual who broke in initially was selfish. Now, if I would have arrested the first one to bring in a ball or something, they would never have brought in any more stuff, and what good would it do. It would have created animosity.

Police discretion allowed policemen like Wilkes to use "initiative," but it had significant effects in the moral realm. On the one hand, it heightened the standards of moral success, for discretion contained the obligation to develop the capacities to use it well. An officer who did not develop the judgment, understanding, and personal relationships that Joe Wilkes did was in danger of feeling morally inadequate because he could not successfully execute this extremely difficult way of keeping "that building from being broken in." Discretion, the perception of an increased range of available means, raised the minimum expectancy of a policeman. It tainted as a shortcoming the more simple reliance on "merely" making an arrest. On the other hand, a less skillful or experienced officer was not expected, either by himself or with others, to accomplish as much as Wilkes. The moral definition of success was lower and easier to attain for the ordinary officer. Only the most skillful, the noble in the profession, were afflicted with the extraordinary obligations of the aristocrat, with *noblesse oblige*.

*Moral Perception.* Moral judgments were deductive in nature. That is, the moral principles by which a policeman regulated himself amounted to major premises in the moral syllogisms of the officer. The facts and the probable outcome of his actions constituted the minor premise. The conclusion was derived from fitting the minor premise into the major premise and in turn dictated whether the action the policeman was going to take would be morally worthwhile.

Wilkes's moral judgment in the case of the burglarized recreation building had this syllogistic form:

1. All "initiative" (i.e., acts which would keep the building from being broken in) was morally valuable. (Major premise)

2. Making the kids "understand" the selfishness of burglary and not reporting them was "initiative." (Minor premise)

---

3. Making the kids "understand" was morally valuable. (Conclusion)

The process by which he fitted the premises together depended upon the distributed middle term, "initiative," the term common to both premises which disappeared in the conclusion. To fit the minor premise into the moral major premise, Wilkes had to characterize his specific actions in terms of the abstraction, "initiative." This process of abstract characterization was often problematic for a policeman because he had a choice among divergent abstractions, into any of which his actions might reasonably be fitted. For example, Wilkes could have perceived his efforts, not as "initiative," but as "softheartedness" or even "favoritism." In either case the facts would have fitted into a different moral major premise (e.g., "softheartedness is an ego trip"), with very different implications for moral worth. Which moral premise was activated depended on choices among alternative ways of seeing things. Moral perception referred to this process of choosing among these plausible abstract middle terms.

To illustrate how policemen encountered the problem of moral perception, let us look at Tony Chacon. When I first talked with him, Officer Chacon was a man of considerable intelligence and fortitude. An officer who could speak English and Spanish, he had not always been so promising a person, at least by his own account. Born in Laconia, raised by a father with great energy and determination, Chacon had misspent his youth meaninglessly in high school. Upon graduation, he had been called up by the army, but he flunked the intelligence test.

> I came out of Edgehill High School in such bad condition that I couldn't pass the Selective Service exam. I told myself I'd better get out of here. So I went to junior college and read *Newsweek* and *Time,* and I made vocabulary lists of words I read and could not understand, and I made a lot of associations with older guys.

Having learned to educate himself, he joined a small-town police department and, after a year's experience, resigned to join the Laconia department. The skill with which he performed his police work and the "benefit" he brought to his beats were important to him: "I ... have pride in [them]."

Chacon talked about a problem of moral perception which had given him particular difficulty:

> Yeah, like this one guy, he kept giving his grandfather a hard time. One day the grandfather took a stick to him and really took it to him and

knocked him unconscious. Well, in the report I made the grandfather the complainant and the grandson the provoker and put in something about self-defense. I figured if the detectives did not like it, they could reverse it. But it wasn't right that the old man suffer trouble on account of that kid . . . .

In those situations you get very personal. Your values get involved. Most of the time it's these domestic situations where the complicated problems arise. And that's why it's so important that you don't get a guy who doesn't give a shit. He's messing around with people's lives and can really wreck them if he's not careful.

Well, it was quite evident that the young man, from previous knowledge of him, was an asshole, and the old man had a nice background, was a good worker. You need just look at their personality, their attitudes, so that any rational man could make up his mind that the old man did not attack this boy without provocation.

Chacon did "give a shit" about this domestic situation, and therefore he perceived the facts in terms of "right" and "wrong," in terms of a moral code, the provisions of which included competing principles: (1) don't let malevolent youths hassle respectable old men; and (2) don't let hysterical old men injure youths who are momentarily frustrated by adolescent feelings of worthlessness. In abstracting the case to fit one of these two premises, Chacon proceeded by analogy. He perceived differences between this particular grandfather and the hysterical old men he had encountered before. Here there was no history of drinking, no prior record of temper tantrums, no early retirement from working life. On the other hand, Chacon recognized in the checkered past of the grandson a significant resemblance to the "assholes" of life. Memories of Chacon's own childhood flitted in and out of his moral consciousness, providing him with the analogues necessary to make these assimilations. Chacon's moral conclusion was that he was dealing with a "malevolent youth" and a "respectable old man." And he intended to take action according to the way he characterized the facts and to the moral principles which were keyed to those characterizations.

The problem of his moral perceptions, however, was "complicated" by the fact that he was a policeman. As a policeman he had a second moral obligation: to square his moral perceptions with the legal implications of the situation. That is, his moral and legal judgments were supposed to parallel one another, not work at cross-purposes. The moral and legal syllogisms were supposed to point to the same actions independently. In the case of Chacon and the disrespectful grandson, this necessity for parallelism created a difficulty, for Chacon's choices of a middle term in the *legal* syllogism were much more confined than in the moral syllogism. He was restricted to assault with a deadly weapon, self-defense, and (for sentencing purposes) circumstances in mitigation. There were no legal equivalents for "grandfather," "old man," "good worker," "asshole," and "disrespectful." In legal terms the perceptible facts were that the grandfather was in control of the "stick," the boy's head was bashed, and the grandfather was unscathed. These facts pointed to the legal conclusion that the grandfather ought to be arrested, not the youth. To resolve this contradiction of law and morals, Chacon "put in" his report some untested inferences about provocation by the grandson. This unsubstantiated story bothered Chacon. He knew he was stretching the truth, yet he could do little in a satisfactory way about it. The choices he had made in formulating his moral perception of the matter had put him in the dilemma of being either a dishonest man or an immoral one (endangering "your job or your respect on it" was the police description of the dilemma).

These moral decisions, the problems they provoked, and the manner in which they were resolved profoundly affected the moral landscape of the individual policeman. The bench marks he began with were eroded or were reestablished to mark out new courses. In turn, these short-term changes forced alterations in the definition of ultimate career goals, and these big changes induced a series of modifications of other moral guideposts immediately at hand. Some events precipitated more critical changes than others—more critical, because they were bigger or more lasting alterations in moral philosophy.

## IV

One such incident involved two men we have encountered—Chacon and the professional, Justice. The story typified the effect of critical events on moral growth. The terrifying aspect of this story was that there was no warning of this profoundly important challenge; all the choices had to be made quickly, spontaneously, without the luxury of months of collective deliberation. Lonely and hurried, these two men were rushed into the task of shaping and fixing their own moral destinies.

In his several years on the department, Chacon had shown no reluctance about resorting to necessary force, and he early developed a reputation as a "stick-man," as one who used his baton too readily. Accurate or not, this reputation was not diminished by a pair of public skirmishes which brought him before Internal Affairs for discipline. Because of his intelligence, his membership in a minority, his bilingualism, his intensity, and his dedication, and the potential for unusual good or ill which these qualities represented, the command officers in the Patrol Division decided to make Chacon a partner of Officer Justice, who as we saw was widely regarded as the best street policeman on the department.

Justice was upset by the decision. He had to vacate "his" beat, a mixed upper- and lower-income area, mainly populated by whites, and accept reassignment to Chacon's beat, then the busiest assignment in town and the area most distant from police headquarters. Worse, he changed supervisors; Justice had little respect for his new sergeant, and Justice's intimidating self-confidence increased his new sergeant's personal insecurities.

Justice and Chacon, however, worked well together. Justice was impressed by the way Chacon developed the beat. Chacon knew his own Puerto Rican and Chicano communities in the intimate and assuring way that Justice had known his former beat. The two men were alike patient and firm. They were craftsmen, and a mutual respect developed between them. They became comfortable, not strained, in their partnership.

That comfort was important. I know of no other relationship which would demand an equal degree of mutual forbearance and trust than a police patrol partnership. Without respect between partners, the work was unbearable.

Patrol partners sat within three feet of each other eight hours a day, five days a week, every week of the year. It was the closest kind of association, in which the smallest annoyance could be magnified into total preoccupation. Imagine the effect, within the confines of a patrol car, of recurrent habits like picking one's nose or one's teeth, cracking knuckles, tapping fingers on the car roof, holding forth in a distasteful one-topic conversation—or of having political differences, overoptimism or dour pessimism, smelly clothes, or a bad stomach.

On top of these petty annoyances must be added the significant problems of interdependence. For example, take driving habits. In the typical partnership, the men daily alternated between driving and doing the paper work. In police work, an officer who was a poor driver did not run the conventional legal risks. He was licensed to drive as fast or as recklessly as he wanted. It chilled the heart to drive with a man for a single eight-hour shift when he customarily traveled thirty miles an hour faster than was prudent down every thoroughfare. It aroused deep emotions to accompany a driver who raced through a quiet, child-filled residential area. In that most terrifying of experiences, the high-speed chase, the sense of loss of control, compounded by doubts about the driving skills of one's partner, were simply horrifying.

Moreover, officers depended on their partners in highly exposed and dangerous situations. "We're dependent on each other" was Justice's laconic summary of the difference between policemen and other workers. Any uncertainty about his partner's ability under pressure multiplied an officer's anxieties.

Furthermore, in this interdependence, differences in techniques of handling the citizenry often embittered the relationship between partners. Some men were mellower, some harder; some were more direct, some more tactful; some were more inclined to arrest, some to temporize. Policemen were humiliated by their partners' different working styles and full of apprehension about their possible consequences.

Finally, partners were responsible for each other's actions. If one officer fouled up and went to disciplinary hearings, his partner was possibly going to have his career damaged as well. ("Subconsciously, you always know when he does something stupid, you'll be in the grease too. If he goes, I go. . . .")

This dynamic of vicarious responsibility stemmed from the moral injunction to "back your partner up," a rule which gave rise to what I have called the complicity privilege. Whenever a matter might involve a public inquiry, every officer was obliged to back up his partner's testimony so far as necessary to defend him against charges of substantial wrongdoing. Either member of a partnership had the right to invoke the other's testimonial loyalty in matters that went to the public (or had the potential to go public; hence, in preliminary inquiries at the district level by the sergeant, the partner's privilege applied).

There were three functions of this complicity privilege. The first was a matter of equity—to compensate for the underdog status of policemen in general. The police job recurrently put officers into situations where they had to make unpopular decisions. Because their actions were coercive ones, they necessarily created antagonisms. As a result, there were always some enemies in the public, persons who wanted retribution. These intense few, with their extreme vindictiveness, applied pressures to any public inquiry that threatened its fairness. In the policeman's view, their presence dimmed the prospects of evenhanded justice. To the problem of due process was added the severity of disciplinary sanctions—termination of employment was always a possibility. Discharging a young officer for a misdeed probably meant the end of his career. Unlike the plumber or the bank executive, the discharged officer found no alternative employers available to hire his services (or at least so he thought). Termination was the equivalent of permanent disbarment for the lawyer or revocation of the doctor's license to practice medicine, decided in a process where mitigating circumstances were much less likely to be taken into consideration than in the case of an errant lawyer or doctor.[3] The complicity privilege functioned to balance the equities between the police and the intemperate segment of the public.

A second function of the privilege was assuring associational privacy. In this respect the complicity privilege resembled the privilege of spouses not to

---

3.    Officer Justice characterized this interplay between the department's injudicious public disciplinary process and the disproportionately heavy sanctions eventuating from it as a "paradox": "You expect more stringent conduct, yet you allow anyone to challenge our decisions, and we could be washed out. Doctors and lawyers have more liberties when they make an error than we do."

testify against one another. In both instances, privilege permitted a pair of persons to let the barriers down between them, to confide in and counsel one another. Such associational privacy was necessary, for both sets of partners, to permit an individual to unite himself with at least one member of the human race without fear of shame or injury. The department could not officially recognize this privilege in its regulations. The result of the discrepancy between the public posture of the department and the moralized practices of the organization was that a policeman could not legitimately invoke a privilege of silence, but had to speak out affirmatively and cover up.

The third function was prudential, an adaptation to the extreme degree of regulation to which police officers were subject. The departmental and legal restraints were so "stringent" that the men were always outside some provision or another—or in fear of becoming so imminently. Regulations pervaded their private and occupational lives. Violations were always occurring. If an officer took an afternoon off to see his son play football, if he gave a friendly lift in his patrol car to a group of juveniles, if he accepted a discount on a set of automobile tires, or if he made a judgment which on hindsight was not optimal, then he was an "outlaw," subject to the threat of being reported by someone with an ax to grind. Where everybody was a wrongdoer, no one escaped the restraints of mutual extortion. The universality of the "dirty linen" that resulted from this state of superregulation functioned in much the same way as an exchange of hostages between enemies. It conduced to a high degree of prudential cooperation.

The privilege of complicity, however, bound only partners. The code did not apply categorically to nonpartners, and an officer was not dishonored if he stated the facts honestly about the misdeeds of an unrelated officer, provided that a personal grudge was not the motive and that the offenses were grave enough.

In Laconia the general rule was that each officer had a fair opportunity to select partners and switch them. If a man's partner was a terrible cross to bear, at least this was a burden freely assumed. The assignment of Chacon to Justice's tutelage was a rare exception to the rule of voluntary partnerships.


## V

One day on a beat adjacent to that of Chacon and Justice, three Laconia police officers responded to a 999, a family beef. The subject of the complaint was a white man who had inflicted severe injury on the woman involved, and the officers intended to make an arrest. Suddenly, the man darted away, jumped in his car, and escaped. An officer put out a radio call, identifying the man and the automobile. Justice and Chacon were the first to catch sight of the fleeing car. On went the red light and siren, and a high-speed chase ensued, during which the two officers witnessed the escaping driver narrowly miss a number of pedestrians, then sideswipe two cars, and finally purposely try to ram a pursuing police car.

Miraculously the driver escaped all his pursuers. However, he apparently had second thoughts and returned to his apartment, placing himself in the custody of the original arresting officers.

Meanwhile Justice and Chacon, having lost his trail, circled back to the address from which the call had originated. Chacon, who was driving, recognized the wrongdoer talking to the police officers, stopped the patrol car, got out, ran at the culprit, and struck him in the face with a blow which knocked him down.

In the subsequent official inquiries into the assault, the reasons for Chacon's actions were disputed. Chacon testified that the arresting officers had failed to handcuff the subject, nor did they then know of the prisoner's attempt to crash into a police car. He had escaped once before, and so long as he was not in cuffs, he was not under sufficient control, in view of his ruthlessness. The sergeant supervising the arresting officers charged that Chacon lost all self-control and had simply brutalized a man who had already given himself up.

Chacon's explanation of his own actions implied a criticism of the arresting officers and their sergeant: they had taken inadequate precautions to secure a dangerous prisoner who had once before escaped them. When the sergeant charged Chacon with brutality in his report of the incident, however, there was no escaping an official inquiry and the joining of fellow police officers in the distressful position of making mutual accusations.

Justice was called to testify twice in the matter; once at the Internal Affairs inquiry (which found that Chacon had acted wrongly and concluded he should be fired) and once before the Civil Service Commission (which unanimously reversed the findings of Internal Affairs and ordered Chacon's reinstatement, over the strong objections of the chief). Justice's unequivocal and unshakable corroboration of his partner's testimony was persuasive and critical in Chacon's exoneration. In fact, it was so good that the commission in its opinion pointed an accusing finger at the complaining sergeant and the arresting officers for taking inadequate security measures.

In testifying as he did, Justice simply did not tell the whole truth: he covered up for his partner, who had in fact lost his self-control. Chacon admitted privately that he had used force, not for security purposes, but to inflict retribution on a man who had tried to harm fellow police officers. What upset Chacon about the Internal Affairs charge was not its injustice, but "the hypocrisy of it all":

> I've been in high-speed chases before, involving Latinos and black guys, and the same sergeant several times has said to us, in a joking way, after

we had apprehended the guy, "Why isn't that guy up in the hospital?" implying that we should have gotten in a few licks before arresting the guy for doing what he did. Now, here's this Anglo driver; he ran down a police car, purposely trying to ram the car (in fact, he actually nicked it); he's hit two other cars. He had driven like crazy. And I admitted it; I hit him. And he wasn't making any complaints against me. But the sergeant made the complaint.

Justice, in covering up, earned the enmity and mistrust of the chief, several command officers, the sergeant, and a substantial portion of the Patrol Division, which sided with the arresting officers against Chacon's counter-allegations.

Chacon found his victory dearly bought. While he gained reinstatement in the department, he was removed from the beat which had meant so much to him and assigned to a nonpolice task, jail duty. Throughout the ranks there was much talk behind his back about his untrustworthiness. Even supervisors who respected his police skills were reluctant to talk to him in a helpful way lest their assistance be construed by a vindictive chief as personal betrayal.

Justice and Chacon were doomed to be pariahs, at least until the memory of the incident faded. And in Laconia, the police organization had a long memory.

## VI

Doubtless, had Chacon made a clean breast of his loss of self-control, he would have been fired from the department. The chief tolerated no street justice; what was more, it was an accepted part of the police code in Laconia that once a man was in sure custody, manhandling him was taboo. Men had been fired for less than Chacon had done. To be sure, there was an outside possibility that the Civil Service Commission, with its civilian membership, might reverse the department's decision on humanitarian grounds or in recognition of Chacon's candor, but the best calculations indicated that the commission would not.

(Moreover, had Justice reversed his initial police report or his sworn testimony before Internal Affairs, he would have been fired for perjury or at least dishonesty. For Justice, who was in the midst of divorce proceedings and taking personal custody of his several small children, discharge from the department would have been a personal disaster.)

It was far too facile to determine Justice's and Chacon's choices on the principle that "Ours is a government of laws, not of men." For one thing, the law was no infallible fount of wisdom. The Laconia department had been faulted for being a repressive department in the past, one which had administered justice without mercy or discretion. The chief himself, in trying to correct the terrible relationship between the department and the community, had admonished his men not to arrest persons who violated the law, but to use reason, sincere judgment, and empathy. The law, as every rookie was taught in the Training Academy, should not override common sense.

For another thing, the goodness or badness of the men who wore the police uniform determined how well the department governed in Laconia. In this regard Chacon was an invaluable police officer. He was a member of a minority on a police department which had few officers from minority groups. He was so skillful in patrolling his beat that the perceptive Justice would say of him: "Chacon really worked this beat like it should be worked. He worked with the people better than I have ever seen any other cop work a Latino beat." In short, the Laconia department was an agency of government consisting of men on whom the legislative and judicial departments had conferred vast discretion to use the law to good or bad effect. How well that agency governed depended on the personality, dedication, and skill of the men who constituted it. Chacon was one of the finest officers Laconia had for this particular moment in history when the minority social revolution was working itself out. If ever a man were inexpendable to a police department, Chacon was that man.

Thus, Justice and Chacon faced a stark and conflicting choice: faithless execution of the laws or certain destruction of a productive public servant.

## VII

If Justice had been the typical police officer, his moral choices would have been far less problematic. If he had been a rookie or an officer whose reputation for integrity had not been established, or if he lacked that commanding presence which made him so impressive to others, he would not have been expected to cover up for Chacon. No one was expected to sacrifice himself in a cause in which he lacked the capacity to make a difference. If their roles had been reversed, Chacon would not have had a responsibility to cover up for Justice. His already impeached reputation would have served to excuse him from involvement in a cover-up.

It was Justice's very virtues, his immense capability, which caused the trouble. He was able to cover up and effectively deceive others into believing what he said. He had the intelligence to construct a story that could not be disproved. Moreover, his reputation for accuracy and fidelity to truth made his testimony unimpeachable. Of the five police and two civilian witnesses to the incident, he was sure to give an account that was the most assured, detailed, and persuasive. Having the capacity to exonerate, he shouldered the burden to use it. He was in the predicament we have called noblesse oblige, the great man's problem of moral discretion.

But what of the moral injunction to tell the truth? How did Justice reconcile his cover-up activities with the moral imperative to be truthful? Or did he see himself acting dishonestly when he failed to disclose Chacon's loss of self-control?

We earlier discussed the importance of what was labeled the moral middle term. The task of moral perception involved making a choice among alternative characterizations of one's actions. The moral worth of the behavior depended on the classification the policeman selected. The selection of this moral middle term was a crucial step in the moral process.

Justice did not perceive his false testimony on behalf of Chacon as "dishonesty." Had he done so, presumably he would have taken a moral step backward. He would have failed to be a "truthful officer." But Justice did not deem his failure to make a full and accurate disclosure of the incident to be a moral shortcoming. It was not lying; it was nondisclosure. Nondisclosure was something a "truthful" officer could do under the circumstances of the Chacon case.

Honest policemen had to fudge on the truth recurrently. For example, Justice had long ago resolved the problem of the critically injured wife— whether to tell the survivor of an auto accident that her spouse had been killed. Because of the uncertain effect of bad news upon her will to live, a truthful policeman was obliged to cover up the real facts—and with skillful deceit convince her that her husband had survived.

A traffic patrolman habitually cited drivers for going 40 miles an hour in a 25-mile-per-hour zone, despite the fact that they were clocked at 50. Such leniency was not considered as an act of untruthfulness.

A good cop in Laconia was praised if he threw away a marijuana joint lawfully seized from a soldier and did not report the infraction. An officer who made an arrest in this situation would have been considered a ding-a-ling for adhering to such a rigid definition of truthfulness.

No policeman that I met felt guilty about placating a potential suicide with the false information that there was nothing to worry about, or about breaking a promise made to a kidnapper. Broken promises under these circumstances did not violate the injunction against untruthfulness.

A good policeman learned how to write a report of an incident in a variety of ways, with a view to manipulating the district attorney into treating a suspect with severity or leniency. Fact was so variegated and manifold that full disclosure was an impossible ideal. Facts were to be reported with at least some regard for their ultimate effects upon the persons to whom the report was made. A truthful officer was obliged to have a feeling for the effects of different versions of the truth, just as it was the job of an advocate to make his case with an eye to the results he wished to produce.[4]

In a sense, all of these actions violated the conventionally understood canons of the criminal law system to "call it the way it is and let the chips fall where they may." The legal definition of honesty as "full disclosure under all circumstances," however, was not morally compelling to most policemen. A principle as unbending as "full disclosure" broke when it collided with competing principles and the exceptional case. It neglected "the other side," the social consequences of an individual's acts. It was a principle which was not responsible for the damage done in its name to the general welfare, to the social organism.

Principally, the major inadequacy of a simple "full disclosure" notion of honesty was that it failed to deal with the paradoxical nature of reality. Particularly, the paradox of irrationality recurrently required policemen to manipulate the presentation of reality in the interest of the general welfare. When the fearlessly ignorant person—say, the suicide or the wino or the juvenile—lacked the capacity to appreciate the implications of the facts, then the truthful policeman had to manipulate his presentation of the truth so as to evoke from the irrational citizen the same response a rational citizen would have made to the full disclosure of reality. Ideally it was a temporary manipulation, enduring only until sober second thoughts set in. You will recall how Bill Douglas dramatically bluffed a bunch of high school kids into fearing arrest because they lacked the self-restraining understanding of the injuries they were doing to Caesar's. So other "truthful" officers bluffed and omitted and covered up and were less than candid in the face of similar irrational circumstances. Such shadings of the truth were not "dishonesty"; rather, they were acts of "integrity"—a responsible adherence to the principle that a policeman's obligation was to convey a deeper truth even if it meant that the truth had to be expressed in metaphorical terms. A cop had to be both judge and advocate. In order to be a worthy policeman, he had to be aware of the real effects of a message on the particular audience and able to frame the message so that it conveyed the subtle nuance of events.

When Justice made his choice to cover up for Chacon, he considered the consequences for the department and the city. At a time when the department needed good officers from minority groups, he felt he was obliged responsibly to consider the provocative context in which Chacon had lost

4. The city had much the same moral problems about absolute truthfulness and competing values. If a policeman made a mistake (e.g., misused his firearm or injured a citizen) and the city admitted it, the city would be exposed to liability in a civil suit brought by the citizen. As Officer Douglas put it, "The city is in a bind. If they admit that the policeman is at fault, they lay themselves open to suit." The result: city officials, truthful ones, frequently withhheld the truth.

control of himself, even if the regulations declared that context irrelevant. In the name of the general welfare, or, in Acton's terms, "for the sake of ... the good cause which prosper[ed]" by his nondisclosure, Justice decided that "the overall picture," keeping the larger social enterprise going, outweighed the principle "to call it the way it is and let the chips fall where they may."

Covering up for Chacon was an act of integrity, in Justice's opinion, because the disciplinary procedures of the department were "irrational." The chief appeared to be a zealot, fearlessly ignorant of the disastrous consequences of the actions he was taking. The chief had displayed a pattern of conduct in disciplining his men which was so ideological and unreal that he seemed mad. Moreover, in tolerating no mitigating circumstances, he was unjust and uncivilized. Such was the reputation the chief himself cultivated, and thus his men appraised him.

Internal Affairs was tainted with irrationality. Incidents had occurred which convinced seasoned patrolmen like Justice that the chief had hounded Internal Affairs into making severe dispositions after it had come to initial conclusions which proved too lenient for the chief. Internal Affairs was seen to lack independence from the chief, who had perverted its impartial adjudicative posture into an administrative weapon aimed directly at the men. The procedures of Internal Affairs did nothing to dissipate the appearance of dependent partiality. Its hearings were not public; accused policemen were not permitted to confront witnesses; there were no written opinions in which the strongest arguments of accused patrolmen were acknowledged and rebutted explicitly; unlike shooting boards on the department there were no impartial jurors (randomly selected police officers sat on shooting boards, but not on Internal Affairs). Internal Affairs fell short of an appearance of the rule of law. In Justice's view, it had no legitimacy.

Thus, Justice reckoned, Internal Affairs, under the control of a zealous chief, was an irrational institution. For Justice, the cover-up for Chacon was the only means by which the effects of this irrational institution could be abated. The department needed time to recalculate its earlier and faulty decision to fire Chacon. Admittedly, Justice would say, his false testimony was based upon an individual value judgment. Doubtless, there were others who would not perceive the chief and Internal Affairs as "irrational," and hence they would come to a different conclusion, namely, that integrity required full disclosure to the tribunal. But Justice had seen enough to feel confident that the department had to be saved from its own overzealousness. "I have a feeling that the chief likes being hated by his men," Justice said sadly. Such a leader, who defined himself exclusively in terms of the enemies he made, was no more rational than the most alienated adolescent on Laconia's streets. Adhering to his own sense of integrity under these circumstances, Justice tried to obtain the restorative powers of time, to enable the department to reconsider its original decision to fire Chacon. If a cover-up was the only available means to bring this about, then it was morally worthwhile to take the necessary steps to cover up.

But if Justice perceived his actions as "legitimate" (to use Tocqueville's phrase), as an exercise of sincere judgment and hence as an act of integrity, Chacon was not so fortunate. He doubted himself. He perceived his personal act of cover-up in terms of self-protection. Eventually he quieted his self-doubts about giving false testimony by characterizing it as an act of courage in the fight between Us and Them. In the battle between policemen and the rest of the world, no holds were barred. Policemen should not be "snitches" against their fellow soldiers. Rules about truthfulness were ridiculous because the enemies (the citizenry, the judges, the chief) were unscrupulous. In this pugnacious context, a lie was perceived as an act of political bravery. Lying to Internal Affairs was a way of fulfilling one's loyalty to one's team. The principle of not snitching was necessary to overcome the vulnerability of the officer. "Standing up for each other" fortified the good and befuddled the bad.

Justice's and Chacon's different moral perceptions of what they were doing were significant personally. Justice's perception of integrity more strictly limited covering up to circumstances of irrationality; his circumscribed exception was compatible with the general injunction of truthfulness; and in principle it was consistent with acceptable civilized notions about "white lies." On the other hand, Chacon's perception of false testimony as an act of courage was practically unconditional; it applied in any and all police incidents involving patrolmen and supervisorial criticism. It derogated truthfulness as weakness. Such a maxim was unacceptable outside police circles, necessitating its being kept from public view. Chacon's perception of lying as courage equally justified padding a report, framing a suspect, and lying on the witness stand. By failing to limit the propriety of false testimony to conditions of irrationality, Chacon began to destroy his own respect for honesty.

Since Chacon saw no clear boundaries for containing the privilege of dishonesty, his moral process began to stampede. Starting from a point which permitted dishonesty in bargaining with a kidnapper, Chacon found himself expanding the privilege to be dishonest whenever his bargaining position was weak, then whenever it would give an advantage to policemen in general, then whenever it would be personally advantageous, then whenever it could be to his personal profit, and finally whenever his impulses moved him to do so. Under the stress of daily police work, the exceptional privilege to be dishonest soon devastated the rule of truthfulness, like a cancer on the soul.

In my opinion, the different perceptions of the two men were not simply determined by their different statuses as witness and suspect. Had Justice been the accused and Chacon the witness, Chacon would still have perceived his testimony as an act of courage and Justice would have striven to contain his privilege to lie within the principled limits of irrationality—to keep it "an exceptional case." Their different perceptions resulted from their different capacities for moral creativeness.[5] Justice's skill in inventing a personally acceptable basis for reconciling his civilized perception of false testimony as dishonesty and his political perception of it as integrity made it possible for him to save the injunction to be truthful. Chacon's lesser ability to harmonize antithetical moral codes required him to obliterate honesty from its place in his moral code. And that had devastating and widespread implications.

## VIII

Before discussing the capacity for moral creativeness, we must clarify one point. The young patrol officer exposed himself more often to more severe moral problems than any young professional I have ever encountered. An unremitting and unavoidable series of quandaries assaulted the policeman's power of decisiveness, to the point of exhaustion.

Let me list at random a dozen moral conflicts which might beset a patrol officer in a normal week in Laconia. (The reader should always keep in mind that Laconia was among that minority of big-city American departments which had virtually no corruption and was beset by a negligible amount of political influence; if either corruption or political influence had been notably present, the incidence and severity of moral problems would have been compounded in staggering fashion.)

1. A group of retired black men had a friendly floating crap game in backyards. The law was "There shall be no gambling," and the chief took pride in the fact that the department had even put a halt to bingo games at the local churches. Moral questions: Was this crap game gambling or recreation? Could the patrolman break up this game with sufficient diplomacy so that he could reconcile in his own mind the fact that men in country clubs (and even fellow policemen) gambled for the fun of it? Was the securing of the principle of the inviolability of the law worth discouraging old men who had lived good lives?

5. Barnard, *Functions*, p. 279. Robert A, Kagan, in his unusually sensitive study of the administration of the Nixon economic stabilization program, refers to this process of "moral creativeness" as a "judicial mode of rule-application." See his "The Wage-Price Freeze: A Study in Administrative Justice" Ph.D. dissertation, Yale University, Department of Sociology, 1974.

2. A group of six adolescents played as a jazz combo and weekly had to rehearse at their manager's house, which was uphill a mile from the nearest bus stop. Department rules forbade the use of police cars to transport any citizen unless he was a prisoner or critically hurt. Moral questions: Was the friendship of these youths (and the information gained from knowing them) worth more than the insurance trouble and other risks the patrolman would run if he had an accident while the kids were in the car? Was this service or favoritism? Could he "ride the heat" from his supervisor and justify himself in the event he was observed?

3. The mother of a seventeen-year-old girl wanted her daughter's twenty-year-old, longtime boyfriend arrested for statutory rape when she found them in bed together. The regulations provided that a policeman had to arrest any citizen whenever a complainant was willing to sign a criminal complaint. Moral questions: Did the patrol officer have the skill to persuade the mother of the unwisdom of bringing criminal charges? Was this a crime or a grudge complaint? Was the public policy of protecting young ladies through and beyond the onset of their sexuality worth the possibly irremediable harm done to the young man?

4. A rich and rude-middle-aged lady, caught speeding twenty miles over the limit, verbally abused the officer's partner, who was the arresting officer. The arresting officer, who had been beset by financial problems because of the medical bills for an operation on his three-year-old son who had cancer, finally lost his temper and said, "I don't care what you think, lady: just get your ass out of here." She complained, and the partner of the arresting officer was called as a witness before Internal Affairs. Moral questions: Should the partner have characterized his fellow officer's behavior as unfortunate profanity or extraordinary restraint under the circumstances, and, if the latter, was it proper to tell the "truth" in metaphorical terms so that the spirit of departmental regulations was applied rather than their letter? Could the partner tell the "truth" with sufficient skill to convey the whole truth? Was lying to protect a fellow officer who could not afford the lost pay resulting from a short suspension worth jeopardizing his own job and his family's dependence on him?

5. The sergeant"s exam was coming up, and not being particularly apt at bookwork, an officer knew he would need to study in his every spare moment for the next half-year to pass the exam, meaning that he would have to give up his work at a boys' club in a lower-income housing project. Moral question: Was his personal long-term plan for advancement worth the short-term shirking of his responsibility to numerous underprivileged youngsters?

6. A wife in critical condition after an automobile collision asked the officer about her husband, who had been killed in the accident. Moral

questions: Was telling her that her husband was alive and well dishonesty or therapy? Had the officer sufficient skill to tell her a believable untruth now, yet regain her confidence in his integrity later? Was her life worth a lie?

7. A citizen complained about kids playing baseball in the street. The nearest park was a mile away. Moral questions: Was alleviating one adult's temporary irritation—including anxiety for the kids' safety—worth the destruction of the recreational opportunities for a dozen boys? Had the officer the eloquence to stop the game yet retain the kids' friendship and enthusiasm for good lives? Was a publicly financed pavement a convenience exclusive for adults with cars, or was it properly sometimes to be made available to benefit nondrivers?

8. A citizen complained about a juvenile who was ringing doorbells in a neighborhood plagued by burglaries. The officer knew the boy had been arrested for burglary before, yet probable cause to arrest him now was lacking. Moral questions: Was the due process protection afforded this one kid worth the possible burglarization and demoralization of other citizens struggling to live on the straight and narrow? Was it harassment or good preventive police work to scare the devil out of the kid? Did the officer have the skill to lean on the juvenile verbally without talking himself into making a false arrest?

9. The officer caught a young kid, without a previous record, with a couple of sticks of marijuana on his person. Moral questions: If he threw away the marijuana and let the kid go, would he have to do it for the next guy? Had he the skill to release the boy, yet convince him that he could not flout the law and get away with it? Was it a crime or a caper to experiment with marijuana when a kid was young and wanted to test his manhood?

10. An elderly janitor working in the downtown commercial area late at night had been the victim of several strong-arm robberies. He saw a young man, with hat low over his eyes and jacket high around his face and both hands in his pockets, walking toward him. The old man told the youth to stop, but his warning went unheeded. The janitor then pulled out a small revolver—an unlicensed concealed weapon—and fired two warning shots into the street. The young man, who had a record of previous robberies and no money in his pockets, fled and later complained to the police officer that the old man should be arrested. Moral questions: Should the officer have written the report as if the young man were the complainant and the old man the suspect for carrying a concealed weapon (a crime for which all the legal elements were clearly present)? Or should he have made the janitor the complainant and the young man the suspect for attempted robbery (a crime in which the crucial legal element of threat was missing)? Had the officer sufficient skill to withstand the supervisorial heat for not arresting the old

man when inquiry was made? At what point did the public interest in gun control demand that private acts of self-protection be penalized?

11. A kid was caught with forty sticks of marijuana, and he agreed to inform on the person who had sold him the marijuana if he were given a break. However, because he was underage, the Investigation Division later told the arresting officer that the boy's testimony would not stand up in court, and no arrests were ever made on the basis of his information. Moral questions: Should the arresting officer have given the kid his "break" (i.e., cut him loose without trial), even though he had contributed nothing that could be used? Was the possibility that the kid would learn that police did keep their word worth more than the other possibility, that the kid would learn he could violate the law and get away with it?

12. A patrolman pulled over a driver for making an illegal left turn, and then found out that the driver was a judge on the superior court. Moral questions: Were judges morally distinguishable from other citizens? Had the officer the skill to justify giving the judge a citation (or refraining from doing so) to his supervisors and himself? If the department told him to exercise discretion in using his authority to arrest, was it relevant to consider that the citizen was either (a) a notable or (b) the recent subject of a lot of uninformed and unfair political attacks in the city's newspapers as an overlenient sentencer?[6]

These dozen incidents illustrate only the moral predicaments of the normal policeman. With ease, a dozen more could have been added, and some would have been far more profound and disturbing. But these suffice to show five points.

First, such incidents recurred far more frequently and unavoidably than for the average citizen. The ordinary person was not required by either law or morals to be his fellow citizen's keeper. The Good Samaritan at least had the freedom to take a walk; the policeman was obligated to be on hand because he had authority. When he heard a citizen's cry for help, he had to respond. Granted, he might have to assess the merit of the request for assistance, but he had to show up to make that assessment and to do it in the public eye. Moreover, the law obliged him to mind other people's business, to override their private, voluntary arrangements under some circumstances, and to impose larger considerations of the general welfare upon persons used to individualism. Legally, he was to use coercion, not only to control coercion but also to fulfill public purposes he did not always agree with. His job was to

6. The format of these twelve examples parallels a marvelous essay by Stephen K. Bailey, "Ethics and the Policitican" (1960), in *Democracy, Liberalism, and Revolution,* ed. Karl A. Lamb (Palo Alto, Calif.: Freel & Associates, 1971).

be bold—to use the police vernacular, "to be aggressive." As the philosopher among the Laconia policemen put it, "You've got to be open and brazen, as opposed to the fellow who'd like to turn up his collar and take a hike." Admittedly, some policemen did turn their backs on the problems of some citizens, but they did so only at the risk of destroying their self-esteem for being responsible workers.

Second, these problems were not academic, and their solutions rarely were universally popular. There were two or more sides to each moral question, and usually on each side there were expectant citizens. With some justification, the mother of the seventeen-year-old ex-virgin, the partner's wife who was caring for her cancer-stricken child, the neighbor watching the stealthy juvenile ring doorbells, the driver who was ticketed after observing the judge get away with the same violation—all felt that they had been sold down the river. From their points of view, the cop lacked integrity, pride, and humanity and would have acted otherwise had he had those qualities. Moral questions were close questions, but the consequence for the losing side hurt no less because the questions were close. The stakes of police decisions were high, and an adverse decision necessarily caused considerable injury. Therefore, resolving these tough questions, the policeman had to expect reprisals from the losers, and hence he had to prepare means of self-defense—which complicated matters further.

Third, the policeman's moral predicaments often involved "snap decisions." The judge, the irate mother, the surly youngster who had been shot at—all wanted a decision right now, and there was never enough time for thoughtful deliberation on these profound and irreversible choices. Unless the officer had done some anterior thinking in privacy, had "anticipated a problem" in his imagination, he would lack time to think a matter through. Shortness of time imposed disconcerting limitations on rationality.[7]

Fourth, the policeman invariably dealt with his moral problems alone. Except in discussions after the event, when he could use hindsight, he rarely had the opportunity to deliberate with colleagues on the scene and share responsibility. He bore his feelings of guilt by himself: "it's a lonely job; you

7. The typical police lament about the shortage of time took this form: "Unfortunately, you have to make up your mind in a split second, right or wrong. The Supreme Court can take two years to decide what you have to decide in a couple of seconds." Peel, who at the age of twenty-eight was then practically an old-timer with nearly five years of experience on the department, would pass along a helpful piece of wisdom to his younger colleagues. When in doubt, he would say, ask yourself, "Is it going to be a peace-keeping move—and especially in the long run?" What kind of a city would Laconia be in twenty years as a result of choices like this? What kind of a department would develop if a particular alternative, with all its implications, were selected? This developmental rule of thumb, abstract though it was, helped to mitigate the adverse effects of surprise and urgency.

really are all by yourself. I'd call it a singular job.... There is a feeling of loneliness.... It's all in the guy's mind, but it's real."

And, finally, the criteria against which a good policeman had to measure his solutions were numerous and more contradictory than the standards the decent citizen used to evaluate his actions. The major cause of this added complexity, of course, was that the policeman was an instrument of a coercive legal order. A policeman, in practicing and contending with the techniques of threat, was always encountering the paradoxes of coercive power. Hence he was always tempted to simplify his moral choices, to be self-defensive, detached, remorseless, and irrational, and to justify segregating his police life from his personal life. If he did not, his facing up to this increased moral complexity involved "guilt feelings" in nearly every critical decision. The legitimacy, the acceptability to himself, of each exercise of his authority was almost always uncertain.

## IX

We have talked about the transformation of moral attitudes over time. In fact, however, the moral attitudes policemen developed tended to become firmly fixed. Their stability resulted from two causes. They were interdependent, and they were responsible: interdependent in that moral attitudes were related to one another systematically, responsible in that they were the bases for moral actions which were related to one another historically. Moral attitudes were fixed vertically in a system based on proportionality and horizontally in a time sequence based on equality.

Change took place, as it had in Chacon's and Justice's cases, but the implications of change were wide because of this complicated interrelatedness of moral attitudes. Moral change could and often did produce what observant policemen called "degeneration." On the other hand, it could and sometimes did produce growth—a regeneration of morale, responsibility, and joy. But moral change was always complicated because of the responsible and interdependent nature of morals.

We shall postpone the question of responsibility until the next section. Here we want to examine the problem of *systematic interdependence* of moral attitudes and the notion of proportionality.

A policeman's moral system was systematic insofar as its elements were positioned in importance. There were, so to speak, hundred-dollar rules like the injunction to save a fellow officer's life when it was endangered, and there were five-cent rules like the injunction to ticket vehicles parked overnight in zones the street cleaners wanted to sweep. The moral value of each rule was tied to an understanding of cause and effect. Moral value, it could be said, was deduced from a complicated calculus of cost and benefit of action. To be sure, the moral system was adjusted temporarily with various discounts and premiums, the equivalent of what we earlier called "taking into account the exceptional case."[8]

Despite the fact that its complexities ultimately made a shambles of this simplistic price-system metaphor, policemen themselves often strained to express the systematic priorities implicit in their moral attitudes in monetary terms. "I attach values to things," the most eloquent of the policemen put it. If the policeman's job was to lock up the evil and free the suppressed, not every lockup had the same worth, and not every liberation was of equal value.

This scale of values was important to a policeman because according to it he apportioned out his time and his commitment—"how I extend myself," as Justice expressed it. It justified priorities. It rationalized the allocation and hoarding of his energies. The potential frustration of not fulfilling all his many responsibilities was eliminated if he fulfilled the most basic, the most valued responsibility. Thus this system of priorities was an essential protection against devastating feelings of shortcoming.

The policeman's system allowed him to accept the limits of his capacities and to live with limited objectives. It permitted him, for example, to serve proudly as a policeman in a city with a high crime rate. Proportionality—budgeting one's life with a reference to the importance of the tasks to be done—pervaded the policeman's moral thinking. It also produced the interdependence between moral attitudes that was so important a factor in fixing those attitudes permanently.

The notion of proportionality underlined the thinking of the professional Justice. Take his discussion of the exercise of police discretion:

> I've seen good batteries occur right in front of me, where I could take him to jail, but I'd be doing more harm putting him in jail. You see a violation: should I warn him and turn my back on it, or take him to jail because I'm morally bound by my oath to, as a part of law and order. Maybe it's on the basis I know people are getting away with so much more. We have organized crime, and the poor little guy on the street is getting caught. I can pinch him for a red light, but I won't. I can justify it by realizing there is so much more that is below the surface. You have the feeeling that you have only a little fish. It's all disproportionate to what he's doing and how his life is affected.

The guy was "little" because he hurt no one and profited so little from his infraction of the traffic code. Of more importance were the big fish, the ones

8.  Undoubtedly, the legislated weights attached to different activities by the criminal code had some affect on how officers calculated the worth of different rules. But the criminal law was not subtle enough or sufficiently responsive to the problem of priorities in enforcement to help in complicated cases of moral conflict.

who hurt others severely and who enriched themselves by flouting the law. The value of their pursuit, arrest, prosecution, and punishment was the reference point in Justice's mind, and the pursuit, arrest, prosecution, and punishment of others ought to be proportionate to their bigness or littleness. If, for example, the punishment of the big fish was deflated, Justice's moral system systematically devalued the importance of pursuing and punishing "the poor little guy."[9]

This interdependent system of moral priorities, little obligations constructed upon responsibilities of major importance, was in danger of collapse whenever some basic attitude changed. The reverberations caused by altering the value of a major imperative were endless because in subtle and unconscious ways it had been the basis for determining the values of many other moral rules.

Truthfulness, for example, was a basic principle fixed in most of the men's system of morals and would have determined their action in all but the greatest emergencies: a policeman might lie in order to save the life of an injured wife but not to save himself some investigative effort. If, however, he were to change his attitude about truthfulness substantially (as Chacon did), to deflate it into near-worthlessness, other moral imperatives whose priority was fixed in proportion to the importance of truthfulness were diminished in worth as well. Such principles as aggressiveness, courage, cooperation, sharing information among colleagues, and community development—interconnected with truthfulness through the notion of proportionality—fell when truthfulness collapsed. Such collapse might be only momentary; the officer might begin to pick up the "shattered" pieces and reconstruct a new system. It might also be a more permanent breakdown. Temporary or enduring, the collapse was very real. Chacon, who in Justice's mind worked his beat better than any other Latino beat was worked, and who "took real pride" in the unique ways he benefited his community, had lost his sense of personal responsibility after he had been reinstated. Some of that collapse of character grew from a bitterness he felt against the chief. But his own words betrayed a more fundamental change in his system of values:

9.  John Gardiner, in his book on traffic control in Massachusetts, points out the unwillingness of beat officers to write traffic tickets. He concludes that division of labor—creating a traffic section—is the only way to overcome this reluctance of officers to write tickets. I suppose that he is right. When the cop is made a specialist in traffic duty, his systematic comparison of the value of his various jobs is truncated, beheaded. The traffic specialist compares one kind of traffic offense with another; the beat officer, on the other hand, compares one kind of crime with another. In the perspective of the beat officer's larger system, a traffic offense is a crime of a most minor degree. Thus, he feels distressed about handing out traffic tickets. As Justice pointed out, "You don't feel right hassling them and raising their insurance rates when assholes that have shot a policeman are out on probation. I wonder, is it fair?"

The chief was out to get me, to make me do justice for the incident, and they were going to put me on shit details like the wagon. The captain, however, came to me in the middle of the watch and offered to put me back on the beat. I was bitter by then; I had originally thought they would give me back my beat as soon as I was reinstated. . . . But they didn't; they had put me in the jail, then assigned me to the pool, then the wagon; they had taken away my good days off and given me Tuesdays and Wednesdays. Well, if the captain had thought I ought not to be on the wagon, why hadn't he objected at the beginning of the watch? Well, I told him, "No, I want to stay on the wagon." He couldn't understand it. He thought of it as a punishment, but I just felt a little bitter by then, and I wasn't going to give them the satisfaction that what they were trying to do was effective. By then, I had learned what a soft job the wagon is. Tonight, for example, I had brought a couple of books to read, and, to be frank with you, I was going to catch a little sleep.

Just the year before, Chacon had expressed how irked he was by "lazy" officers. Now he was satisfied with "a soft job." Having pardoned himself for violating the major obligation to be truthful, he found it disproportionate to punish himself for less serious violations like catching "a little sleep."[10]

In contrast, Justice did not fundamentally alter his moral system. He retained an adherence to the value of truthfulness, but made an exception to it. He "discounted" the value of truthfulness in the presence of irrationality, but in making this temporary adjustment to circumstances, he preserved the principle in his system. By conditioning it, by bending it with explicitness, Justice left its weight intact.

This process by which some policemen added contextual conditions to what otherwise were rigid universalistic moral absolutes was most important. As I reread the interviews, I was struck by the numerous times some officers used the word "if" (or its contextual equivalent, "when") in the qualifying sense, and how other interviews lacked any such use of these conjunctions. Haig talked in contextually limited terms over and over again. Typically, he would say, "When you are dealing with people in their homes, and when . . . you make the arrest to eliminate the problem for the sake of eliminating the problem, you'll be back next day, having done a bad job in the first place." This carefully qualified rule regarding flexibility and reluctance to arrest under provocative circumstances was explicitly restricted

10.    The anthropologist Alexander Leighton, writing about the wholesale moral collapse which took place among the Issei and Nisei detained at a particular American relocation center during World War II, captured the phenomenon of moral interdependency in this expressive metaphor: "Systems of belief resemble a thick matting of roots under the floor of the forest which if cut may result in the withering of some distant bush or a whole tree." Leighton, *The Governing of Men* (Princeton, N.J.: Princeton University Press, 1945), p. 291.

to private family beefs involving civil problems. It contrasted with Bacon's intransigent standard, "I make it a rule not to back down, ever." Bacon's absolutist construction meant that his rule could bear little stress. If the exceptional case necessitated its violation, it was likely to shatter in time and so would the values interdependent with it.[11]

This moral skill of coping with the exceptional case reminded me of the judicial process. Instead of repealing a rule whenever it conflicts with a second one, judges tend to articulate the qualified circumstances under which the first rule has to give way to the other. Let me illustrate the likeness. In the famous Watergate tapes case, *United States* v. *Nixon, President of the United States,*[12] the Supreme Court held that the principle of executive privilege was outweighed by the necessities of criminal due process in the Watergate criminal conspiracy prosecution then going on. The principle, however, was not expunged. Rather, the court appreciably strengthened the acceptability of the principle of executive privilege by delineating the very grounds to which exceptions were confined. Similarly, Justice's capacity to articulate with definitiveness the limited circumstances under which the principle of truthfulness had to give way to an overriding need permitted him to preserve his adherence to honesty. It required "resourcefulness, energy, imagination, general ability" to create an articulate resolution of a potentially calamitous moral conflict.[13] The success of his efforts maintained his moral code and left his system with its complex scales of proportionality intact.

## X

*Responsibility* was the other characteristic of a policeman's moral system. His moral attitudes were formed from his experience. They conferred moral worth upon deeds which were irreversible. Any change in morals altered the interpretation of that experience. Change converted moral assets into liabilities, and vice versa. In the sense that attitudes determined the

---

11.  Another example of the use of "if" and "when" to circumscribe the implications of moral rules occurred in Peel's description of an exemplary officer he had known: "I remember being with him when we saw two women fighting. I was new on the force, and I was about to dive between them, when he pulled me up short by my collar before I dove in. I thought our job as policemen was to keep the peace, but he just said, 'Let them fight.' Then, as exhaustion set in in the two women, he stepped in and broke it up. And immediately they started talking. What he taught me was to stand back and appraise the situation before acting. He didn't do it always, but *when* the odds were even and it was pretty clear nobody was going to get hurt anyone badly, then he would let them at it.... He felt people had to vent their hostilities." [Emphasis mine.]

12.  418 U.S. 683 (1974).

13.  Barnard, *Functions,* p. 272.

innocence or shamefulness of a man's past, we say that moral attitudes were responsible.

This fact was of the utmost importance to policemen because in their work they hurt others. They jailed citizens, caused them to be fined, injured them physically, denied their claims, humiliated them, accused them, threatened them, and (in a more remote way) even spent their money for them (e.g., to replace damaged police equipment). If a policeman had general ability and was well trained, he inflicted these hurts legally. If he was active, however, he inevitably did make some errors. He was gullible; he drove improperly and caused accidents; he got irritated; he misjudged intentions; he was "off the air" when fellow officers needed him; he lost courage; he used undue force; he made bad arrests. In the thousand challenges which faced him each year, he was bound to err once in a while.

Whether the hurt he inflicted was legitimate or mistaken, however, the policeman lived with himself. He would second-guess his actions afterward, and in those private deliberations he might decide he had erred. Or, acting as his own "Monday morning quarterback," he might resolve his anxieties by deciding he had been right. Whatever the outcome of these deliberations— self-conviction or self-acquittal—their result was that he formulated a principle of right conduct, a maxim in terms of which he signified the worth of his behavior. With this maxim he either cloaked his actions in innocence or draped them in self-inflicted blame. This maxim then became part of his moral baggage.[14]

Take the pugnacious officer Kip, for example. He had demolished a police car on a high-speed chase involving a couple of teen-agers who had been driving a car which did not appear to belong to them.

> We were rolling down Kercheval, and we see this '69 Mustang filled with kids. Significantly, it had no front plate. We do a U-turn, and the driver spots me. We chase them for almost ten minutes. We are almost on them at Boulevard and Elm, and he runs a red light. This little old lady came. So I hit the building and totaled the car. And I'm on the carpet. "Did you have to blow the red light? Is there something you could have done and prevented the chase?" I said, "Look, if you don't want us to chase, put it in an order. The criminal code gives us the power to use necessary force." I was completely justified in what I did.

"On the carpet" in his own conscience as well as before the department safety officer, Kip adjudged that he had measured up to a maxim,

---

14. Doug Haig described this trial of conscience: "I think that every police officer tends to—when a situation goes bad—to blame himself. It's a natural reaction.... So you sit home and you wonder what could I have done. It's good to think about it; and if you get a solution, fine. But if you can't, accept the fact you did the best you could."

tailor-made to the occasion, namely, apprehend every possible infractor by using whatever means not specifically prohibited by an "order." His formulation of this justification contained no qualifications about reasonableness, no allusion to proportionality between the gravity of the crime and the drasticness of the means. He simply shaped this imperative and put himself within its protective embrace. Self-justifying as it was in this instance, however, the maxim was a hard one to live by. Its implications were that no wrongdoers ought to be left on the streets and if he had available any nonprohibited means to squash them, he had a positive obligation to use the means "necessary." The maxim by which he "completely justified" himself established future compulsions to work at a frenzied rate.

This curious result, whereby the maxim of an early act became the precedent which dictated later acts, might be characterized as a behavioral form of *stare decisis,* the legal doctrine which commanded that similar cases be treated similarly. Kip insisted on equal treatment of his citizenry. Like incidents should be treated alike. So far as I could discern, every thoughtful policeman resembled Kip in just this respect. Each compared his conduct in the next case with his conduct in the preceding one and demanded consistency between them. They were much bothered by an unjustifiable inconsistency.

The majority of policemen developed moral maxims which were more subtle than Kip's—principles which permitted fine distinctions. But all policemen made these historical, horizontal comparisons ("You sometimes wonder, if I do it for this guy, will I have to do it for that guy?"). In this respect, there was a profound regard for equality, for the evenhanded application of the law, and an abhorrence of unequal protection.

What were the sources of this dislike of inconsistency? Doubtless, some of the pressures to be consistent were external. His fellow officers expected their colleague to act consistently. They had sized him up as a person who acted in a certain patterned way, and they had come to rely on that consistency. They became aggressively curious whenever his behavior took a turn away from their expectancies.

But the internal pressures to be consistent should not be underestimated. Suppose Kip were to start acting in a new way, no longer driving immoderately after every teen-age joyrider. (The reality was that the cars which juveniles took would be found, usually undamaged, sooner or later, whenever they ran out of gas.) Kip would then have had to tailor a new maxim, justifying to himself (as well as to others) the moderation which had let suspicious characters escape. (As a basis for his new behavior, he might have said something like, "Our job is peace-keeping, and the stopping of small crimes does not justify laying waste a neighborhood.") In the perspective of this new maxim, the earlier auto accident would look bad. The meaning of that unchangeable fact would have changed: what was once a commendable act of bravery and dedication became foolish or vicious immoderation. The delusion of innocence would have been shredded. He would have had to "carry about" guilt feelings, or at least misgivings, for an act he had earlier considered quite proper. Ex post facto condemnation was profoundly depressing, at least if it stigmatized a considerable or critical part of a man's career. It was, in Justice's simple understatement, "kind of rough."[15]

Some of the men were extremely hesitant about writing their first pieces of moral legislation in unconventional terms. Especially in the dubious areas where the use of fear, physical force, callousness, lying, and favoritism were involved, they restricted themselves to the most civilized means they could, even when their restraint was counterproductive. It was as if they were afraid that, by adopting mean means, they would be committed to their use recurrently: damned to abide consistently by their contract with the devil. Among these men there was an anxiety that there could be no turning back, no return to the civilized limitations they were used to, if the first steps away were taken. Ingersoll, for example, refused even to get "stern" in "small things." Only in the exceptional situation where a citizen lied to him did he let himself make threats.[16]

The philosopher Kant urged persons to "act so that the maxim of your will can be valid at the same time as a principle of universal legislation."[17] Policemen in Laconia actually behaved according to a narrow and private variation of Kant's categorical imperative: "Act in such a way as to accord with the maxim of your earlier acts." There were "many philosophies of police work," as one professional pointed out, but any one individual's philosophy was extremely dependable from day to day and increasingly stable as the stays of system and history held fast.[18]

## XI

Of course, the rigidities were not so rigid as the reader might think, were he to take the preceding discussion without qualifications. For one thing, there was slippage in the individual's moral process. It was an internal process, and policemen, some more than others, distorted or forgot critical precedents or simply left some choices in a vague ambiguity. Frequently, when

15. See Joseph Wambaugh, *The Onion Field* (New York: Delacorte, 1973).

16. And recall Haig's willingness to temporize in the crowd scene, in chapter 7, even under circumstances of extreme physical danger to himself.

17. Immanuel Kant, *The Philosophy of Kant,* ed. and trans. Carl J. Friedrich (New York: Modern Library, 1949), p. 222.

18. Morris Cohen was alluding to the interdependence and responsibility of moral attitudes when he pointed out that the denial of any one of them "requires all sorts of other assumptions that conflict or are inconsistent with so many of the assumptions that we cannot change." *A Preface to Logic,* (1944; New York: Meridian, 1956), p. 75.

there was no adversary advocate to appeal one of his moral judgments, the policeman went home and "forgot it."

Second, some policemen risked the dangers of changing their attitude systems, conjuring up pictures of themselves as learning from their mistakes, as persons developing. These men faced moral reappraisal more optimistically: destruction of the delusion of earlier innocence was offset by the sensation of learning and growing. Barber noted in his book on first-term lawmakers that a concept of a "developing self" gave some legislators more latitude to experiment with their moral outlooks.[19] Similarly, some policemen, particularly in their early years, shared a similar sense of development.

Finally, as mentioned before, some of the men were extremely subtle line drawers, capable of formulating new maxims which were not inconsistent with old experience, yet making large exceptions to what past precedents had once appeared to portend. No cases were overruled, so to speak, but the moral maxim which reconciled past and present behavior portended actions of a different order.

But when all these qualifications were stated, I was struck by the responsibility of a policeman to his past and to his own system of philosophy. Knowing the moral codes a man said he abided by, an observer could foresee how he would behave on the next occasion. Once the elements of his philosophy were bolted down with responsibility and system, they were changed rarely thereafter and then only on peril of moral collapse.

Therefore, the experiences which a man had had in his early postadolescence became crucial. When a man reached the age of philosophy, when critical events involving responsibility, guilt, and long-term organizational commitment occurred ever more frequently, when events like marriage and parenthood and self-support combined to mature the individual—that was the time when something significant happened in shaping the human material which was to become a policeman. At least such were the observations of thoughtful officers. While these men agreed there were exceptions, for the most part a person going through this period was too malleable, morally speaking, to be a policeman. Only after his system had somewhat crystallized should he leave the noncoercive, reciprocal, civilized world to become a police officer. Then the restraints implanted in his moral system and stabilized by significant experiences served to limit the temptations, inherent in police work, to strike an open-ended deal with the devil. One professional officer, Rolfe, who had worked for several years in a psychiatric hospital before joining the department, told this insightful story:

> I tried to get into police work when I first got out of the service. . . . Then I was shot down because of a court martial in the service. . . . But I was not ready at age 21 or 22. There are very few individuals who are ready at that

19.  James David Barber, *The Lawmakers* (New Haven: Yale University Press, 1965).

age. Even after military service or after college. It takes a little bouncing around in life to get some background on life. Maturity is damn important on this job. I feel that people change drastically from the time they are 21.... Your opinions change between 21 and 25. I talk with other men on the department, and I'll ask, How did you feel about religion and politics when you were that age and how do you feel now. And it's invariable. There's a fantastic difference in their outlooks and their goals in life. At 21 you are still at a point in life when you are finding yourself and getting a direction. I know myself, the value I got from working in a hospital, especially the last year when I worked with a lot of psychiatric patients. I was close to humanity there. I love to work with people. If you have a job learning to work with people, it's a good springboard into police work. I think you're better equipped. I know there are exceptions: there always are.

In Rolfe's view, it was important that, before becoming a policeman, a person had equipped himself with a sense of "direction," that he had fixed his moral cement of experiencing "humanity," and that the exposure to it had come in nonpolice "work with people." Thereafter, those early codes of conduct, shaped as they were outside the pressure of police work, worked to resist a morality of unlimited coercive means.

## XII

There were men like Justice who blended their moral systems with what we have called considerations of integrity. Their codes of conduct permitted them to deal comfortably with the paradoxes of coercion. Some made limited exceptions in their codes to accommodate the use of fear, nastiness, ignorance, detachment, and self-defensiveness. Others made general virtues of these extortionate virtues. In both cases, however, these officers enjoyed power, understood it, and used it with very little inner moral turmoil. Their moral codes were integrated.

An integrated morality regarding coercion contained as a central notion the concept of the general welfare. An integrated moralist saw the "second side" of every human event: the implications of individual acts for the social organism. In the phrase "civil liberties," he stressed the word "civil": liberty within an ordered, structured society. He felt that civilization was the matrix of human dignity, achievement, and freedom. He saw individuals in relation to one another. In this sense, he took seriously the importance of the balance of power in the relationships between individual human beings: equal bargaining power was essential to make these relationships productive and fair. The weak, the vulnerable, the peaceful, the dependent were to be secured by civilization. That was the essence of the "police mission." In the name of the general welfare, in the name of providing compensatory help to those otherwise at a disadvantage, the integrated moralist was active, joyful, comfortable with the responsibility of exercising threat.

Other officers, however, were less able to cope with the apparent conflict between the means they were expected to use as policemen and their civilized scruples which condemned fear, nastiness, ignorance, and detachment on principle as morally worthless. Men, like Ingersoll in chapter 2, could not "get it together," as the saying went. They were unhappy using means which they believed to be illegitimate. Their moral codes were conflicted.

The conflicted morality of power stressed, not the compensatory equality of coercion, but individuality and liberty. The conflicted moralist concentrated on the individual and was virtually unconcerned about his context. The social organism, the Establishment, the general welfare—these were secondary notions, not internalized, not orchestrated, not very meaningful. As a result, whenever the conflicted moralist exercised coercion, he noticed the painful effects of his actions on the individual citizen. He saw no offsetting benefits to justify the use of force and perceived no useful implications to compensate for the sacrifice of the citizen. Hence, what was right and what he was authorized to do as a policeman were frequently in conflict. The denial of liberty was the measure of value in his morality. Even incarcerating a citizen who denied liberty to others bothered him. Civilization was not the matrix of human liberty, but the inhibitor of it. The protection of the social organism was a remote, even hypocritical idea. In action, the conflicted moralist appeared to dislike activity, was hesitant, and found the exercise of coercion illegitimate.

## XIII

We said earlier that separating the intellectual and moral components of a policeman's attitudes was artificial but analytically useful. It is now time to reunite what we previously split.

A policeman's moralized attitudes were understandings about human cause and effect which had glued themselves into a moral grid of responsibility and systematic interdependence. The patrolman would set his particular perspective into a moral epoxy of sacrifice and consistency where it functioned to justify historical acts of omission and harm. Increasingly, thereafter, an officer's perspective resisted subsequent attempts to alter it.

Thus, while actions and understandings were initially reflexive in their effects on each other, a policeman's freedom to change his thinking about the human condition sooner or later became circumscribed by the necessity to justify to himself the legitimacy of his past actions. His past was replete with the record of his responses to the paradoxes of coercion. That is, the morally significant actions in his police career, the ones which made him formulate maxims of acceptable conduct, were usually taken under circumstances where he faced citizens who were dispossessed, detached, remorseless, or irrational. Thus his perspective on the human condition tended to be disproportionately influenced by those morally problematic efforts to respond to the four paradoxes of coercion.

Under certain conditions, a youthful policeman was likely to come upon solutions to the paradoxes of coercive power which enabled him to accept the use of coercion as legitimate. However, if his solution to his moral problems required him to blind himself to the tragedy of the human condition, then he became an enforcer. Under other circumstances, a young policeman's choice of responses to paradox left him in conflict about the morality of coercion. Then he would be transfixed by feelings of guilt, would tend to evade situations which aroused those feelings, and would develop a perspective to justify his evasions. This kind of officer became either a reciprocator or an avoider. Finally, some young officers found ways to exercise coercion legitimately without having to deny their "common sense" of the oneness of the human condition. These men became professionals.

In the next chapter we examine three factors, language, learning, and leadership, which seemed to assist young officers to develop professional responses to the paradoxes of coercion and thus to escape being crucified by the events of their past, *sans* growth, *sans* hope, *sans* the possibility of redemption.

# 12

# Causing
# Professionalism

## I

We have just defined two reactions to the propriety of coercion: an integrated
morality and a conflicted morality.

Furthermore, in an earlier chapter, we identified two different understandings, what we called the tragic and the cynic perspectives. You will
recall that the tragic perspective was unitary. Its starting premise was that all
human nature was basically alike. It acknowledged the different play of
cultural and environmental factors on personality. While there might be
individual deviations from the norm, that is, an individual might become
irrational, remorseless, callous, or paranoid, the tragic perspective consigned
these aberrations to classes of exceptions and comprehended them within a
single, encompassing theory of human motivation in which rationality and
aspiration were prime ingredients. The exceptions were seen as the result of
circumstantial abnormalities, to which all persons were susceptible. The

tragic perspective ruled out categorical exceptions and group distinctions as being useless as basic explanations. It prohibited separating the world into Us and Them. It provided the basis for empathy. It saw weakness and strength as inextricably bound. It found the sources of evil and good in the same origins. And it respected the problems and complexities of individual life. In short, the tragic perspective declared a factual equality among individuals: all men had good and bad intermixed, and no one was exempt from the temptations, conflicts, longings, and above all, the sufferings of the human ordeal.

The cynic perspective was dualistic. It presupposed that human nature was best seen as consisting of warring camps. These antagonistic groups were variously defined: victims and victimizers, dumbs and smarts, weaks and strongs, citizens and savages, men and supermen, friends and enemies, strangers and neighbors, even younger and older generations. The point is that the cynic perspective conceived as basically different the very natures of the members of the warring camps. Empathy across enemy lines was impossible. Human nature was simpler, more unequivocal, and more unchangeable in the cynic than in the tragic perspective. Instead of empathy and love, indignation and self-defensiveness were the practical ways to cope. Cynicism denied the premise that "all men are created equal." On the contrary, men were unlike in motivation, aspiration, and rationality: factual inequality existed. In operation, the hallmark of the cynic perspective was a contempt for a substantial sector of the human race. The style of the cynic was generally pejorative.

In chapter 4 I distinguished ten Laconia policemen who combined a tragic perspective with an integrated morality. These men were called professionals because they conformed to the professional political model. They were distinguishable from six reciprocators (who were characterized by a tragic perspective but a conflicted morality), five enforcers (who combined a cynical perspective with an integrated morality), and seven avoiders (who had a cynical perspective and conflicted morality). I refer the reader back to table 1 in that chapter.

I now want to deal with three factors which seem to have fostered the development of the ten professionals. By way of shorthand, let us call the factors language, learning, and leadership. The first denotes an enjoyment of talk. The second refers to the skill of the field sergeants in teaching the men of their squads on the job. The third points to the means available to a chief to affect the inner perspectives and passions of the patrolmen in his department. I have picked out these three factors, not because they are more "basic" than some other causes of professionalism, but because they are within the control of the department. Their force and direction can be influenced. They are factors of opportunity to a police organization.

## II

Policing demanded eloquence. If the twenty-eight young policemen agreed on any one point about their work, it was the vital importance of verbal facility in every aspect of their jobs. "The crux of police work is that ability to talk to people," they would say. There were many uses of eloquence—it was the key to taking charge in public. The professional response to each of the four paradoxes of power was based on eloquence. "Developing the beat," "gambling on the future," "playing the legal gatekeeper," and "using the restorative powers of time" were each distinguished from alternative responses by the heavy reliance they placed on sophisticated linguistic capacities. Lacking a ready and capable ability to talk, an individual policeman simply could not make professional responses and accept the risks inherent in them.

Likewise, eloquence was critical to influence other colleagues within the police department. Moreover, it was the basis of moral self-mastery.

Al Tennison was the orator par excellence in the Patrol Division. There was a poetry and an energy and a directness about everything he said, and his eloquence commanded attention. Born in Boston, Irish and wiry, a tough former marine, the son of a cashier in a CPA firm (he would say of his father, "He used to wear a belt *and* suspenders: what kind of a man is that?"), Tennison was a perfectly astounding speaker. He talked fast, said much, shaped ideas like an artist, tumbled one thought after the other, piled example upon example, distinguished and assimilated human wants, and dominated situations with his language.

He was also outspoken, proud, and impulsive. Of the twenty-eight young policemen, he stood out as the most frequently injured in street encounters (eight hospitalizations in five years). He was regarded as a "red shirt," a troublemaker, by members of the administration, and his membership on the grievance committee of the Police Officers' Association increased the significance of his public commentary. He would commit rhetorical excesses—not frequently, but often enough to fill himself with chagrin and, later, self-ridicule.[1] Tennison tended to intimidate his superiors, and the more self-confidence he developed, the more his superiors left him unsupervised and unrecognized. At the same time, the less heed the department paid to his unlimited array of suggestions, the more resentment he harbored. At last, embittered by the chief's distrust of him and feeling that the bed he had

---

1. I once heard Tennison tell two dozen police officers how he had made an undercover purchase of a lot of amphetamines from a dope dealer. "The guy said it would cost me 38 thousand dollars. All I gave him was my .38." This lapse into the jargon of TV made him suddenly pause, wince, and shake his head at himself.

made in the department was becoming increasingly uncomfortable, he quit to join a federal drug enforcement program.

But if he was a "red shirt" and a tough cop, he also was appreciated on his beat and admired by his peers as a policeman who had integrity and a sense of responsibility to his inner moral standards. Three of the other twenty-seven officers explicitly acknowledged his importance to their own development (only Peel was mentioned as often). Sergeants regarded him as a man of utmost versatility, who could be trusted to perform well the widest variety of police tasks. If any officer had charisma, it was Tennison.

The term "bullshitting" was the policeman's modest word for a capacity to talk. It encompassed skills of instruction (creating distinctions, identifying causes, projecting consequences, and providing perspective), argumentation (thinking on one's feet, summarizing another's intellectual position, speaking with conviction), manipulation (uttering credible threats and arriving at respectable compromises), and inspiration (touching the moral senses of others). Bullshitting required a moral and factual vocabulary. It was a capacity to express in the vernacular the most impalpable of emotions and to describe the most concrete of realities. And it consisted in its most powerful moments of the skill to use words with intense drama, as Tennison did when he described the funeral of a policeman and the emotions it evoked in him:

> It's real to see your best friend lying in a coffin, with his uniform on, his
> star—your friend. That's a dead cop. That's just like a dead law. It's like
> a piece of the law that has been torn right out of the book because some
> egomaniac ... shot him down. You say to yourself, "That could be me."
> It makes you face yourself. It causes—what shall we call it—introspection.
> That's why we're a fraternity.

Al Tennison's poetry made things very "real."

Tennison used his quick eloquence continually on the streets. He manipulated, argued with, taught, and inspired his citizenry. Imagine yourself surrounded by an apprehensive or curious or angry crowd, and try to think of how you might talk your way to a successful outcome. Here is how Tennison said he had handled various kinds of crowd scenes.

> I've got a thousand tricks. If he's grandstanding, if he's calling everybody
> pigs and motherfucking pigs, I turn to the crowd. There are ladies there;
> they've got feelings. They don't like it. I turn to the crowd and say,
> "You're the jury; how would you feel about this case?" Those women,
> those black women, have feelings. I've seen people quiet a guy down and
> take him right over to my car and say, "Why don't you just get in the car?"
> In effect, they're doing my police job for me. And people come out of their
> houses, waving a rolling pin at the guy. Why do they do it? They also want
> law and order. People know they have to have some kind of structured
> society.

Or you pick the loudest mouth in the crowd, and you make fun of
him. And they'll laugh at him, and pretty soon he leaves. Or I talk to the
most concerned citizen, who says, "What are you doing to the brother?"
He's owed an explanation; I don't say, "None of your business, and get
out of here." I tell him, "He's racing down your street where your kids
are." I try to show him I'm working for him, not for myself. Or if a guy
refuses to sign a citation, I say, "You know, you'll ultimately have to sign
this ticket, even if you have to spend a night in jail, and even if I have
to fill out all these reports. You'll either hurt me or hurt yourself; so why
don't you sign it now, and tell your story in the court?" "You're right,"
he'll say, sooner or later. "How can you beat it?" I'll tell him, "If you think
I'm wrong, tell it to the court."

Tennison put his eloquence to a wide variety of uses in these incidents—
shifting the crowd's role from partisan advocates to neutral jury, making fun,
redefining a situation, establishing a commitment to execute a threat,
pointing out legal avenues to resolve conflict, saving another's face. Most
important, he used his eloquence in public to defend himself from appearing
corrupt, partisan, petty, and foolish. His talking skills permitted him to face
demanding and uncomfortable situations feeling secure about his ability to
take charge. "You have to be willing to expose yourself," Tennison would
say, "you've got to be open and brazen as opposed to the fellow who'd like to
turn up his collar and take a hike." Eloquence was a precondition of
boldness—the determination to take risks, to buck heavy odds.

The point is not whether Tennison actually was as effective as he implied
he was. The point is that these situations actually happened on the streets
and frequently, and an alternative to violent control of each of them—
perhaps the only alternative—was eloquence. It was an alternative available
only to policemen who had honed their rhetorical powers.

Moreover, Tennison used his ability to take charge of conversations with
his fellow officers. Tennison had no qualms about correcting other policemen. This is how he described his methods of passing on criticism:

It's like a pig pile in football. You know what a pig pile is like. I don't like
to see people jumping in for the sake of jumping in. It's overkill, like using
an atomic bomb to shoot down a village. So I say to a policeman who I
think has overstepped himself, "Imagine a photo of what you have just
done." If they could only realize what they look like to the public, maybe
they'd think twice before they did it again. So I go to the radio afterwards
and put out a 940, "Meet with an officer." "I want a 940 with beat G."
That's meet an officer. It sounds official when you hear it on the radio, but
it may mean, "Let's have a cup of coffee together." And so we'll meet over
coffee, and I'll say, "I want to run a situation by you."
    Take the other day. My partner and I had gone into a coffee shop, and
we were lining up to pay for our coffee when two guys come barging in

through the back door of the coffee shop (how they got there I still can't
figure) and help themselves to some coffee and doughnuts, right in front
of this crowd of us. So I put out a 940 for these guys, and we sit down, and
I say, "I want to run a situation by you. It's a busy coffee shop, with people
lining up for service, and two policemen barge through the back door and
help themselves." And pretty soon the guy is saying, "That's me." "Well,"
I'll ask, "how does it sound to you as an observer?" "Well, I never saw it
that way." And I don't think he'll ever do it again. . . . You got to make
sure they don't think you are acting superior, but you can teach old dogs
new tricks, as a rule, if you go about it the right way.

Tennison took the risks of taking the lead in these matters—the risks of
evoking resentment, rebuke, antagonism. A few patrolmen feared to criticize
the actions of a fellow officer lest someday they would be in a dangerous and
dependent position and be betrayed by him. Many policemen preferred to
keep their noses out of other officers' business, often even when they were
ashamed of their own timidity. Not Tennison. Eloquence gave him the
self-confidence that he could accomplish the mission of colleague criticism
and avoid its risks. As a result of his success, he obtained a position of
recognized and accepted influence within the ranks of the Patrol Division.

Finally, eloquence permitted him to explain and justify his actions to
himself. He retained his personal sense of integrity, a sense of conformity to
his own personal moral codes while staying within the law. For example,
Tennison's beat included the red-light district in Laconia, a collection of
run-down hotels that served prostitutes. So-called victimless crimes, offenses
with willing or implicated customers, presented crucial moral choices to
policemen. To a unique degree, victimless crimes compelled policemen to
resort to extremely intrusive and coercive means of surveillance, which
offended people who felt their harmless conduct did not deserve police
attention. Moreover, the enforcement of laws against victimless crimes
created moral difficulties for policemen, who found it hard to justify the
encroachments on personal freedom implied by "morals laws."[2]

Every policeman had to resolve his indecision about morals offenses.
Failure to do so caused policemen to feel they were letting things slide, to lose
their sense of integrity, and to feel guilty. Tennison had made his decision,
for example, about harassing prostitutes:

Nine out of ten times I go the legal way. I'm not going to commit a crime.
I won't break the law to enforce the law. But I put weights on things. I
attach values to things. I ask, "What will happen if a citizen scores on the
date?" I used to set back and watch what went on and tighten my jaw until

2.  See Herbert L. Packer's brilliant discussion of victimless crimes in part 3 of *The Limits
of the Criminal Sanction* (Stanford, Calif.: Stanford University Press, 1968), pp. 247-366.

it was sore. But now I've learned to let my presence be known at times when I think it will do the most good. I stand on the corner among nine prostitutes, shooting the gas. Who's going to come by? The means don't always fit the end, and so forth. A person should be able to support what he does with the law, and never be outside the law. But the law isn't black and white. Just take a look at my favorite example of this, Penal Code Section 836: "A peace officer may . . . arrest a person . . . whenever he has reasonable cause to believe that the person to be arrested has committed a public offense in his presence." "May," "believe," "reasonable." There's your discretion. Those words are the name of the game. Nothing is black and white. Discretion. Judgment.

Repeatedly "shooting the gas" with the women violated the spirit of the criminal law, as some citizens interpreted it. It violated the normal way the Laconia police administrators expected patrol officers to perform their duties. Tennison, however, had acquired the verbal ammunition to quiet any outside criticism of what he was doing and his own self-doubts as well. He had talked himself into feeling what he was doing was legitimate, and he was willing to defend his actions in public or in his own conscience. The result was that he could be utterly candid about what he did and at the same time retain his sense of worthiness.

"Words are important" was Tennison's favorite motto. If his self-description was accurate, Tennison did not develop his mastery of the rhetorical craft until after he came on the department. However, like the nine other professionals under study, he revealed, at the time he was recruited to the department, an enjoyment of dialogue, a confidence in his ability to convince through language, and an appreciation of the importance and pleasures of talk.

At the time he applied to the department, each of the twenty-eight officers had been asked, "If you had the opportunity, and if nothing of the kind existed in the community where you live, would you prefer to found: (a) a debating society or forum; (b) a classical orchestra?" Each candidate had been instructed to distribute three points between the two alternatives, depending on their relative acceptability. Giving three points to one alternative and none to the other meant the candidate preferred the former and cared little about the latter. Giving two points to one alternative and only one to the other meant the candidate slightly preferred the first alternative to the second. The directions and the format were ambiguous enough to permit a strong inclination for one alternative to be scored three, even though the candidate also liked the second choice. The results are shown in table 4.

Of the ten professionals, seven indicated the strongest preference for founding a debating society, and none had a disinclination for doing so. Of the eighteen nonprofessionals, only one expressed a strong preference. Among the seven avoiders, five were disinclined to get involved in forensic activities.

Table 4                                                   Preference to Found a Debating Society

|  | Strong Preference (3) | Some Preference (2) | Disinclination (0 or 1) | Totals |
|---|---|---|---|---|
| Professionals | 7 | 3 | 0 | 10 |
| Reciprocators | 1 | 4 | 1 | 6 |
| Enforcers | 0 | 3 | 2 | 5 |
| Avoiders | 0 | 2 | 5 | 7 |
|  | 8 | 12 | 8 | 28 |

|  | (Andros, Chacon, Douglas, Justice, Patch, Peel, Wilkes) | (Bentham, Rolfe, Tennison) |  |
|---|---|---|---|
|  | (Hughes) | (Haig, Hooker, Ingersoll, Lancaster) | (Wrangel) |
|  |  | (Bacon, Kane, Kip) | (Carpasso, Russo) |
|  |  | (Longstreet, Thayer) | (Booth, Garfield, Nary, Rockingham, Tubman) |

Table 5                                                   Debate Preference and Scores on
                                                          Standardized Vocabulary Test

|  | High Vocabulary (40–50) | Medium Vocabulary (34–39) | Low Vocabulary (0–33) | Totals |
|---|---|---|---|---|
| Strong debate preference | 3 | 0 | 2 | 5 |
| Some debate preference | 2 | 3 | 2 | 7 |
| Disinclination to debate | 2 | 4 | 2 | 8 |
|  | 7 | 7 | 6 | 20 |

As measured on the 50-question vocabulary section of the Army General Classification Test: 40 or more correct answers marked the applicant as having a high vocabulary attainment; 33 or fewer correct answers marked the applicant as having a low vocabulary attainment.

If the answers to this somewhat ambiguous question were acceptable evidence of an enjoyment of talk, did this enjoyment correlate with any other qualities of the applicants? Interestingly enough, it did not correlate with high vocabulary attainment as measured on a standardized vocabulary test. Only twenty officers of the twenty-eight took the vocabulary test, but the results were not strongly related either to the answers on the debate question or to the kind of policeman the applicant came to be (see tables 5 and 6).

Not surprisingly, this preference for debate did correlate with minimal college exposure at the time of coming on the department. Seven of the eight applicants with a strong preference for debate had had one year of college or more at the time (see table 7). But there was no correlation whatever with the *completion* of junior college or the equivalent two years in a college or university (see table 8).

Such correlation, or lack of it, raises the question of the importance of an eligibility requirement of two years of college for police work. (Far more sophisticated and extensive work has been done on this subject than is possible with the limited data afforded by this study.)[3]

If completion of two years of college had been required for appointment on the department, only nine of the twenty-eight Laconia officers would have been eligible (among them, Tennison). Of those nine there would have been five professionals, two reciprocators, one enforcer, and one avoider. The other side of the story, however, would have been that five professionals would not have been eligible, along with four reciprocators. The costs of an eligibility requirement of two years of college appeared very great.[4]

On the other hand, many police officers seriously took up college studies once they were appointed to the department (including Tennison, who completed his last two years of college and obtained his B.A. five years after his appointment). The motivation to begin or resume college education was high. The law required any officer who had had no college exposure at all to take a minimum of two college courses after coming to the department. The department also provided some economic incentives to all officers to go to college. Often college courses attracted a policeman because they were likely to be helpful in preparing for a test for promotion within the department. But most important, the problems of police life motivated the officer to take college courses and repaid the extraordinary effort he made in attending college on a part-time basis. College courses increased verbal confidence, if we take the police officers' self-reports as evidence. They opened new concepts and provided the verbal handles to grasp ideas. Moreover, they provided evaluation of a man's power to communicate.

The thoughtful Peel, reflecting on the importance of language to police work, remarked:

> Verbal and language skills are so important. A guy can go all the way
> through the academy without picking up a dictionary. I've seen it happen,

---

3.  E.g., Louise Berman Wolitz, "An Analysis of the Labor Market for Policemen" (doctoral dissertation, University of California at Berkeley, Department of Economics, 1974).

4.  Such a requirement seems particularly problematic when one thinks that there is no evidence about the level at which eligible applicants who would have had to be appointed to fill the ranks would have performed.

and it shows. He needs the exposure to a college environment. You've got to know the right way to express yourself before you can recognize the wrong way. And it enables him to bend from the right way to speak when it's appropriate. In arresting a guy, in letting the guy know what he's arrested for, you're very proficient as a policeman in the language of the text; you have to translate the language of the text to fit the content of the situation.

His overall point was that a "college environment" was crucial to developing a good policeman's linguistic skills, but college experience could come after appointment to the police department. Peel even went so far as to argue that college experience without the necessary hunger to educate oneself was of much less value than college after the police experience had whetted the appetite for it.

With college: you don't want to make them go to college. That's putting the cart before the horse. You want them to become so interested in their work that they want to understand more about the world, and then they go back to college because they want to.

| Table 6 | | | Police Types and Scores on Standardized Vocabulary Test | |
|---|---|---|---|---|
| | High Vocabulary | Medium Vocabulary | Low Vocabulary | Totals |
| Professionals | 3 | 1 | 2 | 6 |
| Reciprocators | 2 | 2 | 1 | 5 |
| Enforcers | 1 | 1 | 2 | 4 |
| Avoiders | 1 | 3 | 1 | 5 |
| | 7 | 7 | 6 | 20 |
| | High (Andros, Rolfe, Justice) | Medium (Bentham) | Low (Chacon, Patch) | |
| | (Hughes, Wrangel) | (Hooker, Lancaster) | (Ingersoll) | |
| | (Kane) | (Russo) | (Bacon, Carpasso) | |
| | (Tubman) | (Booth, Garfield, Rockingham) | (Nary) | |

As measured on the 50-question vocabulary section of the Army General Classification Test: 40 or more correct answers marked the applicant as haveing a high vocabulary attainment; 33 or fewer correct answers marked the applicant as having a low vocabulary attainment.

Table 7                                      Debate Preference and a Minimum of
                                              One Year of College

|                        | Strong Preference (3) | Some Preference (2) | Disinclination (0 or 1) | Totals |
|------------------------|:---------------------:|:-------------------:|:-----------------------:|:------:|
| One year of college    | 7                     | 6                   | 4                       | 17     |
| No full year of college| 1                     | 6                   | 4                       | 11     |
|                        | 8                     | 12                  | 8                       | 28     |

The question of what motivated policemen to be "so interested in their work" as to want to expand their understanding and their verbal skills brings us to the next basic cause of professionalism: on-the-job learning. In a police department the nature of that learning depended upon one crucial person, the officer's sergeant. To the question of the sovereignty of the sergeants we now turn.[5]

## III

"The sergeant is the cornerstone of the organization, the keystone." "The sergeant is the crucial man in the department." "You think of men in their squads: they adapt to their sergeants." "It boils down to the sergeant.... If he's a crappy leader . . . , it always runs downhill right onto the men." "You may have an inept sergeant; there is no way to tell him he is, and get him to shape up—there is no system built into the department that can do that."

Thus patrol officers talked about the importance of their sergeants. From their vantage points, the person that dominated their understanding of reality and purpose was their immediate supervisor, the patrol sergeant. The chief, the deputy chief in charge of the Patrol Division, and the watch commander were, in comparison, remote and minute men, seen from afar and infrequently. The patrol officer saw none of them as being so crucial to his own development, for good or ill, as his sergeant. The reasons for the sovereignty of the sergeants were not hard to see.

The city of Laconia, on each of the three watches, would send out five squads of patrol officers to police the streets. Each of these squads was under the supervision of a sergeant and was assigned to patrol a discrete geographical area called a district.

Some of these sergeants were old-timers, on the department for ten and fifteen years. Others were extremely young. Beyond the fact that a man was

5.  In *The Autobiography of Malcolm X* (with the assistance of Alex Haley; New York: Grove Press, 1964), there is an essay on education in which Malcolm X argues the importance of two factors in an education: broadening one's "word-base" and engaging in the exhilaration of "debate" (pp. 169–90).

Table 8                                    Debate Preference and a Minimum of
                                           Two Years of College

|  | Strong Preference (3) | Some Preference (2) | Disinclination (0 or 1) | Totals |
|---|---|---|---|---|
| Two years of college | 3 | 4 | 2 | 9 |
| Less than two years of college | 5 | 8 | 6 | 19 |
|  | 8 | 12 | 8 | 28 |

| | | |
|---|---|---|
| (Andros, Justice, Wilkes) | (Hooker, Rolfe, Tennison, Thayer) | (Carpasso, Wrangel) |
| (Chacon, Douglas,* Hughes, Patch, Peel) | (Bacon,* Bentham,* Haig,* Ingersoll,* Kane, Kip,* Lancaster, Longstreet*) | (Booth, Garfield,* Nary,* Rockingham, Russo,* Tubman*) |

*Signifies no complete year of college.

not eligible for promotion to sergeant until he had had three years of experience, seniority counted for nothing in the departmental decisions about promotion. In Laconia, such decisions turned on the ranked results of a written exam (subject to a rarely invoked veto by the administration to block the promotion of an unequivocally inept candidate). The higher the exam score, the higher the candidate stood on the eligibility list for the next available opening.

Under the sergeant's supervision were the eleven men who worked the several beats in the district. As we earlier noted, each district contained a cross-section of the city's population. Laconia was longer east to west than it was wide north to south. Its northern edge ran along the river and its northern areas were flat and contained the oldest parts of town, predominately industrial and characteristically populated by the poor and minority groups. As one went south, geography and social status reached increasingly higher elevations. By the time the city crested in the Laconia hills along its southern boundary, the population had become rich and white.

Each district stretched from north to south and so contained the total social spectrum. The hillside beats within each district were always lonelier, whiter, and quieter than the riverside ones. Several of the busiest beats along the northern edge were patrolled by two cars, but generally one car was assigned to a beat. Within any squad, beat assignments were allotted on the basis of seniority: the rule was that the veteran got his preference, and the rookies divided the leftovers.

This combination of beat diversity within the district and the rule of seniority within the squad usually had this result: the youngest and most inexperienced members of the squad worked the busiest flatland areas in the north, the older and more experienced officers worked the districts south-ward, and the veteran cruised the hilltop on the southern border. Virtually every squad contained several different generations of officers.[6]

The way of assigning patrol officers to particular beats partially explained the great influence of the sergeant. The men called this system of manpower allocation within the division "the slave market." The metaphor alluded to the power exercised by the sergeants—the buyers.

Sergeants who had vacancies on their squads bid against one another for the "best" candidates in the available pool. The pool of available men consisted of four groups—the rookies, the undesirables, men recently transferred to Patrol from other divisions within the department, and those experienced officers who wished to leave their present squads for one reason or another. In a variety of ways sergeants developed means of assessing the capacities of the prospects under consideration. The capability of a rookie temporarily assigned to a squad for training would be well known to the squad members. Scuttlebutt, productivity sheets, evaluations, reports from the beat about the skills of "the relief man," provided what the sergeants considered useful information.

The metaphor of the slave market also expressed the involuntary condition of the typical patrol officer. Every rookie was first and invariably assigned to the Patrol Division and had to earn his way into other units of the department—Juvenile, Traffic, Training, Research, Investigation, Special Operations. Consequently, every man in the crucial initial stages of his career found himself dependent on pleasing some sergeant in order to escape from the wallflower status in the pool to a permanent assignment.

As a general rule, a sergeant would transfer out of Patrol after three years, and the new sergeant appointed to replace him would inherit a squad not of his own choosing. Nonetheless, because the turnover rate was so rapid among the numerous busy flatland beats, he was assured of having, in a relatively short time, the opportunity to affect the predominant character of the squad. Younger officers were continually seeking better beats, willing to transfer to new squads to do so, and leaving openings to be filled by the sergeant with men he persuaded to join him. Every new squad member thereafter would

---

6. This simplified picture can be made slightly more accurate by noting three factors. First, there was a select cadre of old-timers who walked skid row and the commercial districts nearby. Second, a special group of officers constituted a saturation patrol which the administration thrust into "high crime" areas, like a tactical reserve. And third, there were relief squads which replaced permanent squads on their days off: characteristically these relief squads were generally considered less desirable assignments than having a "permanent" beat of one's own.

take up his work in association with this discretely selected cadre of slightly older officers. Reflecting the preferences and the mode of operation of their sergeant, these officers would indoctrinate the latest member in the ways and views of the squad. Thus, the slave market gave the sergeant the opportunity to shape his squad in his own image and perpetuate itself. Every choice of manpower allocation within Patrol permitted the sovereignty of the sergeants to operate.[7]

There was a second device which gave added force to the patrol sergeant's organizational influence. He had the sole responsibility for making annual and even more frequent evaluations of the members of his squad. These evaluations were routinely required. Particularly in the early stages of a young policeman's career, these appraisals affected his career in critical ways. A bad set of evaluations meant purgatory: he lost his options, he earned a "reputation" among any potential "buyer" of his services, if his performance was rated poor. Through this process of evaluation, each new member of the squad came to a full appreciation of what his sergeant was looking for. Aggressive patrolling? Playing hunches? More street identifications and field contacts? Due process? Generous allocation of time to family crises? More sharing of information? The sergeant had a decisive and sanctioned means of communicating his preferences to his men.

Take Russo, the extremely young man whose cynic views and remorseless activity we earlier detailed. At the time he took his police training, the academy course lasted only four months; within one month of graduating from it he had received a permanent beat assignment. The sergeant who selected him submitted this six-month evaluation:

> You have shown a steady improvement in your ability to take charge of a situation, and I feel that as you gain experience and self-confidence, you will develop into a fine officer. I am pleased to have you assigned to my district.

A month and a half later, a second evaluation cited an example of police work which had pleased the sergeant:

> Your work has been good and has shown consistent improvement. During this period you . . . have shown yourself able to deal effectively with the citizens you come in contact with. I commend you on your recent arrest of two strong-arm robbery suspects. You showed above standard initiative and ingenuity in cruising the area searching for suspects after taking the complainant's report and in pursuing the suspects when they broke and ran. Together with covering officers, the suspects were tracked to a nearby

7. Some squads were more desirable than others because they enjoyed weekends off. Squads which had weekdays off tended to have younger, less privileged officers in their ranks than those squads whose regular days off fell on Friday, Saturday, and Sunday.

apartment and taken into custody [sic]. These suspects are believed
responsible for a series of extremely vicious attacks on elderly women, and
this problem seems to have ended with their arrest. Good work!

Then a month later a third evaluation mentioned some bad police work.

Your work has been satisfactory in most respects; however, your reports
do not reflect a check for witnesses. We have discussed the need for field
contact reports, and I expect to see improvement in this area.... When
dealing with prisoners and the public, your manner is good, but you need
to be more inquisitive and not hesitate to ask questions until you are satisfied you have obtained the true facts.... I feel you are developing that
"sixth sense" that is the mark of an outstanding officer. It is partly this
ability to detect persons or situations deserving closer scrutiny, and
following up on them. You have made several good arrests from seemingly
innocent stops. Good work.

In these evaluation reports the sergeant's idea of good police work was
repeatedly formulated and the officer's work appraised in light of it—
aggressiveness, suspicion, a minimax judgment, "a sixth sense." At least
arguably, some sergeants might insist that there were other standards of
good police work which were not mentioned by Russo's sergeant: for
example, not jacking up a neighborhood, using the "edge of fear" of arrest
without arresting, calming family beefs, developing the beat, learning
additional bits of the law outside the penal code. The omission of these
considerations was of crucial importance in Russo's development of his
understanding of the police mission. At the least, we can say that there was a
striking degree of congruence between Russo's later perception of what
constituted good and bad police work and his sergeant's understanding of
what constituted praiseworthy and unsatisfactory accomplishment as com-
municated through this highly threatening process.

But the patrol sergeant had at his disposal far more than threats with
which to influence his men. He had a monopoly of rewards. He had resources
which he effectively bartered in exchange for submission. He had the
respectability and the proximity to give a pat on the back. He had the
organizational know-how to help an officer frame a letter asking the
administration for special consideration: the timing of his vacation, the
taking of an extra day off, exoneration in any special inquiry, getting
permission to take a second job on the outside to earn additional income.
The sergeant had knowledge of especially dangerous circumstances in the
district. He had a sophisticated knowledge of the penal law that cut through
conundrums.[8] He assisted in particularly risky or delicate street encounters

8.  E.g., imagine a young policeman faced with decisions on whether to arrest, and for what,
    in this typical execution of the Murphy confidence game. The officer received a complaint

which had begun gradually to slip out of control. He could show the officer a repertoire of personal techniques which made work with the public easier. He could "take the heat" from above; that is, he could serve as an advocate for any man whose conduct was being criticized by the public or the administration. He provided explanations of baffling events: the arrangement of the social classes, the predominance of certain political forces, the processes and purposes of the police department. He could take men relatively new to the city away to his favorite duck-hunting area. And finally, he could give meaning and excitement to his men's work. Officer Douglas described the effect of a patrol sergeant on him.

> The district that was good was supervised by Sergeant Aurelis. He is a fantastic policeman. Fantastic mind. He keeps book on everybody. He'd go throughout his district and gather information. He was a huge guy. We'd feed all our information to him. He was a huge computer in which we'd store the information, and he would feed us it back when we needed it. He made you interested. He personally made you motivated. It was fun working with him.

In short, a sergeant could enrich his men in every conceivable way—with skills, knowledge, safety, self-respect, freedom from blame, friendship, better jobs, extra money, and even a sense of moral context. The sergeant offered these products of his time and experience to his men, and if the men voluntarily took advantage of these riches, the sergeant received undying and grateful credit.

In one sense, being able to withhold these favors might seem to constitute a form of punishment, but the patrol officer generally felt gratitude for a favor dispensed, not resentment at any withholding of these rare resources. Somehow the men tended to recognize that a resourceful sergeant was entitled to dispense his surplus of resources to whom he chose, exacting in return a degree of cooperation in both behavior and outlook. The sergeant enjoyed the advantages of reciprocity with his men: "interdependence," as one patrolman contentedly phrased it.

Finally, the sergeants exercised sovereignty within the department because they met so little resistance when they did so. Conceivably two sources of

---

about the suspect and his girl friend, who approached the complainant in a supermarket parking lot and offered to sell a color television cheap. The television, in a carton wrapped tightly in cellophane, papered with official-looking documents, like "Retail Price $295," was for sale "for $65." In fact the box contained a chunk of concrete and a piece of glass which, when seen through a crack in the carton, looked like a TV tube. The complainant had neither offered nor accepted the offer to buy the TV. In fact, his television had been stolen in a burglary a week before, and thinking the suspect was a burglar trying to convert his larceny into profit, he had called the police. With what crime should the suspect be charged?

opposition might have developed, the first from the administration, the second from the old-timers, those who by their practical superiority or their independence of organizational rewards and punishments were in a position to counteract the hegemony of the sergeants.

The administration, however, had virtually no control over which officers were promoted to sergeant, or, for that matter, over which sergeants were promoted to lieutenant. Such promotions were tightly controlled by civil service: there was a written examination on topics set publicly. Nor did the administration have freedom to punish sergeants in the Patrol Division. It could not threaten to transfer them to undesirable jobs because the job of a sergeant in Patrol, with its relative discomforts and difficulties, was widely regarded as the most undesirable job a sergeant could be required to take. Sergeants who wanted to be in the Patrol Division were in short supply. A sergeant, content to stay in Patrol, enjoyed the invulnerability of the dispossessed and the detached: having no hopes, he exposed no hostages.

Furthermore, there was the democratic ethos of decentralized administration: the conventional wisdom in the most thoughtful police circles was that the more discretion and responsible judgment that could be delegated to a patrol sergeant, the more active and useful a man he was likely to be. Largely this belief grew from necessity. For all practical purposes it was impossible for a superior to supervise a patrol sergeant's activity. Formal evaluations of patrol sergeants were attempted, but the lieutenants and the captains doing them had nowhere near enough information to do more than the most perfunctory job. Trust was given to patrol sergeants because there was little alternative. Their personal morale, their internalized sense of standards, were widely regarded as the only formidable check on their broad discretion. In every organization a level of responsibility is sooner or later reached where ongoing and close supervision becomes impractical and other ways—moral ways—of guaranteeing performance become paramount. In the police organization, the patrol sergeant attained that level.

The administration could place few checks on the patrol sergeants directly; and it did not have the time, the information, or the resources to exercise much countervailing influence directly on the patrolmen under the sergeants. Compared to the sergeant's rich bag of incentives, the chief could offer little of value to a large number of individual officers—certainly not promotion or added income or physical safety. In the next section, we will analyze what an impoverished and remote administration was capable of doing. For now it is enough to note that the police administration was unable to oppose the influence of the patrol sergeants, directly or indirectly, through reward or punishment.

The second source of potential resistance to the sovereignty of the sergeants was the aristocracy of the Patrol Division, the old-timers, the men who sat in the back row in lineups, whose ridicule and noncomformist example could devastate the respectability of all but the most adept sergeants. Because their assignments (if they were content with them) were permanent, because they could not be transferred or forced to quit their particular beats, because promotion was closed to them by the requirements of civil service, they were secure from retaliation from their supervisors. Because hilltop beats were equally distributed among districts, there were old-timers in every squad.

These extremely secure old-timers had the invulnerability to resist their sergeants. They could, if necessity called, humiliate, undercut, and at times wrest command of a district from an inept or officious sergeant. The veteran enforcer, Bee Heywood, told a story of one such mutiny in the ranks, organized by a group of veterans:

> Sergeants will come on the job, a new sergeant, and right away he's telling us everything to do. He's ignoring the way the patrolman has done the job before. "It's gotta be done this way." Well, one way to handle it, we decided, we'd call on the sergeant. We made him supervise, though he didn't know it. So he comes up to me one day, and he says, "What's with these dumb guys? They don't do anything on their own. They don't ever let me get a bite to eat." "You want to know the truth of it sergeant," I says. "You're a little excitable, and if you want a little peace of mind, you gotta change your ways. You treat your men as if you're the only one who knows anything when you butt in so much. A man takes pride in knowing what he knows. If a man accepts responsibility, let him take it."

The balance of power between old-timers and sergeants tended to stay intact. Yet the trouble with old-timers as a source of direct resistance to the sovereignty of the sergeants was that they were old-timers. A gerontocracy really had less at stake in the long run. Men who will die soon do not plant trees. You may recall Heywood's lament: "Sometimes it's real unpleasant. It's a real tough job. I don't enjoy it like I used to. As you get older, you don't want bitter fights, quarrels, enemies. As you get older, you want a little more peace, friends; you want to get away from all the strife." The old-timers did not want to interrupt their peaceful coexistence with their sergeants unless it was absolutely necessary. So long as the sergeants kept the old-timers happy—which they could do by leaving them alone in the hilltops—the collective resistance of the old-timers was rarely mobilized as a counterforce to the sergeants.

Moreover, the administration inadvertently weakened the old-timers' restraining influence on the sergeants. Original practice had been that the old-timers were assigned as the first field training officers of each rookie out of the academy. For the first few months of a rookie's experience on the streets, the old-timers had customarily been used to instruct and evaluate the

new recruit's performance in the field, eventually giving approval to the
young officer to go on his own.

In their recollections, many of the professionals and reciprocators
described the deep effect these first veteran training officers had had upon
them. Their words of wisdom were still remembered and could be repeated
verbatim. Douglas was typical in his recall of "my first cop":

> He'd been around twenty years or so. And he said to me, "The first thing
> when you contact someone, you're nice; you're nice to everyone, every-
> body. It doesn't make any difference who he is, whether he's raunchy and
> flea-bitten: you're nice. You can be nasty if he gets nasty, but not before. If
> you come on heavy, you can't back off." . . . He was one of the most cour-
> teous men you'll ever meet. He had the good fortune to be a large man; so
> perhaps he didn't have to be tough. You can't do it always, but it's surpris-
> ing how often he could find time to do it. [9]

The example of the "first cop" had given Douglas the assurance to resist the
pressures of his supervisors: he "knew" they did not have a monopoly on
acceptable practice, and it left him feeling free to shape his own mode of
operation.

Toward the end of the interview period, the chief changed this practice. He
sought to assert some control of his own over the first field training, partly to
strengthen his influence vis-à-vis the sergeant's hegemony, partly because of
a misguided feeling that the old-timers set a bad example for the trainees. He
selected certain exemplary "younger" officers, gave them a short training
course, and assigned them the responsibility of introducing the rookies to the
real world. Professionals like Justice and Wilkes, along with reciprocators
like Haig and Ingersoll, were selected, and they served for a brief time.
Before long, however, they began to resign. There were no monetary
incentives to compensate them for their additional training responsibilities,
and they did not derive much satisfaction from the job. Their avuncular
senses never got engaged. Soon the administration was going to the bottom of
the barrel to man the field training officer program. It made some bad
choices (in one instance the disastrous Garfield was selected). The program
began to break down. Already having interfered with the natural influence of
seniority, the administration found itself in an even weaker position. The
vacuum left by the breakdown of the artificial field training program

---

9. Hooker spoke in much the same way, in chapter 6: "He was an old-timer. The thing
that caught my eye was that he was fantastic with people. He was easygoing, without riling
them up. He didn't have anybody resisting him. I'm talking of 999s, family squabbles.
He was really good with them. He was real easygoing, good with people. At the end, he
said, 'Hooker, I know there are a lot of things I didn't show you. We didn't make many
car stops or arrests, and we didn't stop people walking along the streets. I don't believe
in it. You'll have to learn that from someone else.'"

strengthened even more the sergeants' monopoly of influence within the department. The old-timers' countervailing influence was undercut, and nothing substantial was created to replace it. The administration's efforts to bolster its own powers turned out only to weaken the resistance of its one ally, the aristocracy of the old-timers, leaving the sergeants even more powerful.

There were two distinct advantages to the sovereignty of the sergeants. One was diversity; different sergeants, in making use of the slave market, assembled squads that were different. Sergeants had different preferences for the kind of men they wanted to supervise. Peel recalled his own experience:

> There was something very distinctive about our district. We had high pro-
> ductivity—no matter what you measured: high felony arrests, high traffic
> citations, high drunks, all that. But the key to our district was the fact that
> we had an older sergeant who picked younger men who were right guys.
> He ended up, for example, with valedictorians from four academy classes.
> They were really bright fellows. . . . You see, the men are allocated to the
> districts at manpower meetings. This old sergeant took advantage of the
> fact that the younger men were not terribly popular. But he took the top
> of the young men, and then he maintained very close liaison with all of us.

Other sergeants preferred veterans, or big men, or aggressive officers, or passive ones.

This diversity had several results. First, it provided the conditions of human inventiveness. It was stimulating. Having so many different operations within one department, officers saw they had choices and that things could be different. The range of acceptable ways of doing police work expanded because there were so many alternative examples of successful police work already being practiced. Second, through processes of consultation, competition, and persuasion, ideas that had met the test of practical experience were spread to other nooks and crannies of the department. The process of this dissemination was uneven, and frequently the ideas were altered in transition. For example, Peel's radical educational practices were never imitated in toto, and efforts made by others to re-create some aspects of his program of developmental education bore scant resemblance to their progenitor. Nonetheless, the norm that Traffic units bore an important responsibility to help Patrol in doing its routine work did gain increased currency among Traffic cops ("First, you're a policeman, then a Traffic cop"). The communication between squads was not always direct, from sergeant to sergeant, although it sometimes was. Just as frequently, the message was delivered by a man transferred to a new squad, who would bring old notions from his previous squad and seek through persuasion to preserve what he deemed best in his former situation. Thus, diversity, combined with mobility, gave men perspective, choice, and the motivation to proselytize and participate in the governance of their squads.

The second result of the sovereignty of the sergeants was the articulation of a theory of decentralization, which made the entire system of trial and error legitimate. Decentralization as a theory consisted of an argument based on efficiency: the most efficient arrangement in a police department was to delegate the discretion to decide down to the smallest possible unit capable of managing a matter. Efficiency, so the argument asserted, depended upon establishing a process for making rational decisions, and the quality of any decision was directly related to the success by which bits of information could be combined within a frame of reference: the more informed the decision the better, assuming that the context relating these bits to one another was substantially equivalent across units. Bits of information needed a context of understanding in order to be meaningful and useful. The tendency within a police department subscribing to decentralization was for the administration to try to convey the larger context down to the men who had the facts, rather than forcing the men to transmit their bits of information up to the frame of reference possessed by some superior class. Thus, decentralization provided the ethos within the police bureaucracy to educate and develop its every member, even the most inexperienced patrol officer. In a bureaucracy where the pattern of legitimate control was centralization, the administration retained a monopoly of understanding the big picture. Where decentralization was the prevailing belief, the impulse was reversed, and the desirable objective was defined in terms of the development of many well-rounded human beings, all of whom had the big picture.

The oligarchy of the sergeants had disadvantages. One was the lack of uniform street justice within the city. Citizens received different treatment less on the basis of their race or their wealth (although the paradox of dispossession should lead the reader to expect that this latter distinction should have some importance) than on the basis of the district they happened to live in. The individual sergeant made a difference in how the public was dealt with. For example, the easternmost district at certain times during the study had an unrivaled reputation for toughness and high activity. "District V ought to have a radio channel all its own," patrolmen would say, an observation reflecting not only the high crime rate in the area but also the aggressiveness and gangbuster gusto which the sergeants in that district demanded of their squads. Policemen who were inclined to this style of policing (the kind who would say, "What I like best is the worst beat with a little leeway") sought assignment to that district. Those who were disturbed by that kind of remorselessness sought to be transferred to districts where jacking up the neighborhood was considered out of bounds. To the extent that diversity and decentralization permitted gross differences in treatment of the citizenry, the law did not provide an adequate measure of equal protection. The resulting consequences were the baleful twins, citizen alienation and police demoralization.

Second, diversity by itself did not assure that the best examples of police conduct would thrive and the worst would perish and disappear. Theoretically, and in fact, it was possible that any single squad's example of incompetence, corruption, ruthlessness, or laziness might infect other districts. One illustration of this pathology involved quotas.

The chief despised any definition of good police work which smacked of numbers of arrests. The few policemen who had ever discussed this matter of "productivity" with him for any length of time came away convinced that the chief's outlook was, "You don't arrest unless you absolutely have to." Indeed, the chief let it be known that a large number of arrests for certain kinds of offenses (particularly charges of resisting arrest) would be deemed to indicate ineptitude. By his lights quotas were deplorable and had no place within his police department. Unquestionably, the majority of the sample of young policemen we have been studying shared his view. Only the five enforcers—Bacon, Carpasso, Kane, Kip, and Russo—adhered to the belief that quantity of arrests and quality of police work were practical equivalents.

Yet most squads behaved as if quotas were prescribed, and most of the men in Patrol and Traffic worried about falling short of some vague minimum number of felony arrests, traffic violations, and drunk arrests. Typically the kindly Ingersoll took a half hour of his patrol time to wait at a traffic ticket "duck pond" in order to "get our ticket." Longstreet described the pressures to get arrests in more unequivocal terms. Speaking of the expected productivity of a Traffic cop, he observed: "We are expected now to write 260 tickets in a six-week watch. It's gone up. It used to be 240, eight a day." Perhaps there were a few squads where the quota system was eliminated in practical effect. Diversity, however, did not expand these "good" examples, i.e., good from the chief's perspective. On the contrary, far from there being an increase in the number of squads responding positively to the chief's expressed deemphasis of arrests, new sergeants who might have been expected to disabuse their men about the quota system actually seemed to enforce that system.

In part the department's own practices inadvertently stifled the diffusion of the "good" examples and gave life to the bad. By providing each officer with a form on which to tabulate and report the numbers and kinds of arrests he had made, the administration set in motion an unmistakable implication that there were quotas. The "activity sheet," as this form was called, preserved a tangible record of the law enforcement aspects of each policeman's work; the department took no other steps to tabulate descriptions of different aspects of police work—how a policeman dealt with family beefs, how he teamed with fellow squad members, how he developed his beat. Thus, a prudent policeman, knowing that this numerical kind of information would be available to anyone who wished to use it, for better or worse, sought to nullify all conceivably damaging inferences which could be drawn from his quantitative record. He neutralized the activity sheet by keeping it above suspicion, by adhering to modal numbers of arrests, and by shying from extremes. He went out, as Ingersoll did, and "got our ticket."

Then too officers knew that a patrol sergeant who was lazy or inept, and thus had no firsthand knowledge of the work performed by his men, tended to document his evaluations with these activity sheets. In the case of an ignorant sergeant, the availability of these sheets biased his thinking toward some quantitative definition of good police work, regardless of the chief's abhorrence of it. As happens so frequently in life, the means determined the ends: the activity sheets altered the organizational purpose.

Haig had such a sergeant, considered throughout the department as completely incompetent. At the end of Haig's third month on his squad, his sergeant wrote this evaluation: "Quantity is less than your capabilities would warrant. You have the ability to perform above standard work, but you have not shown the enthusiasm to reach your potential. A more energetic approach to your duties, greater drive in all-around productivity ... would improve your rating." Haig's reaction to this invitation to make more arrests ("greater drive in all-around productivity") was demoralization, pushing him deeper into disfavor. Other officers took an easier way out and got along by going along. Thus the quota system could be said to have a life of its own, defying the preferences of the chief and most of the men. The worst practices began to spread throughout Patrol, instead of the best's circulating ever more broadly.

The third major disadvantage of the sergeants' sovereignty stemmed from the timidity of some of the sergeants. Not all the patrol sergeants were worthy to have so much independence. We should not have expected from sergeants as a class a distribution of attitudes toward authority substantially different from the range of attitudes held by other police officers. We should have expected that some sergeants would be corrupted by their power and that some would simply take a hike, bothered by the implications of having to exercise power. In fact, there were a substantial number of sergeants who avoided supervising their squads. They simply grew timid about their men. Why?

The timid sergeant was threatened by the evaluation process to which he was subject. As he saw it, if his men did not obey his orders, if they embarrassed him, their actions would reflect on him and lower his supervisor's evaluation of him. Thus he began to try to curry favor with his squad by overlooking their misdeeds or inaction. This often turned into blatant, studied ignorance of his men and what they were doing. Squad members quickly sensed this kind of sergeant and took advantage of his vulnerable dependence upon them. They knew they held their sergeant's reputation hostage. The ransom they exacted for their cooperation was a permanent surrender of his authority to evaluate or punish them. In Patrol this surrender of responsibility occurred more frequently than might have been expected because so many sergeants wished to transfer out of Patrol as quickly as possible. The long and changing hours of Patrol, the bad working conditions, and the lower intellectual status of Patrol compared to Investigation prompted sergeants to seek escape from Patrol. Wanting so eagerly to be transferred made them vulnerable to their squads' subtle extortionate demands. Where sergeants were sovereign but unwilling to rule, a learning vacuum occurred. In squads like these, the men went uncorrected, untaught, and unschooled, left to cope with the problems and paradoxes of power by themselves, their tendency to the cynic perspective unchecked, their anxieties about power unrelieved.

## IV

In contrast to the sergeants, the chief had little leverage on patrol officers. They did not depend on him for anything. He did not promote them: civil service took care of that. He could transfer an infinitesimal number of them because there were so few favorable positions outside Patrol open to men who had not yet made sergeant. He could not offer pay differentials within any one rank. He could not even get the city to grant extra increments of salary to an officer willing to take on added responsibilities (hence the field training officer program began to collapse for lack of sufficient incentive pay). He could from time to time reorganize some part of the department, thereby opening up new positions for people who saw things his way; organizational change, however, was unsettling and diminished in utility the more often it occurred. The chief had few credit items to exchange. He simply had too little in the way of resources to reward or purchase individual acceptance of his influence.

If he had any one major source of gentle influence, it was the credit he gained in keeping the department free from external influences. The chief's business, from the patrolman's point of view, was to attend to the external relations of the department, dealing with the city manager, the city council, and business and political groups. In the late 1960s and early 1970s, when police departments were thrust into the public spotlight, the men in the Laconia police ranks appreciated the chief's ability to keep outsiders from intruding upon the department. The chief's one major credit within the ranks came from the men's acknowledgment of his success in this important respect.

Nonetheless, freedom from external interference was a collective good, not severable and distributable to particular individuals in discrete packages. In this respect the chief had no patronage. Compared to the Patrol sergeants, the chief could offer little individual inducement.

If he could not reward, however, he could punish. He could threaten great injury to his men. He could detect infractions of the laws and regulations and discipline those who committed them. This he did with a vengeance. He developed an internal disciplinary process as imposing and forbidding as that of any police department in the country. He assigned his Internal Affairs a full investigative staff. He devoted a major part of his time to reviewing its conduct. He treated it as directly responsible to him, on several occasions requiring it to change findings and recommendations which he regarded as unduly lenient. He made sure that the decisions of Internal Affairs had the widest possible publicity throughout the department. Moreover, he saw to it that the procedures of inquiry and the rules of evidence employed by Internal Affairs favored the public complainant against the policeman: there was no confrontation or cross-examination of witnesses; complaints could be made anonymously; there was no presumption of innocence or rule of reasonable doubt; the officer was not permitted to invoke the privilege against self-incrimination; legal counsel could not represent him before Internal Affairs; the officer was not permitted to propose findings of fact or rules of law. There was no independent jury. The opinions, although in writing, never set forth the strongest contentions of the policeman in his own defense and attempted to rebut them systematically. The chief decided whether and in what degree to punish the officer, suspending him (each day of suspension amounted to a fine of at least $60), demoting him, or dismissing him. By any standards of due process, Internal Affairs was an inquisitorial and tyrannical institution.[10]

There were certain safeguards, of course. Appeals of dismissals in particular were possible, first to the Civil Service Board (as in Chacon's case) and then to the courts. The Police Officers' Association, once aroused, could

---

10. In contrast to Internal Affairs, several other disciplinary devices existed in the department which provided a significant measure of due process. As a consequence, each of them had a high degree of openness, participation, and acceptance among the men. Among these devices were (1) the shooting board (whenever a police firearm was discharged, accidentally or otherwise, the department established a panel to inquire into the causes and justification of the shooting); (2) a conflict management panel (an ad hoc panel of command and field officers was convened to examine any officer with an excessive number of 603s—charges against citizens for resisting arrest); and to a lesser degree (3) a safety board (a panel of officers and civilians specialized in Traffic matters examined every substantial motor vehicle accident involving police officers). In varying measure each of these different panels comprised members independent of the administration; the subject officer participated in the presentation and examination of all evidence; and the disciplinary purpose of the inquiry was expressly supplemented by an educational function, not only of the officer under examination but also of those officers on the panels.

finance these appeals and otherwise seek to organize collective opposition to particularly tyrannical actions. Nonetheless, throughout the officer ranks, the chief's Internal Affairs loomed large as a frightening and ubiquitous prosecutor. Longstreet summed up this sentiment: "I'll tell you. I worry about the men upstairs." The men left no doubt about the worry the chief's remorseless, disciplinary practices caused in them. Internal Affairs terrified them. Furthermore, the chief's detractors and those who sang his praises alike agreed that his reign of terror had succeeded in tempering the most offensive practices of those policemen who had been inclined to brutality, rudeness, or venality. The disciplinary process had produced so many harsh examples that the most hardened enforcer was convinced that the jig was up for blatant and unjustifiable misconduct. Longstreet, who once relished the old days of bar brawls and jacking up "the high crime areas," summed up the effects of the chief's punitive practices as they had affected him: "I'm so polite, it's sickening. But I'll take it [i.e., the public's incivility toward policemen] because of Internal Affairs."

But if some undesirable practices were curbed, there were dangers and definite limits inherent in an exclusively punitive basis of administrative control. Those limits might best be summed up as the contradiction in using tyrannical coercion to extort respect for the rule of law.[11]

Internal Affairs, as the chief used it, was a political instrument: it was not neutral (plainly it was the chief's administrative right arm); it was not fair (the procedures and rules of evidence violated every basic assumption of due process); it was harsh (dismissals occurred with relative frequency); it was crazy (mitigating circumstances on the policeman's behalf were deemed irrelevant).

The chief's reign of terror evoked at least five seriously counterproductive responses. First, the policemen came to treat Internal Affairs as an unscrupulous enemy. The lack of dispassionate neutrality entitled good men to lie to it and deceive it and try to beat it. Justice's response to Internal Affairs in the Chacon case illustrated the antagonism it evoked. It aroused responses of vengeance, mistrust, cunning, and ignorance. By abjuring the limits of judicial inquiry, Internal Affairs lost its moral entitlement to be treated fairly in return. Men who would not have felt right about lying in a courtroom found themselves justifying purposeful deception in defiance of the naked force of Internal Affairs.

Second, the reign of terror infected the men with overcautiousness in their everyday street activity. They shied away from troublesome situations, preferring (in Longstreet's terms) to "kiss it off" rather than run the risk of

---

11.   On this provocative topic, see Byron Jackson's Ph.D. dissertation on "Police Leadership" (Department of Political Science, University of California, Berkeley; to be completed).

taking action and exposing themselves to public complaint. Administration coercion, to the degree it was practiced in Laconia, could restrain active misconduct and purposeful violence. It could do little to motivate proper conduct and to detect inaction. Longstreet personified the tendency to avoidance which official intimidation prompted. Some cops simply stopped working, whether from vengeance, demoralization, or fear. How widespread or enduring these reactions were was hard to assess. Inactivity was difficult to measure, and a variety of counterforces against avoidance were begun in the wake of the introduction of this reign of terror. Nonetheless, policemen, sensitive and observant ones, perceived the effects of fear.

Third, the reign of terror appeared to inhibit "taking a chance," the trial and error necessary to a young policeman's development. It made the young officer too responsible too quickly, forcing him to adhere to a proclaimed way of doing things rather than encouraging him to discover an appropriate way for himself. There is a great amount of learning that comes from rediscovering the wheel. Internal Affairs, in the zealous ways it policed the policemen, imposed a radical restriction on the liberty of young policemen to experience the varying results of different procedures. That was the point Peel made with this anecdote about one of his younger squad members:

> He saw a couple jaywalking: rather than ticket both of them, he cited the man and flippantly made some remark to her like he was "just dragging her along." Well, she broke down into tears; apparently her father had just died. It may have been the wrong thing to say, but he had tried to handle the matter with intelligence and humor, but Internal Affairs criticzted him for not behaving in "a businesslike manner." That was awful. For you don't want your men treating the citizenry and behaving like automatons and detached machines.

It was the long-range development of the policeman which suffered the most from the chief's intrusive surveillance. In Peel's mind, a strict and punitive reaction by the department simply discouraged independent judgment.

Fourth, Internal Affairs encouraged secrecy. Men clammed up. The costs of disclosure were too great. The result was to isolate the chief and administrators close to him from informal sources of intelligence about how his men felt, what they were thinking, what their problems and accomplishments were.

Fifth, what made the reign of terror so effective was the chief's reputation for being harsh, irrational, detached, and remorseless. To make the threat of Internal Affairs effective, he had to establish the reality of his cruelty. The difficulty of such a posture was that it concomitantly increased the status of some of the worst cynics in the ranks among their fellow officers. The cynics, accounting for the chief's behavior in a dualistic and satanic context, could point to the chief's statements and punitive actions to support their theories of what was going on in the department and outside it. Their explanations fomented mistrust of and opposition to every action of the chief. At the same time, some of the chief's postures undercut his potential adherents, those who liked and could argue for his larger purposes. Insofar as the chief used means which galvanized his detractors and reduced the influence of his supporters, his punitive processes worked at cross-purposes to his effort to expand his influence.

Retaliation, demoralization, curtailed experimentation, secrecy, and disillusionment were some of the most severe costs of the wholesale use of the purely punitive process. Reliance on cruel discipline ultimately produced sharply diminishing returns and would have been disastrous except for the fact that the chief supplemented his terrifying actions with acts of moral leadership, which reinstilled principle, morale, willingness to take risks, candor, and faith. To the matter of how the chief accomplished these creative acts of leadership and maintained some system of cooperation within the police organization, we now turn.

## V

The chief was not a charismatic or inspiring person. He was not a policeman's policeman. He had limited experience as a field officer, having risen through the ranks in desk units like Research and Development and Training. His personality was brittle, minimally resilient when buffeted by criticism. His youthful shyness had transformed itself into an abhorrent habit of denigrating and humiliating his subordinates. He treated his policemen often as if they were not made of human stuff. He had no ear for the problems of the heart. On the other hand, he was highly intelligent, farsighted, courageous, and determined. An encounter with the more vicious aspects of his character, however, tended to blind the observer to these virtues. In many ways, he was the last person from whom one could expect moral leadership in a police department.

Yet, among the twenty-eight young men of our sample, morale was good and was improving. Despite the fact that they had organizational criticisms and suffered personal disappointments, most of the men worked hard, with a sense of personal satisfaction. They felt they were members of the best department in the country, and they acted like it. They were proud they worked in accordance with the law, including Supreme Court decisions and the chief's stringent regulations. They appreciated their incorruptibility. They were proud of the increasing number of policemen from minority groups and proud of the quality of the men who wanted to be on their police department. By any measure their morale—their willingness to make sacrifices for the collective effort—was high.

The undeniable point was that, despite the chief's personal lack of grace and his frequent resort to punitive control of his men, he administered a department infused with a sense of purpose from which his men derived dignity and moral meaning.

The secret of the chief's success in moral matters was his use of the policeman's appetite for understanding. In the seven years in which he served as chief, he expanded the Training Division in personnel and curriculum. He extended the duration of the academy course for recruits from ten weeks to thirty-eight weeks. He created a series of courses for sergeants, lieutenants, jailors, communications dispatchers, the Vice squad, personnel interviewers, advanced officers (men who had been on the department for three years or more), and field training officers. In short, just about every major unit of the department except Juvenile, Investigation, and Traffic was systematically brought in for continuing professional education. In batches of twenty men, Training incessantly conducted introductory and two-week refresher courses. Discussions, problem sets, simulation, and lectures: the techniques were always changing, but the education never ceased.

The chief participated in every aspect of the training programs. His ideas and influence pervaded the curriculum. He also tried to meet once with each class of trainees, whether rookies or veterans. Ironically, although the chief could not countenance criticism elsewhere, he often reveled in the contention invited in classrooms. While he otherwise appeared remote and tense, in the classroom he was relaxed and familiar. Where he tended to humble and defeat subordinates in day-to-day affairs, he encouraged and inspired men in classrooms. He had found an institutional structure which permitted him to rely confidently on his intelligence, without the defensiveness and embittering vindictiveness which infected his conduct under other circumstances.

More important, the men he selected to conduct Training complemented his strengths. They gradually developed a new style of teaching police courses. It was a style inviting participation, discussion, argument, and questioning in every class. Under the chief's regime, the courses no longer predominantly consisted of lectures and increasingly took on the appearance of seminars. The recruits, for example, were evaluated for class participation. The advanced officers and the sergeants were encouraged to contend, to play the devil's advocate, and to question department policy.

None of these matters went so smoothly as this brief description might make it sound. Busy men were used to being told and ruminating about topics later and privately, instead of having to make an effort to talk about them publicly in classrooms. Sometimes the chief woke on the wrong side of the bed, and the discussions turned into confrontations "where civility went down the drain," as Rolfe put it. Some Training officers fell short of infusing their classes with enthusiasm, balanced skepticism, or motivation. Nevertheless, the pattern was set, and the effects were undeniable. The administration, through Training, provided the men with understanding and, in doing so, endowed old activities with new meaning.

Two examples will suffice. In the refresher course for sergeants, the men were exposed to a concept of organizational theory called the Blake-Mouton grid. Simply put, the grid consisted of a two-dimenional evaluation of supervisors, the two dimensions being group task accomplishment (efficiency) and concern for subordinates (affection). The dimensions were scaled in nine-degree increments, and the sergeants were introduced to this measure by using the grid to evaluate themselves and discussing the evaluations with the class.[12] A "9:1" sergeant was a go-getter, little concerned about the individual feelings of his men but outstanding at eliciting squad productivity. A "1:9," on the other hand, was the archetypical kindly sergeant, solicitous of his men's personal well-being but not overly concerned about his squad's collective effort. When the first class of sergeants was subjected to this concept, the vernacular of policemen within the department suddenly began to change. The locker room talk began to abound with "1:9s" and "9:1s" and "5:5s" and "9:4s," terms applied not only to sergeants but also to chiefs, patrol officers, and citizenry. Imitation, conventional wisdom has it, is the sincerest form of flattery: the widespread use of these terms was an utterly honest acknowledgment of the contribution of Training to the men's well-being.

This language provided a neat handle for a number of important observations policemen had been accumulating but could not express. It provided a vocabulary of degree about which the policemen's vernacular vocabulary was more equivocal and less systematic. (These scores took the place of such endearing, local terms as "General Joe," "Hysterical Harry," and "the Human Computer.") The terms also helped the sergeants understand their job by factoring out the dual but separate criteria of external performance and inner growth and at the same time provided an easily remembered way to describe the relationship between these separate, equally desirable, but often antithetical goals. For the sergeants this simple expression of measures of success was revitalizing. Previously some sergeants had often been discouraged and felt inadequate because their men did not feel the same warmth for them that other squads felt for their sergeants. The "9:1" grid offered this kind of sergeant assurance that he was very much an effective supervisor and that his value to the department was legitimately measured in terms other than the affection of his men. Ironically, a frequent consequence of that reassurance was to relax him, whereupon he began paying greater attention to the personal concerns of his men. The sergeant

12.   Shades of Peel's work with his Traffic squad!

who enjoyed developing his men was enabled, by the evaluative concept contained in the grid, to contend with his own self-doubts about the propriety of his enjoyment. Whatever the dynamics in any individual case, the effect was to shore up the self-confidence of the sergeants.

At the other end of the ranks, the patrol officers (many of whom would someday become supervisors) grasped terms which gave them perspective on the supervisor's job. The language of the grid conveyed to them, in ways the vernacular categories of sergeants had not, a feeling for the complexity of a patrol sergeant's job, and it corrected unrealistic expectations.

A second example. In the field training officer program, Training sought to describe what the recruits were exposed to in the expanded academy curriculum. Among other things, the field training officers read a paper on "The Police Subculture," prepared by one of the Training sergeants for orienting the recruits to their new life. In the field training officer class, the paper provoked discussions of considerably greater intensity than ever took place among the recruits. One consequence was that Training invited these older officers to criticize and add to the paper. It gave the experienced officers great satisfaction to participate in shaping what was taught to the rookies. It thus allayed a widespread mistrust previously directed at the Training Division. This mistrust originally came from Training's close identification with the chief, and usually took the form of a voiced suspicion among old-timers that the chief was talking down the experienced officers to the rookies. The class on police subculture revealed that the administration was not the enemy of the ranks but a rather wise and appreciative associate. It showed the administration paying enough attention to the humanity of the men to understand them. At the same time, the topic of police subculture permitted a discussion of departmental and personal goals.

"New ideas and old experience: together they're a pretty valuable tool." In that homely sentence one professional characterized the importance of leadership. Ideas, the most inexhaustible means of influence, neutralized some of the bitterness against the chief and provided a means of redirecting the resourceful advantages of the sergeants. It required, at least in Laconia, an extensive institutional mechanism, the Training Division. As the men changed from year to year, their intellectual needs changed as well, requiring new substance in the curriculum.[13]

13.  The professional Rolfe made this observation: "We are starting to get a different type of guy as a police officer. And perhaps these social awareness blocks are perhaps of less significance than they used to be. You know, now these guys have had four years of college, and maybe some postgraduate training, and then they took off a couple of years.... Not the majority, but we have a few. They have had no military service, but they have had all the social issues of the day.... Imagine a guy who comes on now at 21, 22: he was ten years old in 1960, and he has had lots of exposure. Some of these things

But the process was important and was established—argument, exchange of experiences, openness, the whetting of the appetite for ideas, the recognition of problems, and the time for detached reflection.

"The Training Division is the heart of the department in one way," Rolfe liked to say. In many ways his metaphor was right. Training was the administration's successful attempt to respond to the moral matters in men's hearts. Training dealt as much with the moral as with the intellectual perplexities of being a policeman. Without a feeling that the world mattered, policemen often surrendered to the worst effects of the paradoxes of power. The Training Division, however, provided the motives, the tools, the stimulation, and the sanctuary which busy men needed to get perspective on their lives, to redefine purposes, to challenge old assumptions, and to become morally creative. The effect was profound.

> The morale is up in this department. It all started with the sergeants' school, I think. (And also the fact that we were paying attention to our men with the field training officer schools. . . .) It just showed that we were doing something at last. But when the chief came into the sergeants' school and said, "We are giving back to you the authority you surrendered many years ago," that really did something.

Thus, the administration reinvigorated its men.

I think Rolfe's observation, that the device which had the most profound effect on the department was the sergeants' school, is very instructive. In schooling his sergeants, the chief capitalized on their natural sovereignty, legitimated it, and persuaded them to use it to inspire and instruct the men in their squads. The supplying of moral leadership to men in their daily lives could take a most subtle and roundabout course, but it was of supreme importance, whether done directly or indirectly. Without moral meaning, without what McCleery would call "a controlling definition of a confused

---

can get a little repetitive. I taught a course called Civil Protest. It was a course a university professor developed and taught; then Sergeant Ford did, and then it was handed to me. I was low man on the totem pole. It had some very interesting aspects. It developed the matter historically: 1640, 1740, the American Revolution as a form of social protest, and all that. But these guys we have as trainees, they aren't dummies. So the second time I taught it, I cut out the lecture, and led them into a discussion. I started off by saying that maybe we should rehearse a few things they knew and then think about them in a new light. Now they were policemen, and what did social protest mean to them as policemen. That was a success. These guys are very sophisticated, very good. . . . What they now lack, men before them had in abundance. The men we had before, you know, they may have been brought up on a farm and been shooting since they were knee-high, or they'd all been in the service. But some of these rookies have never had a gun in their hands before. . . . I talked this observation over with the rangemaster, and we suddenly started teaching the basics of firearms. They learn well once I understood that. It's probably easier to teach them to shoot well than if they had to unlearn old tricks—if you know where to start teaching them. . . . Up here we are changing all the time, and it's interesting."

situation,"[14] the "blooming, buzzing confusion of the world" aroused "continual fear and danger of violent death; and the life of man, [became] solitary, poor, nasty, brutish, and short."[15]

## VI

I hope by this time, reader, that you have developed strong feelings about the chief. His men did. While they granted him intelligence, in their eyes he was uncivilized, not gentle; vindictive, not forgiving; detached, not sympathetic; an ideologue, not rational; above all, unfair, not evenhanded. He was, in short, cruel, or at least fearsome.

At the same time, he brought about universally appreciated improvements in the department. Even his detractors acknowledged that they worked in a good department which was getting better.

The chief, in many ways, personified one of the themes of this book: that conventionally perceived cruel means can and do bring about good ends under some circumstances. In fact, the case can be made that only cruelty could have accomplished what was achieved in Laconia. A gentle, forgiving, sympathetic, enlightened chief simply would not have been able to extort from his officers the sort of attention, effort, and sacrifice which they eventually gave in order to transform themselves into an incorruptible, enlightened, skillful, fair organization. The chief, I am tempted to say, was the ultraprofessional, who took brutal advantage of his "edge of fear" to teach his men that they could be better than they thought they could be.

I hope you will examine your reactions to the chief and then reread Machiavelli's story of the city of Capua with which this book opens. Boldness, the political arrogance to strive to master the unmasterable, is not normally an attractive and endearing quality. So often it can slip beyond the pale of civilized decency and human endurance, as it probably had in Capua. Even when it does not, however, we come to hate the seeming pride and barbarity of professional political persons, who contract with the devil of coercion to shape events. It is only when they are displaced that we find that civilization "fare[s] ill" in their absence. It is only then that we can fully appreciate the benefits and the very necessity of this paradoxical thing we have called coercion.

Perhaps you will keep the story of the chief in mind as you attempt to

14.  Richard McCleery, "Correctional Administration and Political Change," in Lawrence Hazelrigg, *Prison within Society* (Garden City, N.Y.: Doubleday Anchor, 1967), pp. 113–49, 129. My discussion of leadership owes much to McCleery's brilliant article on the effects of reform in an Hawaiian prison.
15.  The words are those of William James and his intellectual progenitor, Thomas Hobbes.

reconcile in your own philosophy the place of coercive power in the human condition.

## VII

There needs to be said a brief word about the rule of law, a final footnote on this discussion of the causes of police professionalism. Policemen in Laconia worked in a context pervaded by law. They felt checked by Supreme Court decisions, legislative limitations, and departmental regulations. They knew that a violation of any of these could cause them to be taken before judges to answer for it. Moreover, they were aware of the license which the law conferred on them, the borders within which they could work legitimately and free of sanctions, the extent of their freedom. In short, as men under the rule of law, they knew whence came their help and their affliction.

The most important effect of this pervading legal ambiance was the limits it imposed on moral obligation. All the policemen knew that their unquestioned jurisdiction stopped at the penal code. They could not take command of human conduct which was not criminal. Avoiders like Tubman and Garfield used these limits of the penal code to kiss off legitimate requests for help on the grounds that police did not handle civil matters. Nonetheless, however often this distinction between civil and criminal was misused, the distinction was of vital importance. Every policeman needed limits to what was expected of him.

To recognize that there were human problems which a policeman could not handle well was the beginning of the development of a professional. As a result of this insight, he began to define his worth in less pretentious terms. In turn this less exalted standard of success meant that he felt no guilt for failing to fulfill what were impossible responsibilities. Some of the men had such a high degree of interpersonal skill that they could handle what we earlier called matters of moral discretion better than other officers, and so they plunged into matters technically noncriminal. Nonetheless, there were some matters which no policeman, not even the adept Justice, could handle. No policeman could knit some marriages together, or shape up some juveniles who had no will to be shaped up. No policeman could increase the incomes of most impoverished persons. To a very real degree, no reasonable amount of policing could stop any particular house from being burglarized. The police could not put a complete halt to pot-smoking or prostitution or gambling. And so on. To the extent that any officer felt he had a responsibility to guarantee the citizenry's freedom from suffering, he inevitably suffered feelings of shortcoming.

The rule of law, therefore, was crucial in mitigating guilt by minimizing obligation. It defined the circumstances under which police were forbidden to help others. The containment of moral responsibility by the rule of law was no mean achievement, because a policeman, to use Tocqueville's felicitous phrasing, was constantly being "canvassed by a multitude of applicants"[16] who exhorted him to use his authority on their behalf. Unless some acceptable way were devised to limit the purposes to which he could put his unique coercive means, he had few defenses against the pressures to use them: for collecting bills, enforcing building codes, rousting drunks, counseling families in trouble, calming neighborhoods, shaping up kids.

One of the subtle uses of the law, then, was to free policemen from these unrealistic responsibilities and often contradictory supplications. The rule of law set out whom and to what degree they could help and, at the same time, set limits on their responsibility. In short, the law gave policemen a sanctuary from public blame and self-criticism.

Policemen often had trouble adjusting to the reality of legal and personal limitation. They were often so moved by the suffering of their citizenry as to want to serve, and they felt discomfited that "nothing could be done." In fact, often something could be done, but not by policemen using their coercive authority. What the best professionals did was increase their understanding of the resourcefulness of individuals and the society within which they lived. Paradoxically, knowledge of the civil law helped these practitioners of criminal law. Not that it made them paraprofessional attorneys in their own right, but knowing what the rest of the legal system was about enabled them to unlock the gates to its resources. Policemen were relaxed when they became aware of the help available from other social institutions. The separation of powers took them off the horns of the dilemma of having to misuse their power or forsake their felt obligation to help. The knowledge of civil law increased their confidence to "pass the buck" to new institutions, without suffering the self-stigma of callousness or cowardice.

Limiting moral responsibility was an important effect of the rule of law. Without this means of defining self-limits, without some patent enforcement mechanism obliging men with power to restrain their resort to it, I find it inconceivable that power could improve a wielder of it: it could only crush him with its burdens, especially if he were one who wanted to be helpful.

16.   Alexis de Tocqueville, *Democracy in America,* trans. Henry Reeve (New York: Vintage, 1945), 1:261.

# Implications
# 4

So what? Does a microscopic study of twenty-eight young policemen in a modest-sized American police department have any larger significance?

I want briefly to take up two implications. The first is the more immediate meaning for police institutions. What choices does a police chief have? The second is of broader political compass, a response to the crucial question, does power tend to corrupt?

# 13

# The Chief's Choices

There is no way to eliminate a patrolman's discretion. He *must* work alone, or with one other patrolman at most, and he must handle chaotic situations. The solution is to make the patrolman a person who is capable of handling the discretion and responsibility that is intrinsic to his job.

*Chief James F. Ahern*
New Haven Police Department
1972

All long-term politics are institutional.

*Karl Popper*
The Open Society and Its Enemies
1950

## I

The basic condition of patrol work was that it was lonely, dangerous, and preoccupied with human suffering. It therefore depended on an extraordinarily high degree of personal morale. No policeman worked at his utmost unless he felt that what he was doing was both effective and right. No amount of punitive supervision could compel the kind of boldness which a self-respecting policeman voluntarily displayed in assisting the suffering. No system of economic rewards could compensate for the dangers to which a morally compelled policeman willingly risked sacrificing himself.

The problem of coercion, however, was that it was morally depleting. Police authority created antagonisms with other individuals unprecedented in each patrolman's life. Possessing authority, he confronted the four paradoxes of power and found himself vulnerable to the dispossessed, the indifferent, the remorseless, and the irrational. He discovered that the restraints of his civilized moral codes checked his impulses to respond effectively and in kind, leaving his work ineffectively accomplished. Faced with the apparent predicament of being either a man of innocence or a policeman of accomplishment, he was tempted to chuck his innate moral baggage. If he did so, he found that he threw out his old understandings, interfused as they were with his moral attitudes. In short, the exercise of authority demoralized him.

A chief of police who understood the demoralizing consequences of power concentrated his efforts on mitigating them. An exemplary department like Laconia's functioned to replenish the morale of its patrolmen by providing them with the intellectual and moral nourishment necessary to restore their souls. At least that happened as a general rule. Replenishment sometimes occurred on purpose and as a result of instituted practices like training; sometimes it occurred "by accident" and even in spite of administrative actions. Then there were the exceptions. Some men became so isolated from the department or so set apart in an immune enclave within it that replenishment did not happen at all.

In other parts of the book we have described several of the devices which the department instituted to cope with the depleting effects of power: the extensive recruit-training program (with its historical and sociological perspectives on cities), the field training officer program (for instructors of recruits in the field), the advanced officers training program (for officers with three or more years of experience), the shooting boards and the conflict management hearings (involving patrol officers in inquiries into incidents involving violence), and the Violence Prevention Unit. Each of these institutions had substantial effects on the morale of those policemen who were involved in it.

Yet if I were to recommend to police chiefs one institution critical to this restorative process, it would be the extensive education of patrol sergeants. From the patrolman's point of view, the critical persons in the process of moral replenishment were their sergeants. On a daily basis, patrolmen's actions and understandings were invisible to the rest of the department. Among their superior officers, only their sergeants had the opportunity to appreciate the moral and intellectual development of individual patrolmen.

The patrol sergeants were educators of their men by circumstances, for the squad was the natural school of patrolmen. The department which best educated these natural educators best served its patrolmen. The best education of a sergeant consisted of schooling him in philosophy, sociology, rhetoric, and law. This is why.

A patrol sergeant had to learn how to teach his men about moral complexity and how to harmonize competing considerations implicit in the obligations to exercise coercive authority. He had to be able to explain, in terms of the patrolman's own experience, the conflicts between civility, departmental objectives, personal goals, and coercive effectiveness. He had to know how to facilitate the process by which individual patrolmen integrated solutions to these conflicts into their existing moral systems. He had to understand the importance of preserving the strength of old moral restraints while accommodating new, coercive considerations. He had to appreciate the importance of free discussion in the process of moral accommodation and the role of the devil's advocate to make the strongest arguments possible for competing points of view. He had to understand how to create a sanctuary in which his officers could debate the wisdom of departmental regulations before accepting them in their moral systems. He had to help them develop a notion of the general welfare. In this sense a sergeant was a teacher of philosophy.

A patrol sergeant was also obliged to deal with his men's understandings of themselves, their department, their city, and human suffering. He had to learn how to help men divulge their presuppositions about human nature, about society, and about the appropriate place of coercion in that society, thereby permitting them to examine their presuppositions in light of the happenings around them. He had to learn how to let his men gain confidence in their understandings by permitting them to make experimental applications of their assumptions and then encouraging them to analyze the discrepancies between prediction and outcome. He had to appreciate the importance of concepts for an individual's learning, recognizing that experience was a great teacher, and that the groupings into which individual experiences were catalogued were important. He had to learn how to permit personal experiences to be reconstructed in a variety of perspectives, through discussion, so that a policeman could see what could have happened but did not. In this sense a sergeant was a teacher of sociology.

A patrol sergeant was further required to deal with his men's ability to express themselves. Language skill was absolutely critical to all techniques of influencing others, whether through extortion, reciprocity, or exhortation. He had to learn how to observe or engage his men in debate and to detect and correct weaknesses in expression. He had to educate his men in the abundance of terms available for capturing nuance and measuring matters of degree. He had to teach them to want to use language effectively and to instill in them the confidence to use and enhance their natural mode of discourse. In this respect the sergeant was a teacher of rhetoric.

Finally, he had to teach his men the law. He had a responsibility for grasping not only the criminal law but the civil law as well, at least to the extent that he could convey to his men how citizens gained access to the resources of the legal system. He had to be able to orient his men to the legal framework of insurance and tort law, property, contract, licensing, and taxation. And most critical, he had to educate his men about the nature of the legal process and their identification with its historical development. In this respect the sergeant was a teacher of the law.

In short, each patrol sergeant had to be an educator of great versatility and skill. He had to teach directly, and he had to inspire his men to want to teach themselves, to go to college, and to keep on learning about human affairs from their citizenry. The prescription may sound impossible, but the fact was that the patrol sergeant was already performing the functions of moralist, sociologist, rhetorician, and law professor for his men, without the formal education which might have enabled him to be a better educator of powerful men.

To accomplish his job competently, a patrol sergeant needed to receive an education commensurate with his key importance; the training of sergeants had to be as effective as the training of recruits. The department also had to provide monetary incentives and build reputations so that the best men would want to be patrol sergeants. The proposal is a modest one, but it would be costly. I believe the benefits would justify the sacrifice which departments and taxpayers would have to make in order to implement it.

## II

In contrast to this suggestion to deal directly with the basic problem of coercion, recommendations have been frequently made to sidestep the phenomenon of moral depletion. Perhaps the best formulated one came from Miami Police Chief Bernard L. Garmire and his department's consulting psychiatrist, Jesse G. Rubin. Garmire and Rubin noted the policeman's problem of power: the exposure to extreme moral conflict and the possibility of moral collapse.[1] Their solution was a simple one: instead of educating patrolmen toward some internal harmonizing of multiple moral obligations, a department should make an external division of jobs:

> Since no policeman can concurrently fulfill all the roles expected of him, police departments should divide into several sections [i.e., neighbor-hood police teams and a crime-fighting tactical group], each of which is assigned a clear, primary policing role. . . . If police roles can be clarified, simplified, and specialized, men can be recruited and trained specifically

1. Garmire's language was, "One person simply cannot reasonably be expected to master both roles [i.e., the role of law enforcer and that of community servant] intellectually and jump psychologically from one to another in an instant's notice. . . . The multiplicity of roles that officers must fill contributes significantly to police fatigue and stress." Robert F. Steadman, ed., *The Police and the Community* (Baltimore: Johns Hopkins University Press, 1972), pp. 4-5.

for each role. The policemen will then have a better chance of shaping his emerging identity to fit realizable role expectations, limited in number.[2]

I shall call this suggestion the morally oversimplified solution to the problem of coercion: to divide a police department into two camps, men and powerful men. This particular formulation of the morally oversimplified solution contains some revealing ambiguities. Nowhere in the argument of Garmire and Rubin is it made clear how the antagonisms incident to the exercise of police authority can be eliminated from neighborhood policing and confined to crime-fighting.

But if, for sake of argument, we assume a department could devise a "clarified, simplified, and specialized" division of labor, we are left with the final problem, what happens to the souls of those specialists who handle antagonism? How do they maintain a civilized perspective? How do they extend the circle of their understanding? How do they grasp the meaning of the whole picture? What prompts them to be active, to be brazen, to risk dangers of failure?

Garmire and Rubin fail to mention changes in personality that could result from this specialization. No doubt, this omission stemmed from the presuppositions implicit in their version of the morally oversimplified solution, namely, once young men emerge from their "identity crisis," the process of moral and intellectual development stops.[3] The deterministic assumption that human nature becomes fixed after some minimum number of years of policing is pivotal to the morally oversimplified solution. There is a kernel of truth in the assumption. The responsibility and systematic interdependence of moral attitudes which a policeman develops through his exposure to the paradoxes of coercion do give a degree of fixity to "the kind of man" a policeman becomes. But changes consistently go on inside the human soul, induced sometimes by accident, sometimes by institutions, and sometimes by personal determination. Policemen grow and shrink throughout their lifetimes. They may be stunted in their growth by such a limited set of experiences that certain options are forever lost. But all nonetheless change, and change constantly. The morally oversimplified solution, by creating an organizational niche for nurturing enforcers who will change into the most radical Machiavellians, to use Weber's term, magnifies the likelihood of

---

2. Jesse G. Rubin, "Police Identity and the Police Role," in ibid., pp. 15, 40-41.

3. "About two years after entering the force, he will have settled into a work role that will determine for better or worse the kind of policeman—and the kind of man—he is to become. Should these years intensify the normal 'growing pains' of young manhood, rather than help resolve them, the cadet will fail to achieve the mature psychological integration necessary for functioning at a professional level" (ibid., pp. 12-13).

corruption by coercive power. It does not solve the problem of coercive power—how to keep the coercively powerful from becoming wicked.[4]

The proper solution to the problem of coercive power is not to eliminate the contradictory demands of civility and coercion but to provide the understanding and the moral strength which will enable policemen to harmonize the two. Police departments can try to adapt to a given state of human frailty or they can make human beings less frail. Within human limits, the imperative in a free society must always be to strengthen the human being. Discussion, understanding of the world and the job, and moral self-knowledge—these become the central instruments of shoring up the moral strengths of mankind.[5]

Let me say one final word about police reform. Knowledgeable policemen have insisted that the two urgent problems which bedevil American police departments are graft and political influence.[6] From what I have read and heard, I believe they are right. Where graft and undue political influence exist, complicity, unequal justice—whether in the form of favoritism or of racism—and a personal sense of meaninglessness inevitably occur. Moreover, the perverted uses of authority seem to defeat measures to make little improvements, preoccupying and misdirecting creative energies.

But one must never confuse urgency with importance. If graft and political

---

4.  Nicholas Pileggi provided an unsettling description of the effects on men who were specially recruited and trained for a crime-fighting tactical group. See his "'Gestapo' or 'Elite'?: The Tactical Patrol Force," *New York Times Magazine,* 21 July 1968, reprinted in Jerome Skolnick and Elliott Currie, *Crisis in American Institutions* (Boston: Little, Brown, 1970), pp. 402–11. Furthermore, Peel provided rebuttal to the morally over-simplified solution while discussing specialization and civilianization (the latter term refer-ring to the increased use of nonpolice in desk jobs, like communications, research, and criminalistics): "I would be careful of specialization and careful of civilianization. Now I'm a civilian, but I'm in the police force too. But the thing has been to shut certain jobs off to policemen. It cuts down diversification. It cuts down experience. If planning and research were limited to civilians, I would not have had that broadening experience. A policeman is a civilian, yet I know a policeman who had to quit to become a criminalist. A patrolman, now, can be a property custodian or a criminalist. There's a lot of difference in the jobs and in the skills and demands the jobs require. And that allows a man to go as high as he wants as a patrolman. Interchangeability of jobs—that's a nice feature of the job. But if you classify the position, then the individual is stuck. Civil service and all that starts going into effect, and that fosters mediocrity. If you have the same job for 20 years, then you can't be too excited about it. It seems to me. And with specialized units, they rele-gate the overall policing job to a secondary position to the special unit's objectives. The guy in the property room gets more concerned about whether the property room is neat than whether the police have the right equipment. I'd provide a much broader grid, a pattern, for a man to progress in the department."

5.  The reader is referred to Dahrendorf's eloquent and moving admonition to remember the soul of the whole man: "Never forget ... the superior rights of ... the person over his role-playing shadow." Ralf Dahrendorf, *Essays in the Theory of Society* (Stanford, Calif.: Stanford University Press, 1968), p. 87.

6.  E.g., James F. Ahern, *Police in Trouble* (New York: Hawthorn, 1972).

influence were rooted out of American police departments by a wave of reform, we would not have solved the important social issues of increasing public safety, infusing hope among the inhabitants of the cities, and developing conditions under which graft and influence could not reroot themselves. We would not have alleviated the problem of coercive power, which influences these phenomena so directly. If one decade concentrated only on the urgent problems but ignored the underlying problem of the wicked effects of coercive power, the next decade would find graft and influence back again, along with new maladies. Graft and influence are both cause and symptom, as much the consequence of the spiritual difficulties of the individual policeman as the breeder of them.

A study like this one, describing what one department experienced when graft and influence virtually disappeared for a time, helps anticipate the problems which become visible when reform efforts succeed. A description of the Laconia department, momentarily lucky enough to be without either graft or undue political influence, provides a realistic vision of what could be—warts and all, difficult problems and matchless opportunities interfused. The challenge and the complexity of the future may convince policeman and citizen alike that reform may be worth it, without exciting those overoptimistic expectations which defeat reforms in the long run.

# 14                                Does Coercive Power
                                    Tend to Corrupt?

Power tends to corrupt, and absolute power corrupts absolutely. Great men are almost always bad men, even when they exercise influence and not authority; still more when you superadd the tendency or the certainty of corruption by authority.

*Lord Acton*
1887

It is impossible that the people should take a part in public business without extending the circle of their ideas and quitting the ordinary routine of their thoughts. The humblest individual who cooperates in the government of society acquires a certain degree of self-respect; and as he possesses authority, he can command the services of minds more enlightened than his own. He is canvassed by a multitude of applicants, and in seeking to deceive him in a thousand ways, they really enlighten him. He takes a part in political undertakings which he did not originate, but which give him a taste for undertakings of the kind. New improvements are daily pointed out to him in the common property, and this gives him the desire of improving the property which is his own. He is perhaps neither happier nor better than those who came before him, but he is better informed and more active.

*Alexis de Tocqueville*
Democracy in America
1835

## I

Does coercive power tend to corrupt? Or does the "superaddition of authority" result in enlightenment and self-respect, as Tocqueville asserted? This study of twenty-eight powerful men sheds some light on these questions and, in doing so, illuminates much about the snares of politics and the development of persons who assume the mantle of authority—politicians, if you will.

True, the policemen you have read about were not politicians in the conventional sense. They were not presidents or popes, statesmen or labor leaders. They were ordinary policemen patrolling the streets of a single city. They did not affect so many citizens as a president. They did not have the capacity to invoke such deathly sanctions as members of a national security council. The repercussions of their decisions were not so widespread as those of a labor leader's.

Yet calming an apprehensive or resentful populace is a problem common to presidents and patrolmen alike. Pacifying a dispute between husbands and wives involves much the same techniques statesmen use to contain outbreaks between embittered nations. And police officers threatening arrest find themselves stumbling into some of the same pitfalls which often trip labor leaders who threaten to stop production. The difficulties of exercising authority are rarely proportional to the importance of the matter requiring its application. As we have seen, often the little problems present the most baffling predicaments to powerful persons.

Alike, policemen and politicians engage in getting others to submit to events under coercion and do so recurrently. Alike they are victims of coercion and have to devise defenses against it. If there is any important difference between them, it derives from the fact that policemen use, and are subject to, threats more directly than politicians. The offices of patrolmen are on the curbside instead of off corridors. They are streetcorner politicians.

## II

Tocqueville, as we have noted, observed that "men are not corrupted by the exercise of power . . . , but by the exercise of power which they believe to be illegitimate."[1] His point was that political persons were not debased by the inescapable necessities of coercive power—dispossession, detachment, re-morselessness, and madness. Rather, they were corrupted by their inability to reconcile these implications of exercising coercive authority with their personal congenital standards of decency. Politicians were bewildered by the conflict between the practices of extortion and the principles of civility; they found their belief in the nobility of their cause and their instinct for innocence working at cross-purposes; they were impaled on the dilemma of power—they had either to violate their most profound codes of self-restraint or suffer political defeat.

Tocqueville's insight was that the process of corruption by power started with feelings of profound guilt at having to act harmfully. Persons with authority constantly bore the burden of feeling they had double-crossed one set of obligations or another. The corrupted man of power, Tocqueville argued, was the one who overcame the moral conflict raging within him by annihilating his civilized principles. By simplifying the complexity of the codes to which he was responsive, he rid himself of the paralyzing agony of

1. Alexis de Tocqueville, *Democracy in America*, trans. Henry Reeve (New York: Vintage, 1945) 1:9.

deciding between irreconcilable obligations. He denied the principles of legitimate conduct in order to flee from his sense of wrongdoing. The result, however, was the subversion of human self-restraint and an unconditional victory for the demon of politics. The ideals, the noble "cause" of political action, might well remain in the mind of the politician. But if he obliterated the ethical guideposts of human remorse and sympathy, he then expunged the very perspective which might have prevented him from succumbing to the bad effects of coercive power. In the long run he would come to destroy all tender sensibility and to harm the very hostages—mankind, civilization, and its gentling institutions—which he had set out to save in the first place.

## III

If the anticipated outcome of political power is personal corruption, we would expect human resourcefulness to begin to do something about averting such a disaster. Indeed, it is plain that some, perhaps most, political figures in civilized countries no longer suffer the wicked form of personal deterioration Lord Acton called corruption. They develop otherwise.

One sees in modern politics, for example, increasing recourse to reciprocity. Reciprocity consists of transforming extortionate relationships into exchange relationships. This entrepreneurial approach manifests itself in phrases like "the power broker" and "the influence peddler." By submitting to a system of mutual claims under reciprocal sanctions, the reciprocating politician trades leniency for favors in return; he surrenders his power for advantages.

It is also possible to detect in civilized, democratic politics a political style which might be called avoidance. Avoidance results from man's natural inclination to avoid distasteful things if he can help it, best summarized in a bureaucratic context by Parkinson's law of triviality, "The time spent on any item of the agenda will be in inverse proportion to the sum involved."[2]

## IV

One way to domesticate power is to convert it into an exchangeable asset—something to be given away in a quid pro quo transaction. The literature of politics details the phenomenon of people with power agreeing to surrender it (more or less permanently) in order to obtain the opportunity to enter into continuing and rewarding reciprocal relationships, premised not on threats but on promises. Power then becomes "currency."[3] It is used as a

---

2. Quoted in Anthony Downs, *Inside Bureaucracy* (Boston: Little, Brown, 1967), p. 84.
3. Karl Deutsch, *Nerves of Government* (New York: The Free Press, 1963), p. 120.

"resource" to be traded on the marketplace for such valuable things as respect, affection, and wealth. Metaphors of reciprocity abound in political science literature—"power brokers," "influence peddlers," as we earlier said, but also many more "political entrepreneurs," "the trade of favors," "logrolling," "functionalism."[4]

Threats and promises are similar in at least one analytic respect. In both reciprocal and extortionate relationships, the parties are in contingent interdependence with one another. If the first party takes some action, the second party will reciprocate, as the saying goes. In this respect severity—threatening to use coercive power to injure *unless* some action is taken—resembles leniency—promising to give up the coercive power to hurt *if* some action is taken. But in practice there is a vital distinction between them. In reciprocity, there is the mutually pleasant prospect of the parties' relationship continuing. In extortion, there is pervasive antagonism.

One consequence of the desire to maintain cooperation among reciprocating parties is that the power holder who momentarily forbears from using his coercive power tends to surrender it permanently. Compulsions occur which do not happen in extortionate relationships. The desire to continue together, to enrich one another, constrains the use of coercive power ever after.

For one thing, parties to a reciprocal deal lose their killer instinct. They begin to luxuriate in their possessions, indulge their instinct to join human associations, crave goodwill, and enjoy gentlemanly reputations. To return to a reliance on extortion, to have to measure up once again to the paradoxes of coercive power, requires an exorbitant sacrifice. Morally, men ensnared in reciprocal relationships seem to lose the stomach to be ruthless. Having so much to lose, they tend to exalt "prudence" above all virtues.

An additional compulsion results if the original deal fell outside the law or the sanctuary of social acceptance. The parties then expose themselves fatally to each other's blackmailing capacities. Each can coerce the other on pain of revelation to submit to the demands of reciprocity. Each has let his guard down; each is over the other's barrel. There is a balance of power between outlaws. Making an illegal deal is the modern equivalent of the bilateral exchange of hostages; both parties have exposed themselves to mutually unavoidable sanctions.

Whatever the reasons, the exchange form of influence often drives out coercive forms of influence. Reciprocity tends to replace extortion under some circumstances.

---

4. As Alvin Gouldner has pointed out, much of the theory of political sociology, particularly under the influence of Talcott Parsons's emphasis on functionalism, presupposes reciprocal relationships exclusively. Alvin W. Gouldner, "The Norm of Reciprocity: A Preliminary Statement," *American Sociological Review* (April 1960), 25:161-78.

It is important to note that reciprocal politics need not necessarily lead to graft. The benefits resulting from a good deal may be distributed in two quite different ways. An official may enjoy the benefits of his leniency in a private way, may pocket his profits, may internalize his economies (as the economists put it); then we call him a crooked politician. We frown upon him because he fills his bank accounts at the expense of the society which delegated him the coercive power he dealt away. On the other hand, the benefits of the bargain may be shared with the society; the power holder may receive in exchange for his leniency a collective good such as greater productivity or community peace and order, which everybody enjoys. When a power holder externalizes the economies resulting from his surrender of the community's power to threaten, we tend to approve of him, to call him a diplomat and a statesman.

What conditions permit a power holder to profit from being lenient?

For one thing, reciprocity takes great social skills. Skills in striking a good bargain require empathy, for example. In a bargain the power holder must understand the other party sufficiently well to obtain the best terms of exchange. In setting the trade ratios, he must teach himself about the values and the situation of his partner in trade: what the value of his leniency is to the other, what the other thinks about his bargaining position, and so on. A reciprocator must sharpen his interest in the meaning of his own actions and possessions for the affairs of others. One condition of reciprocity as a mode of using power is a high degree of social awareness.

A second condition of effective reciprocity is stability. Continuity is the key to an exchange relationship. The participants' familiarity with each other's needs and resources and sequential building of trust facilitate reciprocal relationships significantly. Common understandings result in the development of norms and voluntarily accepted limits. Exchange values stabilize, diminishing bickering. Stability increases efficiency.

A third condition is a system of coercive sanctions which function to enforce promises and adjudicate disputes over the terms of the agreements. If the deal falls outside the law, resort to courts is impossible. Then some other effective mode of arbitration in which the power of the participants is balanced has to be devised to compel compliance and fair bargaining. We have mentioned two such devices so far: the compulsions of conspiracy to keep an illegal deal secret and the mutual exchange of hostages. But we should be remiss if we did not mention legitimate political deals and the importance of institutionalization. Men of power have developed a system of moral and social sanctions in which political bargains are recurrently enforced with great certainty. A legislature is the epitome of the reciprocal way of politics, and Richard Fenno's sensitive description of what he calls the "internal control mechanisms" at work in the House Appropriations Committee shows how political reciprocity is enforced legitimately and systematically in the legislative marketplace in the absence of a judicial presence.[5]

## V

If the four paradoxes of power are distressing to civilized persons and if power cannot be converted into the currency of reciprocity, then one would expect a person, on having power thrust upon him, to shun it. Despite the capacity to hurt others, the will is lacking, and the person in authority avoids every opportunity to be powerful. He will not follow through.

Evidence is plentiful that avoidance of power is perhaps the most prevalent of the responses to power. Think of the abundance of imaginative phrases in our everyday language describing this phenomenon: "Keeping out of trouble," "avoiding responsibilities," "minding your own business," "not getting your fingers burned," "too hot to handle," "not rocking the boat," "keeping your nose clean," "washing your hands of the affair," "not making waves."[6]

What conditions permit persons who have power to refuse to use it? The opportunities to avoid exercising power are available whenever the power holder is not subject to reprisal for self-limitation. Whenever inaction is likely to be condemned less severely than the effort to exercise power, avoidance is a possibility. For a variety of reasons, nonfeasance is less likely than malfeasance to excite those "fast and powerful feedbacks" with which organizations prod us to do our duty properly.[7]

For one thing, nonevents are harder to detect. Complainants need to have a perspective on what could have happened to see the consequences of something which never happened. There may be other reasons why inaction is so hard to supervise.

A second condition of nonuse of power is the widespread acceptability of avoidance in Western civilization. Conditions of affluence have defanged people. The pie has been made sufficiently large that a substantial majority of people no longer need to extort from each other to survive. In a context

---

5. Richard F. Fenno, Jr., "The House Appropriations Committee as a Political System: The Problem of Integration," *American Political Science Review* (June 1962), 56:310-24.

6. James Sterling Young, *The Washington Community: 1800-1828* (New York: Harcourt Brace, 1968), is a description of an entire community of men in the seat of power who could not abide power. A century and a half later, Jeffrey Pressman found a similar community, in which the entire city council consisted of "shrinking violets," men reluctant to pay the opportunity costs of power, unwilling to cope with conflict, suffer insults and the cuts of politics, or reshape their moral codes of responsibility. Jeffrey L. Pressman, "Preconditions of Mayoral Leadership," *American Political Science Review* (June 1972), 66:511-24.

7. Downs, *Inside Bureaucracy,* p. 218.

where coercion is less obviously necessary, the purposeful hurting of people has become a distasteful thing.

To an undemanding environment, there is added an ethic which approves avoidance behavior: Christianity. The religion of Christ made a virtue out of shrinking violets (or lilies of the field). The Sermon on the Mount tells mankind that it is brave to be "meek," to be "merciful," to let others "revile you, and persecute you," to "agree with thine adversary," to "turn the other cheek," to "love your enemies," to "forgive men their trespasses," and to "take no thought for your life" or "for the morrow." This extraordinary private ethic scorns persons who exert power on others unless they have mastered themselves "first": "First cast out the beam out of thine own eye; and then shalt thou see clearly to cast out the mote out of thy brother's eye."[8]

## VI

If coercive power cannot be traded or evaded, however, then does it tend to make wicked those who have to exercise it? It had a tendency to do so in the case of those enforcer policemen who were disinclined to the avoidance or reciprocating response. There is no earthly reason to think that politicians can escape the same effects. Coercive power—authority—tempts all individuals who have it to use coercion instead of resorting to persuasion or reciprocity. A person who can threaten is seduced into trying to save both the time of talking others into seeing matters anew and the costs of compensating them for sacrificing themselves. Giving an individual the opportunity to use coercion, moreover, inflicts on him the perpetual necessity to maintain a defense against those who are frightened by, or invulnerable to, his threats. Furthermore, his civilized network for gathering information begins to break down. In the midst of the antagonisms which coercive power evokes, political survival often appears incompatible with civilized traditions, and unfortunate choices are made as a result. Of course, coercive power tends to corrupt in politics. To accept the mantle of authority is to sign a pact with the

8. Matt. 7:5. John Stuart Mill's critique of Christian morality must certainly be the most eloquent. He wrote (in part): "Christian morality (so called) has all the character of a reaction; it is, in great part, a protest against Paganism. Its ideal is negative rather than positive; passive rather than active; Innocence rather than Nobleness; Abstinence from Evil, rather than energetic Pursuit of Good: in its precepts (as has been well said) 'thou shalt not' predominates unduly over 'thou shalt.'. . . It holds out the hope of heaven and the threat of hell, as the appointed and appropriate motives to a virtuous life: in this falling far below the best of the ancients, and doing what lies in it to give to human morality an essentially selfish character, by disconnecting each man's feelings of duty from the interests of his fellow creatures, except so far as a self-interested inducement is offered to him for consulting them." John Stuart Mill, *On Liberty* (1859; New York: Appleton-Century-Crofts, 1947), p. 49.

devil, as Weber warned, and "Anyone who fails to see this is, indeed, a political infant."[9]

## VII

But to say that coercive power has a tendency to corrupt is to look only at the liability side of the ledger. It is a little like asking, Does agriculture tend to deplete the soil? Of course it does, but the food which is produced warrants exhausting the land. Moreover, the depleting effects of growing crops may be minimized by understanding the process of depletion and then redressing the balance between productivity and soil replenishment by "artificial" means.

So, too, with coercive power. Good comes of it, and the tendency to corruption can be abated by understanding its dynamics and reinvigorating powerful persons with understanding and purpose, with what Weber liked to call perspective and passion.

What good comes of coercion? One good—the one which policemen so obviously perform—is the control of abusive coercion. Threats are necessary to regulate the employment of threats in daily life. The policeman and the government he represents reduce the advantages which the remorseless and the strong naturally have over the sensitive and the civilized. Coercive power preserves civilization against coercive power. Without persons in authority, those who might have been protected would have to find ways of protecting themselves. They would have to go into sanctuary or learn how to develop their own private modes of power. The community would become "politicized", and each citizen would find his own shelter, minimize himself, and cultivate his own self-defensive suspicions. In Hobbes's memorable language, where authority is absent,

> every man is enemy to every man; the same is consequent to the time, wherein men live without other security, than what their own strength and their own invention shall furnish them withal. In such condition, there is no place for industry: because the fruit thereof is uncertain: and consequently no culture of the earth; no navigation, nor use of the commodities that may be imported by sea; no commodious building; no instruments of moving, and removing, such things as require much force: no knowledge of the face of the earth; no account of time; no arts; no letters; no society; and which is worst of all, continual fear and danger of violent death; and the life of man, solitary, poor, nasty, brutish, and short.[10]

9.  Max Weber, "Politics as a Vocation," in *From Max Weber: Essays in Sociology,* ed. and trans. H. Gerth and C. Wright Mills (New York: Oxford University Press, 1946), p. 123.
10.  Thomas Hobbes, *Leviathan,* pt. 1, chap. 13.

But coercion has another use: equality. It is necessary to correct the deficiencies of civilization, particularly the tendencies of the two civilized means of interpersonal control, exchange and exhortation, to magnify natural human inequalities.

Exchange as a means of inducing human cooperation is fine. Its practice is so tender, its results frequently so productive, and the moral development of the economic man so much gentler than that of the powerful man. But in a world where natural inequalities occur, pure exchange does not minimize those inequalities. Quite the contrary, in a world geared exclusively to reciprocity, the rich use their freedom to get richer and the poor, alas, use theirs to become poorer. The haves have things which they wish to trade for things in the possession of the other haves—wealth, education, talent, and strength. In pure exchange conditions, however, the have-nots have no resources to bargain with. Therefore they become useless to the marketplace. Their departure from the earth would be little noted by the financiers and the productive. Such is the plight of the underdeveloped, be they nations or individuals. Having no resources, the dispossessed of the world are left out of the marketplace, and they perish. Extortionate power can be the great corrective of this tragic condition. It enables the have-nots to get something from the haves for nothing. Coercion can facilitate equality by enabling the dispossessed to accumulate and assume their seats in the marketplace.

It was Balzac who said, "Behind every great fortune there is a crime," thereby tipping his hat to the idea that threat was indispensable to bring about economic redistribution. He might have continued, "And behind general good fortune, there is coercion."

The result of using coercion to equalize conditions—"to make the lives of other men better," as Theodore White put it in his eloquent epitaph to Robert Kennedy[11]—may in the long run benefit rich and poor alike. Such is one interpretation of the New Deal. In bringing about the enrichment of the dispossessed of the 1930s and 1940s, the "soak-the-rich" practices of the New Deal rectified an imbalance of economic distribution which had already begun to undermine the profitability of the marketplace. Furthermore, the example of the New Deal is a reminder that coercive power need not be uncivilized or criminal. A nation can, with luck, create extortionate institutions which play Robin Hood acceptably.

Similarly, with the civilized technique of exhortation, its practice is sometimes so elevating, the sense of solidarity it sometimes creates so fulfilling, and the moral development it sometimes promotes so harmonious

11.   Theodore H. White, *The Making of the President 1968* (New York: Atheneum, 1969), p. 181.

that it has an immediate appeal. But in a world where there exists unequal access to the moral rostrums (the "bully pulpits," as Teddy Roosevelt called them), the questions left unresolved are, how to select the particular exhorters and how to change them if their preachments turn out to be cockeyed. The solidarity of a community responding to the urgings of its best and its brightest seems to come about "naturally" in times of emergency and cataclysm. But in normal times solidarity tends to overripen into conformity and to squash the free-spirited. As with the pathologies of reciprocity, coercive power can be the great corrective of the bad effects of exhortative controls. It can call moral leaders to account for irresponsibility and inertia. With coercive power, followers can frighten moral leaders into thinking more precisely and usefully about universal problems, on danger of extermination. Again, the conditions by which leaders may be threatened need not be uncivilized, and a nation may, with luck, establish coercive institutions (like free elections) which play the role of regicide and assassin.

Of course, it must be said that, while extortionate power can equalize conditions, it need not. Indeed, those that have possessions or status—the aristocracy, so to speak—often struggle to control the instrumentalities of coercive power. It has always struck me that their objective is less to exploit political institutions for their own enrichment than to neutralize the bad effects of letting the weapons of politics fall into the hands of the have-nots. Where the aristocracy controls powerful institutions, they are more likely to be of a "do-nothing" than of an exploitative nature. The fault of aristocratic power lies more in its lack of energy than in its tendency to corruption.

Although coercive power need not conduce to equality, the point is that it can serve as a continuing corrective to nature's tendency to disperse skill, talent, health, and luck unequally. Thus, the problem of coercive power can be solved not by eliminating all capacity to use threat, but by mitigating some of its worst effects. By devising institutions to offset the depleting moral effects of coercion, mankind perhaps can employ it both to maintain a civilization and also to correct its tendency to magnify its own grossest inequalities.

## VIII

How can the tendency to corruption be abated? What can maintain in political persons a tragic perspective on human suffering? What can reinvigorate their passion to use coercion for the general welfare in the face of personal danger without becoming radically Machiavellian?

On the basis of the development of professional policemen in Laconia and our understanding of the conditions which made their development possible, four propositions strike me as important.[12]

1. The more a powerful figure enjoys talking, the less cynic his perspective and the more comfortable he feels about using coercion. It is easy to forget how critical eloquence is in the effective exercise of coercion. Yet, as the reader will recall, the police professional responded to each of the paradoxes of power with techniques available only to a person who could communicate skillfully. It was not bullying talk, the kind which some debaters might use to overwhelm or befuddle. It was social talk, which taught and framed choices. Coercion often prompted fear, which got the attention of others. If a political figure were to obtain the ear of others because he evoked fear and then could not express himself meaningfully when he had their attention, his resort to fear would have been for naught. Furthermore, if he was an irrepressible teacher and learner, he displayed his own understanding of the human condition, at once guiding others and being guided by their responses. Insofar as institutions, like legislatures, political campaigns, safeguards for free speech, and law schools, value and cultivate the talents of political figures for meaningful public utterance, they mitigate the tendency of power to corrupt. Of course, eloquence can be abused; so an enjoyment of talk is not a sufficient safeguard against corruption. However, a pleasure in using language to associate with others strikes me as absolutely essential in escaping the depleting effects of power.[13]

2. The more exposure a political figure has had to the contemplation of human suffering, the less cynic his perspective. The political figure is an object of constant supplication to alleviate human suffering and human need. This recurrent experience is unique to men of power and poses dreadful choices in adapting to it. Fortunately, civilization has preserved the profoundest reflections on the subject of human tragedy by chroniclers of the human condition. Their contemplations on the theme of tragedy constitute the liberal arts. The individual who enters and participates in politics without taking advantage of the historical, social, and moral perspectives bequeathed to him by civilization's profoundest thinkers does so at his peril.[14]

12.  A study of twenty-eight policemen, all of whom were young and deemed by psychiatrists fit to wield power, cannot tell us much about those profoundly subconscious disturbances within political figures which psychohistorians have found so worth their while to analyze. To the reader interested in psychiatric analyses of political figures, I recommend Alexander L. George and Juliette L. George, *Woodrow Wilson and Colonel House* (New York: John Day, 1956) and James David Barber, *The Presidential Character* (Englewood Cliffs, N.J.: Prentice-Hall, 1972). The reader should also watch out for Erik Erikson's forthcoming biography of Thomas Jefferson.

13.  I think it no accident that our most corrupted president was our most tongue-tied and least social. I am referring to former President Nixon's inability to enjoy what policemen call "bullshitting."

14.  I am not one to insist that higher education in the liberal arts is a panacea for all ills. Yet I have always thought Gibbon quite wrong when he insisted that that sophisticated

3. The longer his political apprenticeship, the more comfortable the political figure will feel about using coercion. If Tocqueville was right to insist that it was not power that corrupted but the feeling that its exercise was illegitimate, the more association an individual has had with powerful persons before he assumes the responsibilities of power, the more opportunities he has to reflect on the meaning and subtlety of the general welfare, which justify power, and the limits of civility, which check it. To adapt a phrase of John Stuart Mill, political figures need to be socialized into politics by a "government of leading strings."[15] In this regard, such institutions as the seniority system of legislatures (formal or otherwise), the *cursus honorum* built into political party careers, the development of political families like the Adamses, the Roosevelts, and the Kennedys, and the preservation of vicarious political experience in biography and memoirs play their indispensable roles. Tocqueville's profoundest insight about the importance of widespread political participation hinged on what he deemed to be the necessity that older generations inculcate younger ones with an awareness of the subtleties, opportunities, and dangers of power.[16]

4. The more emphasis the legal system places on liberty, the more comfortable a political figure will feel about being in a position of authority. Coercion is the instrument of equality and the enemy of liberty. In times when the demands of equality seem more imperative than the protection of liberty, the limits on coercion imposed in the name of freedom are eroded. At such times political figures are left bereft of those legal and social taboos which once justified them in pursuing limited or moderate goals. They are then pushed by events to use coercion more vehemently. At such times the

---

and complex political entity called the Roman Empire declined and fell because of the private and ignoble ideas of Christianity. If one factor were to be selected to explain its deterioration, it would be the absence of a public system of higher education to preserve and pass on the legacy of civilization to its citizenry.

15. John Stuart Mill, *Considerations on Representative Government* (New York: Liberal Arts Press, 1958), p. 33. The essay was composed for the most part in 1860.

16. E.g., Tocqueville's discussion of the political apprenticeship which citizens served by being jurors is as follows: "The jury teaches every man not to recoil before the responsibility of his own actions and impresses him with that manly confidence without which no political virtue can exist. It invests each citizen with a kind of magistracy; it makes them all feel the duties which they are bound to discharge towards society and the part which they take in its government. By obliging men to turn their attention to other affairs than their own, it rubs off that private selfishness which is the rust of society.

"The jury contributes powerfully to form the judgment and to increase the natural intelligence of a people; and this, in my opinion, is its greatest advantage. It may be regarded as a gratuitous public school, ever open, in which every juror learns his rights, enters into daily communication with the most learned and enlightened members of the upper classes and becomes practically acquainted with the law, which are brought within the reach of his capacity by the efforts of the bar, the advice of the judge, and even the passions of the parties" (*Democracy in America*, 1:295-96).

governed tend to regard as weakness their governors' inclination to temper power with talk and compensation. Insofar as the rule of law handcuffs a politician with visible restraints, mutually agreed to by all other political figures, the compulsions to violate these libertarian taboos are reduced. As a consequence the antagonisms which are evoked by the prospect of unbridled power are alleviated. The law, insofar as it effectively harmonizes the civilized morality responsive to liberty and the coercive morality responsive to equality, functions to prevent corruption by power.

In the long run, what must be counted on to reinvigorate the souls of individuals depleted by the exercise of coercive power is a passion for freedom, made articulate in constant social discussion, interpreted within a tragic perspective which presupposes free will, reflected on by a government of political mentors, and institutionalized by the law. At least, that was the lesson twenty-eight young American policemen taught me about the problem of coercive power.

# Methodological Note

## I

"Power tends to corrupt" and "the office makes the man" are two aphorisms which delight the soul of a social scientist. Each is "true." Each is a premise for many important decisions. And they are mutually contradictory—which is what makes them so intriguing.

The social scientist is often accused of proving the obvious. "Anybody with any common sense knows that. Why waste time belaboring it?" Yet almost every obvious truism has an opposite which is usually no less apparent. "Birds of a feather flock together." "Opposites attract." "Taxes dampen inflation." "Taxes force producers to raise prices." "There is nothing new under the sun." "Nothing is ever the same."

The pairing of contradictions invites the social scientist to deepen his understanding. It beckons him to wonder about the different circumstances under which each is true. When does power corrupt the officeholder, for example, and under what conditions might it make him better?

Typically, social science inquiry is provoked by this need to reconcile opposites. The social scientist sniffs out contradictory pairs because he senses that, in reconciling them, he will arrive at a fuller and more satisfying explanation of human nature than he had had before. Morris Cohen, the eloquent logician and philosopher, coined the word "polarity" to describe the pairing of contradictions:

> To make logic applicable to empirical issues, we must employ the principle of polarity. By this I mean that the empirical facts are generally resultants of opposing and yet inseparable tendencies like the north and south poles. We must, therefore, be on our guard against the universal tendency to simplify situations and to analyze them in terms of only one of such contrary tendencies. This principle of polarity is a maxim of intellectual research, like the principle of causality, against the abuse of which it may serve as a help. If the principle of causality makes us search for operating causes, the principle of polarity makes us search for that which prevents them from producing greater effects than they do.[1]

1. Morris Cohen, *A Preface to Logic* (1944; New York: Meridian, 1956), pp. 87-88.

## II

If it is typical that polar maxims isolate fruitful questions, it is equally typical that the social scientist will encounter a predictable set of methodological hurdles in his research of "contrary tendencies." This short note is about some of those hurdles.

I want to discuss six in particular, especially as they relate to this study of the contrary tendencies of coercive power to make officeholders both wicked and virtuous. The six methodological problems are: (1) establishing the *controlled experiment;* (2) resolving the *dependent-variable problem;* (3) translating intellectual concepts into operational terms (otherwise known as the *validity problem*); (4) turning self-evaluations into evidence (otherwise known as the *reliability problem*); (5) proving *inferences;* and (6) spinning out wider *implications.*

1. *The Controlled Experiment:* The hallmark of the social scientific method of explanation is explicit comparison. The controlled experiment embodies the comparative method. The social scientist establishes two similar groups (called an *experimental* group and a *control* group), subjects the experimental (but not the control) group to the influence of the "explanatory" factor, and treats any resulting dissimilarity between the two groups as the effect of the explanatory factor.

In symbols, the effect of the explanatory factor, $X$, is the difference between $d_x$ and $d_c$ (referring to the development of the experimental and control groups, respectively).

Table 9                              Controlled Experiment

|  | Explanatory Factor X | |
|---|---|---|
|  | Before | After |
| Experimental Group | Persons with $v$ virtues | $v + d_x$ |
| Control Group | Persons with $v$ virtues | $v + d_c$ |

$X$, then, "explains" $(v + d_x) - (v + d_c)$.

A primitive application of this classic controlled experimental format to the problem of corruption by power would involve selecting two samples of similar persons, exposing one group to the conditions of power and isolating the other group from those conditions. Then, after a time, the experimenter would compare the different developments of the empowered and the nonpowerful groups in terms of their vices and virtues.

However, this simpleminded application of the controlled experimental method would advance knowledge very little, principally because the explanatory factor (power) would be much too complex and the context of interaction between power and personality much too loosely controlled. Assume, for example, that our experimental group consisted of ten persons, and assume further that we could measure virtue and vice along one dimension. Suppose that half the persons in the experimental group grew in office ten units' worth (virtue), while the other five subjects deteriorated in office ten units' worth (vice). The aggregate change among the powerful persons in this experimental group is zero. If we were to suppose that none of the persons in the nonpowerful control group changed a whit, being unaffected by power in their before and after states, the control group aggregate score would also be zero. The differences between the two groups, and among the individuals in the experimental group, would thus be obscured by our primitive application of the experimental format.

The cause of this obscurity would be the unrefined quality of the explanatory factor—power. The contrary tendencies in power would not have been "factored out." Applied to the subjects at the same time, the contrary tendencies would be working at cross-purposes, canceling each other out, in some way or another.

A less primitive application of the controlled experiment would be needed to break the notion of empowerment into its contrary tendencies. One of the tendencies would have to be controlled while the other was being manipulated and compared. To increase the subtlety of his research, the social scientist would have to alter the makeup of the control and experimental groups, on the one hand, and to refine his explanatory factor, on the other.

First, he would not constitute his groups with equally virtuous persons, but with (1) equally virtuous persons who were (2) equally powerful and were (3) working under equivalent conditions. (In the language of social science, he would apply three "controls" instead of only the one of equal virtue).

Second, he would take as an explanatory factor, not power, but a critical factor hypothesized, for some reason or another, to magnify one or the other of the contrary tendencies within power (e.g., the inspiration to defend one's fatherland against military attack).

The difficulty with reaching this level of refinement, however, is in picking out the explanatory factor on which to structure the experiment. In the preliminary but indispensable stage of exploring for a hypothesis, conventional application of the classic experimental form is no help. Premature use of the classic form, in fact, is a waste of time, like using a screwdriver to separate wheat from chaff. While conventional application of the classic form is good at persuasively tightening the argument, it is inefficient in conjuring up hypotheses.

But an adaptation of the controlled experiment can help in exploring for shrewd guesses about explanation. The adaptation is to invert the classic format.

In inverting the controlled experiment model, the typical social scientist begins at the end point. That is, he looks at the "after"-math, the equivalent of $v + d_x$ and $v + d_c$. In the context of the power and personality question, he groups a single set of powerful persons according to their differences in vices and virtues at the end of the experiment. (To be consistent with the rest of the book, let us call these two groups the "corrupted" and the "professional"). He then makes an important working assumption. Somewhere, back in time, the persons in these two groups "began" with equal virtue *and* equal power *and* equivalent conditions. (That is, he *assumes* that he has applied all three of his controls.) He then goes on to assume that some explanatory factor (at this point he knows not what) intervened differentially in the development of these two groups, and their corrupted and professional end points are attributable to the absence and presence, respectively, of that intervening condition.

Table 10                                      Inverted Controlled Experiment

|  | Explanatory Factor X? | |
| --- | --- | --- |
|  | Before | After |
| Experimental Group | Assumed: Persons with *v* virtues, *p* power, and *c* context | Professional |
| Control Group | Assumed: Persons with *v* virtues, *p* power, and *c* content | Corrupted |

By comparing the nature and background of these two groups, he explores for the character of that intervening factor, *X:* the explanation.

All this may sound simpleminded, but by reminding ourselves that comparison underlies the exploratory as well as the corroborative phase of the social scientists' method, we come to see the critical importance of the working assumption of "before"-hand sameness, i.e., that the groups started out in an equal condition in the near or distant past, "before" the explanatory factor came into the picture to make them different. The magnitude of this assumption is what makes social scientists humble about any conclusions they reach.

All this is by way of explaining why policemen were attractive subjects with which to explore the problem of power and personality. A city's policemen, having gone through the identical selection process, working under the same departmental conditions, meeting a single citizenry, empowered by the same laws and regulations, were just what a social scientist needed. In contrast to the judiciary (where the informal processes of selection vary so greatly from judge to judge), governors (who work under such varying organizational conditions), and legislators (who come from such different districts), the members of a local police department start out more comparable. That is a blessing for a social scientist, with his nagging doubts about the working assumption of "before"-hand sameness.

Two other factors make police attractive subjects for a study of power and personality. First, in popular parlance, they are described as powerful persons. No matter how much academic dispute there may be over the meaning of "power" (and there is a lot), no one denies that the authority of the revolver is *a* basis of "power." Second, etymologically the word "police" (like "politics") derives from the Greek word *polis,* the polity or city-state. Policemen and persons of politics, alike, are entrusted with a public (and potentially terrifying) asset, the license to inflict harm. They have "authority," which is given to them in the name of the general welfare. Authority distinguishes policemen and politicians, as instruments of legal coercive power, from the unauthorized and the nonpolitical, citizens less directly identified with the *polis.*

In the study I treated the policemen who developed vices as the control group of our inverted controlled experiment and policemen who developed professionally as the experimental group. The comparison of these two groups led to a conclusion about $X$, the explanatory factor which intervened differentially in their two cases. $X$ was language, through which and upon which two other factors, learning and leadership, played critical parts.

This use of the experimental format is necessarily more problematic than its use in the corroborative phase of inquiry. In the real world in which the social scientist is supposed to work, however, this inverted format may be a good compromise between a total waste of time and a total lack of comparative rigor.

2. *The Dependent-Variable Problem:* The "dependent variable" is the thing to be explained by the explanatory factor. It is the difference between the two groups in the "after"-math, $d_x - d_c$. In this study the dependent variable was vice or virtue. But vicious or virtuous what?

The basic choice was whether to explain attitudes or actions. I chose to explain changes in attitudes rather than changes in active behavior for two reasons. First, character has always struck me as more fundamental than behavior. That is, it is easier to predict how a person will act by knowing what he thinks than to predict what he will think by knowing how he acts. Second, Lord Acton's famous aphorism about power and corruption is about the pervasive changes which occur enduringly in a person who accepts the mantle of authority. It is not referring to the circumstantial, ephemeral, and singular changes in behavior. Acton was talking about those changes in character which lead an individual to *premeditate* his wicked deeds. That is why I chose to explain a policeman's moral, intellectual, and emotional vices and virtues.

3. *The Validity Problem:* The validity problem is concerned with the coordination between the intellectual concept and its operational definition. In this study, the validity problem dealt with the translation of moral, intellectual, and emotional "virtue" into the professional political model. Chapter 4 goes into some detail to explain why the validity problem was handled in this way. The logic of Max Weber's argument convinced me that there was a connection between the abstract meaning of political virtue, in all its shades, and his specific model, combining a tragic sense and a moral calm. One test of the validity of this translation of the shadow into reality is exposure. I have always felt that the best methodological check for invalidity is to submit one's assumptions about operational equivalents to those persons who "know" most about the concept in some of its shades. One such group would be the police themselves, and I submitted my conclusions to a few policemen in whom I had considerable confidence. Their acceptance of my operational definition of virtue somewhat alleviated my qualms about the validity problem.

4. *The Reliability Problem:* The professional political model was a tool which I applied to the sayings of the policemen I interviewed. If what an officer *said* about human nature and coercion approximated the combination of perspective and passion which Weber asserted was appropriate for persons undertaking the vocation of politics, I classed him as a person having virtuous attitudes, as a professional. Insofar as other policemen's sayings "substantially" departed from the model, they were tagged as having nonvirtuous attitudes, as an enforcer, a reciprocator, or an avoider.

The reliability problem concerns how much confidence a social scientist can place in his assumption that a policeman's *sayings* are reflective of his attitudes. Would different researchers, talking with the same policemen, questioning them about the same general subject matter, arrive at the same conclusions about their attitudes?

For a variety of reasons, the sayings I elicited could have been unreliable. The policemen could have lied. Or my questions could have been inept. Or my overt or subconscious responses to their remarks could have lacked neutrality and thus been an alien influence in the interview situation. And so on.

The principal methodological check which I employed against unreliability was to let others independently conduct their own research on the same policemen. One researcher rode and talked with two of the men in the sample (Wilkes and Peel), and we later compared notes, coming to much the same conclusions about them. Moreover, over a third of the twenty-eight-man sample submitted to written psychological tests, the Minnesota Multiphasic Inventory (MMPI). The analyzing psychologist and I then wrote down our independent assessments of the men, hers on the basis of the MMPI, mine on the basis of the structured interviews, and compared them. Our compatible conclusions convinced me that the sayings of the policemen were reliable.

I further sought to establish the reliability of what the men told me by sampling their testimony. I compared the description of what they said they did with my observations of what they really did in the field (in the follow-ups a year or more after the interviews). If an officer did not act as he had said he acted, I tended to impeach his testimony about what he had said he thought and felt. If his behavior in the field accorded with what he had said earlier, I relied on his sayings. (I might add, I found that the actions of the men almost invariably accorded with what they had said they did.)

5. *Proving Inference:* In an exploratory study such as this, the weakest link is likely to be the assertions about cause. Establishing a social scientist's inferences in a convincing manner must usually await the more rigorous corroborative phase. Chapter 12, therefore, is the weakest part of this book, because the causes of professionalism are not systematically tested. I am sure, however, that the best solution to the problem of inference in a study like this one is to assert one's surmise as clearly and in as much detail as possible. (James Thurber's moral about the lamb who reported that the wolves intended to be peaceful comes to mind: "Don't get it right; get it written.") These assertions then provide a suitable and sizable target for skeptics. "Proof" so often consists of surviving the skeptical and freely given criticism of scholars as they compete with each other in their searches for the best explanation.

6. *Implications:* When social scientific inquiry is done, when explanations have been explored, articulated, corroborated, and measured, the social scientist comes to the question, "So what?" Does the explanation go beyond the case and reveal something basic about the human condition? Every social scientist worth his salt claims to root his explanation in the nature of Everyman. In going back to the fundamentals, he tries to illuminate those fundamentals. His explanation has broad implications when it exposes what is universal and timeless in the singular events of his case. The credo of social science is best summed up by those remarkable words of President Lincoln as he contemplated the meaning of the Civil War: "What has occurred in this case must ever recur in similar cases. Human nature will not change. In any future great national trial, compared with the men of this, we shall have as

weak and as strong, as silly and as wise, as bad and as good. Let us therefore study the incidents of this, as philosophy to learn wisdom from, and none of them as wrongs to be revenged."[2] I have attempted to root an understanding of the policeman's development in the unchanging nature of mankind—guilt, redemption, morals, understanding, and coercion—and I have tried, throughout the book, but particularly in the last chapter, to describe why we can learn wisdom from the policeman's experience.

I do not believe any piece of social science has ever licked all six of these methodological problems to everyone's satisfaction. I do believe, however, that the task is still worth the undertaking, largely because in my own heart I know how much my intellectual forebears' efforts have helped explain ourselves to ourselves. I have faith, too, that succeeding generations will somehow benefit from this generation's attempts to understand the mysterious alchemy of human affairs.

## III

The method of selection of the twenty-eight-man sample was discussed in the first chapter of the book. Were these twenty-eight dissimilar from the larger Laconia police population? We had data about all police officers who were trained from February 1963 through March 1970—about four hundred men. Some of these four hundred were no longer in the department; some had been promoted to sergeant or into administrative ranks. The twenty-eight-man sample was slightly younger at date of coming on the department than the average among the four hundred men (23.7 years old to 24.2 years old), slightly more were married when they came on the department (78.5% to 69.02%), more agnostic (28.57% to 10.59%), and less Catholic (17.86% to 33.50%), slightly less educated (39.29% had not completed a year of college at the time they entered the department compared with 32.27% of the four hundred-man population), less likely to have views like John Kennedy (46.43% to 52.97%), and more likely to have views like Richard Nixon (21.43% to 11.14%). The sample scored slightly better on intelligence tests, was slightly shorter, and had less military experience (35.75% as compared with 25.91% had no experience). In all other measurable respects similarities existed.

To see the reasonable resemblance between the sample and the population, the interested reader might want to compare the figures in tables 11 through 13. Table 11 shows that the sample scored higher in the 50 to 55 category, but only slightly. To take two more illustrations of the representativeness of the sample, let us compare the results on two attitude tests (see tables 12 and 13). Table 12 shows that the sample is slightly less "theoretical" and more "social" than the population, but the differences are negligible. A further comparison can be made, contrasting the sample and the population with respect to four occupational interests pertinent to police work (see table 13). The sample is again slightly higher in "social service" preference, but the

2.  Quoted in Shelby Foote, *The Civil War: A Narrative* (Random House: New York, 1974), 3:1060.

similarities are sufficient to make me conclude that the sample did not substantially distort the characteristics of the younger field officers in the Laconia Police Department.

| Table 11 | Otis Intelligence Test | |
|---|---|---|
| Intelligence Score | 28-man sample | 344-man population |
| | Percentage | Percentage |
| 40 or lower | 3.57% | 6.39% |
| 41–45 | 10.71 | 10.47 |
| 46–50 | 17.86 | 28.78 |
| 51–55 | 39.29 | 27.03 |
| 56–60 | 17.86 | 16.86 |
| 61–65 | 7.14 | 8.14 |
| 66 or higher | 3.57 | 2.03 |

Table 12      Allport-Vernon-Lindzey Study of Values Test

| Values | 28-man sample | | | 392-man population | | |
|---|---|---|---|---|---|---|
| | Percentage High | Percentage Average | Percentage Low | Percentage High | Percentage Average | Percentage Low |
| Theoretical | 11% | 48% | 41% | 13% | 57% | 30% |
| Economic | 22 | 63 | 15 | 23 | 59 | 18 |
| Aesthetic | 7 | 67 | 26 | 18 | 58 | 24 |
| Social | 30 | 51 | 19 | 18 | 61 | 21 |
| Political | 41 | 52 | 7 | 41 | 49 | 10 |
| Religious | 19 | 51 | 30 | 20 | 54 | 26 |

Table 13      Kuder Vocational Preference Record

| Preference | 28-man sample | | | 400-man population | | |
|---|---|---|---|---|---|---|
| | Percentage High | Percentage Average | Percentage Low | Percentage High | Percentage Average | Percentage Low |
| Mechanical | 31% | 50% | 19% | 35% | 49% | 16% |
| Persuasive | 19 | 65 | 16 | 24 | 53 | 23 |
| Social Service | 58 | 34 | 8 | 36 | 54 | 10 |
| Clerical | 0 | 35 | 65 | 1 | 43 | 56 |

# Bibliographical Essay

## I

There are many instructive books on American police. A teacher mounting a brief course on police might choose as follows: (1) PHILOSOPHY, Herbert L. Packer, *The Limits of the Criminal Sanction* (Stanford, Calif.: Stanford University Press, 1968); (2) HISTORY, Roger Lane, *Policing the City: Boston 1822-1885* (Cambridge: Harvard University Press, 1967); (3) DESCRIPTION, Jonathan Rubinstein, *City Police* (New York: Farrar, Straus & Giroux, 1973); (4) PIONEERING SOCIAL SCIENCE, William A. Westley, *Violence and the Police* (Cambridge: M.I.T. Press, 1970); and (5) POLICY, George E. Berkeley, *The Democratic Policeman* (Boston: Beacon, 1969).

But a course based on such a list would miss so much. It would miss the three important novels of Joseph Wambaugh, *The New Centurions* (Boston: Little, Brown, 1970), *The Blue Knight* (Boston: Atlantic-Little Brown, 1972), and particularly *The Onion Field* (New York: Delacorte, 1973), It would not cover how a department's organization can affect its performance, a topic subtly treated by John A. Gardiner, *Traffic and the Police* (Cambridge: Harvard University Press, 1969). It would not address the topic of police from the perspective of the victims of abusive police power, as does Paul Chevigny, *Police Power* (New York: Pantheon, 1969). Nor would it deal with policemen in unconventional settings, as does the brilliant work of Gresham M. Sykes, *The Society of Captives* (New York: Atheneum, 1966).

Moreover, if I had to pick the particular books which I think the reader would find most useful for understanding the modern American policeman, I would name four without hesitation: the graceful and pathbreaking work of Michael Banton, *The Policeman in the Community* (New York: Basic Books, 1964); the insightful work of Jerome Skolnick, *Justice without Trial* (New York: Wiley, 1966); the effort of a veteran policeman to supplement his experience with social survey information, Arthur Niederhoffer, *Behind the Shield* (Garden City, N.Y.: Doubleday, 1967); and the illuminating comparative work of James Q. Wilson, *Varieties of Police Behavior* (Cambridge: Harvard University Press, 1968), perhaps the most important book in transforming police thinking about their institution. The findings of these four books coincided with my own findings (and in their way assured me that what I observed in Laconia was probably happening in other big cities). Let me briefly describe some of their findings, along with those of other writers where pertinent.

## II

*The Avoider.* Recall a few of the conditions of the avoidance response: (1) an ethical disinclination to hurt and attendant moral conflict in the exercise of power; (2) low self-defensive skills, resulting in low self-confidence; and (3) meager supervision of inaction.

Niederhoffer, among others, found that the men he questioned were motivated to become policemen by a desire to be of service to people. He found, also, that most policemen began with the feeling "that force is a necessary evil which is one of the more unattractive aspects of the police job."[1]

The conflict between initial motives and the work which policemen have to do after donning the uniform was so great in some instances that Banton found that some policemen quit the force "after only a short spell of duty because they felt so guilty at having arrested people."[2] Banton noted that a favorite device for avoiding moral conflict was for policemen to try to convince a wrongdoer that he had done wrong, to get the criminal to agree to the punishment: "The preference of policemen for taking actions which even the people who suffer them have to concede are morally right, seems to be a fundamental factor in explaining why the police are so often reluctant to enforce the law."[3] In short, considerable evidence exists that policemen are no more inclined than the rest of the civilized population to hurt others, and moral conflicts are as real a problem for them as for any other individual.

All four books agree that police work in the field is frightening. Danger lurks unpredictably in every encounter. Niederhoffer summed up his own impressions of twenty years of police duty in New York City: "The hostility and fear ... almost palpably press against a policeman in lower-class areas."[4] The overwhelming inclination of some policemen was to avoid trouble.

There were few bad personal consequences of inaction. To be sure, Skolnick described the informal supervision by the men themselves of the norm "to stand up to danger," which moved patrolmen to risk danger to help their fellow officers.[5] But formal supervision was meager at best. Even the best supervisor found it difficult to show that a goldbrick was not on the job.

Sometimes, as Wilson showed, whole departments institutionalized this pattern of avoidance. *Varieties of Police Behavior* described "the watchman style" of three New York (Albany, Amsterdam, and Newburgh) police departments in the early 1960s as one of ignoring infractions, tolerating deliberately illegal acts, expecting less orderly

---

1.  Niederhoffer, *Behind the Shield,* p. 142.
2.  Banton, *Policeman,* p. 149.
3.  Ibid., p. 147.
4.  Niederhoffer, *Behind the Shield,* p. 131.
5.  Skolnick, *Justice,* pp. 57-59.

conduct from certain groups, and steering clear of private disputes (assaults among friends and families, businessmen's collecting debts, etc.). Undertrained, afraid of an incident, the typical watchman defined for himself an increasingly smaller scope of police responsibilities. Wilson reported that personal avoidance was reinforced by a department's desire "not to rock the boat" and flourished where the supervisorial attitude was one of indifference. "Off the record, we don't care."[6]

The results of police inaction for the civilian populace were very great, however. In Newburgh a black lawyer provided Wilson with this description of what happened:

> We can't get police protection in this [black] community. They ignore the crowds. There's a bar next to where my parents live. . . . Every night there'll be a big crowd, especially in the summers, that will gather in the streets in front of this place. Sometimes we'll have to call the police four or five times before they even come. When they do come, they often get out of their cars and just start joking with the people standing there. The police are supposed to break up these crowds and move them along, but they don't do it.[7]

The strong, the mean, the indifferent, the victimizers of the world had free access to their prey where the police were avoiders.

## III

*The Reciprocator.* Reciprocity in police work depends on a number of factors, among which are: (1) personal skills sufficient to exchange leniency for value; (2) continuing or stabilized relationships where familiarity between parties to the exchange is possible; and (3) the existence of a balance of power between the parties. The advantages of a reciprocating response for a policeman who was motivated to serve mankind was that his police skills were of service to others. Hence, they were marketable and could be a source of personal profit. If he liked to get into "private" or civil matters, the policeman's lot offered him golden opportunities. Moreover, he could bestow upon the citizen the reciprocal of his authority, his leniency, the power not to hurt. For doing so, he could get affection and the reputation of Joe Good Guy. He might aso take bribes. (The literature reveals an aspect of the reciprocator not in evidence in Laconia: graft. Gene Radano's recollections as a patrolman walking the beat in New York contained a portrait of a reciprocator, a man of remarkable eloquence and human insight. This "intelligent, witty, friendly, and warm" officer used his social skills to "milk the tit," to use the New York vernacular.)[8] The scholar Gardiner wondered why policemen fixed tickets when money was not involved and concluded that ticket fixing was "an easily effective form of patronage," convertible into discount prices at the clothier and the liquor store, public support in case of trouble, and friendship with economic and political notables.[9]

6.  Wilson, *Police Behavior,* p. 163.
7.  Quoted in ibid., pp. 161-62.
8.  Gene Radano, *Walking the Beat* (New York: Collier, 1969), chap. 15.
9.  John A. Gardiner, *Traffic and the Police,* pp. 122-23.

This tendency to reciprocity flourished where the policeman and the citizen had a continuing relationship—in police departments with precincts and no rotation of beats, in homogeneous suburban communities, in prisons.[10] As Banton pointed out in a slightly different context, reciprocity could replace coercion only where "uniform and predictable modes of action can develop," where there were "common understandings," where both policeman and citizen knew "their behavior will be correctly interpreted by each other."[11]

Once this relationship was established, the more services the policeman could do, the better position he was in. The reciprocator could poke his nose about looking for opportunities to be of service: acting as a collection agent for merchants, serving as the informed bouncer at a bar, staking out a lookout on citizens' homes, acting as a taxi driver for elderly women, overlooking infractions of the law.

The compulsions to continue these deals might come from any of several sources. One was the policeman's vulnerability once he had entered into an illicit bargain. Speaking of the sharing of profits between police and gamblers and prostitutes, one observer put it: "Once persons in positions of power accept the offer of the vice organizations to share in the profit, then they are, of course, vulnerable. . . . The fact that the 'vice lords' are themselves vulnerable means the law enforcers can bargain, but it does not mean that they can disregard what the vice leaders demand."[12]

A legal form of reciprocity, however, could result from the influence of police leadership. Wilson examined two departments where reciprocity was administration policy in the early 1960s. The two communities, Nassau County and Brighton, New York, were then essentially homogeneous, and outsiders were rarely encountered. Common understandings of the meaning of each department's service behavior were held by both policemen and citizens, since the communities were not divided along class or social lines. The characteristics of what Wilson called "the service style" were frequent intervention on an informal basis, concentration on providing services, an expectation by citizens and police chiefs alike that patrolmen would act in a reciprocating manner, like department store salesmen. One official thought of himself as having "to sell police services to the public at large."[13]

## IV

*The Enforcer.* The exercise of coercive power, we have said, caused the holder of authority to have (1) increasingly meager and biased information and (2) enhanced belief in the efficacy of coercion. The literature on police, if it agrees on any one point, emphasizes the tendency of police to lose contact with the complexity of reality and to

10.   Gresham Sykes, *Society of Captives,* chap. 3.
11.   Banton, *Policeman,* p. 168.
12.   William Chambliss, ed., *Crime and the Legal Process* (New York: McGraw-Hill, 1969), p. 92.
13.   Wilson, *Police Behavior,* p. 205.

grow ever more reliant on the exercise of force: policemen, the sociologists Werthman and Piliavin assert, "soon become defensively cynical and aggressively moralistic."[14]

Banton, Wilson, and others each discussed the nature of the policeman's normal information network: the victim, who invariably "emphasizes the moral wrong that he or she has suffered and not the legal wrong, if any"; "the informer system"; the "civilians who fear us and play up to us." (Tocqueville once said, "Next to hating their enemies, men are most inclined to flatter them.")[15] The point Banton made was how many people were not in this network: the decent bystander who was scared off by the authority of the policeman over him; the violator himself; the "potentially dangerous"; even the patrolman's fellow officers, who would prefer not to confront him with disagreeable information in view of their potential dependence on him in a future tight spot.

This biased information got fed into a belief system, which in turn further sifted out and discarded certain information. The police system of beliefs would tend to be premised on the concepts and assumptions of the law enforcement code, McNamara argued. The officer would begin to classify people entirely in legal categories rather than characteristics relevant to other moral codes: a man was a fleeing felon or a "402 suspect," not a human being. Legal pigeonholing led to the imputation of "additional characteristics" which might not be really there.[16]

Moreover, the policeman tended to ignore the adverse effects of using police coercion and give credence only to evidence of the usefulness of strict enforcement of the law. Banton noted that policemen came to believe that a way of cutting crime was to increase the number of drunk arrests "because drunks, being defenseless, were often robbed."[17] As the pressures to believe in absolute law enforcement mounted, internal conflicts would occur in the individual policeman between strict enforcement and the bad consequences of it. At that point, some officers chucked aside their older ideas of self-restraint and responsibility, leaving themselves vulnerable, as Niederhoffer put it, to a "standing temptation to use violence."[18] When conditions became personally adverse, they began acting preemptively, preventing their own possible victimization by striking first.

Wilson's observations in the early 1960s of departments with a legalistic (or enforcer) style illustrated how admirable departments, in pursuing admirable reforms, simply overlooked the job of dealing with the moral deterioration of their men. Both Oakland, California, and Highland Park, Illinois, were reform departments, having eliminated graft. Concentrating on how their men behaved, the reform-minded administrators ignored how their men felt. As Wilson stated it, a "good man" was defined in Oakland as one who "finds it possible to play the police

14.  Carl Werthman and Irving Piliavin, "Gang Members and the Police," in *The Police: Six Sociological Essays*, ed. David Bordua (New York: Wiley, 1967), p. 57.
15.  Alexis de Tocqueville, *Democracy in America*, trans. Henry Reeve (New York: Vintage, 1945), 1:187.
16.  John H. McNamara, "Uncertainties in Police Work," in Bordua, *Police*, p. 170.
17.  Banton, *Policeman*, p. 57.
18.  Niederhoffer, *Behind the Shield*, p. 113.

role impersonally—to distinguish between what a policeman must do and his feelings about doing it."[19]

## V

*The Professional.* Until recently literature dealing with police was bereft of sophisticated portraits of any individual patrolmen who grew in office.[20] We find some interesting references in the literature. Banton made some acute observations of some skillful police work. Both Wilson and Banton suggested that size and self-confidence helped a patrolman to get a citizen's voluntary cooperation: the citizen was able to submit to an officer of stature with less loss of self-respect than to a policeman who appeared to be a "nobody."[21]

Moreover, the capacity to talk, to open up communication between citizen and officer, was pointed to as important. McNamara said it enabled policemen to recognize "the values of citizens" and to devise ways of getting compliance without forcing the citizen to lose face.[22]

Nonetheless, I think it fair to say that at present we lack scholarship concerning the development of professional policemen. The police literature does not contain descriptions of how policemen come to reconcile the sometimes necessary extortionate practices of authority with their previously felt obligations to be reasonable, kind, empathetic, and creative. It provides no explanation of how the professional policeman maintains a complex sense of "right" and "wrong" without a loss of self-esteem or of belief in civility. The literature does not tell us how a policeman can develop a morality enabling him to be mean opportunistically without becoming mean compulsively.

Moreover, the police literature says nothing about the professional policeman's sense of place, time, and purpose, or of how he cultivates an awareness of the trends of past and future, or of his development of a standard of success for his individual actions in keeping with both the limits of his individual capacities and his impulse for public service. The literature points to the necessity that a policeman have such a social, historical, and ethical perspective and how it would be useful in compensating for the unique distortions of information which befall the policeman—distortions resulting from a steady diet of life's pathologies, from the organizational necessities of maintaining intensely high morale (to overcome fear, hardship, and frustration), and from the authority of office. The literature simply has not described the means of acquiring such a perspective.

19. Wilson, *Police Behavior,* p. 187.
20. This long-existing vacuum has been almost single-handedly filled by one author, Joseph Wambaugh. His two novels, *The New Centurions* and *The Blue Knight,* portray the moral and intellectual development of a most interesting group of fictionalized policemen. But my favorite work is his *The Onion Field,* an insightful study of the moral collapse of a truly professional policeman. What makes this book the more compelling is that it is a true story of the nonfiction-novel genre which Truman Capote made familiar with *In Cold Blood.*
21. Wilson, *Police Behavior,* p. 33; Banton, *Policeman,* p. 175.
22. McNamara, "Uncertainties," p. 174.

# Index